Buddha Śākyamuni

The Buddha of our time

Guru Rinpoche

Also known as Padmasambhava, the Lotus-born, he is the "Second Buddha" who established Buddhism in Tibet. He is shown here in the form known as "Prevailing Over Appearances and Existence" (*Nangsi Zilnön*), the name meaning that, as he understands the nature of everything that appears, he is naturally the master of all situations.

THE SACRED LITERATURE SERIES

THE WORDS OF MY PERFECT TEACHER

The Sacred Literature Series of
the International Sacred Literature Trust

Other titles in the series

AUSTRALIAN ABORIGINAL TRADITIONS
Warlpiri Dreamings and Histories

◆

BUDDHISM
The Recorded Sayings of Zen Master Joshu

◆

CHRISTIANITY
On the Life of Christ: Kontakia of St Romanos

◆

INDIAN TRADITIONS
In the Dark of the Heart: Songs of Meera

◆

JAINISM
That Which Is: Tattvartha Sutra

◆

JUDAISM
Gates of Light: Sha'are Orah
Yemenite Midrash

◆

SIKHISM
The Name of My Beloved: Verses of the Sikh Gurus

◆

SUFISM
Solomon's Ring: The Life and Teachings of a Sufi Master

◆

TAOISM
Lao-tzu's Treatise on the Response of the Tao

Further titles in preparation

༄༅། རྫོགས་པ་ཆེན་པོ་ཀློང་ཆེན་སྙིང་ཏིག་གི་སྔོན་འགྲོའི་
ཁྲིད་ཡིག་ཀུན་བཟང་བླ་མའི་ཞལ་ལུང་
ཞེས་བྱ་བ་བཞུགས་སོ།།

པདྨ་ཀཱ་རའི་སྒྲ་བསྒྱུར་མཐུན་ཚོགས་ནས་
སྒྲ་བསྒྱུར་ཞུས།།

KUNZAN LAMA'I SHELUNG

The Words of My Perfect Teacher

PATRUL RINPOCHE

Translated by the Padmakara Translation Group

With forewords by the Dalai Lama and Dilgo Khyntse Rinpoche

Yale
UNIVERSITY PRESS
New Haven & London

First Yale University Press edition 2011.

Yale University Press books may be purchased in quantity for educational, business, or promotional use. For information, please e-mail sales.press@yale.edu (U.S. office) or sales@yaleup.co.uk (U.K. office).

The Library of Congress has cataloged the original edition as follows:

O-rgyan- 'jigs-med-chos-kyi-dban-po, Dpal-sprul, b. 1808
[Kun bzan bla ma'i źal lun. English]
The words of my perfect teacher / Patrul Rinpoche : translated by the Padmakara Translation Group ; with a foreword by the Dalai Lama and Dilgo Khyntse Rinpoche—2nd ed.
p. cm. —(Sacred literature series)
Includes bibliographical references and index.
ISBN 0-7619-9026-7 (alk. paper). —ISBN 0-7619-9027-5 (alk. paper)
1. Rdzogs-chen (Rñin-ma-pa) 2. Jig-med-rgyal-ba 'I-my-gu, ca 1750–1825.
I. Title. II Series.
BQ 7662.4.072513 1998 98-23830
294.3'420423–dc21 CIP

ISBN 978-0-300-16532-6 (pbk.)

Printed in the United States of America.

10 9 8 7

To the teachers
of the past, the present and the future

INTERNATIONAL
SACRED
LITERATURE
TRUST

The International Sacred Literature Trust was established to promote understanding and open discussion between and within faiths and to give voice in today's world to the wisdom that speaks across time and traditions.

What resources do the sacred traditions of the world possess to respond to the great global threats of poverty, war, ecological disaster and spiritual despair?

Our starting-point is the sacred texts with their vision of a higher truth and their deep insights into the nature of humanity and the universe we inhabit. The translation programme is planned so that each faith community articulates its own teachings with the intention of enhancing its self-understanding as well as the understanding of those of other faiths and those of no faith.

The Trust particularly encourages faiths to make available texts which are needed in translation for their own communities and also texts which are little known outside the tradition but which have the power to inspire, console, enlighten and transform. These sources from the past become resources for the present and future when we make inspired use of them to guide us in shaping the contemporary world.

Our religious traditions are diverse but, as with the natural environment, we are discovering the global interdependence of human hearts and minds. The Trust invites all to participate in the modern experience of interfaith encounter and exchange which marks a new phase in the human quest to discover our full humanity.

Contents

PART ONE
THE ORDINARY OR EXTERNAL
PRELIMINARIES

♦

Chapter One
The difficulty of finding the freedoms
and advantages

♦

Chapter Two
The impermanence of life

♦

Chapter Three
The defects of saṁsāra

♦

Chapter Four
Actions: the principle of cause and effect

♦

Chapter Five
The benefits of liberation

♦

Chapter Six
How to follow a spiritual friend

PART TWO
THE EXTRAORDINARY OR INTERNAL PRELIMINARIES

♦

Chapter One
Taking refuge, foundation stone of all paths

♦

Chapter Two
Arousing bodhicitta, the root of the Great Vehicle

◆

Chapter Three
Meditating and reciting on the teacher as Vajrasattva to cleanse all obscurations

◆

Chapter Four
Offering the maṇḍala to accumulate merit and wisdom

◆

Chapter Five
The kusāli's accumulation: destroying the four demons at a single stroke

♦

Chapter Six
Guru Yoga, entrance-way for blessings, the ultimate method for arousing the wisdom of realization

PART THREE
THE SWIFT PATH OF TRANSFERENCE

♦

Chapter One
Transference of consciousness, the instructions for the dying: Buddhahood without meditation

List of Illustrations

Padmasambhava

Foreword

THE DALAI LAMA

Jig-me Gyal-wai Nyu-gu, who was one of the eminent disciples of Jig-me Ling-pa, the exponent of Dzog-pa Chen-po Long-chen Nying-thig, gave an oral instruction on Long-chen Nying-thig and his disciple Dza Pal-trul Rinpoche transcribed it, giving it the title: KUNSANG LA-MAI ZHAL-LUNG.

It is said in the Great Perfection teachings that one cannot become enlightened through a contrived mind; rather, the basic mind is to be identified, in relation to which all phenomena are to be understood as the sport of the mind. One then familiarises oneself continuously and one-pointedly with this ascertainment. However, to have a full understanding of this is it is not sufficient merely to read books; one needs the full preparatory practice of the Nying-ma system and, in addition, the special teaching of a qualified Nying-ma master as well as his blessings. The student must also have accumulated great merit. That is why great Nying-ma-pa masters like Jig-me Ling-pa and Do-drup-chen worked so hard.

Translation of such works containing the Dzog-chen preliminaries will be of immense value these days. I congratulate the Padmakara Translation Group for having produced this work in English and French. I am sure this authentic preliminary work will benefit all those who are interested in Dzog-chen.

November 23, 1990

The Dalai Lama

Longchenpa (1308-1363)

The most brilliant teacher of the Nyingma lineage. Longchen Rabjampa gathered together the *Heart-essence* teachings of Padmasambhava, Vimalamitra and Yeshe Tsogyal. He transmitted all these teachings to Jigme Lingpa in a series of visions as the *Heart-essence of the Vast Expanse*.

Foreword

by Dilgo Khyentse Rinpoche

The Words of My Perfect Teacher, a Guide to the Preliminaries for the Heart-essence of the Vast Expanse from the Great Perfection, sets out the paths of the four main schools of Tibetan Buddhism without any conflict between them.

It contains all the teachings, including the Steps of the Path for those of the three levels of understanding, along with the Three Main Themes of the Path; the Three Perceptions, preliminaries for the Path and Fruit; the Buddha Nature as the cause, precious human life as the support, the spiritual friend as the impetus, his instructions as the method, and the kāyas and wisdoms as the result, these representing the confluence of the Kadampa and Mahāmudrā traditions; and the Nyingma path in terms of determination to be free through disgust for saṁsāra, faith through confidence in the effect of actions, bodhicitta through striving to help others, and pure perception of the utter purity of everything there is.

For all teachings on all practices, whether preliminaries or main, this text is indispensable. That is why, at this fortunate time in which the Buddha's precious doctrine is beginning to shine its light throughout the world, this book has been translated in the profound hope that—being of enormous worth and little danger, and covering as it does all the essential points of the path—all contact with it may be fruitful, and that it may become the object of study, reflection and meditation. That followers of the Dharma teach or listen to this text is of great importance.

Translators' Acknowledgements

In accordance with Tibetan tradition, the translators would like to thank the teachers of the lineage: the late Dudjom Rinpoche, Dilgo Khyentse Rinpoche and Kangyur Rinpoche, whose extraordinary inspiration and patient explanations form the basis for all our efforts to understand these teachings; and also the numerous other lamas who answered our questions and gave us encouragement—Dodrup Chen Rinpoche, Nyoshul Khenpo Rinpoche, Dzogchen Khenpo Thubten, Zenkar Rinpoche, Khetsun Zangpo Rinpoche, Lama Sönam Tobgyal and many others.

The Padmakara Translation Group is made up of students of Tibetan Buddhism from several countries and disciplines, working under the direction of Pema Wangyal Rinpoche and Jigme Khyentse Rinpoche, at the Centre d'Etudes de Chanteloube in Dordogne, Southwest France.

The history of this particular project runs parallel to the evolution of the group, many of whose members began their study of Patrul Rinpoche's *Kunzang Lamai Shelung* in the mid seventies, both in India and in Europe. They were then taught in detail from it, as the basis for their own practice of the Vajrayāna path during the traditional meditation retreats which started in 1980 at Chanteloube. The text was translated into French by members of the group guided by their Tibetan teachers, and published as *Le Chemin de La Grande Perfection* by the newly-formed Editions Padmakara in 1987.

The first stage of the English version was a draft translation from the French by Michael Dickman. This was the starting point for a new translation from the original Tibetan. It was prepared, with many revisions, by Christian Bruyat, Charles Hastings and John Canti. Stephen Gethin provided editorial help and prepared the index.

The translators are grateful to readers Michal Abrams, Wulstan Fletcher, Helena Blankleder, Rinchen Lhamo, Elissa Mannheimer and Vivian Kurz for their valuable suggestions, and to Jill Heald for help with the typescript.

Finally, our warmest thanks to Kerry Brown of the International Sacred Literature Trust for her constant and patient encouragement.

Preface to the Second Edition

The encouraging need for this book to be reprinted has made possible a number of changes. A preface written by Dilgo Khyentse Rinpoche for the first French edition has been included, as well as a postface written by Jamgön Kongtrul the Great for the very first woodblock printing of this book in Tibetan a century ago. The quality of the illustrations has been improved, the notes and glossary have been expanded and revised, and Sanskrit words have been given their standard transliterated spelling.

However, the principal change is a revision of the text itself, the fruit of a painstaking, detailed re-reading by Pema Wangyal Rinpoche. His numerous comments, clarifications and queries—on average three or four per page—have enabled us to take a critical look at the accuracy of our translation and to bring it closer still to Patrul Rinpoche's original meaning. Readers of the first edition may be assured that we have found no glaring errors in the substance of the instructions and practices explained. Nevertheless, in a text so justly celebrated for its extraordinary wealth of detail and anecdote, it is in those finer details that we hope the translation has gained in authenticity and accuracy.

No translation will ever be definitive. Our hope is that we may continue to improve the translation of this text in the future, particularly since—as testified by the many encouraging letters we have received from all over the world—it is used intensively by many individual readers and Buddhist groups as a tool for study and practice. Had time allowed, we would have liked to undertake a thorough revision of the endnotes in the light of a new translation of one of the principal sources from which they were compiled, Khenpo Ngawang Palzang's *Notes*, currently proceeding under the direction of Alak Zenkar (with the participation of several members of the Padmakara Translation Group, see bibliography). That, unfortunately, will have to await a third edition.

All the changes to this edition were compiled, edited and entered by John Canti, with valuable help from Maria Jesus Hervas, whose assiduous work in preparing a forthcoming Spanish translation uncovered a number of errors and omissions in the English, and from readers Helena Blankleder, Charles Hastings, Steven Gethin and Wulstan Fletcher.

Once again, we are grateful for the continuing interest and support of the Sacred Literature Trust and its successive directors, Paul Seto and Malcolm Gerratt—and especially for their patience, which the delays in the preparation of this second edition must have sorely tested.

Jigme Lingpa (1729-1798

Jigme Lingpa received the transmission of the *Heart-essence of the Vast Expanse* from Longchenpa. He practised them in solitude and subsequently transmitted them to his own students.

Translators' Introduction

The Words of My Perfect Teacher is one of the best-loved introductions to the foundations of Tibetan Buddhism, constantly recommended by His Holiness the Dalai Lama and other eminent teachers. It provides a detailed guide to the methods by which an ordinary person can transform his or her consciousness and set off on the path to Buddhahood, the state of awakening and freedom. The first half of the book contains a series of contemplations on the frustration and deep suffering of saṁsāra, the round of existence based on ignorance and deluded emotions, and the enormous value of our human life, which provides a unique opportunity to attain Buddhahood. The second half explains the first steps of the Vajrayāna, the "Diamond Vehicle" whose powerful methods of transformation provide the distinctive character of the Tibetan tradition of Buddhism.

Patrul Rinpoche's work is not a treatise for experts but a manual of practical advice for anyone sincerely wishing to practise the Dharma. He wrote it in a style that could speak as easily to rough nomads and villagers as to lamas and monks. In fact he claimed that it was not really a literary composition at all, but that he had simply set down the oral instructions of his own teacher as he himself had heard them. The particular magic of the book is that we feel that we are Patrul Rinpoche's own students, listening to his heartfelt advice, based on the oral tradition that he received from his own teacher and the deep experience of years of practice.

He explains everything we need to know to practise the teachings—and also, often with devastating irony, the many mistakes that can be made on the spiritual journey. The language veers from high poetry to broad vernacular. Each point is illustrated by numerous quotations, down-to-earth examples from daily life, and a wealth of stories. Some of these stories go back to the very origins of Buddhism in the 6th century BC and beyond; some are drawn from the extraordinary lives of the great masters of India and Tibet; some concern the doings of the ordinary folk of Patrul Rinpoche's native Kham.

Patrul Rinpoche was famous for the direct way he probed the depths of his students' minds. He was a firm believer in Atīśa's dictum, "The best spiritual friend is the one who attacks your hidden faults." Although his work is clearly adapted to his particular audience, with a little effort of transposition we can see that human nature remains remarkably the same regardless of time and culture. We feel that the recesses of our own character are exposed and we are forced to question our own habits of thought and open our minds to new possibilities.

In his concluding chapter the author describes his work as follows:

> In writing down these instructions I have not been guided primarily by aesthetic or literary considerations. My main aim has simply been to record faithfully the oral instructions of my revered teacher in a way that is easy to understand and useful for the mind. I have done my best not to spoil them by mixing in my own words or ideas. On separate occasions my teacher also used to give numerous special instructions for exposing hidden faults, and I have added whatever I have been able to remember of these in the most appropriate places. Do not take them as a window through which to observe others' faults, but rather as a mirror for examining your own. Look carefully within yourself to see whether or not you have those hidden faults. If you do, recognize them and take them out of their hiding place. Correct your mind and set it at ease on the right path...

For Vajrayāna Buddhism, enlightenment is not a remote ideal but something which, with the appropriate methods and a supreme effort, can be achieved here and now, in this very life. In Tibet's living wisdom tradition, every scripture, every meditation practice and training for the mind, is passed on from teacher to student, and then internalized till it becomes an integral part of that person's experience. One of the words for spiritual practice in Tibetan is *nyamlen*, literally "taking into experience." Someone who can be considered a lineage holder, a truly qualified spiritual teacher, must have actually attained realization. Patrul Rinpoche held a continuous line of transmission coming down from the Buddha himself. This lineage has been passed on unbroken, from one realized teacher to the next, until the present day.

Patrul Rinpoche and the tradition he inherited

In the Nyingmapa school, to which Patrul Rinpoche belonged, and which is the oldest tradition of Tibetan Buddhism, there are two kinds of transmission. There is the Kahma, (*bka' ma*) or oral lineage, passed on from teacher to student over the centuries, and there is the miraculous direct lineage of Terma (*gter ma*) or Spiritual Treasures. These were hidden in the eighth century by Padmasambhava and his great woman disciple Yeshe Tshogyal, to be discovered in later ages at the appropriate moment. *The Words of My Perfect Teacher* is an explanation of the

Jigme Gyalwai Nyugu

Patrul Rinpoche's perfect teacher. Patrul Rinpoche heard his explanation of the *Heart-essence of the Vast Expanse* many times, and claimed that *The Words of My Perfect Teacher* was nothing more or less than a faithful compendium of what he had heard on those different occasions.

preliminary practices of the *Longchen Nyingtik* (*klong chen snying thig*), *The Heart-essence of the Vast Expanse*, a spiritual treasure discovered by Rigdzin Jigme Lingpa (1729-1798).

Jigme Lingpa was a prodigy who became immensely learned with almost no study, through arousing his wisdom mind in a series of long meditation retreats. He received the *Heart-essence of the Vast Expanse* in a series of visions of Longchenpa, a great lama of the fourteenth century.

Longchenpa systematized the Nyingmapa doctrines in his astonishing *Seven Treasures* (*mdzod bdun*, see bibliography) and other works, which cover all aspects of the Buddhist teachings, and in particular discuss fully the subtleties of Dzogchen, the Great Perfection. He also wrote extensively on the teachings of the other schools, but these works have been lost. Although Longchenpa lived several centuries before him, he was in fact Jigme Lingpa's principal teacher.

Jigme Lingpa first practised and mastered the teachings he had discovered, and then passed them on to a few close disciples who were capable of becoming pure holders of the doctrine. One of these was Patrul Rinpoche's teacher, Jigme Gyalwai Nyugu, who after spending a considerable time with Jigme Lingpa in central Tibet, returned to Kham (the eastern region of the country). There he undertook the practice of what Jigme Lingpa had taught him, living on a remote mountainside in a mere depression in the ground, without even a cave for shelter, and with only wild plants for food. He was indifferent to comfort and convenience, determined to let go of all worldly considerations and concentrate on the goal of ultimate realization. Gradually disciples gathered around him, living in tents on the windswept hillside. One of these was the young Patrul, who received from him, no less than fourteen times, the teachings contained in this book. Subsequently Patrul also studied with many other great lamas of the day, including the highly unconventional Do Khyentse Yeshe Dorje, who directly introduced him to the nature of the mind.

Throughout his life Patrul Rinpoche emulated the uncompromising simplicity of his master. Although he had been recognized in his childhood as an incarnate lama, or *tulku*—his name is an abbreviation of Palgye Tulku—and would normally have had a high position in a monastic establishment, he spent his life wandering from place to place, camping in the open, in the guise of an ordinary beggar. If he was offered gold or silver he would often just leave it lying on the ground, thinking that wealth was only a source of trouble. Even when he had become a famous teacher, he would travel around unrecognized, living in the same simple and carefree manner. There is even a story of a lama he met on his travels who, thinking he was a good fellow who might benefit from such an extraordinary teaching, taught him this very text. On another occasion he travelled with a poor widow, helping her to cook and to take care of her children, carrying them on his back. When they arrived at their destination, Patrul Rinpoche excused himself, saying he had something important to do. The woman heard that the great Patrul Rinpoche was teaching at the monastery. She went there to watch, and was amazed to see her travelling companion on the throne instructing a vast assembly. At the end of the teaching he asked that all the offerings be given to her.

To his students he was immensely kind, but also immensely tough. He treated beggars and kings in exactly the same way. In all situations his only interest was to benefit others, and he would always say whatever would be most useful, regardless of social niceties.

The stages of practice

The Words of My Perfect Teacher belongs to a category of literature known as "written guides" (*khrid yig*), which emulate and supplement the oral explanations needed to elucidate a meditation text. In this case the text in question is the preliminary practice of the *Heart-essence of the Vast Expanse*.

The *Heart-essence of the Vast Expanse* cycle of teachings that Longchenpa passed on to Jigme Lingpa has become one of the most widely practised in the Nyingmapa school. It contains a complete Vajrayāna path, starting at the beginner stage with the preliminary practices (*sngon 'gro*). Then comes the main practice (*dngos gzhi*), which has three principal parts, the generation phase (*bskyed rim*) the perfection phase (*rdzogs rim*), and the Great Perfection (*rdzogs pa chen po*).

The preliminary practices have an outer and an inner section, and our text is accordingly divided into two. The first part, the ordinary or external preliminaries, deals with 1) the freedoms and advantages offered by human life, 2) impermanence, 3) the sufferings of saṁsāra, 4) how karma, the principle of cause and effect, applies to all our actions, 5) the benefits of liberation and 6) how to follow a spiritual teacher. These elements are fundamental for a proper understanding of Buddhist values. They are general because they are the fundamentals of Buddhism in general. The contemplations in this section can be practiced by anyone, Buddhist or not.

The second part, the inner preliminaries, starts with taking refuge—learning to rely on the Buddha, the Dharma (his teaching) and the Saṅgha (the Buddhist community). This is the basis of Buddhist commitment common to all traditions. Next comes the development of bodhicitta, the "mind of enlightenment." This attitude of unconditional love and compassion, that seeks to bring all beings to perfect freedom, is the basis of the Mahāyāna. It is followed by practices to purify the effects of one's past negative actions and accumulate the positive energy necessary to progress on the path. These practices use more fully the techniques of visualization and mantra specific to the Vajrayāna approach.

Finally comes the Guru Yoga, uniting one's mind with the mind of the teacher. Guru Yoga is the very root of the Vajrayāna, where the purity of the link between teacher and disciple is of paramount importance. Also included here is the practice of *phowa*, or transference of consciousness, a shortcut method to enable those who are unable to pursue the path to the end to be liberated nonetheless at the time of death.

For the practices in Part Two, it is necessary to have the guidance of a qualified teacher. Indeed this is advisable for any spiritual practice. In precommunist Tibet almost all Tibetans considered themselves Buddhists, and they would try to follow Buddhist ethics, make offerings and recite some prayers and mantras. This remains largely true even in occupied Tibet today. A smaller number of those who are Buddhists in this general sense then take the decision to pursue the spiritual journey actively, and it is such people who would undertake these practices, usually repeating each element one hundred thousand times.

Next come the practices of the generation and perfection phases, culminating in the Great Perfection. In the Tibetan tradition the inner journey is mapped with astonishing precision. For each stage of the practice there are oral explanations and explanatory texts. Vajrayāna is a science of the mind, in which an expert teacher fully understands the significance of each experience, and the solution for each error. Our present text does not go into the details of the rest of the path, but we shall give a brief overview here, to give an idea of the progression that follows on from the preliminaries.

The preliminary practice

The outer preliminaries comprise the four contemplations which turn away from saṁsāra.

The inner preliminaries are 1) taking refuge, 2) bodhicitta, 3) purification through the practice of Vajrasattva, 4) accumulation of merit through the offering of the maṇḍala, and 5) Guru Yoga.

Sometimes there are additional elements, as in the *Heart-essence of the Vast Expanse*. The ritual text may be quite long or very short. This, however, is the general structure.

The generation phase

In the generation phase one learns to develop an enlightened vision of the world by visualizing oneself as a Buddha, and one's surroundings as a pure Buddhafield, while reciting the appropriate mantra. This process is at first artificial, something which is developed or generated, but the visualizations correspond to the visionary experience of enlightened beings. By adopting these new habits of perception, one can weaken the ordinary habits of gross perception based on ignorance and emotional tendencies, and put oneself in touch with a more subtle level of experience. These practices take the form of *sādhanas*, the ritual texts for which are sometimes extraordinarily poetic.

The perfection phase

Once the sacred vision has become a living experience, the perfection phase completes the process, taking it to a more interior level by working with the subtle energies of the body, through mastery of the breath, physical postures and other yogas.

The Great Perfection

In the generation and perfection phases one acquires the illustrative wisdom (*dpe'i ye shes*) through meditation experiences which serve as pointers to indicate the ultimate nature of the mind. In Dzogchen—the Great Perfection—the nature of the mind is introduced directly and suddenly by the teacher. This is an immediate experiential recognition of the Buddha-nature itself. The subsequent practice consists essentially in getting used to that experience and developing it in an increasingly vast way. Here one acquires real or absolute wisdom (*don gyi ye shes*), the direct experience of ultimate truth.

In a sense, each level of practice builds on the previous one, but at the same time it further strips away the layers of delusion, leaving an ever more denuded experience of reality. Each practice is also a complete path in itself, in which—for those who have the wisdom to see it—all the others are included. Even the preliminaries, and indeed the individual elements of the preliminaries, can, in themselves, constitute a complete path to enlightenment.

In particular, the Guru Yoga is the essence of all paths. The teachers of the lineage often say that all practices should be done in the manner of Guru Yoga. Total openness and devotion to a realized teacher is the most sure and rapid way to progress.

Patrul Rinpoche expresses this capital importance of the spiritual teacher in the very title of this book, Kunzang Lamai Shelung, which we have freely translated as *The Words of My Perfect Teacher.*

Kunzang means "everywhere perfect" or "always perfect." It is the abbreviated form of Kuntuzangpo (in Sanskrit, Samantabhadra), the primordial Buddha, source of all lineages. Kuntuzangpo is shown iconographically as a naked Buddha, the deep blue colour of the sky. However this symbol does not represent a person, but the Buddha-nature itself, the unchanging purity of the mind which is the fundamental nature of all beings. Normally this nature is hidden, and it is the teacher who has realized it himself who can lead us to discover it within ourselves, in all its glorious nakedness. Lama literally means, "there is nothing higher." This is the Tibetan expression for the Indian word Guru. Both these words have become overused in common speech, but, as Patrul Rinpoche explains, for us, the spiritual teacher is like the Buddha himself. He brings us the transmission of the Buddhas of the past, embodies for us the Buddhas of the present, and, through his teaching, is the source of the Buddhas of the future. Patrul Rinpoche says that the Guru Yoga is in a sense superior to the generation and perfection phases, because it directly opens the way to ultimate wisdom through the teacher's blessings.

The origins of this translation

The Tibetans have preserved all aspects of Indian Buddhism intact from the eighth century to the twentieth. This has not been, however, a mere static preservation of sacred treasures. The Buddha Dharma was the main preoccupation of Tibet's best minds for centuries, giving rise to an extraordinary range of philosophical, poetic, academic and inspirational literature, as well as a distinctive and magnificent artistic and architectural heritage. But above all, the Tibetans used the Buddhist teachings for their true purpose, as a tool for transforming the human mind, and thousands of practitioners, some of them famous teachers, others unknown yogīs, accomplished their final goal.

One might imagine that Tibet's greatest glories belong to the remote past, and that recent centuries represent a period of decline, but this is by no means the case. In fact each century (including the present one) and each generation has produced its share of spiritual giants. The nineteenth century, for example, saw a particular kind of renaissance. Patrul Rinpoche was a participant in the *rimé* or non-sectarian movement, inaugurated by Jamyang Khyentse Wangpo, Jamgön Kongtrul and others, which sought to break down the barriers that had crystallized between the different Buddhist schools, by studying and teaching them all impartially.

This spirit is still alive today, exemplified by His Holiness the Dalai Lama, and the late Dilgo Khyentse Rinpoche, who was the incarnation of Jamyang Khyentse Wangpo.

Dilgo Khyentse Rinpoche, like Patrul, came from Eastern Tibet. He spent twenty years of his life in meditation retreats, often in the simplest conditions. He studied with a vast number of teachers, even meeting some of Patrul Rinpoche's own disciples in his youth. He responded to the terrible destruction in Tibet in the nineteen fifties and sixties by working tirelessly to find, preserve and reprint lost texts, to establish monastic communities in exile, and above all to teach and inspire the new generation. He considered Patrul Rinpoche to be the perfect example of a Dzogchen practitioner, and encouraged and helped the translators of this book, which he considered to be the perfect guide for students embarking on the Buddhist path.

Our translation comes directly from within the tradition. In a sense it has its own lineage. Dudjom Rinpoche, Dilgo Khyentse Rinpoche, Kangyur Rinpoche, Nyoshul Khenpo Rinpoche, and the other lamas who taught us the entire text orally—and during the translation gave us their advice on the difficult points of the book—are realized holders of Patrul Rinpoche's teaching.

Although close adherence to the exact words of an original text commands a certain respect in Tibetan circles, we have found that such translations often make ideas which are perfectly lucid and reasonable in Tibetan seem unnecessarily obscure and even bizarre in English. For this book in particular, such a method could never reflect the extraordinary lively vernacular style and humour of the original. So although we have tried to be consistent in our translation of technical terms, we have aimed to reflect not only the words, but also the atmosphere and style, by rendering the ideas in a natural English, keeping as close to the Tibetan as possible, but not at the expense of the clarity and flow of the whole.

Brief explanations that we felt might be helpful to many readers appear as footnotes. There are also a large number of endnotes, not all of which will be of interest to the general reader. However we felt it important to include them, since they contain fascinating comments from the notes of Patrul Rinpoche's disciples, and interpretations of the more difficult points given by Dilgo Khyentse Rinpoche and other teachers. They will help the reader to avoid some common misunderstandings about Buddhist ideas; and for the Buddhist practitioner with some previous knowledge of the subject, these comments give a revealing extra dimension to the book.

A brief historical introduction to Tibetan Buddhism

Gautama the Buddha was born in Northern India in the fifth century BC, the son of a king who brought him up as heir to the throne. His birth and youth were remarkable, and it was clear from the beginning that the young prince Siddhartha was destined to be an extraordinary being. His early life was spent in palatial luxury, with few worries or cares, and he excelled in all the pursuits of his time, both academic and athletic.

Before long, however, he began to doubt the validity of his worldly life. Fleeing his father's palace, he sought a more meaningful life, studying under a number of highly regarded masters of philosophy and meditation. Such was the sincerity of his quest that he rapidly achieved the highest meditational accomplishments that these masters could teach him, but he was still not satisfied. Despite years of strenuous ascetic practice, he found that none of these systems could take him beyond the limits of conditioned existence. He decided to continue his search alone, and through his own efforts finally attained enlightenment at present-day Bodh Gaya. What he discovered was so profound and vast that at first he was reluctant to reveal it to anyone else, fearing that none would understand it. Later however he began teaching, and quickly attracted a large following of disciples, many of whom became highly accomplished in meditation.

The diversity of people who came to the Buddha to receive his teaching and practise his path called for a corresponding diversity in the way in which he taught, and different individuals or groups received different instructions appropriate to their respective temperaments and intellectual abilities. The teachings that the Buddha taught during his lifetime can therefore be broadly divided into three categories—those that were eventually collected together in the Pali Canon and form the basis for what is now known as the Theravāda School, emphasizing moral discipline and ethics; the teachings of the Mahāyāna, or Great Vehicle, which stress compassion and concern for others; and the tantric teachings of the Vajrayāna or Secret Mantrayāna, which use an enormous variety of skilful methods to bring about profound realization in a relatively short time. The latter were given by the Buddha himself only on a limited scale, but he predicted that they would be spread in this world by other enlightened beings, who would appear later. This is why the Vajrayāna is no less a Buddhist teaching than the other two schools, even though it was not widely taught in the Buddha's lifetime.

After his death the differences between the various teachings that he had given became more rigidly apparent as different schools and traditions took shape. The present Theravāda tradition, for example, has its beginnings in a group of the Buddha's disciples which later divided into eighteen schools. The Mahāyāna similarly diversified into a number of traditions, each with their own subtly individual philosophical differences. The same is true for the Vajrayāna, in which there is an immense variety of practices, many of which were originally taught only to a single individual.

During the centuries that followed, these different traditions were gradually propagated all over India and further afield, until Buddhism had extended its influence through much of Central, Eastern and Southern Asia, even as far as Indonesia. Some traditions were lost entirely, others merged into newer forms of Buddhism. By the thirteenth century AD, the arrival of Islam and political changes in Indian society had driven the Buddhadharma from its land of origin, and it was in other countries that the teachings were preserved—the Theravāda in Śrī Laṅkā, Burma, Thailand and Cambodia, the Mahāyāna in China, Japan, Korea and Indo-China, and the Vajrayāna mainly in Tibet. Tibet was doubly fortunate. Not only was it one of the few countries in which the Vajrayāna continued to be practised, it was also the only one in which the full range of teachings, from all three traditions, was transmitted and preserved.

Over the centuries these many strands of the Buddha's teaching have been handed down from master to student in the numerous lineages which comprise the four main schools of Tibetan Buddhism we know today. The members of these lineages were not simply learned scholars who studied the teachings they received, but fully realized individuals who had practised and mastered what had been transmitted to them, and were thus fully qualified to pass on the teachings to their students.

Of these four, the Nyingma school (whose name derives from the Tibetan for "old") follows the traditions which were originally introduced in the eighth century by such Indian masters as Śāntarakṣita, Vimalamitra and Padmasambhava, whom the Tibetans refer to as Guru Rinpoche, "the Precious Master," and handed down through fully realized Tibetan masters such as Longchenpa, Jigme Lingpa and Jamyang Khyentse Wangpo. The lineages which have been passed down to the other three main schools—the Kagyupa, Sakyapa and Gelugpa—were introduced into Tibet after the tenth century following the attempts by an anti-Buddhist king to destroy the Dharma in Tibet. Just as the different forms of

Buddhism in other parts of Asia had been adopted and had evolved to meet the needs of different peoples and cultures, each of these four schools had its origins and development in widely diverging situations—historical, geographical and even political—which served as a prism to split the light of the Buddha's teaching into a many-coloured spectrum of traditions and lineages. (Sadly, some Buddhists have tended to forget that this light has one source, and, as in the world's other great religions, sectarian divisions have sometimes masked the true message of Buddhism.)

The teachings preserved in the lineages of Tibetan Buddhism are contained in the enormous sacred literature of that tradition. The Kangyur, consisting of more than a hundred volumes, contains the scriptures originating from the time of the Buddha, and is divided into the Vinaya, dealing with ethics and discipline, the Sūtras, which are concerned with meditation, and the Abhidharma, which covers Buddhist philosophy. The numerous commentaries on these, and other major Buddhist works written later make up over two hundred volumes of the Tangyur. Both the Kangyur and Tangyur were translated into Tibetan mainly from Sanskrit and comprise the Tibetan Buddhist Canon. In addition to this, a vast number of other works exist: teachings introduced into Tibet from India from the eighth century onwards (including many of the Vajrayāna teachings), and countless commentaries on all three vehicles (Śrāvakayāna, Mahāyāna and Vajrayāna) written by Tibetan masters.

The enormous range of teachings to be found within Tibetan Buddhism can nevertheless be summarized by the Four Noble Truths, which the Buddha expounded shortly after his enlightenment. The first of these points out that our conditioned existence is never free from a state of suffering, never truly satisfactory. Any happiness we have is only temporary and in due course gives way to suffering. The reason for this, as explained by the second truth, is that any action one may do, say or think gives rise to a result which has to be experienced either later in one's life or in a future life. Indeed, rebirth is the result of one's actions, and the conditions into which one is born in one life are directly dependent on the actions one has done in previous lives, and particularly the motives and attitudes involved. This, the principle of cause and effect, explains why, for example, some people remain poor all their lives despite their efforts to become wealthy, while others have everything they could want even though they do nothing to gain it. The second truth goes on to show that the driving force behind our actions is the negative emotions such as hatred, attachment, pride, jealousy and, especially ignorance, which is the root of all the others. This ignorance concerns not only a lack of wisdom in how we act, but the basic ignorance behind how we ordinarily perceive the whole of existence and constantly become caught by our clinging to the idea of our own egos and of the outer world as solid and lasting. Because there is no end to our actions, there can be no end to our continuously taking rebirth in the cycle of conditioned existence. Only when we cease to act through ignorance can this cycle be broken, as shown by the third truth which expounds the cessation of suffering and freedom from conditioned existence.

The fourth truth explains the way through which this can be achieved. This essentially means, on the one hand, the accumulation of positive actions, such as venerating and making offerings to the Buddha, Dharma (his teaching), and Saṅgha (the community of practitioners), and practising charity and so on; and on the other hand, the practice of meditation, which can directly dispel the root ignorance which is the cause of suffering. A practitioner who follows this path with only his own liberation in mind can attain a high degree of realization and become an Arhat (one who has overcome the negative emotions). But this is not full enlightenment. Only those who have as their motivation the good and ultimate enlightenment of all other beings can attain final Buddhahood. Such practitioners, who follow the path of the Great Vehicle based on compassion, are known as Bodhisattvas. A Bodhisattva who moreover practises the profound and skilful teachings of the Vajrayāna is able to become fully enlightened in a very short time.

During his lifetime the Buddha created a community of monks and nuns who became the core for upholding and continuing the teachings. This did not, however, exclude lay men and women as serious followers of the path, and this was reflected in Tibet where, from the 8th century onwards, the community of practitioners comprised two complementary congregations: on the one hand, a very large monastic community, and on the other a strong tradition of practitioners with lay ordination, whether yogīs or householders, many of whom would appear to be leading ordinary lives while following an inner spiritual path and eventually attaining full realization.* Within the Nyingmapa tradition monastic ordination is considered a very useful support for the practice, but by no means the only way to progress in meditation. This is encouraging for those who seriously wish to put the teachings into practice but are unable

* The 'community of red-robed celibates' (*rab byung ngur smrigs sde*) and 'community of the white-clad with long plaited hair' (*gos dkar lcang lo can kyi sde*).

to involve themselves in a monastic lifestyle.

Albert Einstein once pointed out that Buddhism was the tradition that he felt fulfilled the criteria he thought necessary for a spiritual path adapted to the twentieth century. Today modern physicists are drawing conclusions which approach the doctrines the Buddha expounded two thousand five hundred years ago. While the attractions of materialism have had an adverse affect on traditional spiritual life throughout Asia, there are increasing numbers of people in the West who are showing an interest in the possibilities offered by the study and practice of Buddhism.

When the continuity of the Buddhist lineages was threatened by the political changes in Tibet in the nineteen fifties, numerous qualified lamas, who had not only received the proper lineage transmissions from their teachers, but also, through study and meditation, gained full understanding and realization of the teachings, sought to preserve them by bringing them to India. At the same time, some Western visitors to India began to show an interest in these lamas and their spiritual heritage. Since it had been said by Guru Rinpoche that, of the Buddha's teachings, the Vajrayāna would prove especially powerful and effective for individuals living in a time when emotions are stronger than ever, many teachers felt that it would be appropriate to introduce these teachings to the West. The Vajrayāna is particularly flexible and adaptable to the sorts of situations in which modern people find themselves, and, without losing its traditional form, has now been taught to a wide range of people all over the world.

Patrul Rinpoche (1808-1887)

THE WORDS OF MY PERFECT TEACHER

a guide to the preliminaries for the *Heart-essence of the Vast Expanse* from the Great Perfection

Prologue

Venerable teachers whose compassion is infinite and
unconditional, I prostrate myself before you all.

Conquerors of the mind lineage; Vidyādharas of the symbol lineage;
Most fortunate of ordinary beings who,
Guided by the enlightened ones, have attained the twofold goal—
Teachers of the three lineages, I prostrate myself before you.

In the expanse where all phenomena come to exhaustion, you
encountered the wisdom of dharmakāya;
In the clear light of empty space you saw sambhogakāya
Buddhafields appear;
To work for beings' benefit you appeared to them in nirmāṇakāya
form.
Omniscient Sovereign of Dharma, * *I prostrate myself before you.*

In your wisdom you saw the true nature of whatever can be
known;
The light of your love beamed benefit upon all beings;
You elucidated the teachings of the profound path, summit of all
vehicles.
Rigdzin Jigme Lingpa, I prostrate myself before you.

You were Lord Avalokiteśvara himself in the form of a spiritual
friend;
Whoever heard you speak was established on the path to freedom;
To fulfil all beings' needs your activity was infinite;
Gracious root teacher, I prostrate myself before you.

* Longchenpa.

The writings of Omniscient Longchenpa and his lineage contain the Buddha's entire teachings:
The quintessential pith instructions that bring Buddhahood in a single lifetime,
The ordinary, outer, and the inner preliminaries of the path
And the additional advice on the swift path of transference.

May the Buddhas and the teachers bless me
That I may explain definitively as I have remembered them,
Wonderfully profound, yet clear and easy to understand—
The unerring words of my perfect teacher.

This faithful record of my peerless teacher's instructions on the general outer and inner preliminaries for the *Heart-essence of the Vast Expanse* from the Great Perfection is divided into three parts: the ordinary outer preliminaries; the extraordinary inner preliminaries; and, as part of the main practice, the swift path of transference.

Part One

THE ORDINARY OR OUTER PRELIMINARIES

THE DIFFICULTY OF FINDING THE FREEDOMS AND ADVANTAGES

THE IMPERMANENCE OF LIFE

THE DEFECTS OF SAṀSĀRA

ACTIONS: THE PRINCIPLE OF CAUSE AND EFFECT

THE BENEFITS OF LIBERATION

HOW TO FOLLOW A SPIRITUAL FRIEND

Jamyang Khyentse Wangpo (1820-1892)

The first Khyentse. One of the main holders of the *Heart-essence of the Vast Expanse*. He was one of the founders of the ecumenical movement in which the teachings particular to all traditions of Tibetan Buddhism are studied impartially, creating a spiritual renaissance in Tibet. He saved many teachings whose lineages were about to disappear.

CHAPTER ONE

The difficulty of finding the freedoms and advantages

The main subject of the chapter, the teaching on how difficult it is to find the freedoms and advantages, is preceded by an explanation of the proper way to listen to any spiritual instruction.

I. THE PROPER WAY TO LISTEN TO SPIRITUAL TEACHING

The proper way to listen to the teachings has two aspects: the right attitude and the right conduct.

1. Attitude

The right attitude combines the vast attitude of the *bodhicitta*, the mind of enlightenment, and the vast skill in means of the Secret Mantrayāna.

1.1 THE VAST ATTITUDE OF THE BODHICITTA

There is not a single being in saṁsāra, this immense ocean of suffering, who in the course of time without beginning has never been our father or mother. When they were our parents, these beings' only thought was to raise us with the greatest possible kindness, protecting us with great love and giving us the very best of their own food and clothing.

All of these beings, who have been so kind to us, want to be happy, and yet they have no idea how to put into practice what brings about happiness, the ten positive actions. None of them want to suffer, but they do not know how to give up the ten negative actions at the root of all suffering. Their deepest wishes and what they actually do thus contradict each other. Poor beings, lost and confused, like a blind man abandoned in the middle of an empty plain!

Tell yourself: "It is for their well-being that I am going to listen to the profound Dharma and put it into practice. I will lead all these beings, my parents, tormented by the miseries of the six realms of existence, to the state of omniscient Buddhahood, freeing them from all the karmic phenomena, habitual patterns and sufferings of every one of the six realms." It is important to have this attitude each time you listen to teachings or practise them.

Whenever you do something positive, whether of major or minor importance, it is indispensable to enhance it with the three supreme methods. Before beginning, arouse the bodhicitta as a skilful means to make sure that the action becomes a source of good for the future. While carrying out the action, avoid getting involved in any conceptualization,[1] so that the merit cannot be destroyed by circumstances.[2] At the end, seal the action properly by dedicating the merit, which will ensure that it continually grows ever greater.[3]

The way you listen to the Dharma is very important. But even more important is the motivation with which you listen to it.

> What makes an action good or bad?
> Not how it looks, nor whether it is big or small,
> But the good or evil motivation behind it.

No matter how many teachings you have heard, to be motivated by ordinary concerns—such as a desire for greatness, fame or whatever—is not the way of the true Dharma. So, first of all, it is most important to turn inwards and change your motivation. If you can correct your attitude, skilful means will permeate your positive actions, and you will have set out on the path of great beings. If you cannot, you might think that you are studying and practising the Dharma but it will be no more than a semblance of the real thing. Therefore, whenever you listen to the teachings and whenever you practise, be it meditating on a deity, doing prostrations and circumambulations, or reciting a mantra—even a single *maṇi*—it is always essential to give rise to bodhicitta.

1.2 VAST SKILL IN MEANS: THE ATTITUDE OF THE SECRET MANTRAYĀNA

The *Torch of the Three Methods* says of the Secret Mantrayāna:

It has the same goal but is free from all confusion,[4]
It is rich in methods and without difficulties.[5]
It is for those with sharp faculties.[6]
The Mantra Vehicle is sublime.

The Mantrayāna can be entered by many routes. It contains many methods for accumulating merit and wisdom, and profound skilful means to make the potential within us manifest[7] without our having to undergo great hardships. The basis for these methods is the way we direct our aspirations:

Everything is circumstantial
And depends entirely on one's aspiration.

Do not consider the place where the Dharma is being taught, the teacher, the teachings and so on as ordinary and impure. As you listen, keep the *five perfections* clearly in mind:

The perfect *place* is the citadel of the absolute expanse, called Akaniṣṭha, "the Unexcelled." The perfect *teacher* is Samantabhadra, the dharmakāya. The perfect *assembly* consists of the male and female Bodhisattvas and deities[8] of the mind lineage of the Conquerors and of the symbol lineage of the Vidyādharas.

Or you can think that the place where the Dharma is being taught is the Lotus-Light Palace of the Glorious Copper-coloured Mountain, the teacher who teaches is Padmasambhava of Oḍḍiyāna, and we, the audience, are the Eight Vidyādharas, the Twenty-five Disciples, and the ḍākas and ḍākinīs.

Or consider that this perfect place is the Eastern Buddhafield, Manifest Joy, where the perfect teacher Vajrasattva, the perfect sambhogakāya, is teaching the assembly of the divinities of the Vajra Family and male and female Bodhisattvas.

Equally well, the perfect place where the Dharma is being taught can be the Western Buddhafield, the Blissful, the perfect teacher the Buddha Amitābha, and the assembly the male and female Bodhisattvas and deities of the Lotus family.

Whatever the case, the *teaching* is that of the Great Vehicle and the *time* is the ever-revolving wheel of eternity.

These visualizations[9] are to help us understand how things are in reality. It is not that we are temporarily creating something that does not really exist.

The teacher embodies the essence of all Buddhas throughout the three times. He is the union of the Three Jewels: his body is the Saṅgha, his speech the Dharma, his mind the Buddha. He is the union of the Three Roots: his body is the teacher, his speech the yidam, his mind the ḍākinī. He is the union of the three kāyas: his body is the nirmāṇakāya, his speech the sambhogakāya, his mind the dharmakāya. He is the embodiment of all the Buddhas of the past, source of all the Buddhas of the future and the representative of all the Buddhas of the present. Since he takes as his disciples degenerate beings like us, whom none of the thousand Buddhas of the Good Kalpa[10] could help, his compassion and bounty exceed that of all Buddhas.

> The teacher is the Buddha, the teacher is the Dharma,
> The teacher is also the Saṅgha.
> The teacher is the one who accomplishes everything.
> The teacher is Glorious Vajradhara.

We, as the assembly gathered to listen to the teachings, use the basis of our own Buddha-nature, the support of our precious human life, the circumstance of having a spiritual friend and the method of following his advice, to become the Buddhas of the future. As the *Hevajra Tantra* says:

> All beings are Buddhas,
> But this is concealed by adventitious stains.
> When their stains are purified, their Buddhahood is revealed.

2. Conduct

The right conduct while listening to teachings is described in terms of what to avoid and what to do.

2.1 WHAT TO AVOID

Conduct to avoid includes the three defects of the pot, the six stains and the five wrong ways of remembering.

2.1.1 The Three Defects of the Pot

Not to listen is to be like a pot turned upside down. Not to be able to retain what you hear is to be like a pot with a hole in it. To mix negative emotions with what you hear is to be like a pot with poison in it.

The upside-down pot. When you are listening to the teachings, listen to what is being said and do not let yourself be distracted by anything else. Otherwise you will be like an upside-down pot on which liquid is being poured. Although you are physically present, you do not hear a word of the teaching.

The pot with a hole in it. If you just listen without remembering anything that you hear or understand, you will be like a pot with a leak: however much liquid is poured into it, nothing can stay. No matter how many teachings you hear, you can never assimilate them or put them into practice.

The pot containing poison. If you listen to the teachings with the wrong attitude, such as the desire to become great or famous, or a mind full of the five poisons, the Dharma will not only fail to help your mind; it will also be changed into something that is not Dharma at all, like nectar poured into a pot containing poison.

This is why the Indian sage, Padampa Sangye, said:

> Listen to the teachings like a deer listening to music;
> Contemplate them like a northern nomad shearing sheep;*
> Meditate on them like a dumb person savouring food;**
> Practise them like a hungry yak eating grass;
> Reach their result, like the sun coming out from behind the clouds.

When listening to the teachings, you should be like a deer so entranced by the sound of the *vīṇā* that it does not notice the hidden hunter shooting his poisoned arrow. Put your hands together palm to palm and listen, every pore on your body tingling and your eyes wet with tears, never letting any other thought get in the way.

It is no good listening with only your body physically present, while your mind wanders off after your thoughts and your speech lets loose a rich store of gossip, saying whatever you like and looking around everywhere. When listening to teachings, you should even stop reciting prayers, counting mantras, or whatever other meritorious activities you may be doing.

After you have listened properly to a teaching in this way, it is then also important to retain the meaning of what has been said without ever forgetting it, and to continually put it into practice. For, as the Great Sage himself said:

> I have shown you the methods
> That lead to liberation.
> But you should know

* That is to say, meticulously, in their entirety, and without distraction.

** A dumb person can taste, but not describe the flavours he is tasting. In the same way, the taste of true meditation is beyond any description or concepts.

> That liberation depends upon yourself.

The teacher gives the disciple instructions explaining how to listen to the Dharma and how to apply it, how to give up negative actions, how to perform positive ones, and how to practise. It is up to the disciple to remember those instructions, forgetting nothing; to put them into practice; and to realize them.

Just listening to the Dharma is perhaps of some benefit by itself. But unless you remember what you hear, you will not have the slightest knowledge of either the words or the meaning of the teaching—which is no different from not having heard it at all.

If you remember the teachings but mix them with your negative emotions, they will never be the pure Dharma. As the peerless Dagpo Rinpoche says:

> Unless you practise Dharma according to the Dharma,
> Dharma itself becomes the cause of evil rebirths.

Rid yourself of every wrong thought concerning the teacher and the Dharma, do not criticize or abuse your spiritual brothers and companions, be free of pride and contempt, abandon all bad thoughts. For all of these cause lower rebirths.

2.1.2 The Six Stains

In the *Well Explained Reasoning*, it says:

> Pride, lack of faith and lack of effort,
> Outward distraction, inward tension and discouragement;
> These are the six stains.

Avoid these six: proudly believing yourself superior to the teacher who is explaining the Dharma, not trusting the master and his teachings, failing to apply yourself to the Dharma, getting distracted by external events, focussing your five senses too intently inwards, and being discouraged if, for example, a teaching is too long.

Of all negative emotions, pride and jealousy are the most difficult to recognize. Therefore, examine your mind minutely. Any feeling that there is something even the least bit special about your own qualities, whether worldly or spiritual, will make you blind to your own faults and unaware of others' good qualities. So renounce pride and always take a low position.

If you have no faith, the entrance to the Dharma is blocked. Of the four types of faith,[11] aim for faith that is irreversible.

Your interest[12] in the Dharma is the basis of what you will achieve. So depending on whether your degree of interest is superior, middling or inferior you will become a superior, middling or inferior practitioner. And if you are not at all interested in the Dharma, there will be no results at all. As the proverb puts it:

> The Dharma is nobody's property. It belongs to whoever has the most endeavour.

The Buddha himself obtained the teachings at the price of hundreds of hardships. To obtain a single four-line verse, he gouged holes in his own flesh to serve as offering lamps, filling them with oil and planting in them thousands of burning wicks. He leapt into flaming pits, and drove a thousand iron nails into his body.[13]

> Even if you have to face blazing infernos or razor-sharp blades,
> Search for the Dharma until you die.

Listen to the teachings, therefore, with great effort, ignoring heat, cold and all other trials.

The tendency of consciousness to get engrossed in the objects of the six senses[14] is the root of all saṁsāra's hallucinations and the source of all suffering. This is how the moth dies in the lamp-flame, because its visual consciousness is attracted to forms; how the stag is killed by the hunter, because its hearing draws it to sounds; how bees are swallowed by carnivorous plants, seduced by their smell; how fish are caught with bait, their sense of taste lured by its flavour; how elephants drown in the swamp because they love the physical feeling of mud. In the same way, whenever you are listening to the Dharma, teaching, meditating or practising, it is important not to follow tendencies from the past, not to entertain emotions about the future and not to let your present thoughts get distracted by anything around you. As Gyalse Rinpoche says:

> Your past joys and sorrows are like drawings on water:
> No trace of them remains. Don't run after them!
> But should they come to mind, reflect on how success and failure come and go.
> Is there anything you can trust besides Dharma, maṇi-reciters?[15]
>
> Your future projects and plans are like nets cast in a dry riverbed:
> They'll never bring what you want. Limit your desires and aspirations!

> But should they come to mind, think how uncertain it is when
> you'll die:
> Have you got time for anything other than Dharma, maṇi-reciters?
>
> Your present work is like a job in a dream.
> Since all such effort is pointless, cast it aside.
> Consider even your honest earnings without any attachment.
> Activities are without essence, maṇi-reciters!
>
> Between meditation sessions, learn to control in this way all
> thoughts arising from the three poisons;
> Until all thoughts and perceptions arise as the dharmakāya,
> This is indispensable—remembering it whenever you need it,
> Do not give rein to deluded thoughts, maṇi-reciters!

It is also said:

> Don't invite the future. If you do,
> You're like the father of Famous Moon!

This refers to the story of a poor man who came across a large pile of barley. He put it in a big sack, tied it to a rafter, and then lay down beneath it and started to day-dream.

"This barley is going to make me really rich," he thought. "Once I'm rich, I'll get myself a wife ... She's bound to have a boy... What shall I call him?"

Just then, the moon appeared and he decided to call his son Famous Moon. However, all this time a rat had been gnawing away at the rope that was holding up the sack. The rope suddenly snapped, the sack fell on the man and he was killed.

Such dreams about the past and the future will never come to fruition and are only a distraction. Give them up altogether. Be mindful and listen with attention and care.

Do not focus too intently, picking out individual words and points, like a *dremo* bear digging up marmots—each time you seize one item, you forget the one before, and will never get to understand the whole. Too much concentration also makes you sleepy. Instead, keep a balance between tight and loose.

Once, in the past, Ānanda was teaching Śroṇa to meditate. Śroṇa had great difficulty getting it right. Sometimes he was too tense, sometimes too relaxed. Śroṇa went to discuss the matter with the Buddha, who asked him: "When you were a layman, you were a good *vīṇā*-player, weren't you?"

"Yes, I played very well."

"Did your *vīṇā* sound best when the strings were very slack or when they were very taut?"

"It sounded best when they were neither too taut nor too loose."

"It is the same for your mind," said the Buddha; and by practising with that advice Śroṇa attained his goal.

Machik Labdrön says:

> Be firmly concentrated and loosely relaxed:[16]
> Here is an essential point for the View.

Do not let your mind get too tense or too inwardly concentrated; let your senses be naturally at ease, balanced between tension and relaxation.

You should not tire of listening to the teachings. Do not feel discouraged when you get hungry or thirsty during a teaching that goes on too long, or when you have to put up with discomfort caused by wind, sun, rain and so forth. Just be glad that you now have the freedoms and advantages of human life, that you have met an authentic teacher, and that you can listen to his profound instructions.

The fact that you are at this moment listening to the profound Dharma is the fruit of merits accumulated over innumerable kalpas. It is like eating a meal when you have only eaten once every hundred mealtimes throughout your life. So it is imperative to listen with joy, vowing to bear heat, cold and whatever trials and difficulties might arise, in order to receive these teachings.

2.1.3 The Five Wrong Ways of Remembering

> Avoid remembering the words but forgetting the meaning,
> Or remembering the meaning but forgetting the words.
> Avoid remembering both but with no understanding,
> Remembering them out of order, or remembering them incorrectly.

Do not attach undue importance to elegant turns of phrase without making any attempt to analyze the profound meaning of the words, like a child gathering flowers. Words alone are of no benefit for the mind. On the other hand, do not disregard the way in which the teachings are expressed, as being just the words and therefore dispensable. For then, even if you grasp the profound meaning, you will no longer have the means through which to express it. Words and meaning will have lost their connection.[17]

If you remember the teaching without identifying the different levels—the expedient meaning, the real meaning and the indirect meaning—you will be confused about what the words refer to.[18] This may lead you away from the true Dharma. If you remember it out of order, you will mix up the proper sequence of the teaching, and every time you listen to it, explain it, or meditate on it the confusion will be multiplied. If you remember incorrectly what has been said, endless wrong ideas will proliferate.[19] This will spoil your mind and debase the teaching. Avoid all these errors and remember everything—the words, the meaning and the order of the teachings—properly and without any mistake.

However long and difficult the teaching may be, do not feel disheartened and wonder if it will ever end; persevere. And however short and simple it may be, do not undervalue it as just elementary.

To remember both words and meaning perfectly, in the right order and with everything properly linked together, is therefore indispensable.

2.2 WHAT TO DO

The conduct to be adopted while listening to teachings is explained as the four metaphors, the six transcendent perfections, and other modes of conduct.

2.2.1 The Four Metaphors

The *Sūtra Arranged like a Tree* says:

> Noble one, you should think of yourself as someone who is sick,
> Of the Dharma as the remedy,
> Of your spiritual friend as a skilful doctor
> And of diligent practice as the way to recovery.

We are sick. From beginningless time, in this immense ocean of suffering that is saṁsāra, we have been tormented by the illness of the three poisons and their fruit, the three kinds of suffering.

When people are seriously ill, they go to consult a good doctor. They follow the doctor's advice, take whatever medicine he prescribes, and do all they can to overcome the disease and get well. In the same way, you should cure yourself of the diseases of karma, negative emotions and suffering by following the prescriptions of that experienced doctor, the authentic teacher, and by taking the medicine of the Dharma.

Following a teacher without doing what he says is like disobeying your doctor, which leaves him no chance of treating your illness. Not taking the medicine of the Dharma—that is to say, not putting it into practice—is like having innumerable medications and prescriptions beside your bed but never touching them. That will never cure your disease.

These days, people say full of optimism, "Lama, look on me with compassion!" thinking that even if they have done many terrible things, they will never have to endure the consequences. They reckon that the teacher, in his compassion, will toss them up into the heavenly realms as if he were throwing a pebble. But when we speak of the teacher holding us with his compassion, what this really means is that he has lovingly accepted us as disciples, and that he gives us his profound instructions, opens our eyes to what to do and what not to do and shows us the way to liberation taught by the Conqueror. What greater compassion could there be? It is up to us whether or not we take advantage of this compassion and actually pursue the path of liberation.

Now that we have this free and well-endowed human birth, now that we know what we should and should not do, our decision at this juncture, when we have the freedom to choose, marks the turning-point which will determine our fate, for better or worse, far into the future.[20] It is crucial that we choose between saṁsāra and nirvāṇa once and for all and put the instructions of our teacher into practice.

Those who conduct village ceremonies will have you believe that on your death-bed you can still go up or down, as if you were steering a horse by the reins. But by that time, unless you have already mastered the path, the fierce wind of your past actions will be chasing after you, while in front a terrifying black darkness rushes toward you as you are driven helplessly down the long and perilous path of the intermediate state. The Lord of Death's countless henchmen will be pursuing you, crying, "Kill! Kill! Strike! Strike!" How could such a moment—when there is no place to run to and nowhere to hide, no refuge and no hope, when you are desperate and have no idea what to do—how could such a moment be the turning point at which you control whether you go up or down? As the Great One of Oḍḍiyāna says:

> By the time empowerment is being given to the card marked with your name,[21] it's too late! Your consciousness, already wandering in the intermediate state like a dazed dog, will find it very hard to even think of higher realms.

In fact the turning point, the only time that you really can direct yourself up or down as if steering a horse with the reins, is right now, while you are still alive.

As a human being, your positive actions are more powerful than those of other kinds of being. This gives you, on the one hand, an opportunity here and now in this very life to cast rebirth aside once and for all.[22] But your negative actions are more powerful too; thus you are also quite capable of making sure, on the other hand, that you will never get free from the depths of the lower realms. So now that you have met the teacher, the skilful doctor, and the Dharma, the elixir that conquers death, this is the moment to apply the four metaphors, putting the teachings you have heard into practice, and travelling the path of liberation.

The *Treasury of Precious Qualities* describes four wrong notions that must be avoided, which are the opposite of the four metaphors we have mentioned:

> Shallow-tongued men with evil natures
> Approach the teacher as if he were a musk-deer.
> Having extracted the musk, the perfect Dharma,
> Full of joy, they sneer at the samaya.

Such people behave as though their spiritual teacher were a musk-deer, the Dharma were the musk, they themselves the hunters, and intense practice the way to kill the deer with an arrow or a trap. They do not practise the teachings they have received and feel no gratitude toward the teacher. They use Dharma to accumulate evil actions, which will drag them down like a millstone to the lower realms.

2.2.2 The Six Transcendent Perfections

In the *Tantra of Thorough Comprehension of the Instructions on all Dharma Practices*, it says:

> Make excellent offerings such as flowers and cushions,
> Put the place in order and control your behaviour,
> Do not harm any living being,
> Have genuine faith in your teacher,
> Listen to his instructions without distraction
> And question him in order to dispel your doubts;
> These are the six transcendent perfections of a listener.

A person listening to the teaching should practise the six transcendent perfections as follows:

Prepare the teacher's seat, arrange cushions upon it, offer a maṇḍala, flowers and other offerings. This is the practice of *generosity.*

Sweep clean the place or room after carefully settling the dust with water, and refrain from all disrespectful conduct. This is the practice of *discipline.*

Avoid harm to living beings, even the smallest of insects, and bear heat, cold and all other difficulties. This is the practice of *patience.*

Lay aside any wrong views concerning the teacher and the teaching and listen joyfully with genuine faith. This is the practice of *diligence.*

Listen to the Lama's instructions without distraction. This is the practice of *concentration.*

Ask questions to clear up any hesitations and doubts. This is the practice of *wisdom.*

2.2.3 Other Modes of Conduct

All forms of disrespectful behaviour should be avoided. The *Vinaya* says:

> Do not teach those who have no respect,
> Who cover their heads although in good health,
> Who carry canes, weapons and parasols,
> Or whose heads are swathed in turbans.

And the *Jātaka*s:

> Take the lowest seat.
> Cultivate the dignified bearing of thorough discipline.
> With your eyes brimming with joy,
> Drink in the words like nectar
> And be completely concentrated.
> That is the way to listen to the teaching.

II. THE TEACHING ITSELF: AN EXPLANATION OF HOW DIFFICULT IT IS TO FIND THE FREEDOMS AND ADVANTAGES

The main subject of the chapter is explained in four sections: reflecting on the nature of freedom, reflecting on the particular advantages related to Dharma, reflecting on images that show how difficult it is to find the freedoms and advantages, and reflecting on numerical comparisons.

1. Reflecting on the nature of freedom

In general, here, "freedom" means to have the opportunity to practise Dharma and not to be born in one of the eight states without that opportunity. "Lack of freedom" refers to those eight states where there is no such opportunity:

Being born in the hells, in the preta realm,
As an animal, a long-lived god or a barbarian,
Having wrong views, being born when there is no Buddha
Or being born deaf and mute; these are the eight states without freedom.

Beings reborn in hell have no opportunity to practise the Dharma because they are constantly tormented by intense heat or cold.

The *pretas* have no opportunity to practise the Dharma because of the suffering they experience from hunger and thirst.

Animals have no opportunity to practise the Dharma because they undergo slavery and suffer from the attacks of other animals.

The long-lived gods have no opportunity to practise the Dharma because they spend their time in a state of mental blankness.[23]

Those born in border countries have no opportunity to practise the Dharma because the doctrine of the Buddha is unknown in such places.

Those born as *tīrthikas** or with similar wrong views have no opportunity to practise the Dharma because their minds are so influenced by those mistaken beliefs.

Those born during a dark kalpa have no opportunity to practise the Dharma because they never even hear of the Three Jewels, and cannot distinguish good from bad.

Those born mute or mentally deficient have no opportunity to practise the Dharma because their faculties are incomplete.

The inhabitants of the three lower realms suffer constantly from heat, cold, hunger, thirst and other torments, as a result of their past negative actions; they have no opportunity to practise the Dharma.

"Barbarians" means those who live in the thirty-two border countries, such as Lo Khaṭha,[24] and all those who consider harming others an act of faith or whose savage beliefs see taking life as good. These people inhabiting the outlying territories have human form, but their minds lack the right orientation and they cannot attune themselves to the Dharma. Inheriting from their forefathers such pernicious customs as marriage to their mothers, they live in a way that is the very opposite of Dharma practice. Everything they do is evil, and it is in techniques of such harmful activities as killing insects and hunting wild beasts that they truly excel.

* Tīrthika, (*mu rtegs pa*): an adherent of non-Buddhist religious or philosophical traditions, implying the wrong views described on page 110.

Many of them fall into lower realms as soon as they die. For such people there is no opportunity to practise the Dharma.

The long-lived gods are those gods who are absorbed in a state of mental blankness. Beings are born in this realm as a result of believing that liberation is a state in which all mental activities, good or bad, are absent, and of meditating upon that state. They remain in such states of concentration for great kalpas on end. But once the effect of the past actions that produced that condition has exhausted itself they are reborn in the lower realms because of their wrong views. They, too, lack any opportunity to practise the Dharma.

The term "wrong views" includes, in general, eternalist and nihilist beliefs, which are views contrary to, and outside, the teaching of the Buddha. Such views spoil our minds and prevent us from aspiring to the authentic Dharma, to the extent that we no longer have the opportunity to practise it. Here in Tibet, because the second Buddha, Padmasambhava of Oḍḍiyāna, entrusted the protection of the land to the twelve Tenma, the tīrthikas themselves have not really been able to penetrate. However, anyone whose understanding is like that of the tīrthikas, and contrary to that of the authentic Dharma and authentic masters, will thereby be deprived of the opportunity to practise according to those true teachings. The monk Sunakṣatra spent twenty-five years as Lord Buddha's attendant, and yet, because he did not have the slightest faith and held only wrong views, ended up being reborn as a preta in a flower-garden.

Birth in a dark kalpa means to be reborn in a period during which there is no Buddha. In a universe where no Buddha has appeared, no-one has ever even heard of the Three Jewels. As there is no Dharma, there is no opportunity to practise it.

The mind of a person born deaf and mute cannot function properly and the process of listening to the teachings, expounding them, reflecting on them and putting them into practice is impeded. The description "deaf mute" usually refers to a speech dysfunction. It becomes a condition without the opportunity for Dharma when the usual human ability to use and understand language is absent. This category therefore also includes those whose mental disability makes them unable to comprehend the teachings and thus deprives them of the opportunity to practise them.

2. Reflecting on the particular advantages related to Dharma

Under this heading are included five individual advantages and five circumstantial advantages.

2.1 THE FIVE INDIVIDUAL ADVANTAGES

Nāgārjuna lists them as follows:

> Born a human, in a central place, with all one's faculties,
> Without a conflicting lifestyle and with faith in the Dharma.

Without a human life, it would not be possible even to encounter the Dharma. So this human body is the advantage of *support*.

Had you been born in a remote place where Dharma was unheard of, you would never have come across it. But the region you were born in is central as far as Dharma is concerned and so you have the advantage of *place*.

Not to have all your sense faculties intact would be a hindrance to the practice of Dharma. If you are free of such disabilities, you have the advantage of *possessing the sense faculties*.

If you had a conflicting lifestyle, you would always be immersed in negative actions and at variance with the Dharma. Since you now have the wish to do positive actions, this is the advantage of *intention*.

If you had no faith in the Buddha's teachings you would not feel any inclination for the Dharma. Having the ability to turn your mind to the Dharma, as you are doing now, constitutes the advantage of *faith*.

Because these five advantages need to be complete with regard to one's own make-up, they are called the *five individual advantages*.

To practice the real, authentic Dharma, it is absolutely necessary to be a human being. Now, suppose that you did not have the support of a human form, but had the highest form of life in the three lower realms, that of an animal—even the most beautiful and highly prized animal known to man. If someone said to you, "Say *Oṁ maṇi padme hūṁ* once, and you will become a Buddha," you would be quite incapable of understanding his words or grasping their meaning, nor would you be able to utter a word. In fact, even if you were dying of cold, you would be unable to think of anything to do but lie in a heap—whereas a man, no matter how weak, would know how to shelter in a cave or under a tree, and would gather wood and make a fire to warm his face and hands. If animals are incapable of even such simple things, how could they ever conceive of practising Dharma?

Gods and other beings of the kind, however superior their physical form, do not meet the requirements laid down for taking the *prātimokṣa* vows, and therefore cannot assimilate the Dharma in its totality.

As to what is meant by a "central region," one should distinguish between a geographically central region and a place that is central in terms of the Dharma.

Geographically speaking, the central region is generally said to be the Vajra Seat at Bodh Gaya[25] in India, at the centre of Jambudvīpa, the Southern Continent. The thousand Buddhas of the Good Kalpa all attain enlightenment there. Even in the universal destruction at the end of the kalpa, the four elements cannot harm it, and it remains there as if suspended in space. At its centre grows the Tree of Enlightenment. This place, with all the towns of India around it, is therefore considered the central region in terms of geography.

In Dharma terms, a central place is wherever the Dharma—the teaching of Lord Buddha—exists. All other regions are said to be peripheral.

In the distant past, from the time Lord Buddha came into this world and as long as his doctrine still existed in India, that land was central in terms of both geography and Dharma. However, now that it has fallen into the hands of the tīrthikas and the doctrine of the Conqueror has disappeared in that region, as far as Dharma is concerned even Bodh Gaya is a peripheral place.

In the days of the Buddha, Tibet, the Land of Snows, was called "the border country of Tibet," because it was a sparsely populated land to which the doctrine had not yet spread. Later, the population increased little by little, and there reigned several kings who were emanations of the Buddhas. The Dharma first appeared in Tibet during the reign of Lha-Thothori Nyentsen, when the *Sūtra of a Hundred Invocations and Prostrations*, a *tsa-tsa* mould and other objects fell on to the palace roof.

Five generations later, in accordance with prophecies that he would understand the meaning of the sūtra, there appeared the Dharma King Songtsen Gampo, an emanation of the Sublime Compassionate One.* During Songtsen Gampo's reign, the translator Thönmi Sambhota was sent to India to study its languages and scripts. On his return he introduced an alphabet to Tibet for the first time. He translated into Tibetan twenty-one sūtras and tantras of Avalokiteśvara, *The Powerful Secret*, and various other texts. The king himself displayed multiple forms, and along with his minister Gartongtsen, he used miraculous means to defend the country. He took as his queens two princesses, one Chinese and one from Nepal, who brought with them numerous representations of the Buddha's body, speech and mind including the statues called the Jowo Mikyö Dorje and the Jowo Śākyamuni, the actual representatives of the Buddha.[26] The king built the series of temples known as the Thadul and Yangdul, of

* Avalokiteśvara, the Bodhisattva of Compassion.

which the principal one was the Rasa Trulnang.[27] In this way he established Buddhism in Tibet.

His fifth successor, King Trisong Detsen, invited one hundred and eight paṇḍits to Tibet, including Padmasambhava, the Preceptor of Oḍḍiyāna, the greatest of the mantra-holders, unequalled throughout the three worlds. To uphold representations of the Buddhas' form, Trisong Detsen had temples built, including "unchanging, spontaneously arisen" Samye. To uphold the Buddha's speech, the authentic Dharma, one hundred and eight translators, including the great Vairotsana, learned the art of translation and translated all the main sūtras, tantras and śāstras then current in the noble land of India. The "Seven Men for Testing" and others were ordained as monks, forming the Saṅgha, to uphold the Buddha's mind.

From that time onwards up to the present day, the teachings of the Buddha have shone like the sun in Tibet and, despite ups and downs, the doctrine of the Conqueror has never been lost in either of its aspects, transmission or realization. Thus Tibet, as far as the Dharma is concerned, is a central country.

A person lacking any of the five sense faculties does not meet the requirements laid down for taking the monastic vows. Moreover, someone who does not have the good fortune to be able to see representations of the Conqueror to inspire his devotion, or to read and hear the precious and excellent teachings as the material for study and reflection, will not be fully capable of receiving the Dharma.

"Conflicting lifestyle" refers, strictly speaking, to the lifestyles of people born in communities of hunters, prostitutes and so forth, who are involved in these negative activities from their earliest youth. But in fact it also includes anyone whose every thought, word and deed is contrary to the Dharma—for even those not born into such lifestyles can easily slip into them later in life. It is therefore essential to avoid doing anything which conflicts with the authentic Dharma.

If your faith is not in the Buddha's teachings but in powerful gods, nāgas and so forth, or in other doctrines such as those of the tīrthikas, then, no matter how much faith you might place in them, none of them can protect you from the sufferings of saṁsāra or from rebirth in lower realms. But if you have acquired a properly reasoned faith in the Conqueror's doctrine, which unites transmission and realization, you are without doubt a fit vessel for the true Dharma. And that is the greatest of the five individual advantages.

2.2 THE FIVE CIRCUMSTANTIAL ADVANTAGES

> A Buddha has appeared and has preached the Dharma,
> His teachings still exist and can be followed,
> There are those who are kind-hearted toward others.

Those not born in a bright kalpa, one in which a Buddha has appeared, have never even heard of the Dharma. But we are now in a kalpa in which a Buddha has come, and so we possess the advantage of the presence of the particular *teacher.*

Although a Buddha has come, if he had not taught no-one would benefit. But since the Buddha turned the Wheel of Dharma according to three levels, we have the advantage of the *teaching of the Dharma.*

Although he has taught, had his doctrine died out it would no longer be there to help us. But the period during which the doctrine will remain extant has not yet ended, so we have the advantage of the *time.*

Although the teachings still exist, unless we follow them they can be of no benefit to us. But since we have taken up the Dharma, we possess the advantage of *our own good fortune.*

Although we have taken up the Dharma, without the favourable circumstance of being accepted by a spiritual friend we would never come to know what the Dharma is really about. But since a spiritual friend has accepted us, we possess the advantage of his *extraordinary compassion.*

Because these five factors need to be complete with regard to circumstances other than one's own, they are called the *five circumstantial advantages.*

The time it takes for the universe to form, to stay in existence, to be destroyed and to remain in a state of emptiness is called a kalpa. A kalpa in which a perfect Buddha appears in the world is called a "bright kalpa;" while one in which a Buddha does not appear is called a "dark kalpa." Long ago, during the great Kalpa of Manifest Joy, thirty-three thousand Buddhas appeared. A hundred dark kalpas followed. Then, during the Perfect Kalpa, eight hundred million Buddhas appeared, again followed by a hundred kalpas without Dharma. Then eight hundred and forty million Buddhas appeared during the Excellent Kalpa, after which there were five hundred dark kalpas. During the Kalpa Delightful to See, eight hundred million Buddhas appeared, and then there were seven hundred kalpas of darkness. Sixty thousand Buddhas appeared during the Joyous Kalpa. Then came our own kalpa, the Good Kalpa.

Before our kalpa arose, this cosmos of a billion universes was an immense ocean on whose surface appeared a thousand thousand-petalled lotuses. The gods of the Brahmā-world, wondering how this could be, through clairvoyance understood it to signify that during this kalpa one thousand Buddhas would appear. "This will be a good kalpa," they said, and "Good" became its name.

From the time when beings' lifespan was eighty thousand years and the Buddha Destroyer-of-Saṁsāra appeared, and up to the time when beings will live incalculably long and the Buddha Infinite-Aspiration will come, one thousand Buddhas will have taken their place in this world on the Vajra Seat at the centre of the Continent of Jambudvīpa. Each one of them will have attained perfect Buddhahood there and turned the Wheel of Dharma. Therefore our present kalpa is a bright kalpa.

It will be followed by sixty peripheral, bad kalpas, and after that, in the Kalpa of Vast Numbers, ten thousand Buddhas will appear. Then another ten thousand bad kalpas will ensue. In this alternation of bright and dark kalpas, should we happen to be born during a dark kalpa, we would never even hear that there was such a thing as the Three Jewels.

Moreover, as the Great One of Oḍḍiyāna points out, the Secret Mantra Vajrayāna in particular is taught only rarely:

> Long ago, during the very first kalpa, the Kalpa of the Complete Array, the teachings of the Secret Mantrayāna were promulgated by the Buddha known as Once-Come-King and achieved great renown. The teachings we have now, those of the present Buddha Śākyamuni, also include the Secret Mantrayāna. In ten million kalpas' time, during the Kalpa of the Array of Flowers, the Buddha Mañjuśrī will come, as I have come now, to reveal the Secret Mantra teachings on a vast scale. This is so because beings in these three kalpas are suitable recipients for the Secret Mantras, and the reason why the Mantrayāna teachings do not appear at other times is because the beings of those times are not capable of making use of them.[28]

In this Good Kalpa, at the present time when the span of human life is a hundred years, the perfect Buddha Śākyamuni has come to the world, and so it is a bright kalpa.

Suppose that a Buddha had come, but was still in meditation and had not yet taught the Dharma. As long as the light of his Dharma had not appeared, his having come would make no difference to us. It would be just as if he had never come at all.

On attaining total and perfect Buddhahood upon the Vajra Seat, our Teacher exclaimed:

> I have found a Dharma like ambrosia,
> Deep, peaceful, simple, uncompounded, radiant.
> If I explain it no-one will understand,
> So I shall stay here silent in the forest.

Accordingly, for seven weeks he did not teach, until Brahmā and Indra begged him to turn the Wheel of the Dharma.

Furthermore, if those who hold the authentic teaching do not explain it, it is difficult for the Dharma to be of any real benefit to beings. An example is the great Smṛtijñāna of India, who came to Tibet because his mother had been reborn there in one of the ephemeral hells. His interpreter died on the journey, and Smṛtijñāna, who was wandering around the province of Kham unable to speak a word of the language, became a shepherd and died there without having been of very much benefit to anyone. When Jowo Atīśa later arrived in Tibet and learned what had happened, he cried out: "How sad! Tibetans, your merit is weak! Nowhere in India, East or West, was there a paṇḍita better than Smṛtijñāna," and, placing his hands together, he wept.

For us, the Buddha Śākyamuni has turned the Wheel of the Dharma on three levels and, manifesting an inconceivable number of forms according to the needs and capacities of those to be helped, leads disciples through the nine vehicles of his teaching to maturity and liberation.

Even during a kalpa in which a Buddha has appeared and given teachings, once the time for those teachings to endure has come to an end and the authentic Dharma he has taught disappears it is exactly the same as in a dark kalpa. The period between the disappearance of one Buddha's teachings and the next Buddha's teachings being given is described as "devoid of Dharma." In fortunate places where beings have adequate merit, pratyekabuddhas appear, but the doctrine is not taught or practised.

These days we still have the teachings of the Buddha Śākyamuni. Their degree of survival follows a tenfold sequence. First, there are three periods, each consisting of five hundred parts.[29] During this time, there appears the "teaching of the heart of Samantabhadra," which is the *fruit*.[30] Then come three periods of five hundred parts for *accomplishment*.[31] These are followed by three periods of five hundred parts for *transmission*. Finally, one period of five hundred parts arises when *only the symbols are retained*. Altogether, this makes ten periods, each of five hundred parts. At present we have reached the seventh or eighth period. We live in an age of increase in the five degenerations—those of lifespan, beliefs, emotions, time and beings. Nonetheless, the doctrine of transmission and realization does still exist. As it has not died out, we still possess the advantage of *having the Dharma in its entirety.*

That the Doctrine is still present, however, is irrelevant unless you make use of it—just as the rising sun, although it lights up the whole world, does not make the slightest difference to a blind man. And, just as the waters of a great lake cannot quench the thirst of a traveller arriving at its shore unless he actually drinks from them, the Dharma of transmission and realization cannot infiltrate your mind by itself.

To enter the Dharma just to protect yourself from sickness and negative influences in this life, or because you fear the sufferings of the three lower realms in future lives, is called "Dharma as protection against fears," and is not the right way to set out on the path.

To enter the Dharma merely to have food, clothing and so on in this life, or to obtain the pleasant reward of a divine or human rebirth in the next, is called "Dharma as quest for excellence."

To enter the Dharma understanding that the whole of saṁsāra has no meaning, striving to find a way to be free from it, is called "taking up the teaching by arriving at the starting point of the path."

Even if you start practising the Dharma, unless you have been accepted by a spiritual friend it will be of no use. The *Condensed Transcendent Wisdom* says:

> The Buddha and the teachings depend upon the spiritual friend.
> Thus said the Conqueror, supreme embodiment of all good qualities.

The Buddha's teaching is immense, its transmissions are numerous, and it covers an inexhaustible range of topics. Without relying on the pith instructions of a teacher we would never know how to condense the essential points of all those teachings and put them into practice.

Once, when Jowo Atīśa was in Tibet, Khu, Ngok and Drom* asked him: "For someone to achieve liberation and complete omniscience, which is more important—the canonical scriptures and their commentaries, or the oral instructions of the teacher?"

"The teacher's instructions," Atīśa replied.

"Why?"

"Because when it comes to doing the practice—even if you can explain

* Atīśa's three main disciples (see glossary).

the whole *Tripiṭaka* from memory and are very skilled in metaphysics—without the teacher's practical guidance you and the Dharma will part company."

"So," they continued, "is the main point of the teacher's instructions to keep the three vows and to strive to do good with body, speech and mind?"

"That is not the slightest bit of use," Atīśa replied.

"How can that be?" they exclaimed.

"You may be able to keep the three vows perfectly, but unless you are determined to free yourself from the three worlds of saṁsāra it just creates further causes of saṁsāra. You may be able to strive day and night to do good with body, speech, and mind, but unless you know how to dedicate the merit to perfect enlightenment, two or three wrong thoughts are enough to destroy it entirely. You may be teachers and meditators, full of piety and learning, but unless your minds are turned away from the eight ordinary concerns, whatever you do will only be for this present life, and you will not encounter the path that helps for future lives."

This illustrates how important it is to be taken under the care of a teacher, a spiritual friend.

Checking your own life and circumstances for each of the eight freedoms and ten advantages, if you find that all these favourable conditions are present, you have what is known as "human life endowed with the eighteen freedoms and advantages." However, the Omniscient Dharma King Longchenpa, in his *Wish-granting Treasury*, specifies sixteen additional conditions which preclude any opportunity to practise the Dharma—eight intrusive circumstances[32] and eight incompatible propensities[33]—under whose sway it is important not to fall. In his words:

> Turmoil from the five emotions, stupidity, being dominated by evil influences,
> Laziness, being inundated by the effect of past evil actions,
> Enslavement to others, seeking protection from dangers, and hypocritical practice:
> These are the eight intrusive circumstances that leave no freedom.
>
> Being bound by one's ties, flagrant depravity,
> Lack of dissatisfaction with saṁsāra, complete absence of faith,
> Taking pleasure in bad actions, lack of interest in the Dharma,
> Heedlessness of the vows and of the samayas:
> These are the eight incompatible propensities that leave no freedom.

2.3 The eight intrusive circumstances that leave no freedom to practise the Dharma

People in whom the five poisons—that is, negative emotions such as hatred for enemies, infatuation with friends and relatives, and so forth—are extremely strong, may wish from time to time that they could practise some kind of true Dharma. But the five poisons are too strong, dominating their minds most of the time and preventing them from ever accomplishing the Dharma properly.

Very stupid beings, lacking even the slightest glimmer of intelligence, might enter the Dharma but, being unable to understand a single word of the teaching or its meaning, they will never be able to study it or reflect and meditate upon it.

Once people have been taken as disciples by a false spiritual friend who teaches the view and action in a perverted manner, their minds will be led on to wrong paths and will not be in accord with the true Dharma.

People who want to learn the Dharma but are too lazy, without even a trace of diligence, will never accomplish it because they are so ensnared in their own indolence and procrastination.

Some people's obscurations and negative actions are such that, in spite of the effort they put into the Dharma, they fail to develop any of the right qualities in their minds. Their backlog of bad actions has overwhelmed them, and they will lose confidence in the teachings without perceiving that it is all due to their own past actions.

Those who are in servitude to someone else, and have lost their autonomy, may want to take up Dharma; but the person who dominates them does not allow them to practise.

Some people take up Dharma out of fear for this present life—that they might lack food or clothing, or experience other afflictions. But since they have no deep conviction in the Dharma, they give themselves up to their old habits and get involved in things that are not Dharma.

Others are impostors who, through a pretence of Dharma, try to win possessions, services and prestige. In front of others they assume the guise of practitioners, but in their minds they are only interested in this life, so they are far removed from the path of liberation.

These are eight circumstances that render it impossible to continue practising the Dharma.

2.4 The eight incompatible propensities that leave no freedom to practise the Dharma

People who are tightly bound to their worldly commitments, wealth, pleasures, children, relatives and so forth, are so preoccupied with the strenuous efforts entailed by these things that they have no time to practise the Dharma.

Some people lack any scrap of humanity, and their nature is so depraved that they are unable to improve their behaviour. Even a genuine spiritual teacher would find it very difficult to set them on the noble path. As the sublime beings of the past said, "The abilities of a disciple can be shaped, but not his basic character."

A person who feels not the slightest consternation either on hearing of lower rebirths and the ills of saṁsāra, or in the face of this present life's sufferings, has no determination whatsoever to liberate himself from saṁsāra, and therefore no reason to engage in Dharma practice.

To have no faith at all, either in the true Dharma or in the teacher, shuts off any access to the teachings and bars entry to the path of liberation.

People who take pleasure in harmful or negative actions, and who fail to control their thoughts, words and deeds, are devoid of any noble qualities and have turned away from the Dharma.

Some people are no more interested in spiritual values and Dharma than a dog in eating grass. Since they feel no enthusiasm for the Dharma, its qualities will never develop in their minds.

Anyone who, having entered the Basic Vehicle, breaks his vows and commitment to bodhicitta, has nowhere else to go but the lower realms. He will not escape from states where there is no opportunity to practise the Dharma.

Anyone who, having entered the Secret Mantra Vehicle, breaks his samaya commitments to his teacher and spiritual brothers and sisters, will bring about his own ruin and theirs, destroying any prospect of accomplishments.

These are eight propensities that lead one away from the Dharma and snuff out the lamp of liberation.

Before these sixteen factors that leave no opportunity for the practice have been carefully ruled out, people in these decadent times may look as if they have all the freedoms and advantages and are true practitioners of the Dharma. However, the chieftain upon his throne and the lama beneath his parasol,[34] the hermit in his mountain solitude, the man who has renounced the affairs of state, and anyone who might have a high opinion of his own worth—each may think he is practising Dharma, but as long as he is under the sway of these additional limiting conditions, he is not on the true path.

So, before blindly assuming the forms of Dharma, check your own state carefully first to see whether or not you have all thirty-four aspects of the freedoms and advantages. If you do have them all, rejoice and reflect deeply on them over and over again. Remind yourself how, now that you have finally gained these freedoms and advantages that are so difficult to find, you are not going to squander them; whatever happens, you are going to practise the true Dharma. Should you find, however, that some aspects are missing, try to acquire them by whatever means may be possible.

At all times, you should take pains to examine carefully whether or not you have all elements of the freedoms and advantages. If you fail to check, and any one of those elements should be lacking, you will be missing the chance to practise the Dharma truly. After all, even the execution of a single minor everyday task requires many mutually dependent materials and conditions to be brought together. Is it any wonder that the realization of our ultimate goal—the Dharma—is impossible without the conjunction of many interconnected factors?

Imagine a traveller who wants to brew himself some tea. The making of tea involves many different elements—the pot, the water, the wood, the fire, and so on. Of these, just to light the fire alone is impossible without a flint, steel, some tinder, the traveller's hands and so forth. If just one thing is missing, the tinder for instance, then the fact that the traveller has everything else he needs is of no use whatsoever. He simply does not have what it takes to make tea. In the same way, if even one element of the freedoms and advantages is missing, there is no chance at all of practising the true Dharma.

If you check your own mind carefully, you will see that even the basic eight freedoms and ten advantages are very difficult to attain, and that to have all ten advantages is even rarer than to have all eight freedoms.

Someone born as a human, with all his faculties intact and in a central region, but who becomes involved in a lifestyle conflicting with the Dharma and who has no faith in the Conqueror's teaching, only has three of the advantages. Were he to obtain either of the two others, he would still only have four. Now, to have a lifestyle which does not conflict at all with the Dharma is extremely hard. If any of a person's thoughts, words and deeds are negative and his motives are for this life, then in fact, even if he has the reputation of a good and learned man, his lifestyle is in conflict with the Dharma.

The same applies to the five circumstantial advantages. If a Buddha has come, has taught the Dharma and the teachings still exist, yet a person has not entered the Dharma, that person has only three of those advantages. Here again, "entering the Dharma" does not simply mean asking for some teaching and being given it. The starting point of the path of liberation is the conviction that the whole of saṁsāra is meaningless and the genuine determination to be free from it. To travel the path of the Great Vehicle, the essential is to have genuinely aroused bodhicitta. The minimum is to have such unshakeable faith in the Three Precious Jewels that you would never renounce them, even to save your life. Without that, simply reciting prayers and wearing yellow robes is no proof that you have entered the Dharma.

Make sure that you know how to identify each of these freedoms and advantages, and to check whether you have them yourself. This is of crucial importance.

3. Reflecting on images that show how difficult it is to find the freedoms and advantages

The Buddha said that it is more difficult for a being to obtain human birth than it would be for a turtle coming up from the depths of the ocean to put its head by chance through the opening of a wooden yoke tossed around by huge waves on the surface.

Imagine the whole cosmos of a billion universes as a vast ocean. Floating upon it is a yoke, a piece of wood with a hole in it that can be fixed around the horns of draught oxen. This yoke, tossed hither and thither by the waves, sometimes eastward, sometimes westward, never stays in the same place even for an instant. Deep down in the depths of the ocean lives a blind turtle who rises up to the surface only once every hundred years.[35] That the yoke and the turtle might meet is extremely unlikely. The yoke itself is inanimate; the turtle is not intentionally seeking it out. The turtle, being blind, has no eyes with which to spot the yoke. If the yoke were to stay in one place, there might be a chance of their meeting; but it is continually on the move. If the turtle were to spend its entire time swimming around the surface, it might, perhaps, cross paths with the yoke; but it surfaces only once every hundred years. The chances of the yoke and the turtle coming together are therefore extremely small. Nevertheless, by sheer chance the turtle might still just slip its neck into the yoke. But it is even more difficult than that, the sūtras say, to obtain a human existence with the freedoms and advantages. Nāgārjuna expresses this in his *Advice to King Surabhībhadra*:[36]

> It is highly unlikely that a turtle might, by chance, arise through a yoke tossed about on a mighty sea;
> And yet, compared to animal birth there is far less chance than even that
> Of obtaining a human life. Accordingly, O Lord of Men,
> Practise the authentic Dharma to make your fortune fruitful!

And Śāntideva says:

> The Buddha declared that like a turtle that perchance can place
> Its head within a yoke adrift upon a shoreless sea,
> This human birth is difficult to find.

The difficulty of obtaining human birth is also compared to that of getting dried peas thrown at a smooth wall to stick to it, or to that of balancing a pile of peas on the tip of an upright needle—which is hard enough with even one single pea! It is important to know these comparisons, which are from the *Nirvāṇa Sūtra*, and similar ones in other texts.

4. Reflecting on numerical comparisons

When you consider the relative numbers of different kinds of beings, you can appreciate that to be born a human is hardly possible at all. By way of illustration, it is said that if the inhabitants of the hells were as numerous as stars in the night sky, the pretas would be no more numerous than the stars visible in the daytime; that if there were as many pretas as stars at night, there would only be as many animals as stars in the daytime; and that if there were as many animals as stars at night, there would only be as many gods and humans as stars in the daytime.

It is also said that there are as many beings in hell as specks of dust in the whole world, as many pretas as particles of sand in the Ganges, as many animals as grains in a beer-barrel[37] and as many asuras as snowflakes in a blizzard—but that gods and humans are as few as the particles of dust on a fingernail.

To take form as any being of the higher realms is already rare enough, but rarer still is a human life complete with all the freedoms and advantages. We can see for ourselves at any time how few human beings there are compared to animals. Think how many bugs live in a clod of earth in summertime, or ants in a single anthill—there are hardly that many humans in the whole world. But even within mankind, we can see that, compared to all those people born in outlying regions where the teachings have never appeared, those born in places where the Dharma has spread are exceedingly rare. And even among these, there are only a very few who have all the freedoms and advantages.

With all these perspectives in mind, you should be filled with joy that you really have all the freedoms and advantages complete.

A human life can be called a "precious human life" only when it is complete with all aspects of the freedoms and advantages, and from then onwards it truly becomes precious. But as long as any of those aspects are incomplete, then, however extensive your knowledge, learning and talent in ordinary things may be, you do not have a precious human life. You have what is called an ordinary human life, merely human life, hapless human life, meaningless human life, or human life returning empty-handed. It is like failing to use a wish-fulfilling gem despite holding it in your hands, or returning empty-handed from a land full of precious gold.

> To come across a precious jewel
> Is nothing compared to finding this precious human life.
> Look how those who are not saddened by saṁsāra
> Fritter life away!
>
> To win a whole kingdom
> Is nothing compared to meeting a perfect teacher.
> Look how those with no devotion
> Treat the teacher as their equal!
>
> To be given command of a province
> Is nothing compared to receiving the Bodhisattva vows.
> Look how those with no compassion
> Hurl their vows away!
>
> To rule over the universe
> Is nothing compared to receiving a tantric empowerment.
> Look how those who do not keep the samayas
> Jettison their promises!
>
> To catch sight of the Buddha
> Is nothing compared to seeing the true nature of mind.
> Look how those with no determination
> Sink back into delusion!

These freedoms and advantages do not come by chance or coincidence. They are the result of an accumulation of merit and wisdom built up over many kalpas. The great scholar Trakpa Gyaltsen says:

> This free and favoured human existence
> Is not the result of your resourcefulness.
> It comes from the merit you have accumulated.

To have obtained human life only to be wholly involved in evil activities without the least notion of Dharma is to be lower than the lower realms. As Jetsun Mila said to the hunter Gönpo Dorje:

> To have the freedoms and fortunes of human birth is usually said to be precious,
> But when I see someone like you it doesn't seem precious at all.

Nothing has as much power to drag you down to the lower realms as human life. What you do with it, right now, is up to you alone:

> Used well, this body is our raft to freedom.
> Used badly, this body anchors us to saṁsāra.
> This body does the bidding of both good and evil.

It is through the power of all the merit you have accumulated in the past that you have now obtained this human life complete with its eighteen freedoms and advantages. To neglect the one essential thing—the supreme Dharma—and instead just spend your life acquiring food and clothes and indulging the eight ordinary concerns would be a useless waste of those freedoms and advantages. How ineffectual to wait until death is upon you and then beat your breast with remorse! For you will have made the wrong choice, as it says in *The Way of the Bodhisattva*:

> Thus, having found the freedoms of a human life,
> If I now fail to train myself in virtue,
> What greater folly could there ever be?
> How more could I betray myself?

This present life, therefore, is the turning-point at which you can choose between lasting good or lasting evil. If you do not make use of it right now to seize the citadel of the absolute nature within this lifetime, in lives to come it will be very hard to obtain such freedom again. Once you take birth in any of the forms of life in the lower realms, no idea of Dharma will ever occur to you. Too bewildered to know what to do or what not to do, you will fall endlessly further and further to ever lower realms. So, telling yourself that now is the time to make an effort, meditate over and over again, applying the three supreme methods: start with the thought of bodhicitta, do the practice itself without any conceptualization, and dedicate the merit at the end.

As a measure of how much this practice has truly convinced us, we should be like Geshe Chengawa, who spent all his time practising and never even slept. Geshe Tönpa said to him: "You'd better rest, my son. You'll make yourself ill."

"Yes, I should rest," Chengawa replied. "But when I think how difficult it is to find the freedoms and advantages that we have, I have no time to rest." He recited nine hundred million mantras of Miyowa and did without sleep for the whole of his life. We should meditate until exactly that sort of conviction arises in our own minds.

Although I have won these freedoms, I am poor in Dharma,
which is their essence.
Although I have entered the Dharma, I waste time doing other
things.
Bless me and foolish beings like me
That we may attain the very essence of the freedoms and
advantages.

King Trisong Detsen (790-844)

The king who invited the scholar Śāntarakṣita and the Tantric master Padmasambhava to Tibet. He built Samye, Tibet's first monastery, and was responsible for establishing the Buddhist teachings on a firm basis.

CHAPTER TWO

The impermanence of life

Seeing this threefold world as a fleeting illusion,
You have left this life's concerns behind like spittle in the dust.
Accepting all hardships, you have followed in the footsteps of the masters of old.
Peerless Teacher, at your feet I bow.

The way to listen to the teaching is as described in Chapter One. The actual subject matter consists of seven meditations: the impermanence of the outer universe in which beings live, the impermanence of the beings living in it, the impermanence of holy beings, the impermanence of those in positions of power, other examples of impermanence, the uncertainty of the circumstances of death, and intense awareness of impermanence.

I. THE IMPERMANENCE OF THE OUTER UNIVERSE IN WHICH BEINGS LIVE

Our world, this outer environment fashioned by the collective good karma of beings, with its firm and solid structure encompassing the four continents, Mount Meru and the heavenly realms, lasts for a whole kalpa. It is nonetheless impermanent and will not escape final destruction by seven stages of fire and one of water.

As the present great kalpa draws closer to the time of destruction, the beings inhabiting each realm below the god-realm of the first meditative state will, realm by realm, progressively disappear until not a single being is left.

Then, one after the other, seven suns will rise in the sky. The first sun will burn up all fruit-bearing trees and forests. The second will evaporate all streams, creeks and ponds; the third will dry up all the rivers; and the fourth all the great lakes, even Manasarovar. As the fifth sun appears, the great oceans, too, will progressively evaporate at first to a depth of one hundred leagues, then of two hundred, seven hundred, one thousand, ten thousand, and finally eighty thousand leagues. The sea-water that is left will shrink from a league down to an ear-shot, until not even enough remains to fill a footprint. By the time there are six suns all blazing together, the entire earth and its snow-covered mountains will have burst into flames. And when the seventh appears, Mount Meru itself will burn up, together with the four continents, the eight sub-continents, the seven golden mountains, and the circular wall of mountains at the world's very rim. Everything will fuse into one vast mass of fire. As it blazes downwards, it will consume all the infernal realms. As it flares upwards, will engulf the celestial palace of Brahmā, already long abandoned. Above, the younger gods of the realm of Clear Light will cry out in fear, "What an immense conflagration!" But the older gods will reassure them, saying, "Have no fear! Once it reaches the world of Brahmā, it will recede. This has happened before."*

After seven such destructions by fire, rainclouds will form in the realm of the gods of the second concentration, and a yoke's depth of torrential rain will fall, followed by a plough's depth. Like salt dissolving in water, everything up to and including the realm of the gods of the Clear Light will disintegrate.

After the seventh such devastation by water is over, the crossed vajra of wind at the base of the universe will rise up. Like dust scattered by the wind, everything up to and including the realm of the gods of the third meditative concentration will be blown completely away.

Reflect deeply and sincerely—if every one of the billion universes which constitute the cosmos, each with its own Mount Meru, four continents and heavens, is to be simultaneously destroyed in this way, leaving only space behind, however could these human bodies of ours, which are like flies at the end of the season, have any permanence or stability?

* These stages of destruction all take place within one kalpa, but even these long-lived gods can grow old between the first destruction by fire and the seventh, after which their realm—part of that of the second concentration—will be destroyed by water.

II. THE IMPERMANENCE OF BEINGS LIVING IN THE UNIVERSE

From the summit of the highest heavens to the very depths of hell, there is not a single being who can escape death. As the *Letter of Consolation* says:

> Have you ever, on earth or in the heavens,
> Seen a being born who will not die?
> Or heard that such a thing had happened?
> Or even suspected that it might?

Everything that is born is bound to die. Nobody has ever seen anyone or heard of anyone in any realm—even in the world of the gods—who was born but never died. In fact, it never even occurs to us to wonder whether a person will die or not. It is a certainty. Especially for us, born as we are at the end of an era* in a world where the length of life is unpredictable, death will come soon. It gets closer and closer from the moment we are born. Life can only get shorter, never longer. Inexorably, Death closes in, never pausing for an instant, like the shadow of a mountain at sunset.

Do you know for sure when you will die, or where? Might it be tomorrow, or tonight? Can you be sure that you are not going to die right now, between this breath and the next? As it says in *The Collection of Deliberate Sayings*:

> Who's sure he'll live till tomorrow?
> Today's the time to be ready,
> For the legions of Death
> Are not on our side.

And Nāgārjuna, too, says:

> Life flickers in the flurries of a thousand ills,
> More fragile than a bubble in a stream.
> In sleep, each breath departs and is again drawn in;
> How wondrous that we wake up living still!

Breathing gently, people enjoy their slumber. But between one breath and the next there is no guarantee that death will not slip in. To wake up in good health is an event which truly deserves to be considered miraculous, yet we take it completely for granted.

* The end of an era is a period of decline in which life is more fragile.

Although we know that we are going to die one day, we do not really let our attitudes to life be affected by the ever-present possibility of dying. We still spend all our time hoping and worrying about our future livelihood, as if we were going to live forever. We stay completely involved in our struggle for well-being, happiness and status—until, suddenly, we are confronted by Death wielding his black noose, gnashing ferociously at his lower lip and baring his fangs.

Then nothing can help us. No soldier's army, no ruler's decrees, no rich man's wealth, no scholar's brilliance, no beauty's charms, no athlete's fleetness—none is of any use. We might seal ourselves inside an impenetrable, armoured metal chest, guarded by hundreds of thousands of strong men bristling with sharp spears and arrows; but even that would not afford so much as a hair's breadth of protection or concealment. Once the Lord of Death secures his black noose around our neck, our face begins to pale, our eyes glaze over with tears, our head and limbs go limp, and we are dragged willy-nilly down the highway to the next life.

Death cannot be fought off by any warrior, ordered away by the powerful, or paid off by the rich. Death leaves nowhere to run to, no place to hide, no refuge, no defender or guide. Death resists any recourse to skill or compassion. Once our life has run out, even if the Medicine Buddha himself were to appear in person he would be unable to delay our death.

So, reflect sincerely and meditate on how important it is from this very moment onwards never to slip into laziness and procrastination, but to practise the true Dharma, the only thing you can be sure will help at the moment of death.

III. THE IMPERMANENCE OF HOLY BEINGS

In the present Good Kalpa, Vipaśyin, Śikhin and five other Buddhas have already appeared, each with his own circle of Śrāvakas and Arhats in inconceivable number. Each worked to bring benefit to innumerable beings through the teachings of the Three Vehicles. Yet nowadays all we have is whatever still remains of the Buddha Śākyamuni's teaching. Otherwise, all of those Buddhas have passed into nirvāṇa and all the pure Dharma teachings they gave have gradually disappeared.

One by one, the numerous great Śrāvakas of the present dispensation too, each with his entourage of five hundred Arhats, have passed beyond suffering into the state where nothing is left of the aggregates.

In India, there once lived the Five Hundred Arhats who compiled the words of the Buddha. There were the Six Ornaments and Two Supreme

Ones, the Eighty Siddhas, and many others, who mastered all attributes of the paths and levels and possessed unlimited clairvoyance and miraculous powers. But all that remains of them today are the stories telling how they lived.

Here too in Tibet, the Land of Snows, when the Second Buddha of Oḍḍiyāna* turned the Wheel of Dharma to ripen and liberate beings, there lived all his followers, like the twenty-five disciples known as the King and Subjects and the Eighty Siddhas of Yerpa. Later came the Ancient Tradition masters of the So, Zur and Nub clans; Marpa, Milarepa and Dagpo of the New Tradition; and innumerable other learned and accomplished beings. Most of them achieved high levels of accomplishment and had mastery over the four elements. They could produce all sorts of miraculous transformations. They could make tangible objects appear out of nowhere and disappear into nowhere. They could not be burned by fire, be swept away by water, be crushed by earth or fall from precipices into space—they were simply free from any harm that the four elements could bring about.

Once, for example, Jetsun Milarepa was meditating in silence in Nyeshangkatya cave in Nepal when a band of hunters passed by. Seeing him sitting there, they asked him whether he was a man or a ghost. Milarepa remained motionless, his gaze fixed before him, and did not answer. The hunters shot a volley of poisoned arrows at him, but none of their arrows managed to pierce his skin. They threw him into the river, and then over the edge of a cliff—but each time there he was again, sitting back where he had been before. Finally, they piled firewood around him and set it alight, but the fire would not burn him. There have been many beings who attained such powers. But in the end, they all chose to demonstrate that everything is impermanent,** and today all that remains of them is their stories.

As for us, our negative actions, carried along by the wind of negative conditions in the prevailing direction of our negative tendencies, have driven us here into this filthy contraption made up of the four material elements, in which we are trapped and upon which our sentient existence depends—and as we can never be sure when or where this scarecrow of an illusory body is going to disintegrate, it is important that from this very

* Padmasambhava is often referred to as the second Buddha of our era, extending the work of Śākyamuni.

** Such beings are considered to be beyond birth and death. However, like the Buddha Śākyamuni, they choose to die nonetheless to remind beings of impermanence.

moment onwards we inspire ourselves to thoughts, words and deeds which are always positive. With this in mind, meditate on impermanence.

IV. THE IMPERMANENCE OF THOSE IN POSITIONS OF POWER

There are magnificent and illustrious gods and ṛiṣis who can live for as long as a kalpa. But even they cannot escape death. Those who rule over beings, like Brahmā, Indra, Viṣṇu, Īśvara and other great gods living for a whole kalpa, with statures measured in leagues or earshots and a power and resplendence that outshine the sun and moon, are nevertheless not beyond the reach of death. As *The Treasury of Qualities* says:

> Even Brahmā, Indra, Maheśvara and the universal monarchs
> Have no way to evade the Demon of Death.

In the end, not even divine or human ṛiṣis with the five kinds of clairvoyance and the power to fly through the sky can escape death. *The Letter of Consolation* says:

> Great ṛiṣis with their five-fold powers
> Can fly far and wide in the skies,
> Yet they will never reach a land
> Where immortality holds sway.

Here in our human world there have been universal emperors who have reached the very pinnacle of power and material wealth. In the holy land of India, starting with Mahāsammata, innumerable emperors ruled the entire continent. Later the three Pālas, the thirty-seven Candras and many other rich and powerful kings reigned in both eastern and western India.

In Tibet, the Land of Snows, the first king, Nyatri Tsenpo, was of divine descent, an emanation of the Bodhisattva Nivāraṇaviṣkambhin. Then reigned the seven heavenly kings called Tri, the six earthly kings called Lek, the eight middle kings called De, the five linking kings called Tsen, the twelve and a half[38] kings of the Fortunate Dynasty including the five of the Extremely Fortunate Dynasty, and others besides. In the reign of the Dharma King Songtsen Gampo, a magical army subdued all lands from Nepal to China. King Trisong Detsen brought two thirds of Jambudvīpa* under his power, and, during the reign of Ralpachen, an iron pillar was erected on the banks of the Ganges, marking the frontier between

* Here this term would seem to refer to South Asia, Mongolia and China.

India and Tibet. Tibet exercised power in many regions of India, China, Gesar, Tajikistan and other countries. At the New Year festival, ambassadors from all those countries were required to spend one day in Lhasa. Such was Tibet's power in the past. But it did not last, and nowadays, apart from the historical accounts, nothing is left.

Reflect on those past splendours. Compared to them, our own homes, belongings, servants, status, and whatever else we prize, seem altogether no more significant than a beehive. Meditate deeply, and ask yourself how you could have thought that those things would last for ever and never change.

V. OTHER EXAMPLES OF IMPERMANENCE

As an example of impermanence, consider the cycle of growth and decline that takes place over a kalpa. Long ago, in the first age of this kalpa, there were no sun and moon in the sky and all human beings were lit up by their own intrinsic radiance. They could move miraculously through space. They were several leagues tall. They fed on divine nectar and enjoyed perfect happiness and well-being, matching that of the gods. Gradually, however, under the influence of negative emotions and wrong-doing, the human race slowly degenerated to its present state. Even today, as those emotions become ever more gross, human lifespan and good fortune are still on the decrease. This process will continue until humans live no more than ten years. Most of the beings living in the world will disappear during periods of plague, war and famine. Then, to the survivors, an emanation of the Buddha Maitreya will preach abstinence from killing. At that time, humans will only be one cubit tall. From then on their lifespan will increase to twenty years and then gradually become longer and longer until it reaches eighty thousand years. At that point Lord Maitreya will appear in person, become Buddha and turn the Wheel of the Dharma. When eighteen such cycles of growth and decline have taken place and human beings live an incalculable number of years, the Buddha Infinite Aspiration will appear and live for as long as all the other thousand Buddhas of the Good Kalpa put together. His activities for beings' welfare, too, will match all of theirs put together. Finally, this kalpa will end in destruction. Examining such changes, you can see that even on this vast scale nothing is beyond the reach of impermanence.

Watching the four seasons change, also, you can see how everything is impermanent. In summertime the meadows are green and lush from the nectar of summer showers, and all living beings bask in a glow of well-being and happiness. Innumerable varieties of flowers spring up and the whole landscape blossoms into a heavenly paradise of white and gold, scarlet and blue. Then, as the autumn breezes grow cooler, the green grasslands change hue. Fruit and flowers, one by one, dry up and wither. Winter soon sets in, and the whole earth becomes as hard and brittle as rock. Ponds and rivers freeze solid and glacial winds scour the landscape. You could ride for days on end looking for all those summer flowers and never see a single one. And so comes each season in turn, summer giving way to autumn, autumn to winter and winter to spring, each different from the one before, and each just as ephemeral. Look how quickly yesterday and today, this morning and tonight, this year and next year, all pass by one after the other. Nothing ever lasts, nothing is dependable.

Think about your village or monastic community, or wherever you live. People who not long ago were prosperous and secure now suddenly find themselves heading for ruin; others, once poor and helpless, now speak with authority and are powerful and wealthy. Nothing stays the same forever. In your own family, each successive generation of parents, grandparents and great-grandparents have all died, one by one. They are only names to you now. And as their time came many brothers, sisters and other relatives have died too, and no-one knows where they went or where they are now. Of the powerful, rich and prosperous people who only last year were the most eminent in the land, many this year are already just names. Who knows whether those whose present wealth and importance makes them the envy of ordinary folk will still be in the same position this time next year—or even next month? Of your own domestic animals—sheep, goats, dogs—how many have died in the past and how many are still alive? When you think about what happens in all of these cases, you can see that nothing stays the same forever. Of all the people who were alive more than a hundred years ago, not a single one has escaped death. And in another hundred years from now, every single person now alive throughout the world will be dead. Not one of them will be left.

There is therefore absolutely nothing in the universe, animate or inanimate, that has any stability or permanence.

> Whatever is born is impermanent and is bound to die.
> Whatever is stored up is impermanent and is bound to run out.
> Whatever comes together is impermanent and is bound to come apart.
> Whatever is built is impermanent and is bound to collapse.
> Whatever rises up is impermanent and is bound to fall down.
> So also, friendship and enmity, fortune and sorrow, good and evil,

all the thoughts that run through your mind—everything is always changing.

You might be as exalted as the heavens, as mighty as a thunderbolt, as rich as a nāga, as good-looking as a god or as pretty as a rainbow—but no matter who or what you are, when death suddenly comes there is nothing you can do about it for even a moment. You have no choice but to go, naked and cold, your empty hands clenched stiffly under your armpits. Unbearable though it might be to part with your money, your cherished possessions, your friends, loved ones, attendants, disciples, country, lands, subjects, property, food, drink and wealth, you just have to leave everything behind, like a hair being pulled out of a slab of butter.* You might be the head lama over thousands of monks, but you cannot take even one of them with you. You might be governor over tens of thousands of people, but you cannot take a single one as your servant. All the wealth in the world would still not give you the power to take as much as a needle and thread.

Your dearly beloved body, too, is going to be left behind. This same body that was wrapped up during life in silk and brocades, that was kept well filled up with tea and beer, and that once looked as handsome and distinguished as a god, is now called a corpse, and is left lying there horribly livid, heavy and distorted. Says Jetsun Mila:

> This thing we call a corpse, so fearful to behold,
> Is already right here—our own body.

Your body is trussed up with a rope and covered with a curtain, held in place with earth and stones. Your bowl is turned upside down on your pillow. No matter how precious and well loved you were, now you arouse horror and nausea. When the living lie down to sleep, even on piles of furs and soft sheepskin rugs, they start to feel uncomfortable after a while and have to keep turning over. But once you are dead, you just lie there with your cheek against a stone or tuft of grass, your hair bespattered with earth.

Some of you who are heads of families or clan chiefs might worry about the people under your care. Once you are no longer there to look after them, might they not easily die of hunger or cold, be murdered by enemies, or drown in the river? Does not all their wealth, comfort and happiness depend on you? In fact, however, after your death they will

* The butter does not stick to the hair. Only the empty impression of the hair remains.

feel nothing but relief at having managed to get rid of your corpse by cremating it, throwing it into a river, or dumping it in the cemetery.

When you die, you have no choice but to wander all alone in the intermediate state without a single companion. At that time your only refuge will be the Dharma. So tell yourself again and again that from now on you must make the effort to accomplish at least one practice of genuine Dharma.

Whatever is stored up is bound to run out. A king might rule the whole world and still end up as a vagabond. Many start their life surrounded by wealth and end it starving to death, having lost everything. People who had herds of hundreds of animals one year can be reduced to beggary the next by epidemics or heavy snow, and someone who was rich and powerful only the day before might suddenly find himself asking for alms because his enemies have destroyed everything he owns. That all these things happen is something you can see for yourself; it is impossible to hang on to your wealth and possessions forever. Never forget that generosity is the most important capital to build up.*

No coming together can last forever. It will always end in separation. We are like inhabitants of different places gathering in thousands and even tens of thousands for a big market or an important religious festival, only to part again as each returns home. Whatever affectionate relationships we now enjoy—teachers and disciples, masters and servants, patrons and their protégés, spiritual comrades, brothers and sisters, husbands and wives—there is no way we can avoid being separated in the end. We cannot even be sure that death or some other terrible event might not suddenly part us right now. Since spiritual companions, couples and so forth might be split up unexpectedly at any moment, we had better avoid anger and quarrels, harsh words and fighting. We never know how long we might be together, so we should make up our minds to be caring and affectionate for the short while that we have left. As Padampa Sangye says:

> Families are as fleeting as a crowd on market-day;
> People of Tingri, don't bicker or fight!

Whatever buildings are constructed are bound to collapse. Villages and monasteries that were once successful and prosperous now lie empty and abandoned, and where once their careful owners lived, now only birds make their nests. Even Samye's central three-storeyed temple, built by

* i.e. a capital of merit. This concept is explained in Part Two, Chapter 4.

Padampa Sangye (11th-12th centuries)

The famous Indian siddha who spread the teachings throughout India, China and Tibet. He and his disciple Machik Labdrön established the lineages of the Chö teachings in Tibet.

miraculously emanated workers during the reign of King Trisong Detsen and consecrated by the Second Buddha of Oḍḍiyāna, was destroyed by fire in a single night. The Red Mountain Palace that existed in King Songtsen Gampo's time rivalled the palace of Indra himself, but now not even the foundation stones are left. In comparison, our own present towns, houses and monasteries are just so many insects' nests. So why do we attach such importance to them? It would be better to set our hearts on following to the very end the example of the Kagyupas of old, who left their homeland behind and headed for the wilderness. They dwelt at the foot of rocky cliffs with only wild animals for companions, and, without the least concern about food, clothing or renown, embraced the four basic aims of the Kadampas:

> Base your mind on the Dharma,
> Base your Dharma on a humble life,
> Base your humble life on the thought of death,
> Base your death on an empty, barren hollow.*

High estate and mighty armies never last. Māndhātṛi, the universal king, turned the golden wheel that gave him power over four continents; he reigned over the heavens of the Gods of the Thirty-three; he even shared the throne of Indra, king of the gods, and could defeat the asuras in battle. Yet finally he fell to earth and died, his ambitions still unsatisfied. You can see for yourself that of all those who wield power and authority—whether around kings, lamas, lords or governments—not a single one can keep his position forever; and that many powerful people, who have been imposing the law on others one year, find themselves spending the next languishing in prison. What use could such transitory power be to you? The state of perfect Buddhahood, on the other hand, can never diminish or be spoiled, and is worthy of the offerings of gods and men. That is what you should be determined to attain.

Friendship and enmity, too, are far from everlasting. One day while the Arhat Kātyāyana was out on his alms-round he came across a man with a child on his lap. The man was eating a fish with great relish, and throwing stones at a bitch that was trying to get at the bones. What the master saw with his clairvoyance, however, was this. The fish had been the man's own father in that very lifetime, and the bitch had been his mother. An enemy he had killed in a past existence had been reborn as his son, as the karmic repayment for the life the man had taken. Kātyāyana

* i.e. die alone in a remote place where there are no disturbances.

cried out:

> He eats his father's flesh, he beats his mother off,
> He dandles on his lap the enemy that he killed;
> The wife is gnawing at her husband's bones.
> I laugh to see what happens in saṁsāra's show!

Even within one lifetime, it often happens that sworn enemies are later reconciled and make friends. They may even become part of each other's families, and end up closer than anyone else. On the other hand, people intimately linked by blood or marriage often argue and do each other as much harm as they can for the sake of some trivial possession or paltry inheritance. Couples or dear friends can break up for the most insignificant reasons, ending sometimes even in murder. Seeing that all friendship and enmity is so ephemeral, remind yourself over and over again to treat everyone with love and compassion.

Good fortune and deprivation never last forever. There are many people who have started life in comfort and plenty, and ended up in poverty and suffering. Others start out in utter misery and are later happy and well-off. There have even been people who started out as beggars and ended up as kings. There are countless examples of such reversals of fortune. Milarepa's uncle, for instance, gave a merry party one morning for his daughter-in-law, but by nightfall his house had collapsed and he was weeping with sorrow. When Dharma brings you hardships, then however many different kinds of suffering you might have to undergo, like Jetsun Mila and the Conquerors of the past, in the end your happiness will be unparalleled. But when wrong-doing makes you rich, then whatever pleasure you might temporarily obtain, in the end your suffering will be infinite.

Fortune and sorrow are so unpredictable. Long ago in the kingdom of Aparāntaka there was a rain of grain lasting seven days, followed by a rain of clothes for another seven days and a rain of precious jewels for seven days more—and finally there was a rain of earth which buried the entire population, and everyone died and was reborn in the lower realms. It is no use trying, full of hopes and fears, to control such ever-changing happiness and suffering. Instead, simply leave all the comforts, wealth and pleasures of this world behind, like so much spittle in the dust. Resolve to follow in the footsteps of the Conquerors of the past, accepting courageously whatever hardships you have to suffer for the sake of the Dharma.

Excellence and mediocrity are impermanent, too. In worldly life, however authoritative and eloquent you may be, however erudite and talented, however strong and skilful, the time comes when those qualities decline. Once the merit you have accumulated in the past is exhausted, everything you think is contentious and nothing you do succeeds. You are criticized from all sides. You grow miserable and everyone despises you. Some people lose whatever meagre advantages they once had and end up without any at all. Others, once considered cheats and liars with neither talent nor common-sense, later find themselves rich and comfortable, trusted by everyone and esteemed as good and reliable people. As the proverb says, "Aging frauds take pride of place."

In religious life, too, as the saying goes, "In old age, sages become pupils, renunciates amass wealth, preceptors become heads of families." People who early in life renounced all worldly activities may be found busily piling up riches and provisions at the end. Others start out teaching and explaining the Dharma but end up as hunters, thieves or robbers. Learned monastic preceptors who in their youth kept all the Vinaya vows may in their old age beget many children. On the other hand, there are also many people who spend all their earlier years doing only wrong but who, in the end, devote themselves entirely to practising the holy Dharma and either attain accomplishment or, if not, at least by being on the path when they die go on to higher and higher rebirths.

Whether someone appears to be good or bad just at present, therefore, is but a momentary impression that has no permanence or stability whatsoever. You might feel slightly disenchanted with saṁsāra, develop a vague determination to be free of it, and take on the semblance of a serious student of Dharma to the point that ordinary folk are quite impressed, and want to be your patrons and disciples. But at that point, unless you take a very rigorous look at yourself, you could easily start thinking you really are as other people see you. Puffed up with pride, you get completely carried away by appearances and start to think that you can do whatever you want. You have been completely tricked by negative forces. So, banish all self-centred beliefs and arouse the wisdom of egolessness.* Until you attain the sublime Bodhisattva levels, no appearance, whether good or bad, can ever last. Meditate constantly on death and impermanence. Analyse your own faults and always take the lowest place. Cultivate dissatisfaction with saṁsāra and desire for liberation. Train yourself to become peaceful, disciplined and conscientious. Constantly develop a sense of poignant and deep sadness at the thought of

* The wisdom that sees the emptiness of self and phenomena.

the transitoriness of all compounded things and the sufferings of saṁsāra, like Jetsun Milarepa:

> In a rocky cave in a deserted land
> My sorrow is unrelenting.
> Constantly I yearn for you,
> My teacher, Buddha of the three times.

Unless you maintain this experience constantly, there is no knowing where all the constantly changing thoughts that crop up will lead. There was once a man who, after having a feud with his relatives, took up the Dharma and became known as Gelong Thangpa the Practitioner. He learned to control energy and mind,[39] and was able to fly in the sky. One day, watching a large flock of pigeons gathering to eat the offering food he had put out, the thought occurred to him that with an army of as many men he could exterminate his enemies. He failed to take this wrong thought on the path,[40] and as a result when he finally returned to his homeland he became commander of an army.

For the moment, thanks to your teacher and your spiritual companions, you might have a superficial feeling for the Dharma. But bearing in mind what a short time any one person's sentiments last, free yourself with the Dharma while you can, and resolve to practise as long as you live.

If you reflect on the numerous examples given here, you will have no doubt that nothing, from the highest states of existence down to the lowest hells, has even a scrap of permanence or stability. Everything is subject to change, everything waxes and wanes.

VI. THE UNCERTAINTY OF THE CIRCUMSTANCES[41] OF DEATH

Once born, every human in the world is sure to die. But how, why, when and where we are going to die cannot be predicted. None of us can say for sure that our death will come about at a particular time or place, in a certain way, or as a result of this or that cause.

There are few things in this world that favour life and many that threaten it, as the master Āryadeva points out:

> Causes of death are numerous;
> Causes of life are few,
> And even they may become causes of death.

Fire, water, poisons, precipices, savages, wild beasts—all manner of mortal dangers abound, but only very few things can prolong life. Even food, clothing and other things usually considered lifesustaining can at times turn into causes of death. Many fatalities occur as a result of eating—the food might be contaminated; or it may be something eaten for its beneficial properties but becoming toxic under certain circumstances;[42] or it might be the wrong food for a particular individual. Especially, nowadays most people crave meat and consume flesh and blood without a second thought, completely oblivious to all the diseases caused by old meat[43] or harmful meat spirits. Unhealthy diets and lifestyles can also give rise to tumours, disorders of phlegm, dropsy and other diseases, causing innumerable deaths. Similarly, the quest for riches, fame and other glories incites people to fight battles, to brave wild beasts, to cross rivers recklessly and to risk countless other situations that may bring about their demise.

Furthermore, the moment when any of those numerous different causes of death might intervene is entirely unpredictable. Some die in their mother's womb, some at birth, others before they learn to crawl. Some die young; others die old and decrepit. Some die before they can get medicine or help. Others linger on, glued to their beds by years of disease, watching the living with the eyes of the dead; by the time they die, they are just skeletons wrapped in skin. Many people die suddenly or by accident, while eating, talking or working. Some even take their own lives.

Surrounded by so many causes of death, your life has as little chance of enduring as a candle-flame in the wind. There is no guarantee that death will not suddenly strike right now, and that tomorrow you will not be reborn as an animal with horns on its head or tusks in its mouth. You should be quite sure that when you are going to die is unpredictable and that there is no knowing where you will be born next.

VII. INTENSE AWARENESS OF IMPERMANENCE

Meditate single-mindedly on death, all the time and in every circumstance. While standing up, sitting or lying down, tell yourself: "This is my last act in this world," and meditate on it with utter conviction. On your way to wherever you might be going, say to yourself: "Maybe I will die there. There is no certainty that I will ever come back." When you set out on a journey or pause to rest, ask yourself: "Will I die here?" Wherever you are, you should wonder if this might be where you die. At night, when you lie down, ask yourself whether you might die in bed during the night or whether you can be sure that you are going to get up in the morning. When you rise, ask yourself whether you might die sometime during the day, and reflect that there is no certainty at all that you will be going to bed in the evening.

Meditate only on death, earnestly and from the core of your heart. Practise like the Kadampa Geshes of old, who were always thinking about death at every moment. At night they would turn their bowls upside-down;* and, thinking how the next day there might be no need to light a fire, they would never cover the embers for the night.

However, just to meditate on death will not suffice. The only thing of any use at the moment of death is the Dharma, so you also need to encourage yourself to practise in an authentic way, never slipping into forgetfulness or loss of vigilance, remembering always that the activities of saṁsāra are transient and without the slightest meaning. In essence, this conjunction of body and mind is impermanent, so do not count on it as your own; it is only on loan.

All roads and paths are impermanent, so whenever you are walking anywhere direct your steps toward the Dharma. As it says in the *Condensed Transcendent Wisdom*:

> If you walk looking mindfully one yoke's-length in front of you, your mind will not be confused.

Wherever you are, all places are impermanent, so keep the pure Buddha-fields in mind. Food, drink and whatever you enjoy are impermanent, so feed on profound concentration. Sleep is impermanent, so while you are asleep purify sleep's delusions into clear light.[44] Wealth, if you have it, is impermanent, so strive for the seven noble riches.** Loved ones, friends and family are impermanent, so in a solitary place arouse the desire for liberation. High rank and celebrity are impermanent, so always take a lowly position. Speech is impermanent, so inspire yourself to recite mantras and prayers. Faith and desire for liberation are impermanent, so strive to make your commitments unshakeable. Ideas and thoughts are impermanent, so work on developing a good nature. Meditative experiences and realizations are impermanent, so go on until you reach the point where everything dissolves in the nature of reality. At that time, the link between death and rebirth[45] falls away and you reach such confidence that you are completely ready for death. You have captured the citadel of immortality; you are like the eagle free to soar in the heights of the

* Turning someone's bowl over was for Tibetans a symbol that the person had died.

** *'phags pa'i nor bdun*: Faith, discipline, learning, generosity, conscientiousness, modesty and wisdom.

heavens. After that there is no need for any sorrowful meditation on your approaching death.

As Jetsun Mila sang:

> Fearing death, I went to the mountains.
> Over and over again I meditated on death's unpredictable coming,
> And took the stronghold of the deathless unchanging nature.
> Now I have lost and gone beyond all fear of dying!

And the peerless Dagpo Rinpoche says:

> At first you should be driven by a fear of birth and death like a stag escaping from a trap. In the middle, you should have nothing to regret even if you die, like a farmer who has carefully worked his fields. In the end, you should feel relieved and happy, like a person who has just completed a formidable task.
>
> At first, you should know that there is no time to waste, like someone dangerously wounded by an arrow. In the middle, you should meditate on death without thinking of anything else, like a mother whose only child has died. In the end, you should know that there is nothing left to do, like a shepherd whose flocks have been driven off by his enemies.

Meditate single-mindedly on death and impermanence until you reach that stage.

The Buddha said:

> To meditate persistently on impermanence is to make offerings to all the Buddhas.
> To meditate persistently on impermanence is to be rescued from suffering by all the Buddhas.
> To meditate persistently on impermanence is to be guided by all the Buddhas.
> To meditate persistently on impermanence is to be blessed by all the Buddhas.
>
> Of all footprints, the elephant's are outstanding; just so, of all subjects of meditation for a follower of the Buddhas, the idea of impermanence is unsurpassed.

And he said in the *Vinaya*:

> To remember for an instant the impermanence of all compounded

> things is greater than giving food and offerings to a hundred of my disciples who are perfect vessels,* such as the bhikṣus Śāriputra and Maudgalyāyana.

A lay disciple asked Geshe Potowa which Dharma practice was the most important if one had to choose only one. The Geshe replied:

> If you want to use a single Dharma practice, to meditate on impermanence is the most important.
>
> At first meditation on death and impermanence makes you take up the Dharma; in the middle it conduces to positive practice; in the end it helps you realize the sameness of all phenomena.
>
> At first meditation on impermanence makes you cut your ties with the things of this life; in the middle it conduces to your casting off all clinging to saṁsāra; in the end it helps you take up the path of nirvāṇa.
>
> At first meditation on impermanence makes you develop faith; in the middle it conduces to diligence in your practice; in the end it helps you give birth to wisdom.
>
> At first meditation on impermanence, until you are fully convinced, makes you search for the Dharma; in the middle it conduces to practice; in the end it helps you attain the ultimate goal.
>
> At first meditation on impermanence, until you are fully convinced, makes you practise with a diligence which protects you like armour; in the middle it conduces to your practising with a diligence in action; in the end it helps you practise with a diligence that is insatiable.[46]

And Padampa Sangye says:

> At first, to be fully convinced of impermanence makes you take up the Dharma; in the middle it whips up your diligence; and in the end it brings you to the radiant dharmakāya.

Unless you feel this sincere conviction in the principle of impermanence, any teaching you might think you have received and put into practice will just make you more and more impervious[47] to the Dharma. Padampa Sangye also said:

* i.e. perfectly capable of receiving the teachings correctly and making use of them.

> I never see a single Tibetan practitioner who thinks about dying;
> Nor have I ever seen one live forever!
> Judging by their relish for amassing wealth once they don the yellow robe, I wonder—
> Are they going to pay off Death in food and money?
> Seeing the way they collect the best of valuables, I wonder—
> Are they going to hand out bribes in hell?
> Ha-ha! To see those Tibetan practitioners makes me laugh!
> The most learned are the proudest,
> The best meditators pile up provisions and riches,
> The solitary hermits engross themselves in trivial pursuits,
> The renunciates of home and country know no shame.
> Those people are immune to the Dharma!
> They revel in wrong-doing.
> They can see others dying but have not understood that they themselves are also going to die.
> That is their first mistake.

Meditation on impermanence is therefore the prelude that opens the way to all practices of Dharma. When he was asked for instructions on how to dispel adverse circumstances, Geshe Potowa answered with the following words:

> Think about death and impermanence for a long time. Once you are certain that you are going to die, you will no longer find it hard to put aside harmful actions, nor difficult to do what is right.
> After that, meditate for a long time on love and compassion. Once love fills your heart you will no longer find it hard to act for the benefit of others.
> Then meditate for a long time on emptiness, the natural state of all phenomena. Once you fully understand emptiness, you will no longer find it hard to dispel all your delusions.

Once we have such conviction about impermanence, all the ordinary activities of this life come to seem as profoundly abhorrent as a greasy meal does to someone suffering from nausea. My revered Master often used to say:

> Whatever I see of high rank, power, wealth or beauty in this world arouses no desire in me. That is because, seeing how the noble beings of old spent their lives, I have just a little understanding of impermanence. I have no deeper instruction than this to offer you.

So, just how deeply have you become permeated with this thought of impermanence? You should be like Geshe Kharak Gomchung, who went to meditate in the mountain solitudes of Jomo Kharak in the province of Tsang. In front of his cave there was a thorn-bush which kept catching on his clothes.

At first he thought, "Maybe I should cut it down," but then he said to himself, "But after all, I may die inside this cave. I really cannot say whether I shall ever come out again alive. Obviously it is more important for me to get on with my practice."

When he came back out, he had the same problem with the thorns. This time he thought, "I am not at all sure that I shall ever go back inside;" and so it went on for many years until he was an accomplished master. When he left, the bush was still uncut.

Rigdzin Jigme Lingpa would always spend the time of the constellation Ṛiṣi, in autumn, at a certain hot spring. The sides of the pool had no steps, making it very difficult for him to climb down to the water and sit in it. His followers offered to cut some steps, but he replied: "Why take so much trouble when we don't know if we will be around next year?" He would always be speaking of impermanence like that, my Master told me.

We too, as long as we have not fully assimilated such an attitude, should meditate on it. Start by generating bodhicitta, and as the main practice train your mind by all these various means until impermanence really permeates your every thought. Finally, conclude by sealing the practice with the dedication of merit. Practising in this way, strive to the best of your ability to emulate the great beings of the past.

Impermanence is everywhere, yet I still think things will last.
I have reached the gates of old age, yet I still pretend I am young.
Bless me and misguided beings like me,
That we may truly understand impermanence.

Jetsun Trakpa Gyaltsen (1147-1216)

A great scholar and early teacher of the Sakya school.

CHAPTER THREE

The defects of saṁsāra

Understanding that samsaric activities are empty of meaning,
With great compassion, you strive only for the benefit of others.
Without attachment to saṁsāra or nirvāṇa, you act according to the Great Vehicle.
Peerless Teacher, at your feet I bow.

Listen to this chapter with the same attitude as you did the previous ones. It comprises a general reflection on the sufferings of saṁsāra and reflections on the particular sufferings of each of the six realms of being.

I. THE SUFFERINGS OF SAṀSĀRA IN GENERAL

As I have pointed out already, we may now have a life endowed with the freedoms and advantages which are so difficult to find, but it will not last for long. We will soon fall under the power of impermanence and death. If after that we just disappeared like a fire burning out or water evaporating, everything would be over. But after death we do not vanish into nothing. We are forced to take a new birth—which means that we will still be in saṁsāra, and nowhere else.

The term *saṁsāra*, the wheel or round of existence, is used here to mean going round and round from one place to another in a circle, like a potter's wheel, or the wheel of a water mill. When a fly is trapped in a closed jar, no matter where it flies it cannot get out. Likewise, whether we are born in the higher or lower realms, we are never outside saṁsāra.

The upper part of the jar is like the higher realms of gods and men, and the lower part like the three unfortunate realms. It is said that saṁsāra is a circle because we turn round and round, taking rebirth in one after another of the six realms as a result of our own actions which, whether positive or negative, are tainted by clinging.

We have been wandering since beginningless time in these samsaric worlds in which every being, without exception, has had relations of affection, enmity and indifference with every other being. Everyone has been everyone else's father and mother. In the sūtras it is said that if you wished to count back the generations of mothers in your family, saying, "She was my mother's mother; her mother was so and so..." and so on, using little pellets of earth as big as a juniper berry to count them, the whole earth would be used up before you had counted them all. As Lord Nāgārjuna says:

> We would run out of earth trying to count our mothers
> With balls of clay the size of juniper berries.

There is not a single form of life that we have not taken throughout beginningless saṁsāra until now. Our desires have led us innumerable times to have our head and limbs cut off. Were we to try to pile up in one place all the limbs we have lost when we were ants and other small insects, the pile would be higher than Mount Meru. The tears we have wept from cold, hunger and thirst when we were without food and clothing, had they not all dried up, would make an ocean larger than all the great oceans surrounding the world. Even the amount of molten copper we have swallowed in the hells would be vaster than the four great oceans. Yet all beings bound to the realms of saṁsāra by their desire and attachments, with never an instant's remorse, will have to undergo still more sufferings in this endless circle.

Even were we able, through the fortunate result of some virtuous action, to obtain the long life, perfect body, wealth and glory of Indra or Brahmā, in the end we would still not be able to postpone death; and after death we would again have to experience the sufferings of the lower realms. In this present life, what little advantages of power, wealth, good health and other things we enjoy might fool us for a few years, months, or days. But once the effect of whatever good actions caused these happy states is exhausted, whether we want to or not, we will have to undergo poverty and misery or the unbearable sufferings of the lower realms.

What meaning is there in that kind of happiness? It is like a dream that just stops in the middle when you wake up. Those who, as the result of some slight positive action, seem to be happy and comfortable at the moment, will not be able to hold on to that state for an instant longer once the effect of that action runs out. The kings of the gods, seated high on their thrones of precious jewels spread with divine silks, enjoy all the pleasures of the five senses. But, once their lifespan is exhausted, in the twinkling of an eye they are plunged into suffering and fall headlong down to the scorching metal ground of hell. Even the gods of the sun and moon,[48] who light up the four continents, can end up being reborn somewhere between those very continents, in darkness so deep that they cannot see whether their own limbs are stretched out or bent in.

So do not put your trust in the apparent joys of saṁsāra. Resolve that, in this very life, you will free yourself from the great ocean of its sufferings and attain the true and constant happiness of perfect Buddhahood. Make this thought your practice, using the proper methods for the beginning, the main part and the conclusion.

II THE PARTICULAR SUFFERINGS EXPERIENCED BY THE BEINGS OF THE SIX REALMS

1. The eighteen hells

1.1 THE EIGHT HOT HELLS

These eight hells lie one above the other like the storeys of a building, from the Reviving Hell on top, down to The Hell of Ultimate Torment at the bottom. In each the ground and perimeter are like the white-hot iron of a smith—there is nowhere at all where you could safely put your foot. Everything is a searingly hot expanse of blazing, fiery flame.

1.1.1 The Reviving Hell

Here, amidst the burning embers that cover the incandescent metal ground, beings as numerous as the snowflakes of a blizzard are gathered together by the force of their actions. As the actions which drove them there were motivated by hatred, the effect similar to the cause makes them see each other as mortal enemies, and furiously they fight. Brandishing inconceivable weapons—a phantom armoury created by their karma—they strike at each other until everyone is slain. At that time, a voice from the sky says, "Revive!" and they immediately come back to life and start fighting all over again. And so they suffer, continually dying and being revived.

How long do they live there? Fifty human years equal one day in the god realm of the Four Great Kings. Thirty of those days make a month, and twelve months make a year; five hundred such years equal one day in the Reviving Hell, where again, twelve months, each of thirty days, make up a year. They suffer there for five hundred of those years.

1.1.2 The Black-Line Hell

Here Yama's henchmen lay their victims out on the ground of burning metal like so many firebrands and cross-rule their bodies with black lines—four, eight, sixteen, thirty-two and so on—which they use as guidelines to cut them up with burning saws. No sooner have their bodies been cut into pieces than they immediately become whole once more, only to be hacked apart and chopped up over and over again.

As for the length of their life there, a hundred human years correspond to one day for the gods in the Heaven of the Thirty-three, and a thousand years in the Heaven of the Thirty-three is equal to one day in this hell. On that scale, beings there live for a thousand years.

1.1.3 The Rounding-Up and Crushing Hell

In this hell, beings by the million are thrown into vast mortars of iron the size of whole valleys. The henchmen of Yama, the Lord of Death, whirling huge hammers of red-hot metal as big as Mount Meru around their heads, pound their victims with them. These beings are crushed to death, screaming and weeping in unimaginable agony and terror. As the hammers are lifted, they come back to life, only to suffer the same torments over and over again.

Sometimes, the mountains on both sides of the valley turn into the heads of stags, deer, goats, rams and other animals that the hell-beings have killed in their past lives. The beasts butt against each other with their horn-tips spewing fire, and innumerable hell beings, drawn there by the power of their actions, are all crushed to death. Then, once more, as the mountains separate, they revive only to be crushed again.

Two hundred human years are equivalent to one day for the gods of the Heaven Without Fighting. Two thousand years in that realm correspond to one day in the Rounding-Up and Crushing Hell, and the beings in that hell live two thousand years.

1.1.4 The Howling Hell

Here, beings suffer by being roasted in buildings of red hot metal with no exit. They scream and cry, feeling that they will never escape.

Four hundred human years equal one day in the Joyous Realm. Four thousand years in that heaven are equivalent to one day in the Howling Hell, where life continues for four thousand years.

1.1.5 The Great Howling Hell

A vast host of Yama's henchmen, armed and terrifying, shove victims by the million into metal sheds with double walls blazing with fire, and beat them with hammers and other weapons. Both the inner and outer doors are sealed with molten metal and the hell-beings howl in torment to think that, even if they could get past the first door, they would never be able to get through the second.

Eight hundred human years correspond to one day in the Paradise of Joyful Magic. Eight thousand years there equal one day in the Great Howling Hell. Its beings have a lifespan of eight thousand years.

1.1.6 The Heating Hell

Here, countless beings suffer by being cooked in huge iron cauldrons the size of the whole cosmos of a billion worlds, where they boil in molten bronze. Whenever they surface, they are grabbed by the workers with metal hooks and beaten about the head with hammers, sometimes losing consciousness; their idea of happiness is these rare moments when they no longer feel pain. Otherwise, they continually experience immense suffering.

Sixteen hundred human years equal one day among the gods Enjoying the Emanations of Others. Sixteen thousand years of these gods correspond to one day in the Heating Hell, and beings stay there sixteen thousand of those years.

1.1.7 The Intense Heating Hell

The beings in this hell are trapped inside blazing metal houses, and Yama's henchmen impale them through the heels and the anus with tridents of red-hot iron, until the prongs push out through the shoulders and the crown of the head. At the same time their bodies are wrapped in sheets of blazing metal. What pain they suffer! This continues for half an intermediate kalpa, a period of time immeasurable in terms of human years.

1.1.8 The Hell of Ultimate Torment

This is an immense edifice of blazing hot metal, surrounded by the sixteen Neighbouring Hells. In it Yama's henchmen toss incalculable numbers of beings into the centre of a mountain of pieces of red-hot iron, glowing like live coals. They whip up the flames with bellows of tiger and leopard-skin until the bodies of their victims and the fire become indistinguishable. Their suffering is tremendous. Apart from the cries of distress, there is no longer any indication of the presence of actual bodies. They constantly long to escape, but it never happens. Sometimes there is a small gap in the fire and they think they can get out, but the workers hit them with spears, clubs, hammers and other weapons and they are subjected to all the agonies of the seven previous hells, such as having molten bronze poured into their mouths.

Lifespan here is a whole intermediate kalpa. It is called the Hell of Ultimate Torment because there could be no worse torment elsewhere. It is the hell where those who have committed the five crimes with immediate retribution, and practitioners of the Mantrayāna who develop adverse views regarding the Vajra Master, are reborn. No other actions have the power to cause rebirth here.

1.1.9 The Neighbouring Hells

Around the Hell of Ultimate Torment, in each of the four cardinal directions, there is a ditch of flaming embers, a marsh of rotting corpses, a plain of bristling weapons and a forest of trees with razor-edged leaves. There is one of each in the north, south, east and west, making sixteen in all. In each of the intermediate directions—the southeast, southwest, northwest and northeast—stands a hill of iron *śālmali* trees.

The pit of hot embers. When beings have purged most of the effect of actions connected with the Hell of Ultimate Torment and emerge from it, they see, far away in the distance, what looks like a shady trench. They leap into it with delight, only to find themselves sinking down into a pit of blazing embers which burn their flesh and bones.

The swamp of putrescent corpses. Then they see a river. Having been roasted in a brazier for a whole kalpa, they are so thirsty that seeing water fills them with joy and they rush towards it to quench their thirst. But of course there is no water. There is nothing but corpses—corpses of men, corpses of horses, corpses of dogs—all decomposing and crawling with insects as they decompose, giving off the foulest of stenches. They sink into this mire until their heads go under, while worms with iron beaks devour them.

The plain of razors. When they emerge from this swamp, they are thrilled to see a pleasant green plain. But when they get there they find that it is bristling with weapons. The whole ground is covered with slender blades of burning hot metal growing like grass, which pierce their feet with each step. Each foot heals as they lift it—only to be excruciatingly stabbed again as soon as they put it down.

The forest of swords. Once again free, they rejoice to see a beautiful forest and rush towards it. But when they get there, there is no beautiful forest. It turns out to be a thicket whose trees have swords growing on their metal branches instead of leaves. As they stir in the wind, the swords cut those beings' bodies into little pieces. Their bodies reconstitute themselves and are chopped up over and over again.

The hill of iron śālmali *trees.* It is here that loose monks and nuns who have broken their vows of chastity and people who give themselves over to sexual misconduct are reborn. The effect of such actions brings them to the foot of the terrifying hill of iron *śālmali* trees. At the top they can see their former lovers calling them. As they climb eagerly up to join them, all the leaves of the iron trees point downwards and pierce their flesh. When they reach the top, they find ravens, vultures, and the like that dig out their eyes to suck up the fat. Again they see their friends calling them, now from the foot of the hill. Down they go, and the leaves turn upward, stabbing them through the chest again and again. Once they get down to the ground, hideous metallic men and women embrace them, biting off their heads and chewing them until the brains trickle out of the corners of their mouths. Such are the torments experienced here.

Absorb all the details of the pains of the eight hot hells, the sixteen neighbouring and supplementary hells and the hills of iron *śālmali* trees. Withdrawing to a quiet place, close your eyes and imagine that you are really living in the infernal realms. When you feel as much terror and pain as you would if you were really there, arouse the following thought in your mind:

"I feel such intense terror and suffering when I just imagine all that pain, even though I am not actually there. There are countless beings living in those realms right now, and all of them have been my parents in past lives. There is no knowing whether my parents, loved ones and friends of this life will not be reborn there once they die. Rebirth in those realms is caused primarily by actions arising from hatred, and I myself have accumulated an incalculable number of such actions in this present life as well as in all my past lives. I can be certain that I myself will be reborn in those hells sooner or later.

"At present, I have a human life complete with all the freedoms and advantages. I have met an authentic spiritual teacher and received the profound instructions which offer the possibility of attaining the level of the Buddha. So I must do my best to practise the methods that will save me from ever having to be born in those lower realms again."

Over and over again, reflect like this on the suffering of the hells. Confess your past misdeeds with intense remorse and make the unshakeable resolve that, even at the risk of your life, you will never again commit acts which lead to birth in the hell realms. With immense compassion for the beings who are there now, pray that they may all be freed from the lower realms this very instant. Put the teaching into practice, complete with the methods for the beginning, the main part and the conclusion.

1.2 THE EIGHT COLD HELLS

In all these hells, the environment is entirely composed of snow mountains and glaciers, perpetually enveloped in snowy blizzards.

The beings there, all completely naked, are tormented by the cold. In the Hell of Blisters, the cold makes blisters erupt on their bodies. In the Hell of Burst Blisters, the blisters burst open. In the Hell of Clenched Teeth, the biting cold is intolerable and the teeth of the beings there are tightly clenched. In the Hell of Lamentations, their lamenting never ends. In the Hell of Groans their voices are cracked and long groans escape from their lips. In the Hell of Utpala-like Cracks, their skin turns blue and splits into four petal-like pieces. In the Hell of Lotus-like Cracks, their red raw flesh becomes visible, and the cold makes it split into eight pieces. Lastly, in the Hell of Great Lotus-like Cracks, their flesh turns dark red and splits into sixteen, thirty-two and then into innumerable pieces. Worms penetrate the cracked flesh and devour it with their metal beaks. The names of these eight hells derive from the different sufferings that beings endure in them.

As for the lifespan in these cold hells, imagine a container that could hold two hundred Koṣala measures,* filled with sesame seeds. Life in the Blistering Hell lasts as long as it would take to empty that container by removing a single grain every hundred years.

For the other cold hells, lifespan and sufferings increase by multiples

* An ancient measure named after the Indian city of Koṣala (near modern Ayodhyā).

of twenty for each one. Life thus lasts twenty times longer in the Hell of Burst Blisters than in the Blistering Hell; twenty times longer than that in the Hell of Clenched Teeth; and so on.

Take these sufferings upon yourself mentally, and meditate on them in the same way as for the hot hells. Think how unbearably cold it feels to stand naked in the winter wind even for an instant in this present human world. How could you stand it if you were reborn in those realms? Confess your faults and promise never to commit them again. Then develop compassion for the beings actually living in those worlds. Practise as before, employing each of the methods for the beginning, main practice and conclusion.

1.3 THE EPHEMERAL HELLS

The ephemeral hells exist in all sorts of different locations and the sufferings experienced in them also vary considerably. Beings may be crushed between rocks, or trapped inside a stone, frozen in ice, cooked in boiling water or burnt in fires. Some feel that, when someone is cutting a tree, they are the tree having their limbs chopped off. Some suffer through identifying their bodies with objects that are constantly put to use, such as mortars, brooms, pans, doors, pillars, hobs and ropes.

Examples of stories about these hells are the accounts of the fish seen by Lingje Repa in Yamdrok Lake and the frog that the siddha Tangtong Gyalpo found inside a stone.

Yutso Ngonmo, the Blue Turquoise Lake, appeared while the ḍākinī Yeshe Tsogyal was meditating in Yamdrok, when a piece of pure gold thrown by a Bönpo was transformed into water. It is one of the four famous lakes of Tibet, and is so long that to get from its head at Lung Kangchen to where it ends at Zemaguru is a walk of several days. One day the great siddha Lingje Repa was looking into this lake, when he started to weep, exclaiming, "Poor thing! Don't misuse offerings! Don't misuse offerings!"[49]

When the people who were with him asked him to explain, he said, "The consciousness of a lama who misused offerings has been reborn in an ephemeral hell in this lake, and is suffering terribly."

They wanted to see, so the siddha miraculously dried up the lake in an instant, revealing a huge fish so big that its body spanned the lake's entire length and breadth. It was squirming in agony because it was completely covered with small creatures that were eating it alive. Lingje Repa's attendants asked him who it was that had such evil karma, and he replied that it was Tsangla Tanakchen, the Black Horse Lama from Tsang. He was a lama whose speech had had great power and blessing.[50] A mere glance from him was enough to cure someone troubled by spirits. For this reason he was highly venerated in the four provinces of U and Tsang. But when he performed the transference of consciousness at funeral ceremonies, for each "*P'et!*"* he uttered he would take as payment a large number of the horses and cattle belonging to the deceased.

One day the siddha Tangtong Gyalpo was practising the yoga exercises of the channels and energies on a big rock. The rock split in two. Inside there was a huge frog. Innumerable small creatures had attached themselves to it and were eating it alive, making it open and close its black mouth in unbearable pain. When his companions asked why this had come about, Tangtong Gyalpo explained that the being who had been reborn in that form had been a priest who sacrificed animals.

Look at the lamas of today! Each time a patron kills a nice fat sheep and cooks up the gullet, kidneys and other organs along with the meat and blood, serving it piled up with the still quivering ribs of a yak, our lamas pull the shawl of their robes over their heads and suck away at the entrails like babies at their mother's breast. Then they cut themselves slices of the outer meat with their knives and munch them in a leisurely fashion. Once they have finished, their heads emerge again, hot and steaming. Their mouths gleam with grease and their whiskers have acquired a reddish tinge. But they will have a big problem in their next life, in one of the ephemeral hells, when they have to pay back with their own bodies all that they have eaten so many times in this life.

Once Palden Chökyong, High Abbot of Ngor, was at Derge. He posted many monks along the banks of the River Ngulda, commanding them to let nothing pass by. Towards evening, they saw a big tree-trunk floating on the water, so they hauled it in to the bank and took it to the Abbot, telling him that they had seen nothing else.

"That must be it," he said. "Split it open."

Inside they found a big frog being eaten alive by a mass of insects. After doing a purification ritual, the Abbot said that the frog had been a treasurer of Derge named Pogye. Today they might seem all-powerful, but all those chiefs and high dignitaries who dip into the public purse should think about the ephemeral hells and be careful.

At the time of the Buddha, there was a village butcher who made a vow never to kill animals at night. He was reborn in an ephemeral hell. At

* One use of the syllable *P'et* is to project the consciousness in the practice of transference (discussed in Part Three).

night his pleasure knew no bounds. He lived in a beautiful mansion, with four lovely women plying him with food and drink and other pleasures. During the day, however, the walls of the house would transform into blazing hot metal and the four women into terrifying brown dogs who fed on his body.

Long ago, Śroṇa saw an adulterer who had vowed to keep from infidelity during the day. In contrast to the butcher, he suffered only during the night.

There was once a delightful monastery, housing about five hundred monks. When the bell rang around midday and the monks gathered to eat, the monastery would turn into a house of burning metal. The monks' begging bowls, cups and so forth would change into weapons and the monks would beat each other with them. Once the lunch-hour had ended, they would separate and take their places again. In the days of Buddha Kāśyapa, many monks had argued at the time of the midday meal, and this was the fully ripened effect.*

These eight hot hells, eight cold hells, the neighbouring hells and the ephemeral hells are together called the eighteen hell realms. Carefully study their number, the length of time spent in them, their sufferings and the causes of being reborn there, and meditate with compassion on the beings born in them. Strive to ensure that no one, neither yourself nor anyone else, is ever reborn in those realms.

If you are content just to listen and know all this intellectually, without making it a living experience, you will just become one of those obdurate and arrogant practitioners criticized by sublime beings and condemned by the wise.

There was once a monk whose conduct was exemplary but whose pride was enormous. He came to visit Shang Rinpoche, who asked him what Dharma he knew.

"I have listened to many teachings," replied the monk.

"Then tell me the names of the eighteen hells," said Shang Rinpoche.

"The eight hot hells and the eight cold hells... that makes sixteen... and eighteen if you add the Black and Red Hat Karmapas."

It was not lack of respect that caused him to count the Karmapa Lamas with the hells. He had simply forgotten the names of the ephemeral hells and neighbouring hells, and since the Red and Black Hat Karmapas were very well known at the time, impulsively he put them in. Now, whether

* This is explained in the chapter that follows.

or not you have practised the teachings you have received is one thing, but not to know at least the words and terms involved is truly shameful.

2. The pretas

There are two sorts of preta: those who live collectively and those who move through space.

2.1 PRETAS WHO LIVE COLLECTIVELY

These pretas suffer from external, internal or specific obscurations.

2.1.1 Pretas suffering from external obscurations

These pretas are tormented by extreme hunger and thirst. Centuries pass without their even hearing any mention of water. Constantly obsessed with food and drink, they search for them endlessly, without ever finding even the tiniest trace. From time to time, far away, they catch sight of a stream of clear, pure water. But their joints are too fragile to take the weight of their bellies. They get there only with great pain and arrive utterly exhausted—only to suffer even more when they find that the water has completely dried up, leaving nothing but the stony river bed.

Sometimes they see an orchard of fruit trees in the distance. As before, they approach, but when they arrive they find that the huge trees are all dried up and withered. Sometimes they see an abundance of food and drink and other pleasant things, but when they get near they find that it is guarded by a large number of armed men who chase and beat them with their weapons, causing them great pain.

In summer, even the moonlight feels hot and burns them; in winter, even the sun feels icy cold. These sensations torture them terribly.

Once, when Śroṇa was in the land of the pretas, he found their avarice so poisonous that it gave him a fever and his mouth became completely dry. He came across an iron castle at whose door stood a terrifying sombre figure with red eyes.

"Where is there some water?" Śroṇa asked.

At these words, a crowd of pretas, all looking like lumps of burnt wood, came milling around him, begging, "Great perfect being, give us water!"

"I have found none myself," answered he. "It is for you to give me some."

"What do you mean?" replied the pretas. "We were born in this land twelve years ago and until today we have never even heard as much as a mention of water."

2.1.2 Pretas suffering from internal obscurations

These pretas have mouths no bigger than the eye of a needle. Even were they to drink all the water in the great oceans, by the time it had passed down their throats, which are as narrow as a horse-hair, the heat of their breath would have evaporated it. Even were they somehow to swallow a little, their stomachs, which are the size of a whole country, could never be filled. Even if—finally—enough to satisfy them were ever to get into their stomach, it would burst into flames during the night and burn their lungs, their heart, and all their entrails. When they want to move, they cannot lift their gigantic bellies with their grass-like limbs, and this causes them immense suffering.

2.1.3 Pretas suffering from specific obscurations

These pretas have all sorts of different experiences that vary from one to another and are of varying intensity. For example, some have many creatures living on their bodies and devouring them.

Once when he was travelling in the land of the pretas, Śroṇa came to a palace where he met a beautiful woman. Exquisitely formed and bedecked with precious jewels, she was ravishing to behold. To each of the four legs of her throne a preta was tied. She offered Śroṇa something to eat, warning him not to give the smallest scrap to the other pretas even if they begged for it. When Śroṇa started to eat they began to beg. He gave some food to one of them and it turned into chaff; what he gave to the second turned into a lump of iron; the third started to eat his own flesh, and what he gave to the fourth became pus and blood.

When the woman came back, she cried, "Didn't I tell you not to give them anything! Do you think that you are more compassionate than I am?"

"What is the connection between you and these four?" Śroṇa asked her.

"This was my husband; that one was my son, that was my daughter-in-law, and the fourth was my servant."

"What past actions have brought you here?"

"The people of Jambudvīpa are too sceptical," the woman replied. "You will never believe me."

"How could I not believe you, when I am seeing this with my very own eyes?"

So the woman told Śroṇa her story. "I was a brahmin woman in a village. One evening, I had prepared some delicious food because it was an auspicious day. The great and sublime Kātyāyana happened to come by on his alms round. I felt faith in him and gave him an offering of food. Then I thought to myself that perhaps my husband would like to share the merit. 'Rejoice with me that I have given alms to the great and sublime Kātyāyana, the Buddha's heir,' I said to him. But he flew into a rage. 'You have not yet offered food to the brahmins, nor even presented your respects to your family and friends, and there you are giving the first part of the food to this shaven-skulled monk! Why can't he stuff his mouth with chaff?'

"I made the same proposition to my son, who also got angry: 'Why doesn't your bald-head eat lumps of iron?' he yelled.

"That night, my parents sent me over some delicious food, but my daughter-in-law ate it, leaving me the worst bits. When I asked her, 'Did you eat the good food and just leave me the worst bits?' she told me a lie: 'I would rather eat my own flesh,' said she, 'than touch a dish which was meant for you!'

"Similarly, when my servant ate the meal that she was supposed to take over to my family, she told me that she would rather drink blood and pus than steal food from me.

"I myself became a powerful preta because I made the wish to be reborn where I could see what happened to them as a result of their actions. Had I not made such a wish I would have been born amongst the gods of the Heaven of the Thirty-three, having given alms to a sublime being.

"If you ever go to our village, tell my daughter, who is a prostitute, that you have seen her parents and that you have been entrusted to tell her that what she is doing will have negative effects, that it is the wrong way to live and she should give up those evil ways.

"If she doesn't believe you, tell her that in her father's old house there are four iron pots filled with gold, a golden stick and an ablution jar for monks. Tell her to take them and make offerings to the great and sublime Kātyāyana from time to time, and dedicate the merit in our name. This will reduce our karma till it is finally exhausted."

Once, as the Master Jetāri was travelling, he met a female preta with a repulsive body, who was the mother of five hundred children.

"My husband went to Bodh Gaya twelve years ago, looking for food. He still isn't back. If you go there, tell him that if he doesn't come back soon, our children will all have died of hunger."

"What does your husband look like?" asked the Master. "All pretas look alike; how will I recognize him?"

"You can't miss him," said she. "He's got a huge mouth, a squashed nose, he's blind in one eye and has all nine marks of ugliness."

When Jetāri came to Bodh Gaya, he saw a novice monk throwing many food and water *torma* offerings outside. When the novice had gone, a horde of pretas was jostling to get them. Among them was the one he was looking for, so he gave him his wife's message.

The preta replied, "I've wandered around for twelve years but I never got a thing—except once, when a pure monk let fall some snot, but I didn't even get much of that because there were lots of us fighting for it." And during that battle for a bit of snot, the Master added as he related the story, the preta had been terribly wounded by the others.

Mentally take upon yourself the different torments that afflict the pretas wherever they are reborn, especially their hunger and thirst. Think how much you suffer when you do not eat or drink just for a morning. How would you feel if you were reborn in a place where for years you do not even hear any mention of water?

Reflect that the principal causes of rebirth as a preta are stinginess and opposing the generosity of others. We too have committed such acts innumerable times, so we must do whatever we can to avoid being born there. Meditate in this way from the core of your heart with the three methods for the beginning, main part and conclusion.

2.2 PRETAS WHO MOVE THROUGH SPACE

These are the *tsen*, *gyalpo*, *shindre*, *jungpo*, *mamo*, *theurang** and so on, all of whom live out their lives in constant terror and hallucination. Thinking of nothing but evil, they always do whatever they can to bring harm to others, and many of them fall into even lower realms such as the hells as soon as they die. In particular, every week they relive all the pain of their preceding death from sickness, weapons, evil forces, or whatever it was. What they want to do is to offload their pain on others, so wherever they go they do nothing but harm. But they still fail to do themselves any good by it. Even when they happily visit their former friends and loved ones, they only bring them sickness, insanity and other unwelcome sufferings.

These pretas undergo continual torture. Powerful magicians bury them, burn them and perform rituals in which they cast all sorts of imaginary weapons at them.[51] They lock them under the earth in darkness for kalpas, burn them up in offering fires, pound them with mustard seeds, powdered

* Different categories of spirits with no equivalent terms in English.

stones and the like. They split their heads into a hundred pieces and their bodies into a thousand fragments.

Like all pretas, these too have distorted perceptions: in winter, the sun feels cold to them; in summer the moon burns. Some take the form of a bird, a dog or other animal, hideous to look upon. In short, the pretas' sufferings are inconceivable.

Practise as before, meditating with the methods for the beginning, main practice and conclusion. Mentally take on the sufferings of these beings and cultivate love and compassion for them.

3. The animals

There are two categories of animals: those living in the depths and those scattered in different places.

3.1 ANIMALS LIVING IN THE DEPTHS

The great outer oceans teem with fish, reptiles, turtles, shellfish, worms and other creatures, as numerous as the grains of malt in the bottom of a beer-barrel. There are serpents and monsters so big that their bodies can wind many times around Mount Meru. Other creatures are as small as particles of dust or the tip of a needle.

They all undergo immense sufferings. The bigger ones swallow up the smaller ones. The small ones burrow into the big ones and eat them alive in their turn. The big animals all have many tiny ones living inside them, feeding on their flesh. Some of these creatures are born between the continents, where the sun does not shine and where they cannot even see whether their limbs are bent in or stretched out. Stupid and ignorant, they have no comprehension of what to do and what not to do. They are reborn in places where suffering knows no bounds.

3.2 ANIMALS THAT LIVE SCATTERED IN DIFFERENT PLACES

The animals that live in the realms of gods and humans suffer continually from their stupidity and from being exploited, while the nāgas[52] pass their lives in misery being tormented by garuḍas and rains of burning sand. In addition they are stupid, aggressive and poisonous.

The wild animals that share our human world, in particular, live in constant fear. They cannot eat a single mouthful of food without being on their guard. They have many mortal enemies, for all animals prey on each other and there are always hunters, beasts of prey and other threats to life. Hawks kill small birds, small birds kill insects, and so on, continually amassing evil actions in an endless round of killing and being killed.

Hunters are expert in all methods of torturing and killing these animals. They threaten their lives with all sorts of vicious devices—nets, snares, traps and guns. Some animals are killed for their horns, fur, skins and other products of their body. Oysters are killed for their pearls; elephants for their tusks and bones; tigers, leopards, otters and foxes for their fur; musk-oxen for their musk; wild asses and yaks for their flesh and blood. It is a terrible affliction that the very body with which they are born is the reason for their being killed.

As for those animals domesticated by man, they are so stupid that when their executioner approaches, knife in hand, they can only stare wide-eyed, not even thinking of escape. They are milked, loaded down, castrated, pierced through the nose and yoked to the plough. Not one of them escapes this continual round of slavery. Horses and yaks continue to be loaded and ridden even when their backs are nothing but one big sore. When they can go no further, they are whipped and pelted with stones. The fact that they could be in distress or ill never seems to cross their owners' minds.

Cattle and sheep are exploited until they die. Once they are too old, they are sold off or killed by the owners themselves. Whatever the case, they are destined for the butcher and a natural death is unknown to them.

Animals, then, experience inconceivable torments. Whenever you see animals tortured in this way, put yourself in their place and imagine in detail all they have to undergo. Meditate with fierce compassion upon all those reborn as animals. In particular, if you have animals of your own, treat them with kindness and love. Since all animals, right down to the smallest insect, have feelings of pleasure and pain, and since they have all been our fathers and mothers, develop love and compassion towards them, combining your practice with the methods for the beginning, main part and conclusion.

No matter where in these three lower realms beings may be reborn, they experience all manner of intense and long-lasting sufferings. Beings born there are stupid, ignorant and without any idea of Dharma, and can only create further causes for yet more lives in the lower realms. So once reborn there, it is difficult to get out. In this present life of ours, and in other past lives, we have accumulated numerous actions that are certain to lead us to rebirth in those states. So we should apply ourselves with great sincerity to regretting our wrong actions in the past, confessing them and vowing to avoid them from now on.

Thinking with great compassion of the beings who live in those worlds, dedicate to them the effects of all the positive actions you have accumulated throughout the three times. Pray that they may be liberated from those evil realms: "Now that I have met with the Dharma of the Great Vehicle, and have the chance to practise the path that brings true benefit both to myself and to others, I shall practise that Dharma with courage, scorning all difficulties, and lead all those beings of the three lower realms to the Buddhafields." Having cultivated bodhicitta with that thought, pray to your teacher and the deities, asking for their help and support, thinking, "May my teacher and the Three Jewels bless me that I may achieve this aim!" Dedicate the merit to the benefit of beings, thus practising the three supreme methods.

Although rebirth in the three lower realms naturally entails suffering, one might expect that the three higher realms would be happy and pleasant. But in fact even in the higher realms there is no happiness.

4. The human realm

Humans suffer from the three fundamental types of suffering, and also from the four great streams of suffering: birth, old-age, sickness and death. Other human sufferings are the dread of meeting hated enemies or of losing loved ones, and the suffering of not getting what one wants or of encountering what one does not want.

4.1 THE THREE FUNDAMENTAL TYPES OF SUFFERING

4.1.1 The suffering of change

The suffering of change is the suffering that we feel when a state of happiness suddenly changes into suffering. One moment we feel fine, satisfied and full after a good meal, and then suddenly we are wracked by violent spasms because of parasites in our stomach. One moment we are happy, and the next moment an enemy plunders our wealth or our livestock; or a fire burns down our home; or we are suddenly stricken by sickness or evil influences; or we receive some terrible news—and immediately we are plunged into suffering.

For indeed, whatever apparent comfort, happiness or prestige is to be found here in saṁsāra, it lacks the tiniest scrap of constancy or stability, and in the long run can never resist the round of suffering. Therefore, cultivate disenchantment with it all.

4.1.2 Suffering upon suffering

We experience suffering upon suffering when, before one suffering is over, we are subjected to another. We get leprosy, and then we break out in boils, too; and then as well as breaking out in boils we get injured. Our father dies and then our mother dies soon afterwards. We are pursued by enemies and, on top of that, a loved one dies; and so forth. No matter where we are reborn in saṁsāra, all our time is spent in one suffering on top of another, without any chance of a moment's happiness.

4.1.3 The suffering of everything composite[53]

Now, some of us might think that things are going quite well for us at the moment, and we do not seem to be suffering much. In fact, we are totally immersed in the causes of suffering. For our very food and clothing, our homes, the adornments and celebrations that give us pleasure, are all produced with harmful actions. As everything we do is just a concoction of negative actions, it can only lead to suffering. As examples, consider tea and *tsampa*.*

Where tea is grown, in China, the number of small creatures that are killed while it is planted, while the leaves are being picked, and so on, would be impossible to count. The tea is then carried as far as Dartsedo by porters. Each porter carries a load of twelve six-brick packs, taking the weight on a band around his forehead which wears away his skin. But even when his skull shows through, all white, he carries on. From Dotok onwards, *dzo*, yaks and mules take over, their backs breaking, their bellies perforated with cuts, patches of their hair chafed away. They suffer terribly from their servitude. Bartering the tea involves nothing but a series of broken promises, cheating and argument, until finally the tea changes hands, usually in exchange for animal products like wool and lambskins. Now wool, in summer before shearing, is crawling with fleas, ticks and other small creatures as numerous as the strands of wool themselves. During shearing, most of those insects are decapitated, cut in two or disembowelled. Those not killed remain stuck in the wool and suffocate. All of this can only lead to lower rebirths. As for lambskins,

* Tea and *tsampa*, finely ground roasted barley, are the two staples throughout Tibet. Tibetan tea is churned with milk and butter and consumed frequently during the day. Tsampa is mixed with it to make an instant food.

remember that new-born lambs have all their organs of sense, and they feel pleasure and pain. Just as they are enjoying their first instants of life, in perfect health, they are killed. Perhaps they are only stupid animals, but nevertheless they do not want to die—they love life and suffer as they are tortured and slaughtered. As for the ewes whose little ones have been killed, they are a living example of the sorrow experienced by a mother who loses her only child. So when we think about the production and trade of such products, we can understand that even a single sip of tea cannot but contribute to rebirth in the lower realms.

Now look at *tsampa*. Before sowing the barley, the fields have to be ploughed, which forces to the surface all the worms and insects living underground and buries underground all those living on the surface. Wherever the ploughing oxen go, they are followed by crows and small birds who feed incessantly on all those small creatures. When the fields are irrigated, all the aquatic animals in the water are stranded on dry land, while all the creatures living on dry land are drowned. Likewise, at each stage of sowing, harvest and threshing, the number of beings killed is incalculable. If you think about it, it is almost as if we were eating powdered insects.

In the same way, butter, milk and other foods, the "three white foods" and the "three sweet foods" that we consider pure and untainted by harmful actions, are not so at all. The majority of baby yaks, calves and lambs are killed. Those who are not, as soon as they are born and before they have had a chance to suckle even a mouthful of their mothers' sweet milk, have a rope tied round their necks and stay tethered to a stake during pauses on the road, and to each other during journeys, so that every mouthful of milk—their rightful food and drink—can be stolen to make butter and cheese. By taking the essence of the mother's body, so vital for the baby, we leave them half way between life and death. When spring comes around, the old mother animals have become so weak that they cannot even get up from their stalls. The calves and lambs have mostly starved to death. The survivors, weak and skeleton-like, stagger about almost dead.

All the factors we now see as constituting happiness—food to eat, clothes to wear, and whatever goods and materials we can think of—are likewise produced through negative actions alone. The end result of all those things can only be the infinite torments of the lower realms. So everything that seems to represent happiness today is, in fact, the suffering of everything composite.

4.2 THE SUFFERINGS OF BIRTH, SICKNESS, OLD AGE AND DEATH

4.2.1 The suffering of birth

For human beings here in this world, birth is from the womb.[54] The consciousness of a being in the intermediate state first has to interpose itself into the union of the father's semen and mother's blood. It then passes through the painful experiences of the various embryonic stages: the round jelly, viscous ellipse, thick oblong, firm oval, hard round lump,[55] and so on. Once the limbs, appendages and sense-organs have formed, the fetus, trapped inside the dark, rank and suffocating uterus, suffers like someone thrown into prison. When the mother eats hot food, the fetus suffers pain as if being burned by fire. When she eats something cold, it feels as if it is being thrown into freezing water; when she lies down, as if buried under the weight of a hill; when her stomach is full, as if trapped between rocks; when she is hungry, as if falling from a precipice; when she walks about or sits down, as if buffeted about by the wind.

As the pregnancy reaches term, the energy of karmic existence[56] turns the baby's head downwards ready to be born. As the baby is pushed down towards the cervix, it suffers as though a strong giant were holding it by the legs and banging it against a wall. As it is forced through the bony structure of the pelvis, the baby feels as though it were being pulled through the hole in a draw-plate.[57] Should the opening be too narrow, it cannot be delivered and dies. Indeed, both mother and baby may die during labour, and even if they survive they experience all the pain of dying. As the Great Master of Oḍḍiyāna said:

> Both mother and child go halfway to the land of Death,
> And all the mother's joints, except her jaws, are wrenched apart.

Everything the baby experiences is painful. Dropping down on the mattress as it is born feels like falling into a pit full of thorns. Having the encrusted slime wiped off its back feels like being flayed alive. Being washed clean feels like being beaten with thorns. Being taken on to its mother's lap feels like being a little bird carried off by a hawk. Having butter rubbed on the crown of its head[58] feels like being tied up and thrown down a hole. Being put in the cradle is like being put into dirty mud. Whenever the infant suffers from hunger, thirst, sickness and so on, all it can do is cry.

From birth onwards, as we mature in our youth, we have the impression of growth and increase. But what is really happening is that our life is getting shorter, day by day, as we approach closer to death. We get caught up in this life's ordinary undertakings, one after another, none of them ever coming to a conclusion, following each other like ripples on water. As all of them are based only on negative actions, their outcome is sure to be lower rebirths, and endless suffering.

4.2.2 The suffering of old age

As we busy ourselves with these inconsequential and ever-unfinished worldly tasks, the suffering of old age creeps up on us unnoticed. Little by little the body loses its vigour. We can no longer digest the food that we like. Our eyesight dims, and we can no longer make out small or distant objects clearly. Our hearing starts to fail and we can no longer distinguish sounds and speech correctly. Our tongue can no longer taste what we eat or drink, nor articulate properly what we want to say. As our mental faculties weaken, our memory fails us and we lapse into confusion and forgetfulness. Our teeth fall out, so we can no longer chew solid food, and whatever we say becomes an unintelligible mumble. Our body loses its heat and we no longer feel warm in light clothing. Our strength declines and we can no longer carry anything heavy. Although we still have a taste for pleasure and enjoyment we no longer have the energy. As our channels and energies degenerate we become irritable and impatient. Scorned by all, we become depressed and sad. The body's elements get out of balance, bringing a host of illnesses and problems. We have to struggle with all our movements, like walking and sitting, which have become almost impossible tasks. Jetsun Mila sings:

> One, you stand yourself up as if pulling a peg from the ground;
> Two, you creep along as though you were stalking a bird;
> Three, you sit down like a sack being dropped.
> When these three things come together, granny,
> You're a sad old woman whose illusory body's wasting away.
>
> One, from the outside your skin hangs in wrinkles;
> Two, from the inside protrude bones where flesh and blood have shrunk;
> Three, in between you're stupid, deaf, blind and dazed.
> When these three things come together, granny,
> Your face frowns with ugly wrinkles.
>
> One, your clothes are so ragged and heavy;
> Two, your food and drink is insipid and cold;

Three, you sit on your mat propped up with skins on four sides.
When these three things come together, granny,
You're like a realized yogī being trampled by men and dogs.

In old age, when we want to stand up we cannot do it normally all in one movement. We have to put both hands on the floor, as though we were trying to pull a peg out of hard earth. When we walk we stay bent over at the waist and cannot raise our heads; and being unable to pick up and put down our feet very quickly, we creep along gingerly like a child stalking a bird. All the joints in our arms and legs are so arthritic that we cannot sit down gradually. Instead, we let our whole weight crash down at once like a gunny-sack as its sling breaks.

As our flesh wastes away, our skin becomes lax and our bodies and faces are covered in wrinkles. With less flesh and blood around them, all our joints become more prominent. Our cheek-bones and all our other bony protuberances stick out under the skin. Our memory declines, and we become dull-witted, deaf and blind. We cannot think clearly and we feel giddy. With the decline of our physical vigour there is little reason for us to want to look our best, so the clothes we wear are always heavy and ragged. We eat left-overs and have no sense of taste; all the food we eat is cold and insipid. We feel so heavy that it is difficult to do anything. We prop ourselves up in bed on all four sides and cannot get up. By that point, our physical deterioration has brought on depression and terrible mental suffering. All the beauty and brightness of our faces has faded, our skin is covered in wrinkles, and our foreheads are lined with ugly frowns of ill humour. Everyone scorns us, and even if people are stepping over our head, we cannot get up. We no longer react. It is as if we were realized yogīs for whom clean and unclean no longer exist.[59] Unable to bear the suffering of old age, we want to die, but in fact the closer we come to death the more terrified we are of it.

All this makes the suffering that we have to undergo in old age not very different from the torments of beings in the lower realms.

4.2.3 The suffering of sickness

When the four elements that make up our body become imbalanced, all sorts of illnesses—those of wind, bile, phlegm and so on—arise, and sensations of pain and suffering afflict us.

As soon as the first painful twinges of illness strike—however young we may be in body and mind, however strong and radiantly healthy, however much in our prime—we crumple like little birds hit by a stone.

Our strength evaporates. We sink into the depths of our bedding, and any movement, however slight, is difficult. Even to answer when someone asks what is wrong is an effort: our voice seems to come from deep inside and is hard to get out. We try lying on our right side, then on our left, on our back or on our belly. But we can never get comfortable. We lose all appetite for food and drink and cannot sleep at night. In the daytime the days seem endless; at night the nights seem endless. We have to put up with bitter, hot or sour medicines, with bloodletting, cautery and all sorts of other unpleasant treatments. The thought that this illness might suddenly end in death terrifies us. Under the power of morbid influences and our own lack of integrity we may lose control of both body and mind, and on top of our normal deluded perceptions we start to hallucinate. Sometimes the sick even take their own lives. People suffering from diseases such as leprosy and epilepsy are abandoned by all and left to contemplate their fate; they are still alive, but it is as though they were already dead.

Sick people are usually unable to look after themselves. Their illness makes them short-tempered, and they always find fault with what others do for them. They become more and more fussy and critical, and if their sickness drags on and on, people get tired of looking after them and no longer do what they ask. The discomforts caused by their disease torment them continually.

4.2.4 The suffering of death

As death approaches, you collapse into your bed and no longer have the strength to get up. Even when you see food and drink, you feel no desire for it. Tormented by the sensations of dying, you feel more and more depressed and all your courage and confidence evaporate. You experience forebodings and hallucinations of what awaits you. Your time has come for the great moving on. Your family and friends gather around you, but there is nothing they can do to delay your departure—you are going through the suffering of death by yourself, all alone. Nor is there any way for you to take your possessions with you, however limitless they might be. You cannot bring yourself to let go of them, but you know you cannot keep them either. Remorse overtakes you as you remember the negative actions that you have done. When you think of the sufferings of the lower realms, you are terrified. Death is suddenly here. Dread takes hold of you. The perceptions of life slip away, and slowly you grow colder.

When an evil-doer dies, he clutches at his breast, covering his skin with the marks of his finger nails. Remembering all his evil actions, he is frightened of being reborn in the lower realms. He is filled with regret at not having practised the Dharma while he had the freedom to do so, as it is the only thing which would have been useful at the moment of death. When he realizes that, he feels tremendous pain. That is why he beats his breast and covers it with the marks of his nails as he dies. It is said:

> Watch an evil man dying;
> He is a teacher demonstrating to us the effect of actions.

Even before he is dead, the lower realms start to close in on him. Whatever he perceives becomes menacing. All his sensations cause him to suffer. The elements of his body dissolve, his breath becomes hoarse and his limbs go limp. He starts to hallucinate. His eyes roll up, and as he passes beyond this life Death comes to meet him. The apparitions of the intermediate state appear, but he has no protector or refuge.

There is no guarantee at all that our moment to leave this life, naked and empty-handed, will not come today. When that happens the only thing that will truly help us is the Dharma. There is no other refuge. It is said:

> In your mother's womb, turn your mind to the Dharma;
> As soon as you are born, remember the Dharma for death.

Since death comes so suddenly, to young as well as old, we ought to have started practising the Dharma from the very moment of our birth. For only Dharma will help us at the moment of death. But up to now we have forgotten about death, being too busy overcoming our adversaries and helping our friends, taking care of our houses and possessions, occupying ourselves with friends and family. But to pass our time like that, steeped in attachment, ignorance and hatred for the sake of friends and loved ones, is, if you think about it, a great mistake.

4.3 OTHER HUMAN SUFFERINGS

4.3.1 The fear of meeting hated enemies

We could spend all our time looking after our wealth and property, and mount guard over it day and night. But even that would not prevent us from eventually having to share it with our enemies. Brigands by day, burglars by night, wild dogs, wolves, and other fierce animals can all descend on us without warning. Obviously, the more wealth and property we have, the more trouble it takes to acquire it, protect it and try to increase it.

Nāgārjuna writes:

> Amassing wealth, watching over it and making it grow will wear you out.
> Understand that riches bring unending ruin and destruction.

Jetsun Milarepa says:

> In the beginning wealth makes you happy and envied;
> But however much you have, it never seems enough.
> In the middle miserliness tightens its knots around you:
> You can't bear to spend it on offerings or charity.
> Your wealth attracts enemies and negative forces,
> And everything you've gathered gets used up by others.
> In the end, wealth's a demon that puts your life in danger.
> How frustrating to just look after wealth for your enemies!
> I've cast off this millstone which drags us down into saṁsāra.
> I want no more of this devils' lure.

Our sufferings are in direct proportion to the extent of our possessions. For instance, if you owned a horse you would worry that it might be carried off by an enemy or stolen by a thief; you would wonder whether it had all the hay it needed, and so on. Just one horse brings plenty of trouble. If you owned a sheep, you would have one sheep's worth of trouble. If all you had was a bag of tea* you could still be sure of having a bag of tea's worth of trouble.

So reflect and meditate on how important it is to live in peace, following the old adage "without wealth, there are no enemies." Inspire yourself with the stories of the Buddhas of the past and uproot all your attachment to money and property. Live on what you find like the birds, and devote yourself entirely to the practice of Dharma.

4.3.2 The fear of losing loved ones

We who live in this world of saṁsāra all feel attachment for those with whom we identify and hostility toward others. For the sake of our families, followers, compatriots, friends and lovers, we are prepared to undergo all sorts of suffering. None of those with whom we have ties of kin or friendship can live for ever, and sooner or later we are bound to

* This is a free translation of *ja 'khor*, a measure which corresponds to four bricks of pressed Tibetan tea.

be separated from them. They die, or they drift off to other countries, or they are threatened by enemies and other dangers—and the suffering they undergo affects us more deeply than our own. Parents, especially, care very much for their children and are constantly worrying that they might be cold, hungry or thirsty, or that they might fall ill or die. Indeed, they love their children to the point that they would rather die themselves than let them suffer, and for their sake suffer a great deal of anguish.

But although we suffer so much from this dread of being separated from the friends and relatives we love, we should think about it carefully. Can we be so sure that our dear ones are as dear as we think? For instance, our parents claim to love us as their children, but their way of loving us is misguided and has an effect that is ultimately harmful. By trying to give us wealth and property and get us married, they are tightening saṁsāra's hold on us. They teach us everything we need to know about how to get the better of our adversaries, how to take care of our friends, how to get rich, and all the other harmful courses of action that will just make sure that we stay inescapably trapped in the lower realms. They could not do worse than that.

As for our children, both boys and girls, in the beginning they suck the essence out of our bodies, in the middle they take food out of our mouths, and in the end they take wealth out of our hands. In return for our love they rebel against us.

To our sons we give all the wealth that we have earned throughout our lives, without counting the cost and regardless of all the negative activities, suffering and criticism we have had to go through—but they are still not in the least bit grateful. Even if we present them with a full measure of Chinese silver, they are less grateful than any normal person would be if we had given them a pinch of tea-leaves. They just think that whatever belongs to their father automatically belongs to them.

Our sisters and daughters, too, swallow up our fortunes without any gratitude. The more we give them, the more they want. If we have so much as a false turquoise as a counter on our rosary, they will wheedle that out of us as well. At the very best, they contribute to the prosperity of other people, but bring nothing to us. But should things go badly, they return home, bringing dishonour and sadness to their family.*

As for all our other relatives and friends, they treat us like gods—as long as we are prosperous and happy and everything is going splendidly.

* In traditional Asian cultures a bride, accompanied by her dowry, joins her husband's family. If the marriage fails she will return to the house of her parents.

They do whatever they can to help us, and give us all kinds of things of which we have no need. But should we fall on hard times, although we have done them no harm at all, they treat us like enemies and return with malice any kindness we show them.

All this goes to show that there is nothing of any worth in sons, daughters, family and friends, as Jetsun Mila expresses in his song:

> In the beginning, your son is a charming little god;
> You love him so much that you cannot bear it.
> In the middle he ferociously demands his due;
> You give him everything, but he is never satisfied.
> He brings home someone else's daughter,
> Pushing his kindly parents out.
> When his father calls him, he doesn't deign to answer.
> When his mother calls, he doesn't even hear.
> In the end, he is like a distant neighbour.
> You destroy yourself nourishing a swindler like that.
> How frustrating it is to beget your own enemies!
> I've cast off this harness that tethers us to saṁsāra.
> I don't want any of these worldly sons.

He goes on:

> In the beginning a daughter is a smiling little goddess,
> Imperiously monopolizing all your best possessions.
> In the middle, she endlessly asks her due:
> She openly demands things from her father,
> And steals them from her mother on the sly.
> Never satisfied with what she's given,
> She's a source of despair to her kindly parents.
> In the end, she's a red-faced ogress:
> At best, she's an asset to someone else,
> At worst, she'll bring calamity upon you.
> How frustrating she is, this ravaging monster!
> I've cast off this incurable sorrow.
> I don't want a daughter who'll lead me to ruin.

Finally:

> In the beginning friends meet you joyfully, they smile
> And the whole valley rings with "Come in!" and "Sit down!"
> In the middle they return your hospitality with meat and beer,
> Item for item, exactly one for one.

In the end, they cause strife based on hate or attachment.
How frustrating they are, those evil friends with all their quarrels!
I've given up my dining companions of easy times.
I don't want any worldly friends.

4.3.3 The suffering of not getting what one wants

There is not one of us in the world who does not want to be happy and feel good; and yet none of us gets what we want. For instance, a family trying to make themselves comfortable build a house, but it collapses and kills them. A person might eat to satisfy his hunger, but the food makes him ill and endangers his life. Soldiers go to battle hoping for victory, and immediately get killed. A group of merchants go on a trading expedition in high hopes of profit, but are attacked and reduced to beggary. No matter how much effort and energy we expend in the hope of becoming happy and rich in this life, unless actions in our past lives have created that potential we will not even be able to satisfy our immediate hunger. All we will do is to make trouble for ourselves and others. The only result we can be sure of achieving is not to be liberated from the depths of the lower realms. That is why a single spark of merit is worth more than a mountain of effort.

What use are samsaric activities that never come to an end? All the effort we have made throughout beginningless time in saṁsāra trying to get what we want has brought us nothing but suffering. In the past, had we taken all the energy we devoted to worldly aims over the early or later part of just one life and devoted that energy to the Dharma instead, we would already be Buddhas by now. And if not, then at least we would definitely never again be subject to the sufferings of the lower realms.

We should meditate as follows: now that we know the difference between what we should do and what we should not, let us stop putting great hopes in samsaric enterprises that will never be accomplished—and instead practise the true Dharma, in which accomplishment is certain.

4.3.4 The suffering of encountering what one does not want

There is not one of us in the world who wants any of the sufferings described here, and yet they are what we experience all the time, whether we like it or not. There are people, for example, who because of their past actions become the subjects of a particular ruler or the slaves of some rich person. Against their wish, they are completely subordinated to the will of their masters, without a moment's freedom. They might be punished terribly for the smallest mistakes, and there is still nothing they can do. Even if they were being led right now to the execution ground, they would know they could not escape.

We are always encountering what we do not want. As the Great Omniscient One* says:

> You would like to stay with family and loved ones
> Forever, but you are certain to leave them.
> You would like to keep your beautiful home
> Forever, but you are certain to leave it behind.
> You would like to enjoy happiness, wealth and comfort
> Forever, but you are certain to lose them.
> You would like to keep this excellent human life with its freedoms and advantages
> Forever, but you are certain to die.
> You would like to study Dharma with your wonderful teacher
> Forever, but you are certain to part.
> You would like to be with your good spiritual friends
> Forever, but you are certain to separate.
>
> O my friends who feel deep disillusionment with saṁsāra,
> I, the Dharmaless beggar,** exhort you:
> From today put on the armour of effort, for the time has come
> To cross to the land of great bliss whence there is no separation.

Wealth, possessions, health, happiness and popularity are all the effects of past positive actions. If you have accumulated positive actions in the past, all these things will come to you naturally as a result, whether you want them or not. But without those positive actions, no amount of effort will ever get what you want. All you will get is what you want least. So when you practise the Dharma, rely on the inexhaustible wealth of being content with whatever comes. Otherwise, once you start practising, your worldly ambitions for this life are sure to bring you trouble and displease the holy beings. Jetsun Mila sings:

> What the Lord of Men, the Conqueror, mainly taught
> Was how to be rid of the eight ordinary concerns.
> But those who consider themselves learned these days—
> Haven't their ordinary concerns grown even greater than before?

* Longchenpa.

** Tibetan authors often refer to themselves with extreme modesty in this way.

The Conqueror taught rules of discipline to follow
So that one could withdraw from all worldly tasks.
But the monks of today who follow those rules—
Aren't their worldly tasks now more numerous than before?

He taught how to live like the ṛiṣis of old
So that one could cut off ties with friends and relations.
But those who live like ṛiṣis these days—
Don't they care how people see them even more than before?

In short, practised without remembering death,
Any Dharma is useless.

Human beings living in these degenerate times in all four continents of this world, but particularly here in Jambudvīpa, are deprived of even the tiniest opportunity for happiness. Their lives are full of suffering. Nowadays degeneration accelerates with every year that passes, every month and every day, every mealtime, every morning and every evening. The kalpa is going from bad to worse. The Buddha's teaching and beings' happiness are decaying more and more. Think about all this and develop a feeling of disillusionment. Moreover, this continent of Jambudvīpa confers a particular power on the effects of actions[60] which makes everything—good and bad, pleasant and unpleasant, high and low, Dharma or not—highly unpredictable. You should really see for yourself how things are, and be clear in your mind about what has to be done and what should be avoided. Put into practice the Omniscient Longchenpa's advice:

Sometimes look at what you perceive to be favourable;
If you know it's just perception, all you experience will turn out to be helpful.[61]
Sometimes look at what you perceive to be adverse and harmful;
This is vital, making you appalled at the deluded way you see things.
Sometimes look at your friends and the teachers of others;
Distinguishing the good from the bad will inspire you to practise.[62]
Sometimes look at the miraculous display of the four elements in space;
You will see how effort subsides in the true nature of mind.[63]
Sometimes look at your homeland, house and possessions;
Knowing them to be illusory, you will feel disgust at the deluded way you perceived them.

Sometimes look at the wealth and possessions of others;
Seeing how pitiful they are, you will cast off samsaric ambition.
In brief, examining the nature of everything in all its multiplicity,
You will destroy the delusion of clinging to any of it as real.

5. The asuras

The pleasures and abundance enjoyed by the asuras, the demigods, rival those of the gods. However, from previous lives they have a strong propensity for envy, quarrelling and fighting. The effect of those past negative actions is that no sooner do they take their present form than they start to experience intense feelings of envy.

Even within their own realms, there are disputes between territories and provinces, and they spend all their time fighting and quarrelling among themselves over such disagreements.

But worse, looking upwards into the realm of the gods, they can see that the gods have the ultimate in wealth and possessions. They also see that all the gods' wants and needs are provided by a wish-fulfilling tree—whose roots, however, are in their own realm. At that they are seized with unbearable resentment. Donning their armour and grabbing their weapons, they set off to make war on the gods. As soon as the gods see what is happening, they proceed to the Forest of Aggression,[64] and in their turn put on armour and take up arms. The gods keep an elephant with thirty-three heads called Supremely Steady. Their king, Indra, rides on the central head, with his ministers all around him on the thirty-two other heads. Inconceivable divine legions of irresistible splendour surround them, raising their mighty battle cry. As the battle begins, they let loose a rain of weapons—vajras, wheels, spears, giant arrows and so on. Their magical power gives them the strength to haul huge mountains into their laps and hurl them down as missiles. Because of their past actions, gods are seven times taller than men, but demigods are much smaller than gods. Gods can be killed only by cutting off their heads; any other wounds they receive are immediately healed by their divine ambrosia. But demigods die, as humans do, when a vital organ is hit. They are therefore bound to lose the many battles that take place. When, among their other strategies, the gods dispatch an elephant called All-Protector, crazed with liquor, a wheel of swords fastened to its trunk, the demigods die in their hundreds of thousands. Their corpses tumble down the slopes of Mount Meru to fall into the Great Exuberant Lakes below, whose waters are suffused with the colour of blood.

In this realm of the asuras, with their constant fights and quarrels, there is no freedom from suffering. Meditate on their lot from the depth of your heart.

6. The gods

The gods enjoy perfect health, comfort, wealth and happiness all their lives. However, they spend their time in diversions and the idea of practising Dharma never occurs to them. Throughout their lives, which may last a whole kalpa, they do not have that thought even for an instant. Then, having wasted their whole life in distraction, they are suddenly confronted with death. All gods of the six heavens of the World of Desire, from that of the Four Great Kings right up to the one called Enjoying the Emanations of Others, have to undergo the sufferings of death and transmigration.

There are five signs that foreshadow the death of a god. His body's inherent brilliance, usually visible from a league or several miles distant, grows dim. His throne, upon which he never before felt weary of sitting, no longer pleases him; he feels uncomfortable and ill at ease. His flower garlands, which before had never faded however much time passed, wither. His garments, which always stayed clean and fresh however long he wore them, get old and filthy and start to smell. His body, which never perspired at all before, starts to sweat. When these five signs of approaching death appear, the god is tormented by the knowledge that he, too, is soon going to die. His divine companions and sweethearts also know what is going to happen to him; they can no longer approach, but throw flowers from a distance and call their good wishes, saying, "When you die and pass on from here, may you be reborn among the humans. May you do good works and be reborn among the gods again." With that they abandon him. Utterly alone, the dying god is engulfed by sorrow. With his divine eye he looks where he is going to be reborn. If it is in a realm of suffering, the torments of his fall overwhelm him even before those of his transmigration have ended. As these agonies become twice and then three times as intense, he despairs and is forced to spend seven gods' days lamenting. Seven days among the gods of the Heaven of the Thirty-three are seven hundred human years. During that time, as he looks back, remembering all the well-being and happiness he has enjoyed and realizing that he is powerlessness to stay, he experiences the suffering of transmigration; and looking ahead, already tormented by the vision of his future birthplace, he experiences the suffering of his fall. The mental anguish of this double suffering is worse than that of the hells.

In the two highest divine realms,[65] there are no obvious sufferings of death and transmigration. However, when the effect of the actions which sent them there is exhausted, these gods fall into the lower realms as though waking from sleep. Such is their suffering. As Lord Nāgārjuna says:

> Know that even Brahmā himself,
> After achieving happiness free from attachment
> In his turn will endure ceaseless suffering
> As fuel for the fires of the Hell of Ultimate Torment.

Wherever we are born throughout the six realms, therefore, everything has the nature of suffering, everything multiplies suffering, everything is an engine of suffering—and there is nothing other than suffering. It is like a pit of fire, an island of murderous ogresses, an oceanic abyss, the tip of a knife or a cesspit. There is not one tiny moment of peace to be found. According to the *Sūtra of Sublime Dharma of Clear Recollection*:

> Beings in hell suffer from hell-fire,
> Pretas suffer from hunger and thirst,
> Animals suffer from being eaten by each other,
> Humans suffer from having a short life,
> Asuras suffer from wars and quarrels,
> And the gods suffer from their own mindlessness.
> In saṁsāra there is never a pinpoint of happiness.

And Lord Maitreya says:

> Just as there are no good smells in a cesspit,
> There is no happiness among the five classes of beings.[66]

The Great Master of Oḍḍiyāna says:

> It is said that in this saṁsāra there is not as much
> As a pinpoint's worth of happiness to be found.
> But should one happen to find just a little,
> It will contain the suffering of change.

The more you reflect on these and other similar passages, the more you will realize that no matter where you are reborn, from the summit of existence right down to the deepest hell, there is not even the tiniest interlude of real comfort or happiness. It is all without any meaning. Think about saṁsāra and its sufferings until you have no desire for it any more, like someone with a bad liver being offered greasy food.

Do not be content with merely hearing about these torments and understanding them intellectually. Take them upon yourself mentally and experience them with all your imagination until you are really convinced of them. Armed with that degree of certainty, avoiding negative actions and take pleasure in positive ones will come naturally to you without your having to force it.

Nanda, Lord Buddha's cousin, was very attached to his wife and did not want to renounce the world. Even though, by skilful means, Lord Buddha persuaded him to enter the Dharma and become a monk, he did not follow the precepts. He was about to run away, when the Buddha miraculously transported him to the top of a snow-mountain and showed him a one-eyed she-monkey.

The Buddha asked Nanda, "Which do you find more beautiful, this monkey or your wife Puṇḍarīkā?"

"My wife," replied Nanda. "A hundred or a thousand times more!"

"Good," replied the Buddha. "Now let us go to the realm of the gods."

When they arrived, the Buddha sat down and told Nanda to go and have a look around. Each god lived in his own palace, surrounded by many young goddesses, and enjoyed inconceivable pleasure, happiness and abundance. However, there was one palace with numerous goddesses but no god. Nanda asked why, and was told, "In the realm of the humans, there is a man called Nanda, a cousin of the Buddha, who is following monastic discipline. This action will lead him to be reborn among the gods, and this palace will then be his."

Nanda was overjoyed. He went back to the Buddha who asked him, "Did you see the gods' realm?"

"I certainly did!"

"Good. Which do you find more beautiful, your wife or the young goddesses?"

"The daughters of the gods are much more beautiful," replied Nanda; "indeed, their beauty surpasses that of Puṇḍarīkā by as much as her beauty surpasses that of the one-eyed monkey we saw before."

Once back on earth, Nanda observed monastic discipline perfectly.

Then the Buddha addressed the monks. "Nanda has renounced worldly life in order to be reborn in the divine realms," he said, "but all of you have become monks in order to go beyond suffering. You and he are not on the same path. Do not talk to him any more. Do not be intimate with him. Do not even sit on the same seat as him!"

All the monks obeyed, and Nanda was very upset. He thought, "Ānanda is my younger brother; at least he will still have some affection for me." But when he went to see his brother, Ānanda got up from the seat and moved away. Nanda asked him why, and Ānanda told him what the Buddha had said. Nanda was heartbroken.

At last the Buddha came to him and said, "Nanda, will you come to see the hells?" Nanda agreed, and the Buddha transported them both there with his miraculous powers. "Go and look around," he said.

So Nanda set off to explore, visiting all the realms of hell, until in one place he came across an empty pot with a blazing fire crackling inside it and a large number of the Lord of Death's henchmen all around. He asked them why there was no one in the pot.

"There is a young cousin of the Buddha called Nanda," they replied, "who is practising monastic discipline with the intention of being reborn as a god. After enjoying the happiness of a celestial realm, when his merit runs out he will be reborn here."

Nanda was terrified. He returned, and thought things over. To be born among the gods in the future and then to end up in the hell-realms made no sense, so he developed a real determination to seek freedom from saṁsāra. Having seen the hells with his own eyes, he never did anything that transgressed the precepts even slightly, and the Buddha extolled him as the disciple with the best control over the sense-doors.*

We do not need to go so far as to see the hells with our own eyes. A simple picture is enough to frighten us and reinforce our desire for liberation. It is for this reason that the Buddha asked that the five-fold wheel representing saṁsāra be drawn at the doors of the saṅgha's assembly-halls.** As Lord Nāgārjuna said:

> If just to see pictures of the hells, to hear descriptions,
> Or to read and think about them brings you such terror,
> What will you do when you experience there
> The full, inexorable effects of your actions?

Reflect, therefore, on all the different kinds of suffering in saṁsāra. From the depth of your heart, turn away from all the ordinary goals of this life. Unless you give up worldly activities completely, whatever Dharma you may claim to be practising will not be the real thing.

As Atīśa was about to leave this world, a yogī came to him with a question. "After you have gone, should I meditate?"

"Even if you do, will it really be the Dharma?" Atīśa asked him.

* Controlling the sense-doors means not allowing oneself to be seduced by the objects of the senses.

** This diagram can commonly be seen at the entrance of Tibetan temples.

"Well then, should I teach?"

The master answered him with the same question.

"So, what should I do?" asked the yogī.

"All of you should rely entirely on Tönpa and sincerely renounce this life," answered Atīśa.

Another tale tells of a monk who was circumambulating Radreng Monastery when he met Geshe Tönpa. The Geshe said, "Venerable monk, circumambulating is a good thing, but wouldn't it be better to practise real Dharma?"

The monk thought to himself, "Maybe it is more important to read the Mahāyāna sūtras than to circumambulate." So he took to reading the sūtras on the balcony overlooking the outdoor teaching yard.

After a while, Geshe Tönpa told him, "It is a good thing to read the teachings, too, but wouldn't it be better to practise real Dharma?"

The monk thought it over again. "This must mean that it would be better to practise meditation than to read the sūtras." So he put off his reading till another time and began to spend his time sitting on his bed with his eyes half closed.

Once again, Tönpa said to him, "It is a good thing to meditate, too, but wouldn't it be better to practise the real Dharma?"

The monk, at his wits' end, cried out, "Venerable Geshe, what should I do, then, to practise Dharma?"

"Venerable monk," the Geshe replied, "renounce this life! Renounce this life!"

It is all our ordinary activities and commitments limited to this life's concerns that prevent us from getting free from saṁsāra's realms of suffering, now and forever. Apart from an authentic teacher, no-one else can truly show us what has to be done to cut through the moorings that hold us to this life and to attain enlightenment in our future lives. Leave behind all of this life's preoccupations—parents, relatives and friends, companions and lovers, food, wealth and possessions—like so much spit in the dust.* Be satisfied with whatever food and clothes might come your way, and devote yourself wholly to the Dharma. Padampa Sangye says:

> Material objects are like clouds and mist; never think they might last.

* What is implied here (explicit in other chapters) is not a rejection of one's responsibilities to parents, children etc. but a transformation of limited ego-based attachment and preoccupation into a genuine love which also extends to all beings.

Popularity is like an echo; don't pursue esteem, pursue its very nature.
Beautiful clothes are like colours in a rainbow; dress simply and apply yourself to practise.
This body of ours is a sack of blood, pus and lymph; do not cherish it.
Even delicious meals turn into excrement; don't give great importance to food.
Phenomena arise as enemies; stay in hermitages or in the mountains.
The thorns of illusory perception tear at the mind; experience them as being of equal nature.*
Desires and needs all come from yourself; keep to the very nature of mind.
The most precious jewel is within you; do not long for food and wealth.
A lot of talking just brings quarrels; act as if you were dumb.
Mind has its own natural ability;[67] don't just follow the dictates of your stomach.
Blessings arise from the mind; pray to your lama and yidam.
If you stay in one place too long, you will find fault even with the Buddha; don't stay anywhere for long.
You should act in a humble way; abandon pride in your status.
You won't be here for long; practise now without delay.
You are like a traveller in this life; don't build a castle where you are just resting a while.
No action will be of any help; put accomplishment into practice.
You never know when your body will become worm-fodder or simply disappear; don't get distracted by this life's appearances.
Friends and relations are like little birds on a branch; do not get attached to them.
Confident faith is like an excellent foundation; don't leave it in the refuse of negative emotions.
This human form is like a precious wish-granting gem; do not hand it to your enemy, hatred.
Samaya is like a watch-tower;[68] don't contaminate it with faults.
While the Vajra Master is still among you, don't let the Dharma drift into laziness.

* Ultimately all perceptions have the same nature, which is emptiness.

To truly practise and experience the Dharma, it is essential that you realize just how meaningless is everything in saṁsāra. The only way to develop that realization is this meditation on saṁsāra's evils. Reflect on it until you are deeply convinced that saṁsāra is full of suffering.

The sign of the meditation having truly taken root in you is to feel like Geshe Langri Thangpa. One day, one of his close attendants told him, "The others call you Langri Thangpa Gloomy-face."

"How could my face be bright and cheery when I think about all the sufferings in the three worlds of saṁsāra?" the Geshe replied.

It is said that Langri Thangpa only ever smiled once. He saw a mouse trying to move a turquoise that was on his *maṇḍala*. But the mouse could not lift the jewel on its own, so it called, "Tsik! tsik!," and another mouse came along too. One mouse pushed the turquoise while the other pulled. That made Langri Thangpa smile.

This meditation on the sufferings of saṁsāra is the basis and support for all the good qualities of the path. It turns your mind towards the Dharma. It gives you confidence in the principle of cause and effect in all your actions. It makes you turn away from the goals of this life. And it makes you feel love and compassion for all beings.

The Buddha himself, pointing out how important it is to recognize suffering, started each of the teachings of the three turnings of the wheel of Dharma with these words: "Monks, this life is suffering."

Put it into practice until you become completely convinced and certain of it.

I see that saṁsāra is suffering, but crave it still.
I fear the abyss of the lower realms, but continue to do wrong.
Bless me and those who have gone astray like me
That we may sincerely renounce the things of this life.

Gampopa (1079-1153)

Also known as Dagpo Rinpoche. One of the principal disciples of Milarepa and an important master in many of the Kagyu lineages.

CHAPTER FOUR

Actions: the principle of cause and effect*

You renounce evil and take up good, as in the teachings on cause and effect.
Your action follows the progression of the Vehicles.[69]
Through your perfect view you are free from all clinging.
Peerless Teacher, at your feet I bow.

The way this chapter should be explained and studied is with the same attitude as for the others. The subject is explained under three headings: negative actions, which should be abandoned; positive actions, which should be adopted; and the all-determining quality of actions.

I. NEGATIVE ACTIONS TO BE ABANDONED

What causes us to be reborn in the higher or lower realms of saṁsāra is the good and bad actions that we ourselves have accumulated. Saṁsāra itself is produced by actions, and consists entirely of the effects of actions—there is nothing else that consigns us to the higher or lower realms. Neither is it just chance. At all times, therefore, we should

* The Sanskrit word karma (Tib. *las*), now often used in English to denote the result of past actions, in fact simply means "action." However, Tibetans also use the expression *las* in common speech to denote the entire process, or principle, of karmic cause and effect, *rgyu 'bras*, which is the subject of this chapter.

examine the effects of positive and negative actions, and try to avoid all those that are wrong and take up those that are right.

1. The ten negative actions to be avoided

Three of these ten are physical acts: taking life, taking what is not given, and sexual misconduct; four are verbal acts: lying, sowing discord, harsh words, and worthless chatter; and three are mental acts: covetousness, wishing harm on others, and wrong views.

1.1 TAKING LIFE

Taking life means doing anything intentionally to end the life of another being, whether human, animal or any other living creature.

A warrior killing an enemy in battle is an example of killing out of hatred. Killing a wild animal to eat its flesh or wear its skin is killing out of desire. Killing without knowing the consequences of right and wrong—or, like certain tīrthikas, in the belief that it is a virtuous thing to do—is killing out of ignorance.

There are three instances of killing that are called acts with immediate retribution, because they bring about immediate rebirth in the hell of Ultimate Torment without passing through the intermediate state: killing one's father, killing one's mother and killing an Arhat.[70]

Some of us, thinking only of the specific act of killing with our own hands, might imagine that we are innocent of ever having taken life. But to start with, there is no one, high or low, powerful or feeble, who is not guilty of having crushed countless tiny insects underfoot while walking around.

More specifically, lamas and monks visiting their benefactors' houses are served the flesh and blood of animals that have been slaughtered and cooked for them, and such is their predilection for the taste of meat that without the least remorse or compassion for the slaughtered beasts they wolf it all down with great gusto. In such cases, the negative karmic effect of the slaughter falls on both benefactor and guest without distinction.

When important people and government officials travel about, wherever they go, innumerable animals are killed for their tea-parties and receptions. The rich as a rule kill countless animals. Of all their livestock, apart from the odd beast here and there, they allow none to die a natural death but have them slaughtered one by one as they age. What is more, in summer these very cattle and sheep, as they graze, kill innumerable insects, flies, ants and even little fish and frogs, swallowed down with the grass, crushed under their hooves or swamped in their dung. The negative karmic result of all these acts comes to the owner as well as the beast. Compared to horses, cattle and other livestock, sheep are a particularly prolific source of harm. As they graze they eat all sorts of little animals—frogs, snakes, baby birds, and so on. In summer at shearing time, hundreds of thousands of insects carried by each sheep in its fleece all die. In winter at lambing time, no more than half the lambs are kept; the rest are killed at birth. The mother ewes are used for their milk and to produce lambs until they become too old and exhausted, at which point they are then all slaughtered for their meat and skins. And not a single ram, whether castrated or not, reaches maturity without being slaughtered straight away. Should the sheep have lice, millions of them are killed at a time on each sheep. Anyone who owns a flock of a hundred or more sheep can be sure of at least one rebirth in hell.

For every marriage, innumerable sheep are slaughtered when the dowry is sent, when the bride is seen off, and when she is received by her in-laws. Afterwards, every time the young bride goes back to visit her own family, another animal is sure to be killed. Should her friends and relatives invite her out and serve her anything but meat, she affects a shocked loss of appetite and eats with a pretentious disdain as if she had forgotten how to chew.[71] But kill a fat sheep and set down a big pile of breast-meat and tripe before her, and the red-faced little monster sits down seriously, pulls out her little knife, and gobbles it all down with much smacking of lips. The next day she sets off loaded down with the bloody carcass, like a hunter returning home—but worse, for every time she goes out she is sure not to come back empty-handed.

Children, too, cause the death of countless animals while they are playing, whether they are aware of it or not. In summer, for instance, they kill many insects just by beating the ground with a willow-wand or leather whip as they walk along.

So all of us humans, in fact, spend our entire time taking life, like ogres. Indeed—considering how we slaughter our cattle to enjoy their flesh and blood when they have spent their whole lives serving us and feeding us with their milk as if they were our mothers—we are worse than any ogre.

The act of taking life is complete when it includes all four elements of a negative action. Take the example of a hunter killing a wild animal. First of all, he sees an actual stag, or musk-deer, or whatever it might be, and identifies the animal beyond any doubt: his knowing that it is a living creature is the *basis* for the act. Next, the wish to kill it arises: the idea of killing it is the *intention* to carry out the act. Then he shoots the animal in a vital point with a gun, bow and arrow or any other weapon: the physical action of killing is the *execution* of the act. Thereupon the animal's vital functions cease and the conjunction of its body and mind is sundered: that is the final *completion* of the act of taking a life.

Another example: the slaughter of a sheep raised for meat by its owner. First, the master of the house tells his servant or a butcher to slaughter a sheep. The *basis* is that he knows that there is a sentient creature involved—a sheep. The *intention*, the idea of killing it, is present as soon as he decides to have this or that sheep slaughtered. The *execution* of the actual act of killing takes place when the slaughterer seizes his noose and suddenly catches the sheep that he is going to kill, throws it on its back, lashes its legs together with leather thongs and binds a rope around its muzzle until it suffocates. In the violent agony of death, the animal ceases to breathe and its staring eyes turn bluish and cloud over, streaming tears. Its body is dragged off to the house and the final phase, the ending of its life, reaches *completion*. In no time at all the animal is being skinned with a knife, its flesh still quivering because the "all-pervading energy"* has not yet had time to leave the body; it is as if the animal were still alive. Immediately it is roasted over a fire or cooked on the stove, and then eaten. When you think about it, such animals are practically eaten alive, and we humans are no different from beasts of prey.

Suppose that you intended to kill an animal today, or that you said you would, but did not actually do so. There would already be the basis, the knowledge that there is a sentient being, and the intention, the idea of killing it. Two of the elements of the negative action would therefore have been fulfilled, and although the harm would be less heavy than if you had in fact completed the act of killing, the stain of a negative act, like a reflection appearing in a mirror, would nevertheless remain.

Some people imagine that only the person who physically carries out the killing is creating a negative karmic effect, and that the person who just gave the orders is not—or, if he is, then only a little. But you should know that the same karmic result comes to everyone involved, even anyone who just felt pleased about it—so there can be no question about the person who actually ordered that the killing be carried out. Each person gets the whole karmic result of killing one animal. It is not as if one act of killing could be divided up among many people.

* One of the five subtle energies (*rlung*), or "winds," in the body (see glossary).

1.2 TAKING WHAT IS NOT GIVEN

Taking what is not given is of three kinds: taking by force, taking by stealth and taking by trickery.

Taking by force. Also called taking by overpowering, this means the forceful seizure of possessions or property by a powerful individual such as a king having no legal right to them. It also includes plunder by force of numbers, as by an army, for example.

Taking by stealth. This means to take possession of things secretly, like a burglar, without being seen by the owner.

Taking by trickery. This is to take others' goods, in a business deal for example, by lying to the other party, using false weights and measures or other such subterfuges.

Nowadays, the idea that in business or in other contexts there is anything wrong with cheating or trickery to get things from others does not occur to us, as long as we are not overtly stealing. But in fact any profit we may make by deceiving other people is no different from outright theft.

In particular, lamas and monks these days see no harm or wrong in doing business; indeed they spend their whole lives at it, and feel rather proud of their prowess. However, nothing debilitates a lama or monk's mind more than business. Engrossed in his transactions, he feels little inclination to pursue his studies or to work at purifying his obscurations—and anyway there is no time left for such things. All his waking hours until he lies down to sleep at night are spent poring over his accounts. Any idea of devotion, renunciation or compassion is eradicated and constant delusion overpowers him.

Jetsun Milarepa arrived one night at a monastery and lay down to sleep in front of the door of a cell. The monk who lived in the cell was lying in bed thinking about how he was going to sell the carcass of a cow that he planned to have slaughtered the next day: "I'll get that much for the head... the shoulder-blade is worth that much, and the shoulder itself that much... that much for the knuckles and shins..." He went on calculating the value of each and every part of the cow, inside and out. By daybreak, he had not slept a wink but he had it all worked out except the price he would ask for the tail. He got up straight away, completed his devotions and made torma-offerings.

As he stepped outside he came across the Jetsun still sleeping, and disdainfully railed at him, "You claim to be a Dharma-practitioner, and here you are still sleeping at this hour! Don't you do any practice or recitation at all?"

"I don't always sleep like this," replied Jetsun Mila. "It's just that I spent the whole night thinking about how to sell a cow of mine that's going to be slaughtered. I only got to sleep a little while ago..." And so, exposing the monk's hidden shortcomings, he left.

Like the monk in this story, those whose lives at the moment are devoted only to business spend day and night totally involved in their calculations. They are so engrossed in delusion that, even when death comes, they will die still as deluded as ever. Moreover, commerce involves all sorts of negative actions. People who have merchandise to sell, however shoddy in reality, extol its qualities in whatever ways they can think up. They tell outright lies, such as how this or that potential buyer has already offered this much for it, which they had refused; or how they originally bought it for this or that huge sum. Trying to buy something that is already the subject of negotiations between two other people, they resort to slander to provoke disagreement between the two parties. They use harsh words to insult their competitors' wares, to extort debts and the like. They indulge in worthless chatter by demanding ridiculous prices or haggling for things that they have no intention of buying. They envy and covet other people's possessions, trying their best to be given them. They wish harm on their competitors, wanting always to get the better of them. If they trade in livestock, they are involved in killing. So business, in fact, involves all of the ten negative actions except perhaps wrong views and sexual misconduct. Then, when their deals go wrong, both sides have wasted their assets, everyone suffers, and traders may end up starving, having brought harm upon both themselves and their counterparts. But should they have some success, however much they make it is never enough. Even those who get as rich as Vaiśravaṇa still take pleasure in their nefarious business deals. As death finally closes in on them they will beat their breasts in anguish, for their entire human life has been spent in such obsessions, which now become millstones to drag them down to the lower realms.

Nothing could be more effective than trade and commerce for piling up endless harmful actions and thoroughly corrupting you. You find yourself continually thinking up ways to cheat people as though you were looking through a collection of knives, awls and needles for the sharpest tool. Brooding endlessly over harmful thoughts, you turn your back on the bodhicitta ideal of helping others, and your pernicious acts multiply to infinity.

Taking what is not given also has to include the four elements already explained for the negative action to be complete. However, any participation, down to merely offering hunters or thieves some food for their expedition, is enough to bring you an equal share of the effect of the evil action of their killing or stealing.

1.3 SEXUAL MISCONDUCT

The rules that follow are for laypeople. In Tibet, during the reign of the Dharma King Songtsen Gampo, laws based on the ten positive actions were established comprising both rules for the laity and rules for the religious community. Here, we are referring to those restrictions on behaviour destined for laypeople, who, as householders, should follow an appropriate ethic. Monks and nuns, for their part, are expected to avoid the sexual act altogether.

The gravest sexual misconduct is that of leading other people to break their vows. Sexual misconduct also includes acts associated with particular persons, places and circumstances: masturbation; sexual relations with a person who is married, or committed to someone else; or with a person who is free, but in broad daylight, during observation of a one-day vow, during illness, distress, pregnancy, bereavement, menstruation, or recovery from child-birth; in a place where the physical representations of the Three Jewels are present; with one's parents, other prohibited family members, or with a prepubescent child; in the mouth or anus, and so on.

1.4 LYING

Lying is of three sorts: ordinary lies, major lies and phoney lama's lies.

Ordinary lies. These are any untrue statements, made with the intention of deceiving other people.

Major lies. These are statements such as, for example, that there is no benefit in positive actions and no harm in negative ones, that there is no happiness in the Buddhafields and no suffering in the lower realms, or that the Buddhas have no good qualities. They are called major lies because no other lies could have more devastatingly misleading consequences.

Phoney lama's lies. These are all untrue claims to possess such qualities and abilities as, for example, to have attained the Bodhisattva levels, or to have powers of clairvoyance. Imposters nowadays have more success than true masters, and everyone's thoughts and actions are easy to influence. So some people declare themselves masters or siddhas in an effort to deceive others. They have had a vision of a certain deity and made thanksgiving offerings to him, they claim, or they have seen a spirit and chastised it. For the most part these are just phoney lama's lies, so be careful not to believe such cheats and charlatans blindly. Affecting as it does both this life and the next, it is important to place your trust in a Dharma practitioner whom you know well, who is humble and whose inner nature and outer behaviour correspond.

Generally speaking, there are ordinary people who have some degree of concept-bound clairvoyance, but it is intermittent, and only valid some of the time. Pure clairvoyance comes only to those who have reached the sublime levels, and is therefore extremely hard to attain.[72]

1.5 SOWING DISCORD

Sowing discord can be either open or secret.

Openly sowing discord. This is a strategy often used by people who hold some authority. It consists of creating a rift between two people both present by openly telling one that the other said something bad about him behind his back, and going on to describe what the first person said or did to harm the second—and then perhaps asking them both why today they are still behaving as if no such thing had happened between them.

Secretly sowing discord. This means to separate two people who get on well by going to see one of them, behind the other's back, to report what terrible things the second, whom the first cares for so much, has supposedly been saying about him or her.

The worst instance of sowing discord is to cause conflict between members of the Saṅgha. It is particularly serious to cause a rift between a teacher of the Secret Mantrayāna and his disciples, or among the circle of spiritual brothers and sisters.

1.6 HARSH SPEECH

Harsh speech is, for instance, to make rude remarks about other people's unsightly physical flaws, openly calling them one-eyed, deaf, blind, and so on. It includes revealing others' hidden shortcomings, offensive talk of all kinds and, in fact, any words that make other people unhappy or uncomfortable, even if spoken sweetly rather than harshly.

In particular, to speak offensively in front of one's teacher, a spiritual friend or a holy being is a very grave error.

1.7 WORTHLESS CHATTER

Worthless chatter means talking a lot without any purpose: for example, reciting what one imagines to be Dharma but is not—such as the rites of brahmins;[73] or talking aimlessly about subjects that stir up attachment and hatred, like telling tales of prostitutes, singing libidinous songs, or discussing robbery and war. In particular, to disturb people's prayers or recitation by distracting them with a flood of useless words is especially harmful, since it prevents them from accumulating merit.

Pieces of gossip that seem to have come up quite naturally and spontaneously are for the most part, when you look more closely, motivated by desire or hatred, and the gravity of the fault will be in proportion to the amount of attachment or hatred created in your own or others' minds.

While you are saying prayers or reciting mantras, mixing them with irrelevant talk will stop them bearing any fruit, no matter how many you say. This applies especially to the different kinds of gossip that circulate along the rows of the gathered Saṅgha. One single gossip-monger can cause the merit of a whole congregation to be spoiled and the meritorious actions of its benefactors and patrons to be wasted.

In the noble land of India, as a rule, only those who had the highest attainments and were free from all harmful defects had the right to use funds donated to the Saṅgha, and the Buddha permitted no-one else to do so. But nowadays people learn one or two tantric rituals and, as soon as they can recite them, they start to use whatever dangerous offerings[74] they can get. Without having received the empowerments, without having maintained all the samayas, without having mastered the generation and perfection phases and without having completed the requirements of the mantra recitation, to obtain offerings by performing tantric rituals—just chanting the secret mantras perfunctorily like bönpo sorcerers—is a serious transgression. To use these dangerous donations is comparable to eating pills of burning iron: if ordinary people partake of them without having the cast-iron jaws of the union of the generation and perfection phases, they will burn themselves up and be destroyed. As it is said:

> Dangerous offerings are lethally sharp razors:
> Consume them and they'll cut the life-artery of liberation.

Far from having any mastery of the two phases of the meditation, such people, who may at least know the words of the ritual, do not even bother to recite those properly. Worse still, the moment they get to the mantra recitation—the most important part—they start chatting, and let loose an endless stream of irrelevant gossip full of desire and aggression for the whole of the allocated time. This is disastrous for themselves and others. It is most important that monks and lamas should give up this kind of chatter and concentrate on reciting their mantras without talking.

1.8 COVETOUSNESS

Covetousness includes all the desirous or acquisitive thoughts, even the slightest ones, we might have about other people's property. Contemplating how agreeable it would be if those wonderful belongings of theirs were ours, we imagine possessing them over and over again, invent schemes to get hold of them, and so on.

1.9 WISHING HARM ON OTHERS

This refers to all the malicious thoughts we might have about other people. For example, brooding with hatred or anger about how we might harm them; feeling disappointed when they prosper or succeed; wishing they were less comfortable, less happy or less talented; or feeling glad when unpleasant things happen to them.

1.10 WRONG VIEWS

Wrong views include the view that actions cause no karmic effect, and the views of eternalism and nihilism.

According to the view that actions cause no karmic effect, positive actions bring no benefit and negative actions no harm. The views of eternalism and nihilism include all the different views of the tīrthikas, which, although they can be divided into three hundred and sixty false views or sixty-two wrong views, can be summed up into the two categories of eternalism and nihilism.

Eternalists believe in a permanent self and an eternally existing creator of the universe, such as Īśvara or Viṣṇu. Nihilists believe that all things just arise by themselves and that there are no past and future lives, no karma, no liberation and no freedom.[75] As it says in the doctrine of Black Īśvara:

> The rising of the sun, the downhill flow of water,
> The roundness of peas, the bristling length and sharpness of thorns,
> The beauty of the iridescent eyes of peacocks' tails:
> No-one created them, they all just naturally came to be.

They argue that when the sun rises in the east, no-one is there to make it rise. When a river flows downhill, nobody is driving it downwards. No-one rolled out peas to make them all so round, or sharpened all the long and bristling points of thorns. The beautiful multicoloured eyes on a peacock's tail were not painted by anyone. All these things just are so by their own nature, and so it is with everything in this world whether pleasant or unpleasant, good or bad—all phenomena just arise spontaneously. There is no past karma, there are no previous lives, no future lives.[76]

To consider the texts of such doctrines true and to follow them, or even without doing so, to think that the Buddha's words, your teacher's instructions or the texts of the learned commentators are in error and to doubt and criticize them, are all included in what is meant by wrong views.[77]

The worst of the ten negative actions are taking life and wrong views. As it is said:

> There is no worse action than taking another's life;
> Of the ten unvirtuous acts, wrong view is the heaviest.

Except for those in the hells, there is no being who does not shrink from death or who does not value his or her life over anything else. So to destroy a life is a particularly negative action. In the *Sūtra of Sublime Dharma of Clear Recollection*, it is said that one will repay any life one takes with five hundred of one's own lives, and that for killing a single being one will spend one intermediate kalpa in the hells.

Even worse is to take some meritorious work you may be involved in, such as building a representation of the Three Jewels, as an excuse for committing harmful actions such as killing. Padampa Sangye says:

> To build a support for the Three Jewels while causing harm and suffering
> Is to cast your next life to the wind.

It is equally wrong, mistakenly thinking you are doing something meritorious, to slaughter animals and offer their flesh and blood to lamas invited to your house or to an assembly of monks. The negative karmic effect of the killing comes to both givers and receivers. The donor, although providing nourishment, is making an impure offering; those who receive it are accepting improper sustenance. Any positive effect is outweighed by the negative one. Indeed, unless you have the power to resuscitate your victims on the spot, there is no situation in which the act of killing does not defile you as a negative action. You can also be sure that it will harm the lives and activities of the teachers.[78] If you are not capable of transferring beings' consciousness to the state of great bliss, you should make every effort to avoid taking their lives.

To have wrong views, even for an instant, is to break all your vows and to cut yourself off from the Buddhist community. It also negates the freedom in this human existence to practise the Dharma. From the moment your mind is defiled by false views, even the good you do no longer leads to liberation, and the harm you do can no longer be confessed.[79]

2. The effects of the ten negative actions

Each negative act produces four kinds of karmic effect: the fully ripened effect, the effect similar to the cause, the conditioning effect and the proliferating effect.

2.1 THE FULLY RIPENED EFFECT[80]

Committing any one of the ten harmful acts while motivated by hatred brings about birth in the hells. Committing one of them out of desire leads to birth as a preta, and out of ignorance to birth as an animal. Once reborn in those lower realms, we have to undergo the sufferings particular to them.

Also, a very strong impulse—extremely powerful desire, anger, or ignorance—motivating a long and continuous accumulation of actions, causes birth in the hells. Should the impulse be less strong and the number of actions less, it causes rebirth as a preta; and if still less strong and numerous, as an animal.

2.2 THE EFFECT SIMILAR TO THE CAUSE

Even when we finally get out of the lower realm in which the fully ripened effect had caused us to be born, and obtain a human form, we go on experiencing the effect similar to the cause. In fact, in the lower realms, too, there are many different kinds of suffering that are similar to particular causes. These effects that are similar to the cause are of two kinds: actions similar to the cause and experiences similar to the cause.

2.2.1 Actions Similar to the Cause

This effect is a propensity for the same kind of actions as the original cause. If we killed before, we still like to kill; if we stole, we enjoy taking what is not given; and so forth. This explains why, for example, certain people from their earliest childhood kill all the insects and flies they see. Such a predilection for killing corresponds to similar acts performed in their past lives. From the cradle on, each of us acts quite differently, driven by different karmic urges. Some enjoy killing, some enjoy stealing, while others again feel no affinity for such actions and enjoy doing good instead.

All such tendencies are the residue of former actions, or in other words the effect similar to the cause. This is why it is said:

> To see what you have done before, look at what you are now.
> To see where you are going to be born next, look at what you do now.[81]

The same is true for animals, too. The instinct of animals such as falcons and wolves to kill, or of mice to steal, is in each case an effect similar to, and caused by, their former actions.

2.2.2 Experiences Similar to the Cause

Each of the ten harmful actions results in a pair of effects on our subsequent experiences.

Taking life. To have killed in a previous life makes our present life not only short, but also subject to frequent disease. Sometimes newborn babies die as an effect similar to the cause of having killed in a past life; for many lifetimes they may keep on dying as soon as they are born, over and over again. There are also people who survive into adulthood but from their earliest childhood are tormented by one illness after another without respite until their death, again as the result of having killed and assaulted others in a past life. In the face of such circumstances, it is more important to confess with regret the past actions that have brought them about than to find ways to modify each immediate problem. We should confess with regret and vow to renounce such actions; and, as an antidote to their effects, make efforts to undertake positive actions and abandon harmful ones.

Taking what is not given. To have stolen will make us not only poor, but also liable to suffer pillage, robbery or other calamities which disperse among enemies and rivals whatever few possessions we come by. For this reason, anyone who now lacks money or property would do better to create even a small spark of merit than to move mountains to get rich. If it is not your destiny to be wealthy because of your lack of generosity in past lives, no amount of effort in this life will help. Look at the loot most robbers or bandits get from each of their raids—often almost more than the very earth itself can hold. Yet people who live by robbery always end up dying of hunger. Notice, too, how traders or those who appropriate the goods of the Saṅgha fail to profit from their earnings, however great. On the other hand, people now experiencing the effects of their past generosity never lack wealth all their lives, and for many of them this happens without their making the least effort. So, if you have hopes of getting rich, devote your efforts to acts of charity and making offerings!

This continent of Jambudvīpa gives a particular power[60] to the effects of actions, so that what we do early in life is likely to have an effect later in the same life—or even right away if done in certain exceptional circumstances. So to resort to theft, fraud or other ways of taking what is not given in the hopes of getting rich is to do just the opposite of what we had intended. The karmic effect will trap us in the world of the pretas for many kalpas. Even towards the end of this life, it will begin to affect us and will make us more and more impoverished, more and more troubled. We will be bereft of any control over the few possessions that remain to us. Our avarice will make us feel more and more destitute and deprived, however wealthy we may be. Our possessions will become the cause of harmful actions. We will be like pretas that guard treasures but are incapable of using what they possess. Look closely at people who are apparently rich. If they are not using their wealth freely for the Dharma, which is the source of happiness and well-being in this life and in lives to come, or even for food and clothing, they are actually poorer than the poor. Their preta-like experience right now is a karmic effect similar to the cause, resulting from their impure generosity in the past.[82]

Sexual misconduct. To have indulged in sexual misconduct, it is said, will cause us to have a spouse who is not only unattractive, but who also behaves in a loose or hostile manner. When couples cannot stop arguing or fighting, each partner usually lays the blame on the other's bad character. In fact they are each experiencing the effect similar to the cause, resulting from their past sexual misconduct. Instead of hating each other, they should recognize that it is the effect of their past negative actions and be patient with each other. Lord Padampa Sangye says:

> Families are as fleeting as a crowd on market-day;
> People of Tingri, don't bicker or fight!

Lying. The experience similar to the cause from having lied in past lives is that not only are we often criticized and belittled, but also we are often lied to by others. If you are falsely accused and criticized now, it is the effect of your having told lies in the past. Instead of getting angry and hurling insults at people who say such things about you, be grateful to them for helping you to exhaust the effects of many negative actions. You should feel happy. Rigdzin Jigme Lingpa says:

> An enemy repaying your good with bad makes you progress in your practice.
> His unjust accusations are a whip that steers you toward virtue.

> He's the teacher who destroys all your attachment and desires.
> Look at his great kindness that you never can repay!

Sowing discord. The effect similar to the cause of sowing discord is not only that our associates and servants cannot get along with each other, but also that they are argumentative and recalcitrant with us. For the most part the monks following lamas, the attendants of chiefs or the servants of householders do not get along well among themselves, and however many times they are asked to do something, they refuse to obey and argue defiantly. The hired servants of ordinary people pretend not to hear when asked to do chores, even easy ones. The master of the house has to repeat the order two or three times, and it is only when at last he gets angry and speaks harshly to them that they do what they were asked, slowly and grudgingly. Even when they have finished, they do not bother to come back and tell him. They are permanently in a bad mood. But the master is only reaping the fruits of the discord he has sown himself in the past. He should therefore regret his own negative actions, and work at reconciling his own and others' disagreements.

Harsh words. To have spoken harsh words in past lives will not only make everything that is said to us offensive or insulting, but will also have the effect that everything we say provokes arguments.

Harsh language is the worst of the four negative actions of speech. As the proverb puts it:

> Words have no arrows nor swords, yet they tear men's minds to pieces.

To suddenly provoke hatred in another person, or—worse still—to say even a single offensive word to a holy being, causes many lifetimes to be spent in the lower realms without any chance of being released. It is said that a brahmin named Kapila once insulted the monks of the Buddha Kāśyapa, calling them "horse-head," "ox-head" and many other such names. He was reborn as a fish-like sea monster with eighteen heads. He was not released from that state for an entire kalpa and even then was reborn in hell. A nun who called another nun a bitch was reborn herself as a bitch five hundred times. There are many similar stories. So learn to speak gently at all times. Moreover, since you never know who might be a holy being or a Bodhisattva, train yourself to perceive all beings purely. Learn to praise them and extol their good qualities and achievements. It is said that to criticize or speak offensively to a Bodhisattva is worse than killing all the beings in the three worlds:

To denigrate a Bodhisattva is a greater sin
Than killing all the beings in the three worlds;
All such great and futile faults that I have accumulated, I confess.

Worthless chatter. The effect similar to the cause of worthless chatter is not only that what we say will carry no weight, but also that we will lack any resolution or self-confidence. Nobody will believe us even when we speak the truth, and we will have no self-assurance when speaking in front of a crowd.

Covetousness. The effect of covetousness is not only to thwart whatever we most wish for, but also to bring about all the circumstances we want least.

Wishing harm on others. As the result of wishing harm on others, we will not only live in constant fear, but will also suffer frequent harm.

Wrong views. The effect of having harboured wrong views is that not only will we persist in such harmful beliefs, but also our mind will be disturbed by deceit and misconceptions.

2.3 THE CONDITIONING EFFECT

The conditioning effect acts on our environment. Taking life causes rebirth in grim, joyless landscapes full of mortally dangerous ravines and precipices. Taking what is not given causes rebirth in areas stricken by famine where frost and hail destroy crops and trees bear no fruit. Sexual misconduct obliges us to live in repulsive places, full of excrement and dung, muddy swamps, and so forth. Lying will bring us material insecurity, constant mental panic and encounters with terrifying things and situations. Sowing discord makes us inhabit regions difficult to cross, cut with deep ravines, rocky gorges and the like. Harsh speech causes rebirth in a bleak terrain, full of rocks, stones and thorns. Useless chatter causes rebirth on barren and infertile land which produces nothing in spite of being worked; the seasons are untimely and unpredictable. Covetousness will bring about poor harvests and all the many other ills of inhospitable places and times. Wishing harm on others leads to rebirth in places of constant fear with many different afflictions. Wrong views cause rebirth in impoverished circumstances without any refuge or protectors.

2.4 THE PROLIFERATING EFFECT

The proliferating effect is that whatever action we did before, we tend to repeat again and again. This brings an endless succession of suffering throughout all our subsequent lives. Our negative actions proliferate yet further and cause us to wander endlessly in saṁsāra.

II. POSITIVE ACTIONS TO BE ADOPTED

In a general sense, the ten positive actions comprise the unconditional vow never to commit any of the ten negative actions, such as taking life, taking what is not given and so on, having understood their harmful effects.

To take such a vow in front of a teacher or preceptor is not strictly necessary; while to decide on your own to avoid all taking of life from now on, for example—or to avoid taking life in a particular place or at particular times, or to avoid killing certain animals—is in itself a positive act. However, making that promise in the presence of a teacher, a spiritual friend or a representation of the Three Jewels renders it particularly powerful.

It is not enough that you just happen to stop taking life, or stop the other negative actions. What counts is that you commit yourself with a vow to avoid that negative action, whatever happens. Thus even lay people who are unable to abstain completely from taking life can still derive great benefit from taking the vow not to kill for a period each year, either during the first month, the Month of Miracles; or during the fourth month, known as Vaiśākha; or at each full or new moon, or for a particular year, month, or day.

Long ago, a village butcher made a vow in the presence of the noble Kātyāyana that he would not kill during the night. He was reborn in one of the ephemeral hells, where every day he was tormented all day long in a house of red-hot metal. But he spent every night in a palace, happy and comfortable, in the company of four goddesses.

The ten positive actions, then, consist of giving up the ten negative actions and practising their positive antidotes.

The three positive acts of the body are: (1) to renounce killing, and instead to protect the lives of living beings; (2) to renounce taking what is not given, and instead to practise generosity; and (3) to give up sexual misconduct, and instead to follow the rules of discipline.

The four positive acts of speech are: (1) to renounce lying, and instead to tell the truth; (2) to give up sowing discord, and instead to reconcile disputes; (3) to abandon harsh words, and instead to speak pleasantly; and (4) to put an end to useless chatter, and instead to recite prayers.

The three positive acts of the mind are: (1) to renounce covetousness, and instead to learn to be generous; (2) to give up wishing harm on others, and instead to cultivate the desire to help them; and (3) to put an end to wrong views, and instead to establish in yourself the true and authentic view.

The fully ripened effect of these acts is that you will be reborn in one of the three higher realms.

The effect similar to the cause as *action* is that you take pleasure in doing good in all your subsequent lives, so your merit goes on and on increasing.

The effects similar to the cause as *experience* for each of the ten are as follows: for giving up taking life, a long life with few illnesses; for giving up taking what is not given, prosperity and freedom from enemies or thieves; for giving up sexual misconduct, an attractive partner and few rivals; for renouncing lies, praise and love from everyone; for giving up sowing discord, a respectful circle of friends and servants; for giving up harsh words, hearing only pleasant speech; for giving up useless chatter, being listened to seriously; for abandoning covetousness, the fulfilment of your wishes; for giving up harmful thoughts, freedom from harm; and for giving up wrong views, the growth of the right view in your mind.

The conditioning effect is, in each case, the opposite of the corresponding negative effect: you are born in places that have all the most perfect circumstances.

The proliferating effect is that whatever good actions you do will multiply, bringing you uninterrupted good fortune.

III. THE ALL-DETERMINING QUALITY OF ACTIONS

In all their inconceivable variety, the pleasures and miseries that each individual being experiences—from the summit of existence down to the very lowest depth of hell—arise only from the positive and negative actions that each has amassed in the past. It is said in the *Sūtra of a Hundred Actions*:

> The joys and sorrows of beings
> All come from their actions, said the Buddha.
> The diversity of actions
> Creates the diversity of beings
> And impels their diverse wanderings.
> Vast indeed is this net of actions!

Whatever strength, power, wealth or property we may now enjoy, none of it follows us when we die. We take with us only the positive and negative actions we have gathered during our lifetime, which then propel us onward to higher or lower samsaric realms. In the *Sūtra of Instructions to the King* we read:

> When the moment comes to leave, O King,
> Neither possessions, friends nor family can follow.
> But wherever beings come from, wherever they go,
> Their actions follow them like their own shadow.

The effects of our positive or negative actions may not be immediately evident and identifiable; but nor do they just fade away. We will experience each one of them when the right conditions come together.

> Even after a hundred kalpas
> Beings' actions are never lost.
> When the conditions come together
> Their fruit will fully ripen,

as the *Sūtra of a Hundred Actions* says. And in the *Treasury of Precious Qualities* we find the following:

> When the eagle soars up, high above the earth,
> Its shadow for the while is nowhere to be seen;
> Yet bird and shadow still are linked. So too our actions:
> When conditions come together, their effects are clearly seen.

When a bird takes off and flies high up into the sky, its shadow seems to disappear. But that does not mean that the shadow no longer exists. Wherever the bird finally lands, there is its shadow again, just as dark and distinct as before. In the same way, even though our past good or bad actions may be invisible for the moment they cannot fail to come back to us in the end.

Indeed, how could this not be so for ordinary beings like us, when even Buddhas and Arhats, who have rid themselves of all karmic and emotional obscurations, still have to accept the effects of past actions?

One day the armies of Virūḍhaka, king of Śrāvastī, fell upon the city of the Śākyas* and massacred eighty thousand people. At that moment, the Buddha himself had a headache. When his disciples asked him why this was, he replied:

"Many lifetimes ago, those Śākyas were fishermen who lived by killing and eating many fish. One day they caught two big ones, and instead of killing them immediately they left them tied to a pole. As those two fish stranded out of the water writhed in agony, they thought: 'These men

* The Buddha's clan, who lived on the borders of present-day India and Nepal.

are killing us, although we have done them no harm. In return, may the day come when we kill them, without their having done us any harm.' The effect of the two big fishes' thought was that they were reborn as king Virūḍhaka and his minister Mātropakāra, while all the other fish killed by the fishermen became their troops. Today they have massacred the Śākyas.

"At that time, I myself was the child of one of those fishermen and, watching those two tied-up fish writhing in unbearable agony as they dried, I laughed. The effect of that action is that today I have a headache. But had I not achieved the qualities[83] I now possess, I, too, would have been killed by the troops of Virūḍhaka."

On another occasion, the Buddha's foot was injured by an acacia[84] splinter—the result of his having killed Black Spearman during one of his previous lives as a Bodhisattva.*

Maudgalyāyana, of all the Buddha's Śrāvaka disciples, possessed the greatest miraculous powers. Nonetheless, he was killed by the Parivrājikas, because of the power of his past actions. It happened as follows.

The sublime Śāriputra and the great Maudgalyāyana often used to travel to other worlds, such as the hell-realms or the realm of the pretas, to work for the benefit of beings in those worlds. One day, while in the hells, they came across a tīrthika teacher named Pūrṇakāśyapa who had been reborn there and was undergoing a multitude of different torments.

He said to them, "Noble ones, on your return to the human realm, please tell my former disciples that their guru, Pūrṇakāśyapa, has been reborn in hell. Tell them from me that the way of the Parivrājikas is not the way of virtue. The way of virtue lies in the doctrine of the Śākya Buddha. Our path is mistaken; they should abandon it and learn to follow Śākyamuni. And tell them, above all, that whenever they make offerings to the shrine they built for my bones, a shower of molten metal falls upon me. Tell them, I beg you, not to make those offerings any more."

The two noble companions returned to the human realm. Śāriputra arrived first and went to give the tīrthikas their guru's message but, the necessary karmic conditions being absent, they did not listen to him. When Maudgalyāyana arrived, he asked Śāriputra if he had taken to the tīrthikas Pūrṇakāśyapa's message.

"Yes," replied Śāriputra, "but they said not a word."

Maudgalyāyana said, "Since they cannot have taken in what you said, I shall speak to them myself." And he went off to tell them what

* See page 125.

Pūrṇakāśyapa had said.

But the tīrthikas were furious. "Not content with insulting us, he is criticizing our Guru!" they said. "Beat him!" They fell on him, beat him to a pulp, and left him lying there.

Now, until this point not even a concerted attack from all the three worlds together, let alone the blows of the Parivrājikas, could have harmed a single hair of Maudgalyāyana's head. But at that moment, crushed by the weight of his past actions, he succumbed like any ordinary man.

"I could not even think how to use magical powers, let alone do it," he said. Śāriputra wrapped him in his robes and carried him away.

When they came to the Jeta Grove Śāriputra cried out, "Even to hear my friend's death described would be unbearable! How can I watch it happen?" and he passed away into nirvāṇa along with numerous other Arhats. Immediately afterwards, Maudgalyāyana too passed beyond suffering.

Once in Kashmir there lived a monk called Ravati, who had many disciples. He was clairvoyant and had miraculous powers. One day he was dyeing his monk's robes with saffron in a dense stretch of woodland. At the same time, a layman living nearby was searching for a calf that had strayed. He saw smoke rising up from the thick forest, and went to see what was going on.

Finding the monk stoking his fire, he asked: "What are you doing?"

"I'm dyeing my robes," the monk replied.

The layman raised the lid off the cauldron of dye and looked inside.

"It's meat!" he cried, and indeed when the monk looked in the cauldron he too saw what was inside as meat.

The layman led the monk off and handed him over to the king, saying, "Sire, this monk stole my calf. Please punish him." The king had Ravati thrown into a pit.

However, several days later it happened that the layman's cow found her missing calf by herself. The layman went back to see the king and said, "Sire, the monk did not steal my calf after all; please release him."

But the king got distracted and forgot to have Ravati freed. For six months he did nothing about it.

Then one day a large group of the monk's disciples, who had themselves attained miraculous powers, came flying through the air and landed in front of the king.

"Ravati is a pure and innocent monk," they said to the king. "Please set him free."

The king went to release the monk, and when he saw Ravati's debilitated condition he was filled with great remorse.

"I meant to come sooner, but I left it so long," he exclaimed. "I have committed a terrible sin!"

"No harm has been done," said the monk. "It was all the fruit of my own deeds."

"What kind of deeds?" asked the king.

"During a past life I was a thief, and once I stole a calf. When the owner came after me, I ran off, leaving the animal next to a pratyekabuddha who happened to be meditating in a thicket. The owner took the pratyekabuddha and threw him into a pit for six days. As the fully matured effect of my action, I have already been through numerous lives of suffering in the lower realms. The sufferings I have now just experienced in this life were the last of them."

Another example is the story of the son of Surabhībhadra,[85] an Indian king. One day, the prince's mother gave him a seamless silken robe. He did not want to wear it immediately, saying, "I shall put it on the day I inherit the kingdom."

"You never will inherit the kingdom," said his mother. "That could only happen if your father, the king, died. But your father and the teacher Nāgārjuna have the same life force,[86] so there is no chance that he will die as long as Nāgārjuna is still alive. And since Nāgārjuna has power over his own lifespan, your father will never die. That is why many of your elder brothers have already died without inheriting the kingdom."

"So what can I do?" her son asked.

"Go to see the teacher Nāgārjuna and ask him to give you his head. He will agree, because he is a Bodhisattva. I can see no other solution."

The boy went to see Nāgārjuna and asked him for his head. "Cut it off and take it," the Master said. The boy took a sword and struck at Nāgārjuna's neck. But nothing happened. It was as if his blade had cut through thin air.

"Weapons cannot harm me," the Master explained, "because five hundred lifetimes ago I entirely purified myself of all the fully maturing effects of having used weapons. However, I did kill an insect one day while cutting *kuśa* grass. The full effect of that act has not yet played itself out, so if you use a blade of *kuśa* grass you will be able to cut off my head." Accordingly, the boy plucked a blade of *kuśa* grass and severed Nāgārjuna's head, which fell to the ground. Nāgārjuna entered nirvāṇa saying,

> Now I am leaving for the Blissful Land;
> Later I shall return to this very body.[87]

If even exceptional individuals like these have to experience the effects of their own past actions, how can we—whose negative actions amassed throughout beginningless time in our wanderings through the realms of saṁsāra are already innumerable—ever hope to get free from saṁsāra while we still go on accumulating them? Even to escape from the lower realms would be difficult. So let us at all costs avoid the slightest misdeed, however minute, and apply ourselves to doing whatever good we can, no matter how insignificant it may seem. As long as we are not making that effort, each instant of negative action is leading us into many kalpas of life in the lower worlds. Never underestimate the minutest wrong deed, thinking that it cannot do that much harm. As Bodhisattva Śāntideva says:

> If evil acts of but a single instant
> Lead to a kalpa in the deepest hell,
> The evils I have done from time without beginning—
> No need to say that they will keep me from the higher realms!

And in the *Sūtra of the Wise and the Foolish* we find:

> Do not take lightly small misdeeds,
> Believing they can do no harm:
> Even a tiny spark of fire
> Can set alight a mountain of hay.

In the same way, even the smallest positive acts bring great benefit. Do not disparage them, either, with the idea that there is not much point in doing them.

King Māndhātṛi in a past life was a poor man. One day, as he was on his way to a wedding with a fistful of beans in his hand, he met the Buddha Kṣāntiśaraṇa, who was travelling to the village. Moved by intense devotion, he threw him his beans. Four beans fell into the Buddha's begging bowl and two others touched his heart. The maturation of this act was that he was reborn as the universal emperor over the continent of Jambu. Because of the four beans that fell into the bowl, he reigned over the four continents for eighty thousand years. Because of one of the two that touched his heart, he became sovereign over the realm of the Four Great Kings for another eighty thousand years; and because of the second, he shared equally with thirty-seven successive Indras their sovereignty over the Heaven of the Thirty-three.

It is also said that even to visualize the Buddha and throw a flower into the sky will result in your sharing Indra's reign for a length of time difficult to imagine. This is why the *Sūtra of The Wise and the Foolish* says:

Do not take lightly small good deeds,
Believing they can hardly help:
For drops of water one by one
In time can fill a giant pot.

And *The Treasury of Precious Qualities* says:

From seeds no bigger than a mustard grain
Grow vast ashota trees, which in a single year
Can put out branches each a league in length.
But even greater is the growth of good and evil.

The seed of the *ashota* tree is no bigger than a mustard seed, but the tree develops so quickly that its branches grow as much as a league in one year. Yet even this image is not adequate to describe the profuse growth of the fruit of positive and negative actions.

The tiniest transgression of the precepts, too, gives rise to great evils. One day Elapatra, king of the nāgas, came to see the Buddha in the guise of a Universal Emperor.

The Buddha scolded him: "Isn't the harm that you did to the teachings of the Buddha Kāśyapa enough for you? Now do you want to harm mine too? Listen to the Dharma in your own real form!"

"Too many beings will hurt me if I do so," replied the nāga; so the Buddha placed him under the protection of Vajrapāṇi, and he changed into a huge serpent, several leagues in length. On his head there grew a great *elapatra* tree, crushing him with its weight, its roots crawling with insects which caused him terrible suffering.

The Buddha was asked why he was like this, and replied, "Long ago, during the era of the Buddha Kāśyapa's teachings, he was a monk. One day his robe got caught on a big *elapatra* tree growing beside the path and was pulled off. He became extremely angry and, violating his precepts,[88] he cut the tree down. What you see today is the effect of that act."

For all good or bad actions, the intention is by far the most important factor that determines whether they are positive or negative, heavy or light. It is like a tree: if the root is medicinal, the trunk and leaves will also be medicinal. If the root is poisonous, the trunk and leaves will be poisonous too. Medicinal leaves cannot grow from a poisonous root. In the same way, if an intention develops from aggression or attachment and is thus not entirely pure, the action that follows is bound to be negative, however positive it might seem. On the other hand, if the intention is pure, even acts that appear negative will in fact be positive. In the *Treasury of Precious Qualities* it says:

> If a root is medicinal, so are its shoots.
> If poisonous, no need to say its shoots will be the same.
> What makes an act positive or negative is not how it looks
> Or its size, but the good or bad intention behind it.

For this reason there are times when Bodhisattvas, the Heirs of the Conquerors, are permitted to actually commit the seven harmful acts of the body and speech, as long as their minds are pure, free from all selfish desire. This is illustrated by the examples of Captain Compassionate Heart who killed Black Spearman, or of the young brahmin Lover of the Stars who broke his vows of chastity with a young brahmin girl.

Once in a previous life, the Buddha was a captain called Compassionate Heart. He was sailing upon the ocean with five hundred merchants when the evil pirate called Black Spearman appeared, threatening to kill them all. The captain realized that these merchants were all non-returning Bodhisattvas,* and that if one man killed them all he would have to suffer in the hells for an incalculable number of kalpas. Moved by an intense feeling of compassion, he thought: "If I kill him, he will not have to go to hell. So I have no choice, even if it means that I have to go to hell myself." With this great courage he killed the pirate, and in so doing gained as much merit as would normally take seventy thousand kalpas to achieve. On the face of it, the act was a harmful one, since the Bodhisattva was committing the physical act of murder. But it was done without the least selfish motivation. In the short term, it saved the lives of the five hundred merchants. And in the long term it saved Black Spearman from the sufferings of hell. In reality, therefore, it was a very powerful positive act.

Again, there was a brahmin named Lover of the Stars who lived in the forest for many years, keeping the vow of chastity. One day he went begging in a village. A brahmin girl fell so hopelessly in love with him that she was about to kill herself. Moved by compassion towards her, he married her, which brought him forty thousand kalpas of merit.

Taking life or breaking one's vow of chastity are permitted for such beings. On the other hand, the same acts done with selfish motivation, out of desire, hatred or ignorance, are not permitted for anyone.

A Bodhisattva with a vast mind and no trace of personal desire may

* Bodhisattvas who had reached a level where they were no longer obliged to return to samsaric existence.

also steal from the rich and miserly and, on their behalf, offer the goods to the Three Jewels or give them to the needy.

Lying in order to protect someone on the point of being killed, or to protect goods belonging to the Three Jewels, would also be permitted. But it is never right to deceive others in one's own interest.

Sowing discord, for instance between two close friends, one of whom was a wrong-doer while the other loved to do good, would be permitted if there were a danger that the bad one's stronger character would have corrupted the good one. However, it is not permissible simply to separate two people who get along well.

Harsh words could be used, for example, as a more forceful means to bring to the Dharma those on whom a softer approach makes no impression—or in advice given to a disciple in order to get at his hidden faults. As Atīśa says:

> The best teacher is one who attacks your hidden faults;
> The best instruction is one aimed squarely at those hidden faults.

However, harsh words spoken just to insult others are not justified.

Worthless chatter might be used as a skilful means of introducing the Dharma to people who love talking and who cannot be brought to the Dharma otherwise. But it is never warranted simply to create distraction for oneself and others.

As for the three negative mental actions, they are never permitted for anyone because there is no way for intention to turn them into something positive. Once a negative thought has arisen it always develops into something negative.

The mind is the sole generator of good and bad. There are many occasions when the thoughts which arise in the mind, even if they are not translated into speech or action, have a very strong positive or negative effect. So always examine your mind. If your thoughts are positive, be glad and do more and more good. If they are negative, confess them immediately, feeling bad and ashamed that you still entertain such thoughts in spite of all the teaching you have received, and telling yourself that from now on you must do your utmost not to let such thoughts occur in your mind. Even when you do something positive, check your motivation carefully. If your intention is good, act. If your motivation is to impress people, or is based on rivalry or a thirst for fame, make sure you change it and infuse it with bodhicitta. If you are quite unable to transform your motivation, it would be better to postpone the meritorious act until later.

One day Geshe Ben was expecting a visit from a large number of his benefactors. That morning he arranged the offerings on his shrine in front of the images of the Three Jewels particularly neatly. Examining his intentions, he realized that they were not pure and that he was only trying to impress his patrons; so he picked up a handful of dust and threw it all over the offerings, saying, "Monk, just stay where you are and don't put on airs!"

When Padampa Sangye heard this story, he said, "That handful of dust that Ben Kungyal threw was the best offering in all Tibet!"

So always watch your mind carefully. On our level, as ordinary beings, it is impossible not to have thoughts and actions which are inspired by evil intentions. But if we can recognize the wrong immediately, confess it and vow not to do it again, we will part company with it.

Another day, Geshe Ben was at the home of some patrons. At one moment his hosts left the room and the Geshe thought: "I have no tea. I'll steal a bit to brew up when I get back to my hermitage."

But the moment he put his hand in their bag of tea, he suddenly realized what he was doing and called to his patrons: "Come and look what I'm doing! Cut my hand off!"

Atīśa said: "Since taking the *prātimokṣa* vows, I have not been stained by the smallest fault. In practising the precepts of bodhicitta, I have committed one or two errors. And since taking up the Secret Mantra Vajrayāna, even though I have sometimes stumbled, still, I have let neither faults nor downfalls remain with me for as much as a whole day."

When he was travelling, as soon as any bad thought occurred to him he would take up the wooden maṇḍala base[89] he carried with him and confess his bad thought, vowing never to let it happen again.

One day Geshe Ben was at a large gathering of geshes at Penyulgyal. After a while some curd was offered to the guests. Geshe Ben was seated in one of the middle rows, and noticed that the monks in the first row were receiving large portions.

"That curd looks delicious..." he thought to himself, "but I don't think I'll get my fair share."

Immediately he caught hold of himself: "You yoghurt-addict!" he thought, and turned his bowl upside down. When the man who was serving the curd came and asked him if he would like some, he refused.

"This evil mind has already taken its share," he said.

Although there was no wrong at all in wanting to share the feast equally with the other pure monks, it was the self-centredness of his expectant thoughts about getting that delicious curd that made him refuse it.

If you always examine your mind like this, adopting what is wholesome and rejecting what is harmful, your mind will become workable and all your thoughts will become positive.

Long ago, there was a brahmin called Ravi who examined his mind at all times. Whenever a bad thought arose, he would put aside a black pebble, and whenever a good thought arose he would put aside a white pebble. At first, all the pebbles he put aside were black. Then, as he persevered in developing antidotes and in adopting positive actions and rejecting negative ones, a time came when his piles of black and white pebbles were equal. In the end he had only white ones. This is how you should develop positive actions as an antidote with mindfulness and vigilance, and not contaminate yourself with even the smallest harmful actions.

Even if you have not accumulated negative actions during this present life, you cannot know the extent of all the actions you have accumulated in saṁsāra which has no beginning, or imagine their effects which you have still to experience. There are therefore people who, although they now devote themselves entirely to virtue and the practice of emptiness, are nevertheless beset by sufferings. The effect of their actions that would otherwise have remained dormant but later would have resulted in their rebirth in the lower realms, surfaces because of the antidote that they are applying and ripens in this life. The *Diamond Cutter Sūtra* says:

> Bodhisattvas practising transcendent wisdom will be tormented—indeed, they will be greatly tormented—by past actions that would have brought suffering in future lives, but have ripened in this life instead.

Conversely, there are some people who only do harm, but who experience the fruit of some positive action right away, an action that would otherwise have ripened later on. This occurred in the land of Aparāntaka. For seven days there was a rain of precious stones, then for seven days a rain of clothes, and for seven more days a rain of grain. In the end there was a rain of earth. Everyone was crushed to death and took rebirth in hell.

Such situations, in which those who do good suffer and those who do harm prosper, always occur as the result of actions done in the past. Your present actions, good or bad, will have their effects in your next life or in those to follow. For this reason it is vital to develop a firm conviction about the inevitable effect of your actions and always to behave accordingly.

Do not use the Dharma language of the highest views[90] to scorn the principle of cause and effect. The Great Master of Oḍḍiyāna said:

> Great King, in this Secret Mantrayāna of mine, the view is the most important thing. However, do not let your action slip in the direction of the view. If it does, you will fall into the evil views of demons, prattling on about how goodness is empty, evil is empty. But do not let your view slip in the direction of action, either, or you will be caught in materialism and ideology,* and liberation will never come...
>
> That is why my view is higher than the sky, but my attention to my actions and their effects is finer than flour.**

So however fully you have realized in your view the nature of reality, you must pay minute attention to your actions and their effects.

Someone once asked Padampa Sangye, "Once we have realized emptiness, does it still harm us to commit negative acts?"

"Once you realize emptiness," Padampa Sangye replied, "it would be absurd to do anything negative. When you realize emptiness, compassion arises with it simultaneously."

If you want to practise Dharma authentically, therefore, you should give priority to choosing what you do in accordance with the principle of cause and effect. View and action should be cultivated side by side. The sign that you have understood this teaching on the effects of actions is to be like Jetsun Milarepa.

His disciples said to him one day: "Jetsun, all the deeds that we see you doing are beyond the understanding of ordinary beings. Precious Jetsun, were you not an incarnation of Vajradhara, or of a Buddha or Bodhisattva right from the start?"

"If you take me for an incarnation of Vajradhara, or of a Buddha or Bodhisattva," the Jetsun replied, "it shows you have faith in me—but you could hardly have a more mistaken view of the Dharma! I started out by heaping up extremely negative acts, using spells and making hail. I soon realized that there was no way that I would not be reborn in hell. So I practised Dharma with relentless zeal. Thanks to the profound methods

* *dngos po dang mtshan ma*, lit. matter and characteristics. This means that one will never get beyond a conceptual approach.

** *zhib* means fine (like flour) and also meticulous, precise.

of the Secret Mantrayāna, I have developed exceptional qualities in myself. Now, if you cannot develop any real determination to practise the Dharma, it is because you do not really believe in the principle of cause and effect. Anyone with a bit of determination could develop courage like mine if they had that true and heartfelt confidence in the effects of their actions. Then they would develop the same accomplishments—and people will think that they too are manifestations of Vajradhara, or of a Buddha or Bodhisattva."

His belief in cause and effect utterly convinced Jetsun Mila that having committed the harmful acts of his youth he would be reborn in the hells. Because of that conviction, he practised with such determination that it is difficult to find any story either in India or Tibet to equal the tale of his trials and efforts.

So, arouse confidence from the depths of your heart in this crucial point, the principle of cause and effect. Always do as many good actions as possible, no matter how small, applying the three supreme methods.* Promise yourself never to do the smallest negative act again, even if your life is at stake.

When you wake up in the morning, do not suddenly jump out of bed like a cow or a sheep from its pen. While you are still in bed, relax your mind; turn within and examine it carefully. If you have done anything negative during the night in your dreams, regret it and confess. On the other hand, if you have done something positive, be glad and dedicate the merit to the benefit of all beings. Arouse bodhicitta, thinking, "Today I will do whatever positive, good actions I can and do my best to avoid doing anything negative or evil, so that all infinite beings may attain perfect Buddhahood."

At night, when you go to sleep, do not just drop off into unconsciousness. Take the time to relax in bed and examine yourself in the same way: "So, what use have I made of this day? What have I done that is positive?" If you have done some good, be glad and dedicate the merit so that all may attain Buddhahood. If you have done something wrong you should think, "How terrible I have been! I have just been destroying myself!" Confess it and vow never to act that way again.

At all times, be mindful and vigilant that you do not cling to your perceptions of the universe, and the beings within it, as real and solid. Train yourself to see everything as the play of unreal apparitions. To make your mind workable by always keeping it on a good and honest course is

* See page 36.

essentially the aim as well as the outcome of what we have been explaining, namely the practice of the four thoughts that turn the mind from saṁsāra . In this way, all the good actions you do will automatically be linked to the three supreme methods. As it is said:

> A person who does good is like a medicinal plant;
> All who rely on him benefit.
> A person who does harm is like a poisonous plant;
> Those who rely on him are destroyed.

If you have the right state of mind yourself, you will be able to turn the minds of all those connected with you[91] towards the true Dharma. Immense merit for yourself and others will increase without limit. You will never again take rebirth in the lower worlds in which your prospects get worse and worse, but will always have the unique conditions of a god's or human's life. Even the region in which the holder of such a teaching dwells will have merit and good fortune and will always be protected by the gods.

> *I know all the details of karma, but I do not really believe in it.*
> *I have heard a lot of Dharma, but never put it into practice.*
> *Bless me and evil-doers like me*
> *That our minds may mingle with the Dharma.*

Drom Tönpa (1005-1064)

Geshe Tönpa was one of Atīśa's principal disciples and a founder of the Kadampa school, which emphasized a simple lifestyle and training the mind in compassion.

CHAPTER FIVE

The benefits of liberation

Guided by many learned and accomplished sublime beings,
You have practised and experienced the instructions of your teachers.
You point out the sublime path unerringly to others.
Peerless Teacher, at your feet I bow.

The way to listen to this teaching on the benefits of liberation, and to the following chapter on how to follow a spiritual friend, is as explained before.

What is liberation? It is to find freedom from this ocean of suffering called saṁsāra, and to attain the level of a śrāvaka, a pratyekabuddha or perfect Buddhahood.

I. CAUSES LEADING TO LIBERATION

The causes of your attaining liberation are, firstly, making your mind workable through the four reflections that turn the mind from saṁsāra, beginning with the difficulty of finding the freedoms and advantages; and secondly, undertaking all the practices starting from the taking of refuge, which is the foundation of all paths, right up until you perfectly complete the main practice.[92]

The benefits of each of these practices are explained in the relevant chapters.

II. THE RESULT: THE THREE LEVELS OF ENLIGHTENMENT

Whether your attainment is that of a śrāvaka, a pratyekabuddha or perfect Buddhahood, the result is peaceful and cooling, free from the dangerous pathways of samsaric suffering. What a joy that is!

Since, out of all the various paths, it is the Mahāyāna that you have now taken up, all practices—the ten positive actions, the four boundless qualities, the six transcendent perfections, the four concentrations, the four formless states, sustained calm and profound insight—should be done with perfect Buddhahood as your sole aim, and with the three supreme methods: giving rise to bodhicitta as preparation, remaining free of conceptualization during the actual meditation and closing with prayers of dedication.

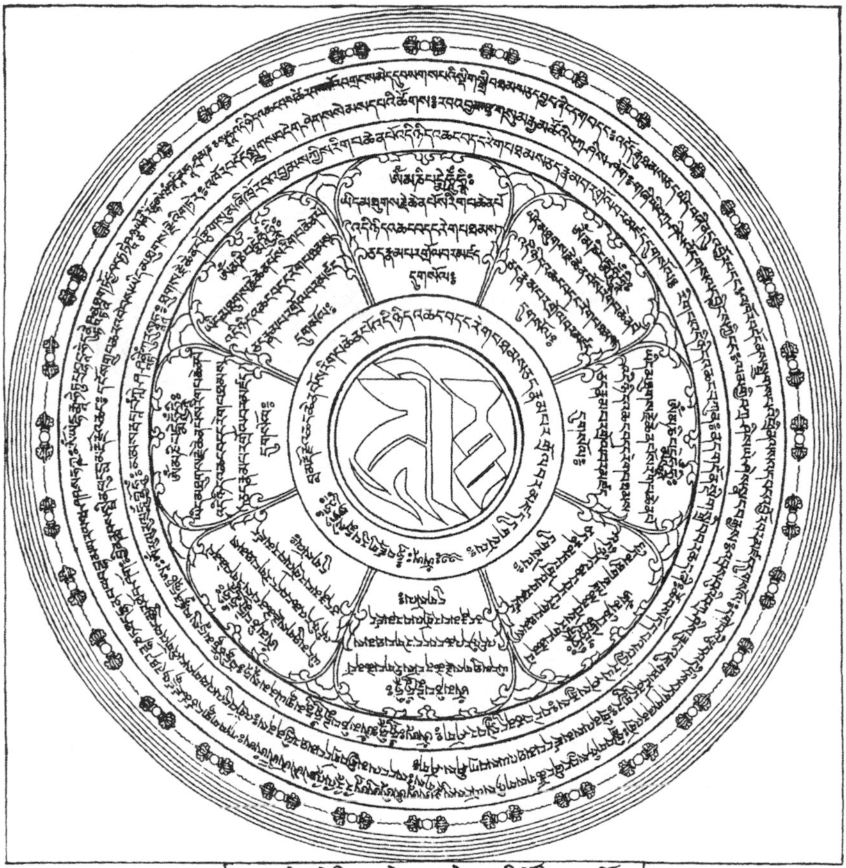

༄༅། །མཆིམ་འཛུའི་ཡང་གཏེར་ཐུགས་ཆེན་པདྨ་ཞི་ཁྲོའི་བཏགས་གྲོལ།

Milarepa (1040-1123)

Tibet's most famous yogi, renowned for his ascetic lifestyle in the high mountains of Southern Tibet, his perseverance in meditation, and the spontaneous songs by which he taught hunters and villagers alike.

CHAPTER SIX

How to follow a spiritual friend

No sūtra, tantra or śāstra speaks of any being ever attaining perfect Buddhahood without having followed a spiritual teacher. We can see for ourselves that nobody has ever developed the accomplishments belonging to the stages and paths by means of their own ingenuity and prowess. Indeed, all beings, ourselves included, show particular talent in discovering wrong paths to take—while when it comes to following the path leading to liberation and omniscience we are as confused as a blind person wandering alone in the middle of a deserted plain.

No-one can bring back jewels from a treasure island without relying on an experienced navigator.* Likewise, a spiritual teacher or companion is our true guide to liberation and omniscience, and we must follow him with respect. This is accomplished in three phases: firstly, by examining the teacher, then by following him, and finally by emulating his realization and his actions.

I. EXAMINING THE TEACHER

Ordinary people like us are, for the most part, easily influenced by the people and circumstances around us. That is why we should always follow a teacher, a spiritual friend.

A reference to adventurers in ancient times who went to seek jewels in faraway islands.

In the sandalwood forests of the Mālaya mountains, when an ordinary tree falls, its wood is gradually impregnated with the sweet perfume of the sandal. After some years that ordinary wood comes to smell as sweet as the sandal trees around it. In just the same way, if you live and study with a perfect teacher full of good qualities, you will be permeated by the perfume of those qualities and in everything you do you will come to resemble him.

> Just as the trunk of an ordinary tree
> Lying in the forests of the Mālaya mountains
> Absorbs the perfume of sandal from the moist leaves and branches,
> So you come to resemble whomever you follow.[93]

As times have degenerated, nowadays it is difficult to find a teacher who has every one of the qualities described in the precious tantras. However, it is indispensable that the teacher we follow should possess at least the following qualities.

He should be pure, never having contravened any of the commitments or prohibitions related to the three types of vow—the external vows of the Prātimokṣa, the inner vows of the Bodhisattva and the secret vows of the Secret Mantrayāna. He should be learned, and not lacking in knowledge of the tantras, sūtras and śāstras. Towards the vast multitude of beings, his heart should be so suffused with compassion that he loves each one like his only child. He should be well versed in ritual practices—outwardly, of the Tripiṭaka and, inwardly, of the four sections of tantras. By putting into practice the meaning of the teachings, he should have actualized in himself all the extraordinary achievements of riddance and realization. He should be generous, his language should be pleasant, he should teach each individual according to that person's needs and he should act in conformity with what he teaches; these four ways of attracting beings enable him to gather fortunate disciples around him.

> All the qualities complete according to purest Dharma
> Are hard to find in these decadent times.
> But trust the teacher who, based on pure observance of the three vows,
> Is steeped in learning and great compassion,
> Skilled in the rites of the infinite pitakas and tantras,
> And rich in the fruit, the immaculate wisdom that comes through riddance and realization.
> Drawn by the brilliant flower of his four attractive qualities
> Fortunate disciples will gather like bees to follow him.

More particularly, for teachings on the profound essence of the Mantra Vajrayāna pith-instructions the kind of master upon whom one should rely is as follows. As set out in the precious tantras, he should have been brought to maturity by a stream of ripening empowerments, flowing down to him through a continuous unbroken lineage. He should not have transgressed the samayas and vows to which he committed himself at the time of empowerment. Not having many disturbing negative emotions and thoughts, he should be calm and disciplined. He should have mastered the entire meaning of the ground, path and result tantras of the Secret Mantra Vajrayāna. He should have attained all the signs of success in the approach and accomplishment phases of the practice, such as seeing visions of the yidam. Having experienced for himself the nature of reality, he himself should be liberated. The well-being of others should be his sole concern, his heart being full of compassion. He should have few preoccupations, for he has given up any clinging to the ordinary things of this life. Concentrating on future lives, his only, resolute thought is for the Dharma. Seing saṁsāra as suffering, he should feel great sadness, and should encourage the same feeling in others. He should be skilled at caring for his disciples and should use the appropriate method for each of them. Having fulfilled all his teacher's commands, he should hold the blessings of the lineage.

> The extraordinary teacher who gives the pith instructions
> Has received empowerments, kept the samayas, and is peaceful;
> Has mastered the meaning of the ground, path and result tantras;
> Has all the signs of approach and accomplishment and is freed by
> realization;
> Has limitless compassion and cares only for others;
> Has few activities and thinks only, resolutely, of the Dharma;
> Is weary of this world, and leads others to feel the same;
> Is expert in methods and has the blessings of the lineage.
> Follow such a teacher, and accomplishment comes swiftly.

On the other hand, there are certain kinds of teachers we should avoid. Their characteristics are as follows.

Teachers like a millstone made of wood. These teachers have no trace of the qualities arising from study, reflection and meditation. Thinking that as the sublime son or nephew of such and such a lama, they and their descendants must be superior to anyone else, they defend their caste like brahmins. Even if they have studied, reflected and meditated a little, they did so not with any pure intention of working for future lives but for more mundane reasons—like preventing the priestly fiefs of which they are the incumbents from falling into decay. As for training disciples, they are about as well suited to fulfilling their proper function as a millstone made of wood.

Teachers like the frog that lived in a well. Teachers of this kind lack any special qualities that might distinguish them from ordinary people. But other people put them up on a pedestal in blind faith, without examining them at all. Puffed up with pride by the profits and honours they receive, they are themselves quite unaware of the true qualities of great teachers. They are like the frog that lived in a well.

One day an old frog that had always lived in a well was visited by another frog who lived on the shores of the great ocean.

"Where are you from?" asked the frog that lived in the well.

"I come from the great ocean," the visitor replied.

"How big is this ocean of yours?" asked the frog from the well.

"It is enormous," replied the other.

"About a quarter the size of my well?" he asked.

"Oh! Bigger than that!" exclaimed the frog from the ocean.

"Half the size, then?"

"No, bigger than that!"

"So—the same size as the well?"

"No, no! Much, much bigger!"

"That's impossible!" said the frog who lived in the well. "This I have to see for myself."

So the two frogs set off together, and the story goes that when the frog who lived in the well saw the ocean, he fainted, his head split apart, and he died.

Mad guides. These are teachers who have very little knowledge, never having made the effort to follow a learned master and train in the sūtras and tantras. Their strong negative emotions together with their weak mindfulness and vigilance make them lax in their vows and samayas. Though of lower mentality than ordinary people, they ape the siddhas and behave as if their actions were higher than the sky.[94] Brimming over with anger and jealousy, they break the lifeline of love and compassion. Such spiritual friends are called mad guides, and lead anyone who follows them down wrong paths.

Blind guides. In particular, a teacher whose qualities are in no way superior to your own and who lacks the love and compassion of bodhicitta will never be able to open your eyes to what should and should not be done. Teachers like this are called blind guides.

Like brahmins, some defend their caste,
Or in pools of fear for their fief's survival
Bathe themselves in bogus study and reflection;
Such guides are like a millstone made of wood.

Some, although no different from all ordinary folk,
Are unthinkingly sustained by people's idiot faith.
Puffed up by profit, offerings and honours,
Such friends as these are like the well-bound frog.

Some have little learning and neglect their samayas and vows,
Their mentality is low, their conduct high above the earth,
They have broken the lifeline of love and compassion—
Mad guides like these can only spread more evil.

Especially, to follow those no better than yourself,
Who have no bodhicitta, attracted only by their fame,
Would be a huge mistake; and with such frauds as these
As your blind guides, you'll wander deeper into darkness.

The Great Master of Oḍḍiyāna warns:

Not to examine the teacher
Is like drinking poison;
Not to examine the disciple
Is like leaping from a precipice.

You place your trust in your spiritual teacher for all your future lives. It is he who will teach you what to do and what not to do. If you encounter a false spiritual friend without examining him properly, you will be throwing away the possibility a person with faith has to accumulate merits for a whole lifetime, and the freedoms and advantages of the human existence you have now obtained will be wasted. It is like being killed by a venomous serpent coiled beneath a tree that you approached, thinking what you saw was just the tree's cool shadow.

By not examining a teacher with great care
The faithful waste their gathered merit.
Like taking for the shadow of a tree a vicious snake,
Beguiled, they lose the freedom they at last had found.

After examining him carefully and making an unmistaken assessment, from the moment you find that a teacher has all the positive qualities mentioned you should never cease to consider him to be the Buddha in person.[95] This teacher in whom all the attributes are complete is the embodiment of the compassionate wisdom of all Buddhas of the ten directions, appearing in the form of an ordinary human simply to benefit beings.

> The teacher with infinite qualities complete
> Is the wisdom and compassion of all Buddhas
> Appearing in human form for beings' sake.
> He is the unequalled source of all accomplishments.

So that such a true teacher may skilfully guide the ordinary people needing his help, he makes his everyday conduct conform to that of ordinary people. But in reality his wisdom mind is that of a Buddha, so he is utterly different from everyone else. Each of his acts is simply the activity of a realized being attuned to the nature of those he has to benefit. He is therefore uniquely noble. Skilled in cutting through hesitation and doubt, he patiently endures all the ingratitude and discouragement of his disciples, like a mother with her only child.

> Expediently, to guide us, he acts just like us all.
> In truth he is completely different from us all.
> His realization makes him the noblest of us all.
> Skilled at cutting through our doubts, he bears with patience
> All our discouragement and lack of gratitude.

A teacher with all these qualities is like a great ship in which to cross the vast ocean of saṁsāra. Like a navigator, he unfailingly charts out for us the route to liberation and omniscience. Like a downpour of nectar, he extinguishes the blaze of negative actions and emotions. Like the sun and moon, he radiates the light of Dharma and dispels the thick darkness of ignorance. Like the earth, he patiently bears all ingratitude and discouragement, and his view and action are vast in their capacity. Like the wish-granting tree, he is the source of all help in this life and all happiness in the next. Like the perfect vase, he is a treasury of all the inconceivable variety of vehicles and doctrines that one could ever need. Like the wish-granting gem, he unfolds the infinite aspects of the four activities according to the needs of beings. Like a mother or father, he loves each one of all the innumerable living creatures equally, without any attachment to those close to him or hatred for others. Like a great river, his compassion is so vast that it includes all beings as infinite as space, and so swift that it can help all who are suffering and lack a protector. Like the king of mountains, his joy at others' happiness is so steadfast that it cannot be shifted by jealousy, or shaken by the winds of belief in the reality of appearances. Like rain falling from a cloud,* his impartiality is never disturbed by attachment or aversion.

He is the great ship carrying us beyond the seas of samsaric
existence,[96]
The true navigator, unerringly charting the sublime path,
The rain of nectar quenching the inferno of emotions and actions,
The sun and moon dispelling the darkness of ignorance.
He is the earth, immensely patient,
The wish-granting tree, source of help and happiness,
The perfect vase containing the treasure of the Dharma.
He provides all things, more than a wish-granting gem.
He is a father and mother, loving all equally.
His compassion is as vast and swift as a great river.
His joy is unchanging like the king of mountains.
His impartiality cannot be disturbed, like rain from a cloud.

Such a teacher is equal to all the Buddhas in his compassion and his blessings. Those who make a positive connection with him will attain Buddhahood in a single lifetime. Even those who make a negative connection with him will eventually be led out of saṁsāra.

Such a teacher is equal to all the Buddhas.
If even those who harm him are set on the path to happiness,
On those who entrust themselves to him with sincere faith
Will be showered the bounty of the higher realms and liberation.

II. FOLLOWING THE TEACHER

Noble one, you should think of yourself as someone who is sick ...

So begins the series of similes in the *Sūtra Arranged like a Tree*. Sick people put themselves in the care of a skilful doctor. Travellers on dangerous paths entrust themselves to a courageous escort. Faced with dangers from enemies, robbers, wild beasts and the like, people look to a companion for protection. Merchants heading for lands across the ocean entrust themselves to a captain. Wayfarers taking the ferry to cross a river entrust themselves to the boatman. In the same way, to be protected from death, rebirth and negative emotions, we must follow a teacher, a spiritual friend.

* Rain falls from a cloud upon whatever lies beneath it, without distinction.

As the sick man relies on his doctor,
The traveller on his escort,
The frightened man on his companion,
Merchants on their captain,
And passengers on their ferryman—
If birth, death and negative emotions are the enemies you fear,
Entrust yourself to a teacher.

A courageous disciple, armoured with the determination never to displease his teacher even at the cost of his life, so stable-minded that he is never shaken by immediate circumstances, who serves his teacher without caring about his own health or survival and obeys his every command without sparing himself at all—such a person will be liberated simply through his devotion to the teacher.

Those who, well armoured and steady of reason,
Serve a teacher regardless of health or of life,
Following his instructions without sparing themselves,
Will be freed by the strength of devotion alone.

To follow the teacher, you should have so much confidence in him that you perceive him as a real Buddha. You should have such discrimination and knowledge of the teachings that you can recognize the wisdom underlying his skilful actions and grasp whatever he teaches you. You should feel immense loving compassion for all those who are suffering with no one to protect them. You should respect the vows and samayas that your teacher has told you to keep, and should be peaceful and controlled in all your deeds, words and thoughts. Your outlook should be so broad that you can accept whatever your teacher and spiritual companions may do. You should be so generous that you can give the teacher whatever you possess. Your perception of everything should be pure, not always critical and tainted. You should restrain yourself from doing anything harmful or negative, for fear of displeasing him.

Have great faith, discrimination, knowledge and compassion.
Respect the vows and samayas. Control body, speech and mind.
Be broad-minded and generous.
Have pure vision and a sense of self-restraint.

The *Sūtra Arranged like a Tree* and other texts also tell us that when following a teacher we should be like the perfect horse,[97] always acting according to the teacher's wishes in every situation, skilfully avoiding anything that would displease him, and never getting angry or resentful even when he reprimands us severely. Like a boat, we should never tire of going back and forth to take messages or do other services for him. Like a bridge, there should be nothing that we cannot bear, however pleasant or unpleasant the tasks he asks us to do. Like a smith's anvil, we should endure heat, cold and all other difficulties. Like a servant we should obey his every command. Like a sweeper,* we should never be proud but take the lowest position. Like a bull with broken horns, we should abandon arrogance and respect everyone.

> Be skilled in never displeasing the teacher,
> And never resent his rebukes, like the perfect horse.
> Never be tired of coming and going, like a boat.
> Bear whatever comes, good or bad, like a bridge.
> Endure heat, cold and whatever else, like an anvil.
> Obey his every order, like a servant.
> Cast off all pride, like a sweeper,
> And be free of arrogance, like a bull with broken horns.
> This, the pitakas say, is how to follow the teacher.

There are three ways to please the teacher and serve him. The best way is known as the offering of practice, and consists of putting whatever he teaches into practice with determination, disregarding all hardship. The middling way is known as service with body and speech, and involves serving him and doing whatever he needs you to do whether physically, verbally or mentally. The lowest way is by material offerings, which means to please your teacher by giving him material goods, food, money and so forth.

> To offer what wealth you may have to the Fourth Jewel,**
> To honour and serve him with body and speech,
> Not one of these actions will ever be wasted.
> But out of the three ways to please him, practice is best.

However incomprehensibly the teacher may behave, always maintain pure perception, and recognize his way of doing things as his skilful methods.

The great paṇḍita Nāropa had already become highly learned and

* In the Indian caste system the sweeper had a very low status, and was expected to behave deferentially to all.

** The teacher, as the embodiment of the Three Jewels, is considered to be the Fourth Jewel. See Part Two, Chapter 1.

accomplished. But his yidam told him that his teacher from previous lives was the great Tilopa, and that to find him he should travel to eastern India. Nāropa set off immediately, but upon arriving in the east he had no idea where to find Tilopa. He asked the local people but they knew nothing.

"Is there nobody in these parts named Tilopa?" he insisted.

"There is someone called Tilopa the Outcaste, or Tilopa the Beggar."

Nāropa thought, "The actions of siddhas are incomprehensible. That might be him." He asked where Tilopa the Beggar lived.

"By that ruined wall over there, where the smoke is coming from," they replied.

When he got to the place that had been pointed out, he found Tilopa seated in front of a wooden tub of fish, of which some were still alive and some dead. Tilopa took a fish, grilled it over the fire and put it in his mouth, snapping his fingers. Nāropa prostrated himself before him and asked Tilopa to accept him as a disciple.

"What are you talking about?" Tilopa said. "I'm just a beggar!" But Nāropa insisted, so Tilopa accepted him.

Now, Tilopa was not killing those fish just because he was hungry and could find nothing else to eat. Fish are completely ignorant of what to do and what not to do, creatures with many negative actions, and Tilopa had the power to free them. By eating their flesh he was making a link with their consciousness, which he could then transfer to a pure Buddhafield.* Similarly, Saraha lived as an arrowsmith, Śāvaripa as a hunter, and most of the other mighty siddhas of India, too, adopted very lowly lifestyles, often those of outcastes. It is therefore important not to take any of your teacher's actions in the wrong way; train yourself to have only pure perception.

> Do not misinterpret how he acts.
> Most of India's siddhas lived
> As common evil-doers, base outcastes,
> More degenerate than the lowest of the low.

People who ignore this point, continually misinterpreting and criticising what their teacher does, would, so it is said, find fault even in the Buddha if they were to live with him long enough.

* The snapping of the fingers is part of a practice for transferring the consciousness of another being to a pure realm. The practice of transference (*'pho ba*) is discussed in Part Three.

The monk Sunakṣatra was the Buddha's half-brother. He served him for twenty-four years, and knew by heart all the twelve categories of teachings in the pitakas.* But he saw everything the Buddha did as deceitful, and eventually came to the erroneous conclusion that, apart from an aura six feet wide, there was no difference between the Buddha and himself.

> Apart from that light around your body six feet wide,
> Never have I seen, in twenty-four years as your servant,
> Even a sesame seed's worth of special qualities in you.
> As for the Dharma, I know as much as you—and will no longer be your servant!

So saying, he left. Thereafter, Ānanda became the Buddha's personal attendant. He asked the Buddha where Sunakṣatra would be reborn.

"In one week's time," the Buddha replied, "Sunakṣatra's life will come to an end and he will be reborn as a preta in a flower garden."

Ānanda went to see Sunakṣatra and told him what the Buddha had said. Sunakṣatra thought to himself, "Sometimes, those lies of his come true, so for seven days I had better be very careful. At the end of the week, I'll make him eat his words." He spent the week fasting. On the evening of the seventh day, his throat felt very dry, so he drank some water. But he could not digest the water properly, and died. He was reborn in a flower-garden as a preta with all nine marks of ugliness.

Whenever you see faults in anything your sublime teacher does, you should feel deeply embarrassed and ashamed of yourself. Reflecting that it is your own mental vision that is impure, and that all his actions are utterly flawless and unerring, strengthen your pure perception of him and increase your faith.

> Without having mastered your own perceptions,
> To look for mistakes in others is an immeasurable error.
> Although he knew the twelve kinds of teachings by heart,
> The monk Sunakṣatra, consumed by the power of evil,
> Saw the Buddha's actions as deceitful.
> Think about this carefully and correct yourself.

When the teacher seems to be furious with you, do not get angry. Instead, remind yourself that he must have glimpsed some fault in you and seen that this is the moment to correct it with such an outburst. When his anger

* *Pitakas*: the three sections of the Buddha's teachings. See glossary: Tripiṭaka.

has abated, go to him, confess your faults and vow not to repeat them.

> If your teacher appears angry, conclude that he has seen
> A fault in you, ripe for correction with his rebukes.
> Confess and vow never to repeat it.
> Thus, the wise will not fall under the power of Māra.

In the presence of your teacher, stand up at once whenever he does, instead of just remaining seated. When he sits down, enquire after his well-being. When you think there might be something he needs, at the right moment bring him whatever would please him.

When walking with him as his attendant, avoid walking in front of him as that would mean turning your back on him. Do not walk behind him, however, because you would be treading on his footprints.* Nor should you walk to his right, since that would be assuming the place of honour. Instead, keep respectfully to his left and slightly behind. Should the road be hazardous, it would not then be wrong to ask his permission to go ahead.

As for the teacher's seat and his conveyance, never tread on his cushion and do not mount upon or ride his horse. Do not open doors violently or slam them shut; handle them gently. Abstain from all expressions of vanity or discontent in his presence. Also avoid lying, unconsidered or insincere words, laughing and joking, playing the fool, and unnecessary or irrelevant chat. Learn to behave in a controlled manner, treating him with respect and awe, and never drifting into casualness.

> Do not remain seated when the teacher stands up;
> When he sits, solicitously bring him all he needs.
> Walk with him neither in front, behind nor on the right.
> To disrespect his mount or seat will spoil your merit.
> Do not slam doors; do not posture vainly or scowl;
> Avoid lies, laughter, ill-considered and irrelevant talk.
> Serve him with composure of body, speech, and mind.

Should there be people who criticize or hate your teacher, do not treat them as your friends. If you are capable of changing the attitude of anyone who has no faith in him or who disparages him, then you should do so. But if that is impossible, avoid being too open or having familiar conversations with such people.

> Do not treat as friends those who criticize

* As the spiritual teacher is Buddha, the place where his foot has trodden is blessed.

Or hate your teacher. Change their mind if you can.
If you speak freely with them, the powerful influence
Of their wrong action will harm your own samaya.

However much time you have to spend with your teacher's entourage or with your vajra brothers and sisters, never feel weary or irritated with them; be easy to be with, like a comfortable belt. Swallow your self-importance and join in with whatever there is to be done, mixing easily like salt in food. When people speak harshly to you or pick quarrels, or when the responsibilities you have to assume are too great, be ready to bear anything, like a pillar.

Like a belt, be a comfortable companion;
Like salt, be easily mixed in;
Like a pillar, untiringly bear any load;
Serve thus your vajra brothers and your teacher's attendants.

III. EMULATING THE TEACHER'S REALIZATION[98] AND ACTIONS

When you are perfectly versed in how to follow your teacher, you should be like a swan gliding smoothly on an immaculate lake, delighting in its waters without making them muddy; or like a bee in a flower garden, taking nectar from the flowers and leaving without spoiling their colour or fragrance. Doing whatever he says without ever feeling bored or tired, be receptive to your teacher and through your faith and steadfastness make sure that you absorb all his qualities of knowledge, reflection and meditation, like the contents of one perfect vessel being poured into another.

Like a swan swimming on a perfect lake,
Or a bee tasting the nectar of flowers,
Without ever complaining, but always receptive to him,
Always wait upon your teacher with exemplary conduct.
Through such devotion you will experience all his qualities.

Whenever your sublime teacher accumulates great waves of merit and wisdom through his Bodhisattva activities, your own participation with the least material offering or effort of body or speech, or even just your offering of joy at the slightest thing he does, will bring you as much merit as springs from his own unsurpassable intention.

Once there were two men travelling to central Tibet. The only food that one of them had was a handful of brown tsampa made from beans.

He gave it to his companion, mixing it with the other's copious supply of white barley tsampa. Several days later, the better-off traveller said to his fellow-voyager, "Your tsampa is probably finished by now."

"Let's have a look," the other said. So they did, and there was still some bean-tsampa left. Although they checked many times, the bean-tsampa was never finished, so that in the end they had to share all the tsampa equally.

Likewise, simply by offering a small material contribution to someone else's positive action, or by participating physically or verbally, you can attain as much merit as they do. Specifically, to serve the teacher's daily needs, to carry messages for him or even just to sweep his room are an infallible way to accumulate merit, so try to do such things as much as you can.

> All action consistent with the aims of a holy teacher
> Truly engaged in the activity of bodhicitta
> And accumulating merit and wisdom, all efforts
> To serve him, carry his messages or even sweep his floor,
> Will be fruitful—this is the best path of accumulating.

Of all the paramount sources of refuge or opportunities for accumulating merit there is none greater than the teacher. Especially while he is giving an empowerment or teaching, the compassion and blessings of all the Buddhas and Bodhisattvas of the ten directions pour into his sacred person and he becomes indivisibly one with all the Buddhas. At such a time, therefore, offering him even a mouthful of food is more powerful than hundreds or thousands of offerings at other times.

In the deity practices of the generation phase, there are many different forms of particular deities on which to meditate, but the nature of all of them is nothing other than your own root teacher. If you know that, the blessings will come swiftly. All the ways in which wisdom develops in the perfection phase depend only on the power of your devotion to your teacher and of his blessings, and consist of giving birth to the wisdom of the teacher's realization within yourself. The essence of what has to be realized at all stages of practice, including those of the generation and perfection phases, is therefore embodied in the teacher himself. That is why all sūtras and tantras describe him as being the Buddha in person.

> Why is he the refuge and the field of merit?
> Because the outer and inner yogas of accomplishing the teacher
> Contain the essence of what is to be realized through the
> generation and perfection phases.

> That is why all sūtras and tantras say he is the Buddha himself.

Although the wisdom mind of a sublime teacher is inseparable from that of all the Buddhas, in order to guide us, his disciples, impure as we are, he has appeared in ordinary human form. So, while we have him here in person, we must try our best to do whatever he says and to unite our minds with his through the three kinds of service.

There are people who, instead of serving, respecting and obeying their teacher while he was still alive, profess now that he has passed away to be meditating on a picture someone has made of him. There are others who claim to be absorbed in the contemplation of the natural state and look for all kinds of profundities elsewhere, instead of praying with devotion that they may receive in themselves the qualities of freedom and realization of the teacher's wisdom mind. This is known as "practising at odds with the practice."

Meeting and being guided by our teacher in the intermediate state can only take place because of a connection already created by our own limitless devotion and the power of the teacher's compassion and prayers. It is not that the teacher comes physically. So, if you lack devotion, however perfect the teacher may be, he will not be there to guide you in the intermediate state.

> Most fools take his portrait and meditate on that
> But do not honour him while he is present in person.
> They claim to meditate on the natural state, but do not know the
> teacher's mind.
> What an affliction to practise at odds with the practice!
> With no devotion, to meet the teacher in the intermediate state
> would be miraculous!

In the first place, you should take care to check the teacher. This means that before becoming committed to him through empowerments and teachings, you should examine him with care. Should you find that he has all the characteristics of a teacher, then follow him. If some of them are lacking, do not follow him. But, from the moment you start to follow him, learn to have faith in him and see him with pure perception, thinking only of his virtues and seeing whatever he does as positive. Looking for flaws in him will only bring you inconceivable ills.

To examine the teacher in a general sense means to check whether or not he has all the qualities described in the sūtras and tantras. In particular, what is absolutely necessary is that he should have bodhicitta, the mind of enlightenment. So examining a teacher could be condensed into just one question: does he or does he not have bodhicitta? If he does, he will do whatever is best for his disciples in this life and in lives to come, and their following him cannot be anything but beneficial. The Dharma taught by such a teacher is connected with the Great Vehicle, and can only lead along the authentic path. On the other hand, a teacher who lacks bodhicitta still has selfish desires, and so cannot properly transform the attitudes of his disciples. The Dharma he teaches, however profound and marvellous it may seem, will end up being useful only for the ordinary concerns of this life. This one question therefore epitomizes all the other points to be checked in a teacher. If a teacher's heart is filled with bodhicitta, follow him, however he might appear externally. If he lacks bodhicitta, do not follow him, however excellent his disillusionment with the world, his determination to be free, his assiduous practice and his conduct may at first appear.

For ordinary people like us, however, no amount of careful examination can reveal to us the extraordinary qualities of those sublime beings who hide their true nature. Meanwhile, charlatans pretending to be saints abound, skilled in the art of deception. The greatest of all teachers is the one with whom we are linked from former lives. With him, examination is superfluous. Simply to meet him, simply to hear his voice—or even just his name—can transform everything in an instant and stir such faith that every hair on our bodies stands on end.

Rongtön Lhaga told Jetsun Milarepa,* "The lama of your past lives is that best of all beings, the king of translators known as Marpa. He lives in a hermitage in Trowolung in the South. Go and see him!"

Hearing the name of Marpa alone was enough to arouse in Milarepa an extraordinary faith from the very depth of his being. He thought, "I must meet this lama and become his disciple, if it costs me my life." He tells us that on the day they were to meet, Marpa had come out on the road to look out for him but was ostensibly just ploughing a field. When Mila first saw him, he did not recognize him as his teacher. Nevertheless for an instant all his restless ordinary thoughts ceased and he stood transfixed.

Generally speaking, the teacher we meet is determined by the purity or impurity of our perceptions and the power of our past actions. So, whatever sort of person he may be, never cease to consider as a real Buddha the teacher through whose kindness you received the Dharma

* Milarepa's story is told in greater detail at the end of this chapter.

and personal guidance. For without the right conditions created by your past actions you would never have had the good fortune of meeting an excellent teacher. Moreover, if your perceptions were impure, you could even meet the Buddha in person and still be unable to see the qualities he had. The teacher whom you have met by the power of your past actions, and whose kindness you have received, is the most important of all.

In the middle phase, actually following the teacher, obey him in all things and disregard all hardships, heat, cold, hunger, thirst and so on. Pray to him with faith and devotion. Ask his advice on whatever you may be doing. Whatever he tells you, put it into practice, relying on him totally.

The final phase, emulating the teacher's realization and actions, consists in carefully examining the way he behaves and doing exactly as he does. As the saying goes, "Every action is an imitation; he who imitates best, acts best." It could be said that the practice of Dharma is to imitate the Buddhas and Bodhisattvas of the past. As the disciple is learning to be like his teacher, he will need to assimilate truly the latter's realization and way of behaving. The disciple should be like a *tsa-tsa* from the mould of the teacher. Just as the *tsa-tsa* faithfully reproduces all the patterns engraved on the mould, in the same way the disciple should make sure he or she acquires qualities identical with, or at least very close to, whatever qualities the teacher has.

Anyone who first examines his teacher skilfully, then follows him skilfully, and finally emulates his realization and actions skilfully will always be on the authentic path, come what may.

> In the beginning, skilfully examine the teacher;
> In the middle, skilfully follow him;
> In the end, skilfully emulate his realization and action.
> A disciple who does that is on the authentic path.

Once you have met a noble spiritual friend with all the requisite qualities, follow him without any concern for life or limb—just as the Bodhisattva Sadāprarudita followed Bodhisattva Dharmodgata, the great paṇḍit Nāropa followed the supreme Tilopa, and Jetsun Mila followed Marpa of Lhodrak.

First, here is the story of how Bodhisattva Sadāprarudita became the disciple of Dharmodgata.* Sadāprarudita was looking for the Prajña-

* The name Sadāprarudita means "Ever Weeping." Dharmodgata means "Sublime Dharma."

pāramitā, the teachings on transcendent wisdom.

One day, his quest led him to a solitary wasteland, where he heard a voice from the skies saying, "O fortunate son, go towards the east and you will hear the Prajñapāramitā. Go without caring about bodily fatigue, sleep or lethargy, heat or cold, whether by day or by night. Look neither to the right nor to the left. Before long you will receive the Prajñapāramitā, either contained in books or from a monk who embodies and teaches the Dharma. At that time, fortunate son, follow and stick to the one who teaches you the Prajñapāramitā, consider him your teacher and venerate his Dharma. Even if you see him enjoying the five pleasures of the senses, realize that Bodhisattvas are skilled in means, and never lose your faith."

At these words, Sadāprarudita set out towards the east. He had not gone far when he realized that he had forgotten to ask the voice how far he should go—and so he had no idea how to find his Prajñapāramitā teacher. Weeping and lamenting, he vowed to ignore fatigue, hunger, thirst and sleep, day or night until he had received the teaching. He was stricken, like a mother who has lost her only child. He was obsessed with a single question: when would he hear the Prajñapāramitā?

At that moment, the form of a Tathāgata appeared before him and praised the quest for Dharma. "Five hundred leagues from here," the Tathāgata added, "there is a city called City of Fragrant Breezes. It is made of the seven precious substances. It is surrounded by five hundred parks and possesses all the perfect qualities. In the centre of that city, at the crossroads of four avenues, is the abode of Bodhisattva Dharmodgata. It too is made of the seven precious substances, and is one league in circumference. There, in the gardens and other places of delight, lives the Bodhisattva, the great being Dharmodgata, with his entourage. In the company of sixty-eight thousand women he enjoys the pleasures of the five senses, over which he has total mastery, blissfully doing whatever he likes. Throughout past, present and future, he teaches the Prajñapāramitā to those who dwell there. Go to him, and you will be able to hear the teachings on Prajñapāramitā from him!"

Sadāprarudita could now think of nothing except what he had heard. From the very spot where he was standing, he could hear the Bodhisattva Dharmodgata teaching the Prajñapāramitā. He experienced numerous states of mental concentration. He perceived the different worlds in the ten directions of the universe, and saw innumerable Buddhas teaching the Prajñapāramitā. They sang the praises of Dharmodgata before disappearing. Full of joy, faith and devotion for Bodhisattva Dharmodgata,

Sadāprarudita wondered how he might come into his presence.

"I am poor," thought he. "I have nothing with which to honour him, no clothes or jewels, no perfumes or garlands, nor any of the other objects with which to pay respect to a spiritual friend. So I shall sell the flesh of my own body and, with the money I receive for it, I will honour the Bodhisattva Dharmodgata. Throughout beginningless saṁsāra, I have sold my flesh innumerable times; an infinite number of times, too, I have already been cut to pieces and destroyed in the hells where my own desires had dragged me—but it was never to receive a teaching like this or to honour such a sublime teacher!"

He went to the middle of the market place and started calling out, "Who wants a man? Who wants to buy a man?"

But evil spirits, jealous that Sadāprarudita was undergoing such trials for the sake of the Dharma, made everyone deaf to his words. Sadāprarudita, finding no one to buy him, went to a corner and sat there weeping, tears pouring from his eyes.

Indra, king of the gods, then decided to test his determination. Taking the form of a young brahmin, he appeared before Sadāprarudita and said, "I do not need a whole man. I need only some human flesh, some human fat and some human bone marrow to make an offering. If you can sell me that, I'll pay you for it."

Overjoyed, Sadāprarudita took up a sharp knife and cut into his right arm till the blood spurted out. He then cut off all the flesh from his right thigh, and, as he was preparing to smash the bones against a wall, the daughter of a rich merchant saw him from the top story of her house and rushed down to him.

"Noble one, why are you inflicting such pain upon yourself?" she asked.

He explained that he wished to sell his flesh so that he might make an offering to the Bodhisattva Dharmodgata.

When the young girl asked him what benefit he would obtain from such homage, Sadāprarudita replied, "He will teach me the skilful methods of the Bodhisattvas and the Prajñapāramitā. If I then train myself in those, I shall attain omniscience, possess the many qualities of a Buddha and be able to share the precious Dharma with all beings."

"It is surely true," said the girl, "that each of those qualities deserves an offering of as many bodies as there are grains of sand in the Ganges. But please do not hurt yourself so! I shall give you whatever you need to honour the Bodhisattva Dharmodgata and come with you myself to see him. In so doing, I will create the root of merit which will enable me to attain the same qualities, too."

When she finished speaking, Indra reassumed his own form and said to Sadāprarudita, "I am Indra, King of the Gods. I came to test your determination. I shall give you whatever you want; you have only to ask."

"Bestow upon me the unsurpassable qualities of the Buddhas!" Sadāprarudita replied.

"That I cannot grant you," said Indra. "Such things do not fall within my domain."

"In that case, there is no need for you to trouble yourself about making my body whole again," said Sadāprarudita. "I shall invoke the blessings of the truth. By the blessings of the Buddhas' prediction that I will never return into saṁsāra, by the truth of my supreme and unshakeable determination, and by the truth of my words, may my body resume its former state!"

At these words, his body became exactly as it had been before. And Indra disappeared.

Sadāprarudita went with the merchant's daughter to her parents' house and there told them his tale. They provided him with the numerous materials he would need for his offering. Then he, together with the merchant's daughter and her parents, accompanied by five hundred female attendants and their whole retinue, set out in carriages towards the east, and arrived in the City of Fragrant Breezes. There he saw the Bodhisattva Dharmodgata preaching the Dharma to thousands of people. The sight filled him with the bliss that a monk experiences when immersed in meditative absorption. The entire party stepped down from their carriages and went to meet Dharmodgata.

Now Dharmodgata, at that time, had built a temple to the Prajñapāramitā. It was made of the seven precious substances, and was decorated with red sandalwood and covered with a filigree of pearls. In each of the four directions had been placed wish-granting gems as lamps and silver censers from which wafted fragrant offerings of black aloe-wood incense. At the centre of the temple were four jewelled coffers containing the volumes of the Prajñapāramitā, made of gold and written in ink of lapis lazuli.

Seeing both gods and men making offerings, Sadāprarudita made enquiries and then, accompanied by the daughter, the merchant and the five hundred attendants, made excellent offerings too.

They then approached Dharmodgata, who was giving teaching to his disciples, and honoured him with all their offerings. The merchant's daughter and her maidens took the vows of sublime bodhicitta. Sadāprarudita asked him where the Buddhas he had seen before had come from and where they had gone. Dharmodgata answered with the chapter explaining that Buddhas neither come nor go.* He then left his seat and went to his own quarters, where he remained in the same continuous state of concentration for seven years.

Throughout this whole period, Sadāprarudita, the merchant's daughter and the five hundred servants renounced both sitting and lying down, staying permanently on their feet. As they stood still or walked around, their minds dwelt only on the moment when Dharmodgata would arise from his concentration and teach the Dharma once more.

When those seven years were nearly at an end, Sadāprarudita heard the gods announcing that in seven days' time Bodhisattva Dharmodgata would arise from his state of concentration and start teaching again. With the five hundred serving maidens he swept, for one league in every direction, the area where Dharmodgata was going to teach. When he started to sprinkle water on the ground to settle the dust, Māra made all the water disappear. So Sadāprarudita cut open his veins and sprinkled his own blood on the ground, and the merchant's daughter and her five hundred attendants did the same. Indra, King of the gods, transformed their blood into the red sandalwood of the celestial realms.

At last, Bodhisattva Dharmodgata arrived and sat upon the lion-throne that Sadāprarudita and the others had so perfectly set up. He expounded the Prajñapāramitā. Sadāprarudita experienced six million different states of concentration and had the vision of an infinite number of Buddhas—a vision which never again left him, even in his dreams. It is said that he now dwells in the presence of the perfect Buddha called He who Proclaims the Dharma with Inexhaustible Melodious Voice.

While following Tilopa, the great paṇḍita Nāropa also underwent immeasurable difficulties. As we saw earlier, Nāropa met Tilopa, who was living like a beggar, and asked him to accept him as his disciple. Tilopa granted this request and took him along wherever he went, but never taught him any Dharma.

One day, Tilopa took Nāropa to the top of a nine-storey tower and asked: "Is there anyone who can leap from the top of this building to obey his Master?"

Nāropa thought to himself, "There is nobody else here, so he must mean me." He jumped from the top of the building and his body crashed to the ground, causing him tremendous pain and suffering.

Tilopa came down to him and asked, "Are you in pain?"

* This means that Buddhas are not bound by concepts of place.

"It's not just the pain," groaned Nāropa. "I am not much more than a corpse..." But Tilopa blessed him, and his body was completely healed. Tilopa led Nāropa off again on their journey.

"Nāropa, make a fire!" Tilopa ordered him one day.

When the fire was blazing, Tilopa prepared many long splinters of bamboo, oiling them and putting them in the fire to harden.

"If you're going to obey your teacher's orders, you'll also have to undergo trials like this," he said, and pushed the splinters under the nails of his disciple's fingers and toes.

Nāropa's joints all became completely rigid and he experienced unbearable pain and suffering. The Guru then left him. When he returned several days later, he pulled out the splinters and huge quantities of blood and pus streamed from Nāropa's wounds. Once again Tilopa blessed him and set off with him again.

"Nāropa," he said another day, "I'm hungry. Go and beg some food for me!"

Nāropa went to a spot where a large crowd of farm labourers were busy eating, and from them he begged a skull-cup* full of soup which he took back to his teacher. Tilopa ate it with enormous relish and seemed to be delighted.

Nāropa thought, "In all the long time I have served him, I have never seen my teacher so happy. Perhaps if I ask again I can get some more."

He set off to beg again, skull-cup in hand. By this time the workers had gone back to their fields, leaving their left-over soup where it had been before.

"The only thing to do is to steal it," Nāropa thought to himself, and he took the soup and ran off with it.

But the labourers saw him. They caught him and beat him up, leaving him for dead. He was in such pain that he could not get up for several days. Again his teacher arrived, blessed him and took to the road with him as before.

"Nāropa," he said another day, "I need a lot of money.[99] Go and steal me some."

So Nāropa went off to steal money from a rich man, but was caught in the act. He was seized, beaten, and again left for dead. Several days passed before Tilopa arrived and asked him, "Are you in pain?" Receiving the same answer as before, he blessed Nāropa, and off they went again.

* *thod phor* (Skt. *kapāla*). A skull cup. The top of a skull is used by some yogīs as a bowl. It symbolizes egolessness.

Nāropa underwent twelve major and twelve minor hardships like these—twenty-four hardships that he had to undergo in one lifetime. Finally, they were at an end.

One day, Tilopa said, "Nāropa, go and fetch some water. I'll stay here and make the fire."

When Nāropa came back carrying the water, Tilopa jumped up from the fire he had been making and grabbed Nāropa's head with his left hand.

"Show me your forehead," he ordered.

With his right hand he took off his sandal and hit his disciple on the forehead with it. Nāropa lost consciousness. When he came to, all the qualities of his teacher's wisdom mind had arisen within him. Teacher and disciple had become one in realization.

As the twenty-four trials undergone by the great paṇḍita Nāropa were, in fact, his teacher's instructions, they became the skilful means by which his obscurations were eliminated. They appear to be just pointless hardships that nobody would think of as Dharma. Indeed, the teacher had not uttered a word of teaching and the disciple had not done a moment of practice, not even a single prostration. However, once Nāropa had met an accomplished siddha, he had obeyed his every command regardless of all difficulties, and in so doing achieved the purification of his obscurations so that realization awakened in him.

There is no greater Dharma practice than obeying one's teacher. The benefits are immense, as we can see here. On the other hand, to disobey him, even a little, is an extremely grave fault.

Once Tilopa forbade Nāropa to accept the post of paṇḍita-gatekeeper at Vikramaśīla.[100] But when Nāropa arrived in Magadha some time later, one of the paṇḍitas who held this position had died. Since there was no one else capable of debating with the tīrthikas, they all begged Nāropa to take the post of protector of the northern gate, and pressed him insistently until he accepted. However, when a tīrthika presented himself for debate, Nāropa argued with him for days on end without being able to defeat him. He prayed to his teacher until finally one day Tilopa appeared to him, looking at him with a piercing gaze.

"You don't have much compassion—why didn't you come earlier?" Nāropa complained.

"Did I not forbid you to take this post of gatekeeper?" Tilopa retorted. "Nevertheless, while you debate, visualize me above your head and make the threatening gesture at the tīrthika!"

Nāropa did as Tilopa had told him, won his debate and put an end to all the arguments of the tīrthikas.

Finally, here is how Jetsun Milarepa followed Marpa of Lhodrak. In the region of Ngari Gungthang, there lived a rich man by the name of Mila Sherab Gyaltsen. This man had a son and a daughter, and it was the son, whose name was Mila Thöpa-ga, "Mila Joy to Hear," who was to become Jetsun Mila. When the two children were still small, their father died. Their uncle, whose name was Yungdrung Gyaltsen, appropriated all their wealth and possessions. The two children and their mother, left with neither food nor money, were forced to undergo many hardships. Mila learned the arts of casting spells and making hailstorms from the magicians Yungtön Throgyal of Tsang and Lharje Nupchung, and brought about the death of his uncle's son and daughter-in-law together with thirty-three other people by making the house collapse. When all the local people turned angrily against him, he caused such a hailstorm that the hail lay on the ground as deep as three courses of a clay wall.[101]

Afterwards, repenting his misdeeds, he decided to practise Dharma. Taking the advice of Lama Yungtön, he went to see an adept of the Great Perfection by the name of Rongtön Lhaga, and asked him for instruction.

"The Dharma I teach," the Lama replied, "is the Great Perfection. Its root is the conquest of the beginning, its summit the conquest of attainment and its fruit the conquest of yoga.[102] If one meditates on it during the day, one can become Buddha that same day; if one meditates on it during the night, one can become Buddha that very night. Fortunate beings whose past actions have created suitable conditions do not even need to meditate; they will be liberated simply by hearing it. Since it is a Dharma for those of eminently superior faculties, I will teach it to you."

After receiving the empowerments and instructions, Mila thought to himself, "It took me two weeks to obtain the main signs of success at casting spells. Seven days were enough for making hail. Now here is a teaching even easier than spells and hail—if you meditate by day you become a Buddha that day; if you meditate by night you become a Buddha that night—and if your past actions have created suitable conditions, you don't even need to meditate at all! Seeing how I met this teaching, I obviously must be one of the ones with good past actions."

So he stayed in bed without meditating, and thus the practitioner and the teaching parted company.

"It is true what you told me," the lama said to him after a few days. "You really are a great sinner, and I have praised my teaching a little too highly. So now I will not guide you. You should go to the hermitage of Trowolung in Lhodrak, where there is a direct disciple of the Indian siddha Nāropa himself. He is that most excellent of teachers, the king of translators, Marpa. He is a siddha of the New Mantra Tradition,[103] and is without rival throughout the three worlds. Since you and he have a link stemming from actions in former lives, go and see him!"

The sound of Marpa the Translator's name alone was enough to suffuse Mila's mind with inexpressible joy. He was charged with such bliss that every pore on his body tingled, and immense devotion swept over him, filling his eyes with tears. He set off, wondering when he would meet his teacher face to face.

Now, Marpa and his wife had both had many extraordinary dreams, and Marpa knew that Jetsun Mila was on his way. He went down the valley to await his arrival, pretending to be just ploughing a field. Mila first met Marpa's son, Tarma Dodé, who was tending the cattle. Continuing a little further, he saw Marpa, who was ploughing. The moment Mila caught sight of him, he experienced tremendous, inexpressible joy and bliss; for an instant, all his ordinary thoughts stopped. Nonetheless, he did not realize that this was the lama in person, and explained to him that he had come to meet Marpa.

"I'll introduce you to him myself," Marpa answered him. "Plough this field for me." Leaving him a jug of beer, he went off. Mila, draining the jug to the last drop, set to work. When he had finished, the lama's son came to call him and they set off together.

When Mila was brought into the lama's presence, he placed the soles of Marpa's feet upon the crown of his head and cried out, "Oh, Master! I am a great sinner from the west! I offer you my body, speech and mind. Please feed and clothe me and teach me the Dharma. Give me the way to become Buddha in this life!"

"It's not my fault that you reckon you're such a bad man," Marpa replied. "I didn't ask you to pile up evil deeds on my account! What is all this wrong you have done?"

Mila told him the whole story in detail.

"Very well," Marpa acquiesced, "in any case, to offer your body, speech and mind is a good thing. As to food, clothing and Dharma, however, you cannot have all three. Either I give you food and clothing and you look for Dharma elsewhere, or you get your Dharma from me and look for the rest somewhere else. Make up your mind. And if it's the Dharma you choose, whether or not you attain Buddhahood in this lifetime will depend on your own perseverance."

"If that is the case," said Mila, "since I came for the Dharma, I will look for provisions and clothing elsewhere."

He stayed a few days and went out begging through the whole of upper and lower Lhodrak, which brought him twenty-one measures of barley. He used fourteen of them to buy a four-handled copper pot. Placing six measures in a sack, he went back to offer that and the pot to Marpa.

When he set the barley down, it made the room shake. Marpa got up.

"You're a strong little monk, aren't you?" he said. "Are you trying to kill us all by making the house fall down with your bare hands? Get that sack of barley out of here!" He gave the sack a kick, and Mila had to take it outside. Later on he gave Marpa the empty pot.[104]

One day Marpa said to him: "The men of Yamdrok Taklung and Lingpa are attacking many of my faithful disciples who come to visit me from U and Tsang, and stealing their provisions and offerings. Bring hailstorms down on them! Since that is a kind of Dharma too, I will give you the instructions afterwards."

Mila caused devastating hailstorms to fall on both these regions and then went to ask for the teachings.

"You think I'm going to give you the teachings I brought back from India at such great cost in exchange for three or four hailstones? If you really want the Dharma, cast a spell on the hill-folk of Lhodrak. They attack my disciples from Nyaloro and are always treating me with downright contempt. When there is a sign that your spell has worked, I shall give you Nāropa's oral instructions, which lead to Buddhahood in a single lifetime and body."

When the signs of the success of the evil spell appeared, Mila asked for the Dharma.

"Huh! Is it perhaps to pay honour to your accumulation of evil deeds that you are claiming to want these oral instructions that I had to search for, never considering the risk to my own body and life—these instructions still warm with the breath of the ḍākinīs? I suppose you must be joking, but I find this a bit too much. Anyone else but me would kill you! Now, bring those hill people back to life and return to the people of Yamdrok their harvest. You'll get the teachings if you do—otherwise, don't hang around me anymore!"

Mila, utterly shattered by these reprimands, sat and wept bitter tears. The next morning, Marpa came to see him.

"I was a bit rough with you last night," he said. "Don't be sad. I will give you the instructions little by little. Just be patient! Since you're a good worker, I'd like you to build me a house to give to Tarma Dodé. When you've finished, I'll give you the instructions, and provide you with food and clothing as well."

"But what will I do if I die in the meantime, without the Dharma?"

Mila asked.

"I'll take the responsibility of making sure that doesn't happen," Marpa said. "My teachings are not just idle boasting, and since you obviously have extraordinary perseverance, when you put my instructions into practice we will see if you can attain Buddhahood in a single lifetime."

After further encouragement in the same vein, he had Mila build three houses one after the other: a circular one at the foot of the eastern hill, a semicircular one in the west and a triangular one in the north. But each time, as soon as the house was half finished, Marpa would berate Mila furiously, and make him demolish whatever he had built and take all the earth and stones he had used back to where he had found them.

An open sore appeared on Mila's back, but he thought, "If I show it to the Master, he will only scold me again. I could show it to his wife but that would just be making a fuss." So, weeping, but not showing his wounds, he implored Marpa's wife to help him request the teachings.

She asked Marpa to teach him, and Marpa replied, "Give him a a good meal and bring him here!" He gave Mila the transmission and vows of refuge.

"All this," he said, "is what is called the basic Dharma. If you want the extraordinary instructions of the Secret Mantrayāna, the sort of thing you'll to have to go through is this..." and he recounted a brief version of the life and trials of Nāropa. "It'll be difficult for you to do the same," he concluded.

At these words Mila felt such intense devotion that his tears flowed freely, and with fierce determination he vowed to do whatever his teacher asked of him.

A few days later, Marpa went for a walk and took Mila with him as his attendant. He went south-east and, coming to a favourably situated piece of ground, he said, "Make me a grey, square tower here, nine storeys high. With a pinnacle on top, making ten. You won't have to take this building down, and when you've finished I'll give you the instructions. I'll also give you provisions when you go into retreat to practise."

Mila had already dug the foundations and started building when three of his teacher's more advanced pupils came by. For fun, they rolled up a huge stone for him and Mila incorporated it in the foundations. When he had finished the first two storeys, Marpa came to see him and asked him where the stone in question had come from. Mila told him what had happened.

"My disciples practising the yoga of the two phases shouldn't be your servants!" Marpa yelled. "Get that stone out of there and put it back where it came from!"

Mila demolished the whole tower, starting from the top. He pulled out the big foundation stone and took it back to where it had come from.

Then Marpa told him, "Now bring it here again and put it back in."

So Mila hauled it back to the site and put it in just as before. He went on building until he had finished the seventh storey, by which time he had an open sore on his hip.

"Now leave off building that tower," Marpa said, "and instead build me a temple, with a twelve-pillared hall and a raised sanctuary."

So Mila built the temple, and by the time he had finished, a sore had broken out on his lower back.

At that time, Metön Tsönpo of Tsangrong asked Marpa for the empowerment of Saṁvara, and Tsurtön Wangé of Döl asked for the empowerment of Guhyasamāja. On both occasions, Mila, hoping that his building work had earned him the right to empowerment, took his place in the assembly, but all he received from Marpa were blows and rebukes and he was thrown out both times. His back was now one huge sore with blood and pus running from three places. Nevertheless, he continued working, carrying the baskets of earth in front of him instead.

When Ngoktön Chödor of Shung came to ask for the Hevajra empowerment, Marpa's wife gave Mila a large turquoise from her own personal inheritance. Using it as his offering for the empowerment, Mila placed himself among the row of candidates but, as before, the teacher scolded him and gave him a thrashing, and he did not receive the empowerment.

This time he felt that there was no further doubt: he would never receive any teachings. He wandered off in no particular direction. A family in Lhodrak Khok hired him to read the *Transcendent Wisdom in Eight Thousand Verses*. He came to the story of Sadāprarudita, and that made him think. He realized that, for the sake of the Dharma, he must accept all hardships and please his teacher by doing whatever he ordered.

So he returned, but again Marpa only welcomed him with abuse and blows. Mila was so desperate that Marpa's wife sent him to Lama Ngokpa, who gave him some instructions. But when he meditated nothing came of it, since he had not received his teacher's consent. Marpa ordered him to go back with Lama Ngokpa, and then to return.

One day, during a feast offering, Marpa severely reprimanded Lama Ngokpa and some other disciples and was about to start beating them.

Mila thought to himself, "With my evil karma, not only do I myself suffer because of my heavy faults and dense obscurations, but now I am also bringing difficulties on Lama Ngokpa and my Guru's consort. Since

I am just piling up more and more harmful actions without receiving any teaching, it would be best if I did away with myself."

He prepared to commit suicide. Lama Ngokpa was trying to stop him when Marpa calmed down and summoned them both. He accepted Mila as a disciple, gave him much good advice and named him Mila Dorje Gyaltsen, "Mila Adamantine Victory Banner." As he gave him the empowerment of Saṁvara, he made the maṇḍala of its sixty-two deities clearly appear. Mila then received the secret name of Shepa Dorje, "Adamantine Laughter," and Marpa conferred all the empowerments and instructions on him just like the contents of one pot being poured into another. Afterwards, Mila practised in the hardest of conditions, and attained all the common and supreme accomplishments.[105]

It was like this that all the paṇḍitas, siddhas and vidyādharas of the past, in both India and Tibet, followed a spiritual friend who was an authentic teacher, and by doing whatever he said achieved realization inseparable from the teacher's own.

On the other hand, it is a very serious fault not to follow the teacher with a completely sincere mind, free from deceit. Never perceive any of his actions negatively. Never even tell him the smallest lie.

Once the disciple of a great siddha was teaching the Dharma to a crowd of disciples. His teacher arrived, dressed as a beggar. The disciple was too embarrassed to prostrate before him in front of the crowd, so he pretended not to have seen him. That evening, once the crowd had dispersed, he went to see his teacher and prostrated to him.

"Why didn't you prostrate before?" his teacher asked.

"I didn't see you," he lied.

Immediately, both his eyes fell to the ground. He begged forgiveness and told the truth, and with a blessing the master restored his sight.

There is a similar story about the Indian mahāsiddha Kṛṣṇācārya. One day, he was sailing at sea in the company of numerous disciples, when the thought arose in his mind, "My teacher is a real siddha, but from a worldly point of view I am better than him, because I am richer and have more attendants."

Straight away, his ship sank into the ocean. Floundering desperately in the water, he prayed to his teacher, who appeared in person and saved him from drowning.

"That was the reward for your great arrogance," the teacher said. "Had I tried to gather wealth and attendants, I would have had them too. But I chose not to do that."

Inexpressible multitudes of Buddhas have already come, but their compassion has not been enough to save us: we are still in the ocean of suffering of saṁsāra. Inconceivable numbers of great teachers have appeared since ancient times, but we have not had the good fortune to enjoy their compassionate care, or even to meet them. These days, the teachings of the Buddha are coming to an end. The five degenerations are more and more in evidence, and although we have obtained human life, we are totally in the clutches of our negative actions, and confused about what to do and what not to do. As we wander like a blind man alone in an empty plain, our spiritual friends, the supreme teachers, think of us with their boundless compassion, and according to the needs of each of us appear in human form. Although in their realization they are Buddhas, in their actions they are attuned to how we are. With their skilful means they accept us as disciples, introduce us to the supreme authentic Dharma, open our eyes to what we should do and what we should not do, and unerringly point out the best path to liberation and omniscience. In truth, they are no different from the Buddha himself; but compared to the Buddha their kindness in caring for us is even greater. Always try, therefore, to follow your teacher in the right way, with the three kinds of faith.*

I have met a sublime teacher, but let myself down by my negative behaviour.
I have found the best path, but I wander on precipitous byways.
Bless me and all those of bad character like me
That our minds may be tamed by the Dharma.

* These are explained at the beginning of the chapter that follows.

Dilgo Khyentse Rinpoche (1910-1991)

One of the incarnations of Jamyang Khyentse Wangpo. He studied with one hundred and twenty teachers and spent a total of twenty years in meditation retreat. He frequently gave teachings, including those of the Great Perfection, to the Dalai Lama. Many of the younger generation of Tibetan lamas consider him their root teacher. He also taught widely in Europe and North America.

Part Two

THE EXTRAORDINARY OR INNER PRELIMINARIES

TAKING REFUGE, THE FOUNDATION STONE OF ALL PATHS

AROUSING BODHICITTA, THE ROOT OF THE GREAT VEHICLE

MEDITATING ON THE TEACHER AS VAJRASATTVA
TO CLEANSE ALL OBSCURATIONS

OFFERING THE MAṆḌALA
TO ACCUMULATE MERIT AND WISDOM

THE KUSĀLI'S ACCUMULATION:
DESTROYING THE FOUR DEMONS AT A SINGLE STROKE

GURU YOGA, ENTRANCE-WAY FOR BLESSINGS,
THE ULTIMATE WAY TO AROUSE THE WISDOM OF REALIZATION

The Refuge Deities

The visualization of the field of merit for taking refuge according to the *Heart-essence of the Vast Expanse*.

CHAPTER ONE

Taking refuge, the foundation stone of all paths

Crowned with the Three Jewels of the outer refuge,
You have truly realized the Three Roots, the inner refuge;
You have made manifest the three kāyas, the ultimate refuge.
Peerless Teacher, at your feet I bow.

Taking refuge,[106] the foundation stone of all paths,[107] is explained under three headings: approaches to taking refuge, how to take refuge, and the precepts and benefits of taking refuge.

I. APPROACHES TO TAKING REFUGE

1. Faith

Just as taking refuge opens the gateway to all teachings and practices, it is faith that opens the gateway to taking refuge. As the first step in taking refuge, therefore, it is important to develop a lasting and stable faith. Faith itself is of three kinds: vivid faith, eager faith and confident faith.

1.1 VIVID FAITH

Vivid faith is the faith that is inspired in us by thinking of the immense compassion of the Buddhas and great teachers. We might experience this kind of faith on visiting a temple containing many representations of the Buddhas' body, speech and mind, or after an encounter with a great teacher or spiritual friend we have just met personally or whose qualities or life-story we have heard described.[108]

1.2 EAGER FAITH

Eager faith is our eagerness to be free of the sufferings of lower realms when we hear them described; our eagerness to enjoy the happiness of higher realms and of liberation when we hear what they are; our eagerness to engage in positive actions when we hear what benefits they bring; and our eagerness to avoid negative actions when we understand what harm they cause.

1.3 CONFIDENT FAITH

Confident faith is the faith in the Three Jewels that arises from the depth of our hearts once we understand their extraordinary qualities and the power of their blessings. It is the total trust in the Three Jewels alone that comes from the knowledge that they are the only unfailing refuge,[109] always and in all circumstances, whether we are happy, sad, in pain, ill, living or dead.* The Precious Lord of Oḍḍiyāna says:

> The faith of total trust allows blessings to enter you.
> When the mind is free of doubt, whatever you wish can be achieved.

Faith, then, is like a seed from which everything positive can grow. If faith is absent, it is as though that seed had been burnt. The sūtras say:

> In those who lack faith
> Nothing positive will grow,
> Just as from a burnt seed
> No green shoot will ever sprout.

Of the seven noble riches, faith is the most important. It is said:

> The precious wheel of faith
> Rolls day and night along the road of virtue.

Faith is the most precious of all our resources. It brings an inexhaustible supply of virtues, like a treasure. It carries us along the path to liberation like a pair of legs, and gathers up everything positive for us like a pair of arms.

* This means that our faith in the refuge will enable us to deal with the experiences of the intermediate state (*bar do*) after death.

> Faith is the greatest wealth and treasure, the best of legs;
> It is the basis for gathering all virtues, like arms.

The compassion and blessings of the Three Jewels are inconceivable, but nevertheless their ability to reach into us depends entirely on our faith and devotion. If you have immense faith and devotion, the compassion and blessings you receive from your teacher and the Three Jewels will be equally immense. If your faith and devotion are just moderate, the compassion and blessings that reach you will also be moderate. If you have only a little faith and devotion, only a little compassion and blessings will reach you. If you have no faith and devotion at all, you will get absolutely nothing. Without faith, even meeting the Buddha himself and being accepted as his disciple would be quite useless, as it was for the monk Sunakṣatra, whose story was told in the previous chapter, and for the Buddha's cousin, Devadatta.

Even today, whenever the Buddha is invoked with sincere faith and devotion, he is there, bestowing blessings. For the Buddha's compassion there is no near or far.

> For all who think of him with faith
> The Buddha is there in front of them
> And will give empowerments and blessings.

And the Great Master of Oḍḍiyāna says:

> For all men and women with faith in me, I, Padmasambhava,
> Have never departed—I sleep beside their door.[110]
> For me there is no such thing as death;
> Before each person with faith, there is a Padmasambhava.

When one has confident faith, the Buddha's compassion can be present in anything. This is illustrated by the tale of the faithful old woman who was helped towards Buddhahood by a dog's tooth.

Once there was an old woman whose son was a trader. He often went to India on business. The old woman said to him one day: "Bodh Gaya is in India, and that's where the perfectly enlightened Buddha came from. Bring me some special relic from India, so that I can do my prostrations to it." She repeated her request many times, but her son kept forgetting and never brought her what she had asked for.

One day, as he was preparing to leave again for India, his mother said to him, "This time, if you fail to bring me something for my prostrations, I shall kill myself in front of you!"

The son travelled to India, concluded the business he had planned, and set off back home, once more forgetting his mother's request. It was only as he was nearing his house again that he remembered her words.

"Now what am I going to do?" he thought to himself. "I haven't brought anything for my old mother's prostrations. If I arrive home empty-handed, she'll kill herself!"

Looking around him, he saw a dog's skull lying on the ground nearby. He pulled out one of the teeth and wrapped it in silk. Arriving home, he gave it to his mother, saying, "Here is one of the Buddha's canine teeth. You can use it as a support for your prayers."

The old woman believed him. She had great faith in the tooth, just as if it really were the Buddha's. She did prostrations and offerings all the time, and from that dog's tooth came many miraculous pearls.* When the old woman died, there was a canopy of rainbow light around her, and other signs of accomplishment.

Now a dog's tooth does not contain any blessings. But the old woman's faith was so strong that she was sure that it really was the Buddha's tooth. Through her faith the tooth was imbued with the Buddha's blessings, until in the end that dog's tooth was in no way different from a real Buddha's tooth.

Once, in the province of Kongpo, there lived a simple-minded fellow who later became known as Jowo Ben. He made a journey to Central Tibet to see the Jowo Rinpoche.**

When he first arrived in front of the statue, there was no caretaker or anyone else about. Seeing the food-offerings and the butter-lamps in front of it, he imagined that the Jowo Rinpoche must dip pieces of the offering cakes in the melted butter of the lamps and eat them. The wicks were burning in the lamps, he supposed, to keep the butter liquid.

"I think I'd better eat some, like Jowo Rinpoche does," he thought to himself, and dunking a piece of dough from the offering *tormas* into the butter, he ate it. He looked up at the smiling face of the Jowo.

"What a nice lama you are," he said. "Even when dogs come and steal the food you've been offered, you smile; when the draught makes your lamps sputter, you still keep smiling. Here, I'll leave you my boots. Please look after them for me while I walk around you."†

* *ring bsrel*: round objects like minute pearls which emerge from the relics of realized practitioners.

** The famous statue of the Buddha in Lhasa. See note 295.

† Eating the offerings and putting his boots up in front of the statue would be considered a scandalous act of sacrilege.

He took off his boots and put them up in front of the statue. While he was circumambulating round the middle pathway that circles the temple, the caretaker saw the boots. He was about to throw them out when the statue spoke.

"Don't throw those boots away. Kongpo Ben has entrusted them to me!"

Ben eventually came back and took his boots.

"You really are what they call a good lama!" he said to the statue. "Next year, why don't you come and visit us. I'll slaughter an old pig and cook it for you and brew you up some nice old barley beer."

"I'll come," said the Jowo.

Ben went back home and told his wife, "I've invited Jowo Rinpoche. I'm not sure exactly when he's coming, though—so don't forget to keep an eye out for him."

A year went by. One day, as she was drawing water from the river, Ben's wife clearly saw the reflection of Jowo Rinpoche in the water.

Straight away she ran home and told her husband: "There's something down there, in the river... I wonder if it's the person you invited."

Ben rushed down to the river and saw Jowo Rinpoche shining in the water. Thinking that he must have fallen into the river, Ben jumped in after him. As he grabbed at the image, he found that he could actually catch hold of it and bring it along with him.

As they were proceeding towards Ben's house, they arrived in front of a huge rock on the side of the road. The Jowo did not want to go any further.

"I do not enter laypeople's homes," he said, and disappeared into the rock.

This place, to which the Jowo himself was seen coming, is called Jowo Dolé, and the river in which the image appeared bears the name of Jowo River. Even nowadays, it is said that this place confers the same blessing as the Jowo in Lhasa, and everyone does prostrations and makes offerings there. It was by the power of his firm faith that Ben experienced the compassion of the Buddha. Although he ate butter from the lamps and food from the offerings, and put his boots up in front of the Jowo—acts which otherwise could only be wrong—the power of his faith made it all positive.

What is more, it is also upon faith alone that actual realization of the absolute truth, the natural state, depends. It is said in a sūtra:

> O Śāriputra, absolute truth is only realized through faith.

As you develop a faith quite beyond the commonplace, by its power the blessings of the teacher and of the Three Jewels will enter you. Then true realization will arise and you will see the natural state as it really is. When that happens you will feel an even more extraordinary and irreversible faith and confidence in your teacher and in the Three Jewels. In this way faith and the realization of the natural state support each other.

Before leaving Jetsun Mila, Dagpo Rinpoche asked him when he should start to teach.

"One day," the Jetsun replied, "You will have a realization that brings you an extraordinarily clear vision of the nature of your mind, quite different from the one you have now. At that time, firm faith will arise in you and you will perceive me, your old father, as a real Buddha. That is when you should start to teach."

Our capacity to receive the compassion and blessings of the teacher and the Three Jewels, therefore, depends entirely on devotion and faith.

Once, a disciple called out to the master Jowo Atīśa, "Jowo, give me your blessing!"

"Lax disciple," Atīśa replied, "give me your devotion..."

So absolute unwavering trust, arising from extraordinary faith and devotion, is indispensable. It opens the door to taking refuge.

2. Motivation

There are three different levels of motivation for taking refuge with this sort of faith.

2.1 THE REFUGE OF LESSER BEINGS

Fear of the sufferings of the three lower realms—the hell realm, the preta realm and the animal realm—motivates us to take refuge simply with the idea of obtaining the happiness of gods and men.

2.2 THE REFUGE OF MIDDLING BEINGS

The knowledge that wherever we are reborn in any of the realms of saṁsāra, high or low, there is no freedom from suffering, motivates us to take refuge in the Three Jewels just with the aim of attaining for ourselves the level of nirvāṇa, peaceful and free from all saṁsāra's sufferings.

2.3 THE REFUGE OF GREAT BEINGS

The sight of all beings plunged in the great ocean of saṁsāra's infinite sufferings and undergoing an unimaginable variety of torments motivates us to take refuge with the idea of establishing them all in the unsurpassable and omniscient state of perfect and complete Buddhahood.

Of these three levels of motivation, here we should choose the way of great beings, taking refuge out of a desire to establish each one of the whole infinity of beings in the state of perfect Buddhahood.

The happiness of gods and men may seem at first sight to be true happiness. In fact, however, it is not free of suffering; and as soon as the effects of the good actions that lead them to those states of happiness are exhausted, they fall back into lower realms. Why strive to achieve the happiness of higher realms if it only lasts for a moment? The śrāvakas' and pratyekabuddhas' nirvāṇa brings peace and happiness, but to ourselves alone; when all beings—our mothers and fathers since beginningless time—are sinking in saṁsāra's infinite ocean of sufferings, not to try to help them would not be right. To take refuge in the Three Jewels with the wish that all beings may attain Buddhahood is, therefore, the way of great beings and the gateway to infinite merit. That is the way we, too, should adopt. It is said in the *Jewel Garland*:

> As there are infinite kinds of beings
> The wish to help them is infinite, too.

II. HOW TO TAKE REFUGE

According to the Basic Vehicle, one takes refuge in the Buddha as the teacher, in the Dharma as the path, and in the Saṅgha as companions along the way.

The general method of the extraordinary Secret Mantra Vehicle is to take refuge by offering body, speech and mind to the teacher, taking the yidams as support and the ḍākinīs as companions.

The special, sublime method of the Vajra Essence is to take refuge in the rapid path whereby one uses the channels as the nirmāṇakāya, trains the energies as the sambhogakāya and purifies the essences as the dharmakāya.

The ultimate and infallible refuge in the indestructible natural state is based on the primal wisdom inherent in the refuge. That wisdom's essential nature is emptiness; its natural expression is clarity; and its compassion is all-pervasive.[111] Taking refuge here means to realize in one's own mindstream, with total confidence, the great inseparability of these three aspects of primal wisdom.

Having gained a clear understanding of all these ways in which refuge should be taken, we now go on to the actual practice of taking refuge. First, visualize the field of merit[112] in the presence of which you will take refuge.

Consider that the place where you are is all a Buddhafield, beautiful and pleasant, made of all sorts of precious substances. The ground is as smooth as the surface of a mirror, without any hills, valleys or irregularities. In the middle, in front of you, grows a wish-fulfilling tree with five great branches spreading from its trunk. Its perfect leaves, flowers and fruit stretch so far to the east, south, west and north that they fill the entire sky, and every branch and twig is hung with a multitude of entrancing jewels and bells of many kinds.

On the central branch is a jewelled throne upheld by eight great lions. Seated upon the throne, on a seat consisting of a multi-coloured lotus,[113] a sun and a moon, is your own glorious root teacher, incomparable source of compassion, embodiment of all past, present and future Buddhas, appearing in the form of the great Vajradhara of Oḍḍiyāna. His body is of a compelling white colour with a rosy gleam. He has one face, two arms and two legs[114] and is seated in the royal posture.* In his right hand he holds a golden five-pronged vajra with the threatening gesture. In his left hand, which rests in the gesture of meditation, he holds a skull-cup containing a vase filled with the ambrosia of deathless wisdom. The lid of the vase is topped by a wish-fulfilling tree. He wears a brocade cloak, monastic robes and a long sleeved blue tunic, and on his head the lotus hat. Seated in union with him is his consort, the white ḍākinī Yeshe Tsogyal, holding a hooked knife and a skull cup.

Visualize him like this in the space before you, facing toward you. Above his head are all the lamas of the lineage, seated one above the other, each not quite touching the one below. The teachers of the general tantra transmission are innumerable, but here we visualize particularly the main figures of the *Heart-essence* lineage of the Great Perfection: Samantabhadra, the dharmakāya; Vajrasattva, the sambhogakāya; Garab Dorje, the nirmāṇakāya; the master Mañjuśrīmitra; Guru Śrī Siṃha; the learned Jñanasūtra; the great paṇḍita, Vimalamitra; Padmasambhava of Oḍḍiyāna and his three closest disciples, the King, Subject and Consort—the Dharma king Trisongdetsen, the great translator Vairotsana and the ḍākinī Yeshe Tsogyal; the omniscient Longchen Rabjampa; and Rigdzin Jigme Lingpa. Each of them should be visualized with their own particular ornaments and attributes. They are all surrounded by an inconceivable multitude of yidam deities of the four sections of tantra and by ḍākas and

* *rgyal po'i rol stabs*: the posture of royal ease, with the right leg half extended and the left bent in.

ḍākinīs.

On the front branch is the Buddha, the Conqueror Śākyamuni, surrounded by the thousand and two perfect Buddhas of this Good Kalpa as well as all the other Buddhas of the past, present and future and of the ten directions. All of them are in the supreme nirmāṇakya form, garbed in monastic robes, bearing all the thirty-two major marks of Buddhahood—the crown protuberance, the wheels marked on the soles of the feet and so on—and the eighty minor signs. They are seated in the vajra posture. Some are white, some yellow, some red, some green and some blue. Inconceivable rays of light stream forth from their bodies.

On the right-hand branch visualize the eight great Close Sons,[115] headed by the Bodhisattva Protectors of the Three Families—Mañjuśrī, Vajrapāṇi and Avalokiteśvara—and surrounded by the whole noble saṅgha of Bodhisattvas. They are white, yellow, red, green and blue. They all wear the thirteen ornaments of the sambhogakāya,[116] and are standing with both feet together.

On the left-hand branch visualize the two principal śrāvakas, Śāriputra and Maudgalyāyana, surrounded by the noble saṅgha of śrāvakas and pratyekabuddhas. All are white in colour, and dressed in the three monastic robes. They too are standing, holding their staffs and alms-bowls in their hands.[117]

On the rear branch visualize the Jewel of the Dharma in the form of piles of books. Topmost of them, encased in a lattice of lights, are the six million four hundred thousand tantras of the Great Perfection, the label of each volume facing towards you.* All these books appear very clearly and distinctly, and resonate with the spontaneous melody of the vowels and consonants.

Between the branches are all the glorious Dharma-protectors, both the wisdom protectors and the protectors constrained by the effect of their past actions.[118] The male protectors all face outwards; their activity is to prevent outer obstacles from coming in, protecting us from hindrances and conditions unfavourable to practising the Dharma and attaining enlightenment. The female protectors all face inwards; their activity is to keep inner accomplishments from leaking out.

Think of all these figures of refuge, with their immeasurable qualities of knowledge, love and power, leading you as your only great guide.

Imagine that your father in this lifetime is with you on your right and

* These are long Tibetan looseleaf volumes, wrapped in cloth, with a cloth label tucked in the left-hand end.

your mother on your left. In front of you, gathered together in an immense crowd covering the surface of the earth, are all beings of the three worlds and the six realms of existence, the first row consisting of all adversaries who detest you and all obstacle makers who harm you. All these beings with you are standing up, with the palms of their hands joined. Expressing respect with your body, do prostrations. Expressing respect with your speech, recite the refuge-prayer. Expressing respect with your mind, cultivate the following thought:

"O Teacher and Three Jewels, whatever happens to me, favourable or unfavourable, pleasant or painful, good or bad, whatever sickness and suffering befall me, I have no other refuge nor protection than you. You are my only protector, my only guide, my only shelter and my only hope. From now on until I reach the very heart of enlightenment,[119] I place all my trust and faith in you. I shall neither seek my father's counsel, nor ask my mother's advice, nor decide on my own. It is you, my teacher and the Three Jewels, that I take as my support. It is to you that I make my offerings. I pledge myself to you alone. I have no other refuge, no other hope than you!"

With this burning conviction, recite the following text:

> *In the Sugatas of the Three Roots, the true Three Jewels,*[120]
> *In the bodhicitta, nature of the channels, energies and essences*
> *And in the maṇḍala of essential nature, natural expression and compassion,*
> *I take refuge until I reach the heart of enlightenment.*[121]

Say this as many times as possible in each session. Until you have said it at least one hundred thousand times, be sure to practise it in distinct sessions[122] and make it your constant and most important practice.

You might wonder why your enemies and obstacle-makers are given precedence over your parents in the refuge practice, since they are visualized at the front of the crowd, while your father and mother are beside you at the back. The reason is that we who have undertaken the Great Vehicle must have the love and compassion of bodhicitta equally for the whole infinity of beings. More particularly, the only way to accumulate an immense amount of merit and not waste all that we have already accumulated is to make patience our main practice. As it is said:

> How could we practice patience if there were no-one who made us angry?

It is the harm caused by enemies and obstacle makers that gives you the opportunity to develop patience. Careful observation will show you that, from the point of view of Dharma, enemies and obstacle makers are kinder to you than your own parents. Your parents, by teaching you all the trickery and deceit necessary to succeed in this world, can prevent you from getting free from the depths of the lower realms in your future lives. So their kindness is not as great as it seems. On the other hand, enemies and obstacle makers are extremely kind to you. It is the adversity your enemies cause you that provides you with a reason for practising patience. They separate you, whether you like it or not, from your wealth and possessions—the bonds that prevent you from ever getting free from saṁsāra and therefore the very source of all suffering. Negative forces and obstacle makers, too, provide you with a focus for the practice of patience. Through the illnesses and sufferings they provoke, many past misdeeds are purified. What is more, enemies and obstacles bring you to the Dharma, as happened to Jetsun Mila, whose uncle and aunt robbed him of all his wealth, and to the nun Palmo, who, because she had been stricken with leprosy by a demon nāga, devoted herself to the practice of Avalokiteśvara and subsequently attained supreme accomplishment. The Omniscient Longchenpa, King of Dharma, says:

> Assailed by afflictions, we discover Dharma
> And find the way to liberation. Thank you, evil forces!
> When sorrows invade the mind, we discover Dharma
> And find lasting happiness. Thank you, sorrows!
> Through harm caused by spirits we discover Dharma
> And find fearlessness. Thank you, ghosts and demons!
> Through people's hate we discover Dharma
> And find benefits and happiness. Thank you, those who hate us!
> Through cruel adversity, we discover Dharma
> And find the unchanging way. Thank you, adversity!
> Through being impelled to by others, we discover Dharma
> And find the essential meaning. Thank you, all who drive us on!
> We dedicate our merit to you all, to repay your kindness.

Not only have your enemies, therefore, been very kind to you in this life; they have also been your parents in past lives. This is why you should give them such an important place in this practice.

When the time comes to conclude the session, visualize that your yearning devotion causes innumerable rays of light to stream out from the refuge deities. The rays touch you and all sentient beings, and, like a flock of birds scattered by a slingstone, you all fly up with a whirring sound and dissolve into the assembly of deities.

Then the surrounding deities melt into light, from the outside inwards, and dissolve into the teacher in the centre, embodiment of the three refuges. All the deities above the teacher's head also dissolve into him. The teacher then dissolves and vanishes into light. Rest for as long as you can in the primordial state free from all elaboration, the dharmakāya, without any movement of thought.

As you arise from this meditation, dedicate the merit to the infinity of beings with these words:

> *Through the merit of this practice,*
> *May I swiftly accomplish the Three Jewels*
> *And establish every single being,*
> *Without exception, on their level.*

Remember the deities of the refuge constantly, in all situations. When you walk, visualize them in space above your right shoulder and imagine that you are circumambulating them. When you sit, visualize them above your head as the support of your prayers. When you eat, visualize them in your throat and offer them the first part of your food or drink. When you sleep, visualize them in your heart centre. This practice is essential to dissolve delusions into clear light.

Whatever you are doing, never separate from a clear mental image of the refuge deities. Entrust yourself with total confidence to the Three Jewels and devote yourself entirely to taking refuge.

III. PRECEPTS AND BENEFITS OF TAKING REFUGE

1. The precepts of taking refuge

The precepts consist of three things to be abandoned, three things to be done, and three additional attitudes which are to be observed.

1.1 THE THREE THINGS TO BE ABANDONED

Having taken refuge in the Buddha, do not pay homage to deities within saṁsāra. In other words, since the gods of the tīrthikas, like Īśvara or Viṣṇu, are themselves not liberated from the suffering of saṁsāra, nor are local gods, owners of the ground, or any other powerful worldly gods and spirits, you should not take them as your refuge for future lives, make offerings to them, or prostrate to them.

Having taken refuge in the Dharma, do not harm others, even in your dreams. Make vigorous efforts to protect them to the best of your ability.

Having taken refuge in the Saṅgha, do not get involved with tīrthikas and other such people who do not believe in the teaching of the Conquerors or in the perfect Buddha who taught it. Although there are no real tīrthikas in Tibet, you should also avoid getting involved with anyone who acts like a tīrthika—who insults and criticizes your teacher and the Dharma, for instance, or who denigrates the profound teachings of Secret Mantrayāna.

1.2 THE THREE THINGS TO BE DONE

Having taken refuge in the Buddha, honour and respect even a tiny piece of broken statue representing him. Raise it above your head,* put it somewhere clean, have faith and perceive it with pure vision, considering it as the true Jewel of the Buddha.

Having taken refuge in the Dharma, respect even a fragment of paper bearing a single syllable of the scriptures. Place it above you head and consider it to be the true Jewel of the Dharma.

Having taken refuge in the Saṅgha, consider anything that symbolizes it, be it no more than a patch of red or yellow cloth, as the true Jewel of the Saṅgha. Honour and respect it, raise it above your head, put it somewhere clean and regard it with faith and pure vision.

1.3 THE THREE SUPPLEMENTARY PRECEPTS

Look upon your teacher, the spiritual friend who teaches you here and now what to do and what not to do, as the true Jewel of the Buddha. Do not even so much as walk on his shadow, and endeavour to serve and honour him.

Consider every word of your sublime teacher as the Jewel of the Dharma. Accept everything he says without disobeying a single point.

Consider his entourage, his disciples and your spiritual companions who have pure conduct as the Jewel of the Saṅgha. Respect them with your body, speech and mind and never upset them, even for an instant.

Particularly in the Secret Mantra Vehicle, the teacher is the main refuge: his body is the Saṅgha, his speech the Dharma and his mind the Buddha. Recognize him, therefore, as the quintessential union of the

* To carry something on the crown of one's head is a sign of veneration.

Three Jewels and see all his actions as perfect. Follow him with absolute trust and try to pray to him all the time. Remember that to displease him with anything you do, say or think is to renounce the entire refuge, so put all your determination and effort into trying to please him all the time.

No matter what happens to you, be it pleasant or unpleasant, good or bad, sickness or suffering, entrust yourself entirely to the Jewel of the teacher. Recognize all well-being as springing from the compassion of the Three Jewels. It is said that everything pleasant and good in this world—even the slightest breeze on a hot day—comes from the compassion and blessings of the Buddha. In the same way, the smallest positive thought arising in your mind results from the inconceivable power of his blessings. In *The Way of the Bodhisattva*, Śāntideva says:

> As when a flash of lightning rends the night,
> And in its glare shows all the dark black clouds had hid,
> Likewise rarely, through the Buddhas' power,
> Virtuous thoughts rise, brief and transient, in the world.

So recognize the Buddha's compassion in everything that helps you and makes you happy.

Whenever you encounter sickness or suffering, when demons and enemies create obstacles, or whatever else may befall you, just pray to the Three Jewels and do not rely on any other methods of dealing with such problems. If you have to undergo medical treatment or make use of a healing ritual, do so in the recognition that those very things are the activity of the Three Jewels.

Learn to have faith and pure perception by recognizing everything that appears as being manifested by the Three Jewels. When you set off to go somewhere, whether to work or for some other reason, go there paying homage to the Buddha, Dharma and Saṅgha of that direction. Make the refuge prayer your constant daily practice, whether you use the text of the *Heart-essence* quoted above or this prayer known as the fourfold refuge, which is common to all vehicles:

> I take refuge in the Teacher.
> I take refuge in the Buddha.
> I take refuge in the Dharma.
> I take refuge in the Saṅgha.

Recommend to other people that they take refuge and encourage them in the refuge practice. Entrust yourself and others to the Three Jewels both for this life and for lives to come, and practise the refuge diligently.

When you go to sleep, visualize the deities of the field of merit, as described above but in your heart, and fall asleep with your mind concentrated upon them. If you cannot do that, think of your teacher and the Three Jewels as being really present by your pillow, full of love and compassion for you. Then fall asleep with faith and pure perception, without losing the thought of the Three Jewels.

When you eat or drink, visualize the Three Jewels in your throat and offer them the taste of everything you eat or drink. If you cannot do that, offer them the first mouthful or sip, thinking, "I offer this to the Three Jewels."

When you have new clothes to wear, before putting them on for the first time lift them up and offer them mentally to the Three Jewels. Then wear them with the thought that the Three Jewels have given them to you.

Whenever you see anything that gives you joy or that you find desirable, offer it mentally to the precious Three Jewels: lovely gardens full of flowers, streams of clear water, beautiful houses, pleasant groves, vast wealth and possessions, beautiful men and women in fine clothes.

When drawing water, throw a few drops into the air and say "I offer this water to the Three Jewels," before pouring it into your container.

All good and desirable circumstances in this life—comfort, happiness, popularity, profit or whatever—spring from the compassion of the Three Jewels. With devotion and pure perception think, "I offer all this to them." Offer to them whatever sources of merit you create—prostrations, offerings, meditation on deities, recitation of mantras and so on—and dedicate them to the benefit of all beings. Make offerings to the Three Jewels as often as you can, on full and new moon days, and in the six periods of the day.* Always observe the special times consecrated to the Three Jewels.

Whatever happens, good or bad, never forget to take refuge in the Three Jewels. Train yourself until you reach the point where even feeling afraid in a nightmare you remember to take refuge, because that means that you will also remember to do so in the intermediate state. In short, place your entire trust in the Three Jewels and never give up the refuge even at the cost of your life.

Once, in India, a Buddhist lay practitioner was taken prisoner by some tīrthikas, who told him: "If you renounce taking refuge in the Three Jewels we won't kill you. Otherwise we'll put you to death."

* *dus drug*, six times: three times in the day and three times in the night.

He replied, "I can only renounce taking refuge with my mouth. I could never do so with my heart." So they killed him.

We should really be like that layman. Once we give up taking refuge in the Three Jewels, then no matter how profound the practices we undertake may be we are no longer even part of the Buddhist community. It is said:

> It is the refuge that makes the difference between a Buddhist and a non-Buddhist.

There are plenty of tīrthikas who avoid harmful acts, meditate on deities, practise on the channels and energies, and who obtain the common accomplishments. But, not knowing the refuge in the Three Jewels, they are not on the path to liberation and will not be free from saṁsāra.[123]

There was not a single one of all the multitude of sūtra and tantra teachings that Jowo Atīśa did not know or had not read. But of all of them, he thought that the refuge was of such primary importance that it was the one thing he used to teach his disciples—to the extent that people nicknamed him the "Refuge Paṇḍita."

So, from the moment you enter the path of liberation and become a Buddhist, practise the taking of refuge along with its precepts, and never give them up even if your life is at stake. As a sūtra puts it:

> Those who take refuge in the Buddha
> Are true lay followers;
> They no longer should seek refuge
> In any other deity.
> Those who take refuge in the sacred Dharma
> Should have no harmful thoughts.
> Those who take refuge in the noble Saṅgha
> Should no longer associate with tīrthikas.

These days, some people claim to be followers of the Three Jewels but do not have the slightest respect for their representations. They consider paintings and statues representing the Buddha or books containing his words to be ordinary goods that can be sold or pawned. This is called "living by holding the Three Jewels to ransom" and is a very severe fault. To point out the ugliness of a drawing or statue of the Buddha or otherwise criticize it, unless you are evaluating its proportions in order to fix it, is also a grave error and should be avoided. To place books containing the scriptures directly on the floor, to step over them, to wet your fingers with saliva to turn the pages and similar disrespectful behaviour are all serious mistakes as well. The Buddha himself said:

> At the end of five hundred years
> My presence will be in the form of scriptures.
> Consider them as identical to me
> And show them due respect.

It is an everyday maxim that one should not put images on top of the scriptures. For it is the representation of the speech of the Buddha, rather than that of his body or mind, that teaches us what to do and what not to do and also ensures the continuity of his doctrine. The scriptures are therefore no different from the Buddha himself, and are particularly sacred.

Furthermore, most people do not think of a vajra and bell* as anything but ordinary objects. They do not appreciate that they are representations of the Three Jewels. The vajra symbolizes the Buddha's mind, the five wisdoms. The bell bears the image of a face which, according to the outer tantras, is that of Vairocana and, in the view of higher tantras, is Vajradhatvishvari. In other words, it bears an image of the Buddha's body. The letters engraved on it are the eight seed-syllables of the eight consorts, and the bell itself symbolizes the Buddha's speech, the sound of the Dharma. So together, vajra and bell fulfil all the criteria of representations of the Buddha's body, speech and mind. More particularly, these two objects contain all the maṇḍalas of the Secret Mantra Vajrayāna, and so are considered extraordinary samaya objects. To treat them with disrespect is therefore a grave fault. Always venerate them.

2. The benefits of taking refuge

Taking refuge is the foundation of all practices. By simply taking refuge you plant the seed of liberation within yourself. You distance yourself from all the negative actions you have accumulated and develop more and more positive actions. Taking refuge is the support for all vows, the source of all good qualities. Ultimately, it will lead you to the state of Buddhahood. And in the meanwhile it will secure you the protection of beneficent gods and the realization of all you wish for; you will never part company from the thought of the Three Jewels; you will remember them from life to life and find happiness and well-being in this present existence

* The vajra and bell are "samaya objects," sacred objects required for the practices of the Vajrayāna (see glossary).

and in rebirths to come. Its benefits are said to be innumerable.

In *The Seventy Stanzas on Refuge*, it is said:

> Indeed, anyone can take the vows,
> Except those who have not taken refuge.

Taking refuge is the indispensable basis for all the vows of the Prātimokṣa, those of a lay practitioner, a novice, a monk and so on. Before generating bodhicitta, receiving the empowerments of the Secret Mantra Vajrayāna, and all other practices, it is essential to take a complete and authentic refuge vow. There is no way to begin even a one-day practice of purification and reparation* without first taking refuge. It is the support for all vows and all good qualities.

To take refuge with a faith fully cognizant of the qualities of the Three Jewels unquestionably brings benefit. But even simply to hear the word "Buddha," or to create any link, tenuous though it may be, with any representation of the Buddha's body, speech and mind can plant the seed of liberation, and in the end will lead to the state beyond suffering. In the Vinaya, the story is told of a dog who chased a pig around a stūpa. Through this "circumambulation," the seed of enlightenment was sown in both of them.

According to another story, three people attained Buddhahood because of a single clay *tsa-tsa*. There was once a man who saw a little clay *tsa-tsa* statue lying on the ground by the road.

"If it stays there," he thought, "the rain will soon ruin it; I'd better do something about it." So he covered it with an old leather shoe sole that had been left lying nearby.

Another person, passing the same spot, thought to himself, "It's not right to have an old shoe sole covering that *tsa-tsa*," and so he took it off.

As the fruit of their good intentions, both the one who covered the *tsa-tsa* and the one who removed the covering inherited kingdoms in their next lives.

> With pure intention, he who covered
> The Buddha's head with a shoe
> And he who then uncovered it again
> Both inherited a kingdom.

Three people—the person who had moulded the *tsa-tsa* in the first place, the person who then covered it with the sole of a shoe, and the person

* *gso sbyong*: a ritual for purifying and repairing errors in keeping the various vows.

who finally uncovered it—all obtained the happiness of higher realms, inheriting kingdoms and so forth, as a temporary benefit, and at the same time progressed towards Buddhahood by sowing in themselves the seed of ultimate liberation.

By taking refuge you distance yourself from all negative actions. Taking refuge in the Three Jewels with sincere and intense faith reduces and exhausts even the evil actions you have already accumulated in the past. And from that moment onwards, the compassionate blessings of the Three Jewels render all your thoughts positive, so that you no longer do anything harmful.

An example is King Ajātaśatru, who killed his father but later took refuge in the Three Jewels. He suffered the agonies of hell for one week and was then freed.

And Devadatta, who had committed three of the crimes which bring immediate retribution, even experienced the fires of hell while he was still alive. But at that moment he had faith in the Buddha's teaching and cried out, "I am determined from the depths of my bones to take refuge in the Buddha!" The Buddha explained that because of these words Devadatta would become a pratyekabuddha called Utterly Determined.[124]

Now, therefore, through the kindness of a teacher or spiritual friend, you have already received the authentic Dharma and have given rise to some slight intention to do good and to stop doing wrong. If you make the effort to practise taking refuge in the Three Jewels, your mind will be blessed and you will increasingly develop all the good qualities of the path, such as faith, purity of perception, disillusionment with saṁsāra and determination to get free from it, faith in the effects of actions, and so on.

On the other hand, no matter how intense your disgust with saṁsāra or your determination to achieve liberation may be now, if you do not bother to take refuge in the teacher and the Three Jewels or pray to them, appearances are so seductive, the mind so gullible and thoughts so quick to deceive, that, even while you are doing good, this can easily turn into something negative. So it is important to know that there is nothing better than taking refuge for cutting the stream of negative actions for the future.

Now for another important point. It is said:

> Demons particularly hate those who persevere in the practice.

And also:

> The more intense the practice, the more intense the demons.

We are in an age of decadence, and people who meditate on the profound meaning and whose good actions are powerful can easily be deceived by the seductions of ordinary life. They are held back by families and friends. They suffer from adverse circumstances like sickness and interference from negative forces. Their minds are invaded by thoughts and hesitations. In many such guises, obstacles to Dharma practice come up and destroy all their merit. But as the antidote to these dangers, if you make a real effort to take refuge sincerely in the Three Jewels, everything that opposes your practice will be transformed into favourable circumstances and your merit will grow unceasingly.

Nowadays householders, announcing that they are going to protect themselves and their flocks from disease for the year, call in some lamas and their disciples—none of whom have received the necessary empowerment or oral transmission, nor practised the basic recitation[125]—to open up the maṇḍala of some wrathful deity.[126] Without going through the generation and perfection phases, they goggle with eyes like saucers and whip themselves into an overwhelming fury directed at an effigy made of dough.* They always perform "red offerings" of flesh and blood, and their cries of "Bring them! Kill them! Just you wait... Hit them!" arouse feelings of violent aggression in everybody who hears them. A closer look at such ceremonies shows that they are as Jetsun Mila says:

> Inviting the wisdom deities to protect worldly beings is like dragging a king off his throne and making him sweep the floor.

Padampa Sangye says:

> They build a Secret Mantra maṇḍala in the village goat-pen and claim that it is an antidote!

Practices of this sort poison the Secret Mantrayāna and transform it into the practices of the Bönpos.[127] Those who perform "liberation" practices should be beyond all self-centred interest. Only such people, acting on a vast scale for the benefit of beings and the teachings, may legitimately liberate enemies and obstacle-makers who are committing the ten pernicious acts. But when such a practice is done with ordinary anger,[128] taking sides, not only will it have no power to liberate the beings at which it is directed, it will also cause rebirth in hell for the people who perform it.

For someone not accomplished in the generation and perfection phases

* Correctly understood, such an effigy symbolizes the false notion of a truly existing self. Here sacred ritual is being used in an external way, contrary to its intention.

and who does not observe the samayas, the performance of the "red offerings" of meat and blood brings realization neither of the wisdom deities nor of the Dharma protectors. Instead, all kinds of malevolent gods and demons gather to partake of the offerings and tormas. They might seem to bring about some immediate benefit, but the final outcome will be a multitude of undesirable consequences.

A far better protection than all of that would be to place your confidence in the Three Jewels. Ask teachers and monks who have pacified and controlled their own minds to recite the refuge a hundred thousand times. You will be brought into the care of the Three Jewels; nothing undesirable will happen to you in this life and all your wishes will be realized spontaneously. Beneficent gods will protect you, and all those who might do you harm—the demons and obstacle makers—will be unable even to approach.

Once someone caught a thief and gave him a beating, accompanying each very hard blow of the stick with a line from the refuge prayer:

"I go for refuge to the Buddha," whack! "I go for refuge to the Dharma," whack! and so on.

Having inculcated those lines firmly into the robber's mind, he let him go. The robber spent the night under a bridge, his mind filled with the words of the refuge prayer, along with the memory of the painful thrashing he had received. While he was lying there a whole troop of demons drew near over the bridge. But then they cried, "There is someone here who takes refuge in the Three Jewels!" and all ran away screaming.

There is no better way to dispel the ills of this life than to take refuge from the bottom of your heart in the Three Jewels. And in future lives it will bring you liberation and omniscience. It is hard to even imagine all the benefits of the refuge. The *Immaculate Sūtra* says:

> If all the merit of taking refuge
> Were to take a physical form,
> The whole of space, entirely filled,
> Would not be enough to contain it.

And in the *Condensed Transcendent Wisdom*:

> If the merit of taking refuge took form,
> All the three worlds could never contain it.
> Could the vast amount of water in all the great oceans
> Ever be measured with a quarter-pint scoop?

What is more, as the *Sūtra of the Heart of the Sun* says:

He who has made the Buddha his refuge
Cannot be killed by ten million demons;
Though he transgress his vows or be tormented in mind,
It is certain that he will go beyond rebirth.

Devote yourself earnestly, therefore, to taking refuge, the basis of all Dharma practices, for its benefits are immeasurable.

I have taken the threefold refuge but have little heartfelt faith.
I follow the threefold training, but have let my commitments slip.
Bless me and all those who are faint-hearted like me
That our faith may be firm and irreversible.

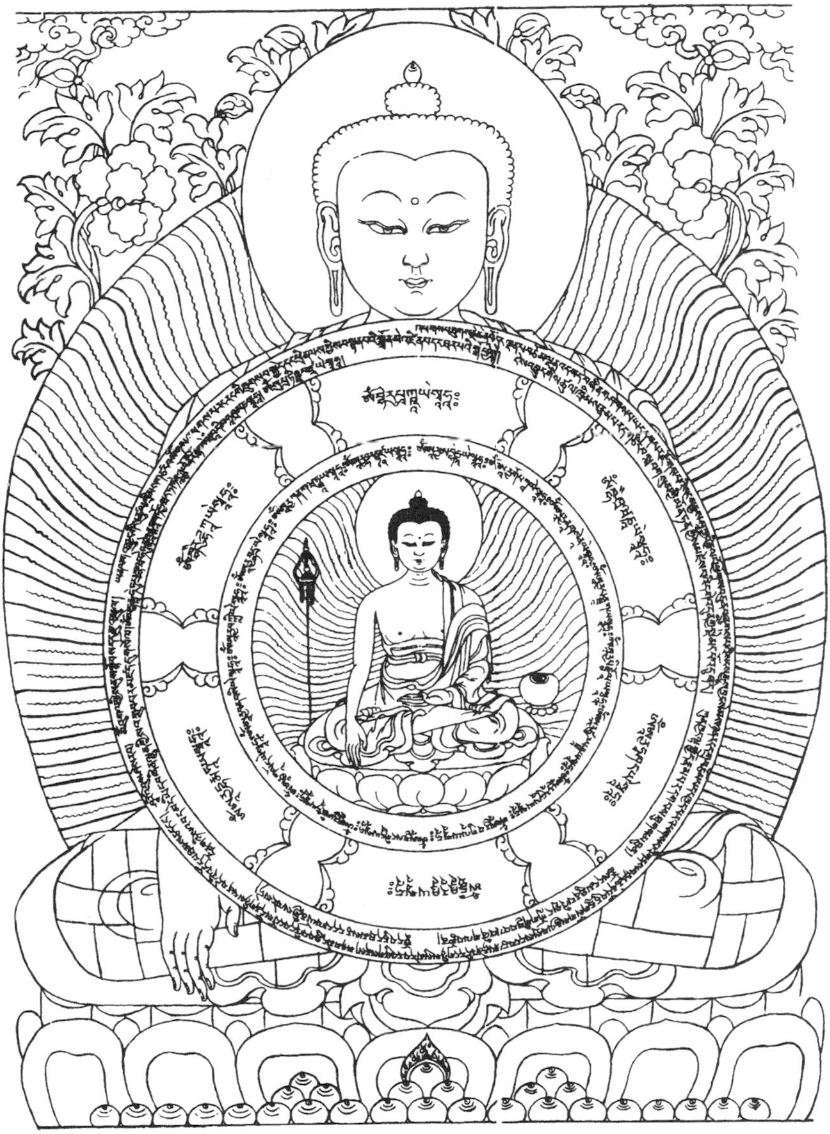

༢ གནམ་ཆོས་མི་འགྱུར་རྡོ་རྗེའི་ཐོར་ཚོམས་གཏེར་ཁ་ལས་བྱུང་བའི་འདུས་པ་མཆོད་པའི་ཐོ་ཐེར་ལོ།

Śāntideva (7th-8th centuries)
Author of *The Way of the Bodhisattva* (*Bodhicaryāvatāra*), the great classic of Indian Mahāyāna literature.

CHAPTER TWO

Arousing bodhicitta, the root of the Great Vehicle

Through your great wisdom, you have realized nirvāṇa.
Through your great compassion, you willingly embrace saṁsāra.
Through your skill in methods you have realized that they are no different.
Peerless Teacher, at your feet I bow.

This chapter has three sections: training the mind in the four boundless qualities; arousing bodhicitta, the mind turned towards supreme enlightenment; and training in the precepts of bodhicitta in aspiration and bodhicitta in application.

I. TRAINING THE MIND IN THE FOUR BOUNDLESS QUALITIES

The four boundless qualities are boundless love, compassion, sympathetic joy and impartiality. Love is usually dealt with first. But when we practise the four one after the other as a training for the mind, we should start by developing impartiality. Otherwise, whatever love, compassion and sympathetic joy we generate will tend to be one-sided and not completely pure. In this case, therefore, we begin with the meditation on impartiality.

1. Meditation on impartiality

Impartiality (*tang nyom* in Tibetan) means giving up (*tang*) our hatred for enemies and infatuation with friends, and having an even-minded (*nyom*) attitude towards all beings, free of attachment to those close to us and aversion for those who are distant.

As things are now, we are very attached to those we think of as part of our own group—father and mother, relatives and so on—while we feel an intolerable aversion towards our enemies and those associated with them. This is a mistake, and comes from a lack of investigation.

In former lives, those whom we now consider our enemies have surely been close to us, ever lovingly at our side, looking after us with goodwill and giving us unimaginable help and support. Conversely, many of those whom we now call friends have certainly been against us and done us harm. As we saw in the chapter on impermanence, this is illustrated by the words of the sublime Kātyāyana:

> He eats his father's flesh, he beats his mother off,
> He dandles on his lap his own unfortunate enemy;
> The wife is gnawing at her husband's bones.
> I laugh to see what happens in saṁsāra's show!

Another example is the story of Princess Pema Sel, daughter of the Dharma King Trisong Detsen. When she died at the age of seventeen, her father went to ask Guru Rinpoche how such a thing could happen.

"I would have thought that my daughter must have been someone with pure past actions," said the king. "She was born as the daughter of King Trisong Detsen. She met all of you translators and paṇḍitas, who are like real Buddhas. So how can it be that her life was nevertheless so short?"

"It was not at all because of any pure past deeds that the princess was born as your daughter," the Master replied. "Once I, Padma, you, the great Dharma King, and the great Bodhisattva Abbot had been born as three low-caste boys. We were building the Great Stūpa of Jarung Khashor. At that time the princess had taken birth as an insect, which stung you on the neck. Brushing it off with your hand, you accidentally killed it. Because of the debt you incurred in taking that life, the insect was reborn as your daughter."[129]

If even the children of Dharma King Trisong Detsen, who was Mañjuśrī in person,* could be born to him in that way as the result of his past

* Trisong Detsen is considered to be an emanation of the Bodhisattva Mañjuśrī.

actions, what can one say about other beings?

At present we are closely linked with our parents and our children. We feel great affection for them and have incredible aspirations for them. When they suffer, or anything undesirable happens to them, we are more upset than we would be if such things had happened to us personally. All this is simply the repayment of debts for the harm we have done each other in past lives.

Of all the people who are now our enemies, there is not one who has not been our father or mother in the course of all our previous lives. Even now, the fact that we consider them to be against us does not necessarily mean that they are actually doing us any harm. There are some we think of as opponents who, from their side, do not see us in that way at all. Others might feel that they are our enemies but are quite incapable of doing us any real harm. There are also people who at the moment seem to be harming us, but in the long term what they are doing to us might bring us recognition and appreciation in this life, or make us turn to the Dharma and thus bring us much benefit and happiness. Yet others, if we can skilfully adapt to their characters and win them over with gentle words until we reach some agreement, might quite easily turn into friends.

On the other hand there are all those whom we normally consider closest to us—our children, for example. But there are sons and daughters who have cheated or even murdered their parents. Sometimes children side with people who have a dispute with their parents, and join forces with them to quarrel with their own family and plunder their wealth. Even when we get along well with those who are dear to us, their sorrows and problems actually affect us even more strongly than our own difficulties. In order to help our friends, our children and our other relatives, we pile up great waves of negative actions which will sweep us into the hells in our next life. When we really want to practise the Dharma properly they hold us back. Unable to give up our obsession with parents, children, and family, we keep putting off Dharma practice until later, and so never find the time for it. In short, such people may harm us even more than our enemies.

What is more, there is no guarantee that those we consider adversaries today will not be our children in future lives, or that our present friends will not be reborn as our enemies, and so on. It is only because we take these fleeting perceptions of "friend" and "enemy" as real that we accumulate negative actions through attachment and hatred. Why do we hold on to this millstone which will drag us down into the lower realms?

Make a firm decision, therefore, to see all infinite beings as your own parents and children. Then, like the great beings of the past whose lives we can read about, consider all friends and enemies as the same.

First, toward all those you do not like at all—those who arouse anger and hatred in you—train your mind by various means so that the anger and hatred you feel for them no longer arise. Think of them as you would of someone neutral, who does you neither good nor harm. Then reflect that the innumerable beings to whom you feel neutral have been your father or mother sometime during your past lives throughout time without beginning. Meditate on this theme, training yourself until you feel the same love for them as you do for your present parents. Finally, meditate until you feel the same compassion toward all beings—whether you see them as friends, enemies or in between—as you do for your own parents.

Now, it is no substitute for boundless impartiality just to think of everybody, friends and enemies, as the same, without any particular feeling of compassion, hatred or whatever. That is mindless impartiality, and brings neither harm nor benefit. The image given for truly boundless impartiality is a banquet given by a great sage. When the great sages of old offered feasts they would invite everyone, high or low, powerful or weak, good or bad, exceptional or ordinary, without making any distinction whatsoever. Likewise, our attitude toward all beings throughout space should be a vast feeling of compassion, encompassing them all equally. Train your mind until you reach such a state of boundless impartiality.

2. Meditation on love

Through meditating on boundless impartiality as described, you come to regard all beings of the three worlds with the same great love. The love that you feel for all of them should be like that of parents taking care of their young children. They ignore all their children's ingratitude and all the difficulties involved, devoting their every thought, word and deed entirely to making their little ones happy, comfortable and cosy. Likewise, in this life and in all your future lives, devote everything you do, say or think to the well-being and happiness of all beings.

All those beings are striving for happiness and comfort. They all want to be happy and comfortable; not one of them wants to be unhappy or to suffer. Yet they do not understand that the cause of happiness is positive actions, and instead give themselves over to the ten negative actions. Their deepest wishes and their actions are therefore at odds: in their attempts to find happiness, they only bring suffering upon themselves.

Over and over again, meditate on the thought of how wonderful it would be if each one of those beings could have all the happiness and comfort they wish. Meditate on it until you want others to be happy just as intensely as you want to be happy yourself.

The sūtras speak of "loving actions of body, loving actions of speech, loving actions of mind." What this means is that everything you say with your mouth or do with your hands, instead of being harmful to others, should be straightforward and kind. As it says in *The Way of the Bodhisattva*:

> Whenever catching sight of others,
> Look on them with open, loving heart.

Even when you simply look at someone else, let that look be smiling and pleasant rather than an aggressive glare or some expression of anger. There are stories about this, like the one about the powerful ruler who glared at everyone with a very wrathful look. It is said that he was reborn as a preta living on left-overs under the stove of a house, and after that, because he had also looked at a holy being in that way, he was reborn in hell.

Whatever actions you do with your body, try to do them gently and pleasantly, endeavouring not to harm others but to help them. Your speech should not express such attitudes as contempt, criticism or jealousy. Make every single word you say pleasant and true. As for your mental attitude, when you help others do not wish for anything good in return. Do not be a hypocrite and try to make other people see you as a Bodhisattva because of your kind words and actions. Simply wish for others' happiness from the bottom of your heart and only consider what would be most beneficial for them. Pray again and again with these words: "Throughout all my lives, may I never harm so much as a single hair on another being's head, and may I always help each of them."

It is particularly important to avoid making anyone under your authority suffer, by beating them, forcing them to work too hard and so on. This applies to your servants and also to your animals, right down to the humblest watchdog. Always, under all circumstances, be kind to them in thought, word and deed. To be reborn as a servant, or as a watchdog for that matter, and to be despised and looked down upon by everyone, is the maturation of the effects of past actions. It is the reciprocal effect of having despised and looked down on others while in a position of power in a past life. If you now despise others because of your own power and wealth, you will repay that debt in some future life by being reborn as their servants. So be especially kind to those in a lower position than yourself.

Anything you can do physically, verbally or mentally to help your own parents, especially, or those suffering from chronic ill health, will bring inconceivable benefits. Jowo Atīśa says:

> To be kind to those who have come from afar, to those who have been ill for a long time, or to our parents in their old age, is equivalent to meditating on emptiness of which compassion is the very essence.

Our parents have shown us such immense love and kindness that to upset them in their old age would be an extremely negative act. The Buddha himself, to repay his mother's kindness, went to the Heaven of the Thirty-three to teach her the Dharma. It is said that even if we were to serve our parents by carrying them around the whole world on our shoulders, it would still not repay their kindness. However, we can repay that kindness by introducing them to the Buddha's teaching. So always serve your parents in thought, word and deed, and try to find ways to bring them to the Dharma.

The Great Master of Oḍḍiyāna said,

> Do not make old people distressed; look after them with care and respect.

In whatever you say and do, be kind to all those older than you. Take care of them and do whatever you can to please them.

Nowadays most people say that there is no way to get on in the samsaric world without harming others. But this is not true.

Long ago, in Khotan, two novices were meditating on the sublime Mañjuśrī.

One day, he appeared to them and said, "There is no karmic link between you and me. The deity with whom you have had a connection in your past lives is the great Avalokiteśvara. He is at present to be found in Tibet, over which he rules as the king.* You should go there to see him."

When the two novices arrived in Tibet and went within the walls of Lhasa, they could see that a large number of people had been executed or imprisoned. They asked what was going on.

"Those are punishments ordered by the king," they were told.

* The king was Songtsen Gampo, the first Buddhist king of Tibet, who is considered to be an incarnation of Avalokiteśvara.

"This king is most certainly not Avalokiteśvara," they said to themselves, and fearing that they might well be punished too, they decided to run away.

The king knew that they were leaving and sent a messenger after them summoning them to his presence.

"Do not be afraid," he told them. "Tibet is a wild land, hard to subjugate. For that reason I have had to produce the illusion of prisoners being executed, dismembered, and so on. But in reality, I have not harmed a single hair on anyone's head."

That king was the ruler of all Tibet, the Land of Snows, and brought kings in all four directions under his power. He vanquished invading armies and kept peace along the frontiers. Although he was obliged to conquer enemies and defend his subjects on such a vast scale, he managed to do so without harming so much as a hair on a single being's head. How could it not be possible for us, therefore, to avoid harming others as we look after our own tiny dwellings, which by comparison are no bigger than insects' nests?

Harming others brings harm in return. It just creates endless suffering for this life and the next. No good can ever come of it, even in the things of this life. No-one ever gets rich from murder, theft, or whatever it might be. They only end up paying the penalty and losing all their money and possessions in the process.

The image given for boundless love is a mother bird taking care of her chicks. She starts by making a soft, comfortable nest. She shelters them with her wings, keeping them warm. She is always gentle with them and she protects them until they can fly away. Like that mother bird, learn to be kind in thought, word and deed to all beings in the three worlds.

3. Meditation on compassion

The meditation on compassion is to imagine beings tormented by cruel suffering and to wish them free from it. As it is said:

> Think of someone in immense torment—a person cast into the deepest dungeon awaiting execution, or an animal standing before the butcher about to be slaughtered. Feel love towards that being as if it were your own mother or child.

Imagine a prisoner condemned to death by the ruler and being led to the place of execution, or a sheep being caught and tied up by the butcher.

When you think of a condemned prisoner, instead of thinking of that suffering person as someone else, imagine that it is you. Ask yourself what you would do in that situation. What now? There is nowhere to run. Nowhere to hide. No refuge and no-one to protect you. You have no means of escape. You cannot fly away. You have no strength, no army to defend you. Now, at this very moment, all the perceptions of this life are about to cease. You will even have to leave behind your own dear body that you have sustained with so much care, and set out for the next life. What anguish! Train your mind by taking the suffering of that condemned prisoner upon yourself.

And when you think of a sheep being led to the slaughter, do not think of it as just a sheep. Instead, feel sincerely that this is your own old mother that they are about to kill, and ask yourself what you would do in such a situation. What are you going to do now that they are going to kill your old mother, even though she has done no harm? Experience in the depth of your heart the kind of suffering that your mother must be going through. When your heart is bursting with the desire to do something right away to prevent your old mother from being butchered on the spot, reflect that although this suffering creature is not actually your father or mother in this present life, it is sure to have been your parent at some time in your past lives and to have brought you up with great kindness in just the same way. So there is no real difference. Alas for your poor parents who are suffering so much! If only they could be free from their distress right now, without delay—this very instant! With these thoughts in your heart, meditate with such unbearable compassion that your eyes fill with tears.

When your compassion is aroused, think how all this suffering is the effect of harmful actions committed in the past. All those poor beings now indulging in harmful actions will inevitably have to suffer too. With this in mind, meditate with compassion on all beings who are creating causes of suffering for themselves by killing and other harmful actions.

Then consider the suffering of all beings born in the hells, among the pretas and other realms of torment. Identify with them as if they were your parents, or yourself, and meditate on compassion with great energy.

Finally, reflect deeply upon all beings in the three worlds. Wherever there is space there are beings. Wherever there are beings, there are negative actions and the resulting suffering. Poor beings, involved only in all that negative action and suffering! How wonderful it would be if each individual being of the six realms could be free from all the perceptions brought about by past actions, all those sufferings and negative tendencies, and attain the everlasting happiness of perfect Buddhahood.

When you start meditating on compassion, it is important to focus first on suffering beings individually, one at a time, and only then to train yourself step by step until you can meditate on all beings as a whole. Otherwise your compassion will be vague and intellectual. It will not be the real thing.

Reflect particularly on the sufferings and hardships of your own cattle, sheep, packhorses and other domestic animals. We inflict all sorts of barbarity on such creatures, comparable to the torments of hell. We pierce their noses, castrate them, pull out their hair and bleed them alive.* Not even for a moment do we consider that these animals might be suffering. If we think about it carefully, the trouble is that we have not cultivated compassion. Think about it carefully: right now, were someone to pull out a single strand of your hair you would cry out in pain—you would not put up with it at all. Yet we twist out all the long belly-hairs of our yaks, leaving a red weal of bare flesh behind, and from where each hair was growing a drop of blood begins to flow. Although the beast is grunting with pain, it never crosses our mind that it is suffering.

We cannot stand having a blister on our hand. Sometimes when our backsides hurt from travelling on horseback we can no longer sit in the saddle and have to ride sidesaddle instead. But it never occurs to us that the horse might be weary or suffering. When it can no longer go on and it stumbles, panting for breath, we still think that it is just being stubborn. We lose our temper and thrash it without a moment's sympathy.

Think of an individual animal—a sheep, for example—that is being slaughtered. First, as it is dragged from the flock, it is struck with paralyzing fear. A blood-blister comes up where it has been grabbed. It is thrown on its back; its feet are tied together with a leather thong and its muzzle bound till it suffocates.** If, in the throes of its agony, the animal is a little slow in dying, the butcher, that man of evil actions, just gets irritated.

"Here's one that doesn't want to die!" says he, and hits it.

Hardly is the sheep dead than it is already being skinned and gutted. At the same time another beast is being bled till it cannot walk straight. The blood of the dead animal is mixed with the blood of the living one and the mixture is cooked up as sausages in the entrails of the one already disembowelled.† Anyone who can eat such things afterwards must be a real cannibal.

* The softer belly hair of the yak, used as wool, is pulled out rather than shorn. Blood from living yaks is used to make sausages.

** In Tibet, it is common to slaughter animals by suffocation.

† As blood-sausages. This follows a local belief that a mixture of the blood of a living animal and the blood of a dead one increases vitality.

Think carefully about the suffering of these animals. Imagine that you yourself are undergoing that suffering and see what it is like. Cover your mouth with your hands and stop yourself breathing. Stay like that for a while. Experience the pain and the panic. When you have really seen what it is like, think again and again how sad it is that all those beings are afflicted by such terrible sufferings without a moment's respite. If only you had the power to give them refuge from all these sufferings!

Lamas and monks are the people who are supposed to have the most compassion. But they have none at all. They are worse than householders when it comes to making beings suffer. This is a sign that the era of the Buddha's teaching is really approaching its end. We have reached a time when flesh-eating demons and ogres are given all the honours. In the past, our Teacher, Śākyamuni, rejected the kingdom of a universal monarch[130] as though it were so much spit in the dust, and became a renunciate. With his Arhat followers he went on foot, begging for alms, bowl and staff in hand. Not only did they do without packhorses and mules, but even the Buddha himself had no mount to ride. That was because he felt that to make another being suffer was not the way of the Buddhist teaching. Could the Buddha really not have been resourceful enough to find himself an old horse to ride?

Our own venerables, however, as they set out for a village ceremony, push a piece of rough twine through the ring-hole gouged in their yak's muzzle. Once they are hoisted into the saddle, they pull with both hands as hard as they can on the yak-hair cord, which digs into the animal's nostrils, causing unbearable pain and making the poor creature rear and plunge. So the rider, with all his strength, whacks it with his whip. Unable to stand this new pain on its flanks, the yak starts to run—but is pulled up again by the nose. The pain in its nostrils is now so unbearable that it stops in its tracks, and has to be whipped again. A tug in front, a whack behind, until soon the animal is aching and exhausted. Sweat drips from every hair, its tongue hangs out, its breath rasps, and it can no longer go on.

"What's the matter with him? He's still not moving properly," the rider thinks and, getting angry, digs the beast in the flanks with his whip handle, until in his rage he digs it in so hard that the handle breaks in two. He stuffs the pieces in his belt, picks up a sharp stone and, turning round in the saddle, slams it down hard on to the old yak's rump... all this because he feels not the slightest compassion for the animal.

Imagine yourself as an old yak, your back weighed down with a load far too heavy, a rope pulling you by the nostrils, your flanks whipped, your ribs bruised by the stirrups. In front, behind, and on both sides you feel only burning pain. Without a second's rest, you go up long slopes, down steep descents, you cross wide rivers and broad plains. With no chance to swallow even a mouthful of food, you are driven on against your will from the early dawn until late in the evening when the last glimmers of the setting sun have disappeared. Reflect on how difficult and exhausting it would be, what pain, hunger and thirst you would experience, and then take that suffering upon yourself. You cannot but feel intense and unbearable compassion.

Normally, those we call lamas and monks ought to be a refuge and a help—impartial protectors and guides of all beings. But in fact, they favour their patrons, the ones who give them food and drink and make offerings to them. They pray that these particular individuals may be sheltered and protected. They give them empowerments and blessings. And all the while they are ganging up to cast out all the pretas and mischievous spirits whose evil rebirth is the result of their unfortunate karma. The lamas performing such ceremonies work themselves up into a fury and make beating gestures, intoning, "Kill, kill! Strike, strike!"

Now surely, if anyone takes harmful spirits as something to be killed or beaten, it must be because his mind is under the power of attachment and hatred and he has never given rise to vast, impartial compassion. When you think about it carefully, those malignant spirits are far more in need of compassion than any benefactors. They have become harmful spirits because of their evil karma. Reborn as pretas, with horrible bodies, their pain and fear is unimaginable. They experience nothing but endless hunger, thirst and exhaustion. They perceive everything as threatening. As their minds are full of hate and aggression, many go to hell as soon as they die. Who could deserve more pity? The patrons may be sick and suffering, but that will help them to exhaust their evil karma, not to create more. Those evil spirits, on the other hand, are harming others with their evil intentions, and will be hurled by those harmful actions to the depths of the lower realms.

If the Conqueror, skilled in means and full of compassion, taught the art of exorcising or intimidating these harmful spirits with violent methods, it was out of compassion for them, like a mother spanking a child who will not obey her. He also permitted the ritual of liberation to be practised by those who have the power to interrupt the flow of evil deeds of beings who only do harm, and to transfer their consciousness to a pure realm. But as for pandering to benefactors, monks and others that we consider to be on our own side, and rejecting demons and wrongdoers as hateful enemies—protecting the one and attacking the other out of attachment and hatred—were such attitudes what the Conqueror taught? As long as we are driven by such feelings of attachment and hatred, it would be futile to try to expel or attack any harmful spirits. Their bodies are only mental and they will not obey us. They will only do us harm in return. Indeed—not to speak of desire and hate—as long as we even believe that such gods and spirits really exist and want them to go away, we will never subdue them.

When Jetsun Mila was living in the Garuḍa Fortress Cave in the Chong valley, the king of obstacle-makers, Vināyaka, produced a supernatural illusion. In his cave, Jetsun Mila found five *atsaras** with eyes the size of saucers. He prayed to his teacher and to his yidam, but the demons did not go away. He meditated on the visualization of his deity and recited wrathful mantras, but still they would not go.

Finally, he thought, "Marpa of Lhodrak showed me that everything in the universe is mind, and that the nature of mind is empty and radiant. To believe in these demons and obstacle-makers as something external and to want them to go away has no meaning."

Feeling powerful confidence in the view that knows spirits and demons to be simply one's own perceptions, he strode back into his cave. Terrified and rolling their eyes, the *atsaras* disappeared.

This is also what the Ogress of the Rock meant, when she sang to him:

> This demon of your own tendencies arises from your mind;
> If you don't recognize the nature of your mind,
> I'm not going to leave just because you tell me to go.
> If you don't realize that your mind is void,
> There are many more demons besides myself!
> But if you recognize the nature of your own mind,
> Adverse circumstances will serve only to sustain you
> And even I, Ogress of the Rock, will be at your bidding.

How, then, instead of having confidence in the view that recognizes all spirits and demons as being one's own mind, could we subjugate them by getting angry?

When clerics visit their patrons, they happily eat all the sheep that have been killed and served to them, without the least hesitation. When they perform special rituals to make offerings to the protectors, they claim that clean meat is needed as an ingredient. For them, this means the still

* *a tsa ra* is a corruption of the Sanskrit *ācārya*, and here means apparitions taking the form of Indian ascetics.

bleeding flesh and fat of a freshly killed animal, with which they decorate all the *tormas* and other offerings. Such fearful methods of intimidation can only be Bönpo or tīrthika rites—they are certainly not Buddhist. In Buddhism, once we have taken refuge in the Dharma we have to give up harming others. How could having an animal killed everywhere we go, and enjoying its flesh and blood, not be a contravention of the precepts of taking refuge? More particularly, in the Bodhisattva tradition of the Great Vehicle, we are supposed to be the refuge and protector of all infinite beings. But for those very beings with unfortunate karma that we are supposed to be protecting we feel not the slightest shred of compassion. Instead, those beings under our protection are murdered, their boiled flesh and blood set before us, and their protectors—we Bodhisattvas—then gleefully gobble it all up, smacking our lips. Could anything be more vicious and cruel?

The texts of the Secret Mantra Vajrayāna say:

> For whatever we have done to upset the siṁha and tramen*
> By not gathering offerings of flesh and blood according to the texts,
> We beg the ḍākinīs of the sacred places to forgive us.

Now here, "gathering offerings of flesh and blood according to the texts" means to gather them as explained in the tantric texts of the Secret Mantrayāna. What are the directives in those texts?

> The five types of meat and five ambrosias
> Are the food and drink of the outer feast gathering.

Offering a feast of flesh and blood according to the texts, therefore, means offering the five meats considered worthy samaya substances for the Secret Mantrayāna—namely, the flesh of humans, horses, dogs, elephants and cows. These five kinds of meat are undefiled by harmful action because these are all creatures which are not killed for food.[131] This is quite the opposite of sticking to concepts of clean and unclean in which human flesh, the flesh of dogs and the like are seen as unclean and inferior, and the succulent, fatty meat of an animal that has just been killed for food is seen as clean. Such attitudes are referred to as:

> Viewing the substances of the five samayas of relishing
> As pure and impure, or consuming them heedlessly,

in other words, having ideas of pure and impure which transgress the

* Symbolic deities of the maṇḍala.

samayas of relishing. Even those five acceptable kinds of meat may only be used if you have the power to transform the food you eat into ambrosia and if you are in the process of practising to attain particular accomplishments in a solitary place. To eat them casually in the village, just because you like the taste, is what is meant by "heedless consumption contrary to the samayas of relishing," and is also a transgression.

"Pure meat," therefore, does not mean the meat of an animal slaughtered for food, but "the meat of an animal that died because of its own past actions," meaning meat from an animal that died of old age, sickness, or other natural causes that were the effect of its own past actions alone.

The incomparable Dagpo Rinpoche said that taking the still warm flesh and blood of a freshly slaughtered animal and placing it in the maṇḍala would make all the wisdom deities faint. It is also said that offering to the wisdom deities the flesh and blood of a slaughtered animal is like murdering a child in front of its mother. If you invited a mother for a meal and then set before her the flesh of her own child, would she like it, or would she not like it? It is with the same love as a mother for her only child that the Buddhas and Bodhisattvas look on all beings of the three worlds. Slaughtering an innocent animal that has been the victim of its own bad actions and offering its flesh and blood to them is therefore no way to please them. As the Bodhisattva Śāntideva says:

> Just as no pleasures can bring delight
> To someone whose body is ablaze with fire,
> Nor can the great compassionate ones be pleased
> When harm is done to sentient beings.

If you perform rituals like the offering prayer to the protectors using only the flesh and blood of slain animals, it goes without saying that the wisdom deities and the protectors of the Buddha's doctrine, who are all pure Bodhisattvas, will never accept those offerings of slaughtered beings laid out like meat on a butcher's counter. They will not even come anywhere near. Instead, powerful evil spirits who like warm flesh and blood and are ever eager to do harm will gather round the offering and feast on it.

For a short while after a practitioner of such "red offerings" has done his work, people may notice some minor benefits. But since the spirits involved are constantly harming others, they are liable to cause sudden problems and sicknesses. Again the practitioner of the "red" rituals will make his appearance and offer flesh and blood, and again that will help for a little while. This is how evil spirits and practitioners of the red rites become inseparable companions who always support each other. Like beasts of prey on the prowl, they roam around, obsessed solely by their urge to consume flesh, gnaw bones, and seek ever more victims. Possessed by evil spirits, practitioners of such rituals lose whatever disillusionment with saṁsāra and thirst for liberation they may have had before. Whatever faith, purity of perception and interest in Dharma they once had, these qualities all fade away until the point comes when even the Buddha himself flying in the sky before them would arouse no faith in them, and even the sight of an animal with all its innards hanging out would arouse no compassion. They are always on the lookout for prey, like killer *rākṣasas* marching to war, their faces inflamed, shaking with rage and bristling with aggression. They pride themselves on the power and blessing of their speech, which comes from their intimacy with evil spirits. As soon as they die they are catapulted straight into hell—unless their negative actions are still not yet quite sufficient for that, in which case they are reborn in the entourage of some evil spirit preying on the life force of others, or as hawks, wolves and other predators.

During the reign of Dharma King Trisong Detsen, the Bönpos made offerings of blood and meat for the king's benefit. The Second Buddha from Oḍḍiyāna, the great paṇḍita Vimalamitra, the great Bodhisattva Abbot and the other translators and paṇḍitas were all completely outraged at the sight of the Bönpos' offerings. They said:

> A single teaching cannot have two teachers;
> A single religion cannot have two methods of practice.
> The Bön tradition is opposed to the law of Dharma;
> Its evil is even worse than ordinary wrongdoing.
> If you permit such practices, we shall go back home.

The paṇḍitas were all of the same opinion without even having to discuss the matter. When the king asked them to preach the Dharma, not one of them came forward. Even when he served them food, they refused to eat.

If we, claiming to walk in the footsteps of the paṇḍitas, siddhas and Bodhisattvas of the past, now perform the profound rites of the Secret Mantrayāna in the manner of Bönpos and cause harm to beings, it will destroy the sublimity of the doctrine and dishonour the Three Jewels, and will cast both ourselves and others into the hells.

Always take the lowest place. Wear simple clothes. Help all other beings as much as you can. In everything you do, simply work at developing love and compassion until they have become a fundamental part of you. That will serve the purpose, even if you do not practise the more outward and conspicuous forms of Dharma such as prayers, virtuous activities and altruistic works. The *Sūtra that Perfectly Encapsulates the Dharma* says:

> Let those who desire Buddhahood not train in many Dharmas but only one.
> Which one? Great compassion.
> Those with great compassion possess all the Buddha's teaching as if it were in the palm of their hand.

Geshe Tönpa was visited once by a monk who was a disciple of the Three Brothers and Khampa Lungpa.*

"What is Potowa doing nowadays?" Tönpa asked the monk.

"He is teaching the Dharma to hundreds of members of the Saṅgha."

"Wonderful! And what about Geshe Puchungwa?"

"He spends all his time fashioning representations** of the body, speech and mind of the Buddha from materials that he and other people have offered."

"Wonderful!" Geshe Tönpa repeated. "What about Gönpawa?"

"He does nothing but meditate."

"Wonderful! Tell me about Khampa Lhungpa."

"He stays in solitude, weeping continually, with his face hidden."

At this Tönpa took off his hat, joined his hands before his heart and, shedding many tears, exclaimed, "Oh, that is really marvellous! That is really practising the Dharma. I could tell you a lot about how good he is, but I know he wouldn't like it."

The reason why Khampa Lhungpa hid his face and cried all the time was that he was constantly thinking about beings tortured by the sufferings of saṁsāra, and meditating on compassion for them.

One day Chengawa was explaining the numerous reasons why love and compassion were so important, when Langri Thangpa prostrated himself before him and said that thenceforth he would meditate on nothing but those two things. Chengawa bared his head and said three times, "What excellent news!"

Nothing could be more effective than compassion for purifying us of negative actions and obscurations. Once long ago, in India, the Abhidharma teaching had been challenged on three separate occasions and was

* See glossary.

** Lit. support. The representations of the Buddha's body refer to statues and paintings, of his speech to sacred texts and other writings, and of his mind to stūpas.

about to disappear. But a brahmin nun named Prakāśaśīlā had the thought, "I have been born as a woman. Because of my low status I cannot myself make the Buddha's doctrine shine forth. So I will couple with men and give birth to sons who can spread the teaching of the Abhidharma."

With a kṣatriya as the father she gave birth to the noble Asaṅga, and with a brahmin to Vasubandhu. As each of her two sons came of age, they asked what their fathers' work had been.

Their mother told each of them, "I did not give birth to you to follow in your father's footsteps. You were born to spread the Buddha's teachings. You must study the Dharma, and become teachers of the Abhidharma."

Vasubandhu went off to Kashmir to study Abhidharma with Saṅghabhadra. Asaṅga went to Kukkuṭapāda Mountain, where he started to do the practice of the Buddha Maitreya in the hopes that he might have a vision of him and ask him for instruction. Six years passed, and although he meditated hard he did not have as much as a single auspicious dream.

"Now it looks as if I will never succeed," he thought, and departed, feeling discouraged. Along the way, he came across a man rubbing an enormous iron bar with a soft cotton cloth.

"What are you trying to do, rubbing like that?" he asked the man.

The man replied, "I need a needle, so I'm making one by rubbing away at this bar."

Asaṅga thought, "He'll never make a needle by rubbing that huge bar with a soft piece of cotton. Even if it could be done in a hundred years, will he live that long? If ordinary people make such efforts for so little reason, I can see that I have never really practised the Dharma with any persistence."

So he went back to his practice. He practised for three more years, still with no sign.[132]

"This time I'm quite certain that I can never succeed," he said, and he took to the road again. He came at last to a rock so high that it seemed to touch the heavens. At its foot, a man was stroking it with a feather dipped in water.

"What are you doing?" Asaṅga asked him.

"This rock is too tall," the man said. "I don't get any sun on my house, which is to the west of it. So I'm going to wear it away till it disappears."

Asaṅga, with the same thoughts as three years before, went back and practised for another three years, still without so much as a single good dream.

Utterly discouraged, he said "Now whatever I do I can never succeed!" and set off once more.

Along the road, he came across a bitch with two crippled hind legs and her entire hind quarters crawling with maggots. Nevertheless, she was still full of aggression, and tried to bite him as she dragged herself along on her forelegs, the rest of her body trailing along on the ground behind her. Asaṅga was swept by deep, unbearable compassion. Cutting off a piece of his own flesh, he gave it to the bitch to eat. Then he decided that he had to rid her of the worms on her hind quarters. Fearing that he might kill them if he removed them with his fingers, he realized that the only way to do it was with his tongue. But whenever he looked at the whole of the creature's body, so rotten and full of pus, he could not bring himself to do it. So he shut his eyes and stretched out his tongue...

Instead of touching the body of the bitch, his tongue touched the ground.

He opened his eyes and found that the bitch had disappeared. In its place stood Lord Maitreya, surrounded by a halo of light.

"How unkind you are," Asaṅga cried, "not to have shown me your face all this time!"

"It is not that I have not shown myself. You and I have never been separate. But your own negative actions and obscurations were too intense for you to be able to see me. Because your twelve years of practice have diminished them a little, you were able to see the bitch. Just now, because of your great compassion, your obscurations have been completely purified and you can see me with your own eyes. If you do not believe me, carry me on your shoulder and show me to everyone around!"

So Asaṅga placed Maitreya on his right shoulder and went to the market, where he asked everyone, "What do you see on my shoulder?"

Everyone replied there was nothing on his shoulder—all except one old woman whose perception was slightly less clouded by habitual tendencies. She said, "You are carrying the rotting corpse of a dog."

Lord Maitreya then took Asaṅga to the Tuṣita heaven, where he gave him *The Five Teachings of Maitreya* and other instructions. When he came back to the realm of men, Asaṅga spread the doctrine of the Great Vehicle widely.

Since there is no practice like compassion to purify us of all our harmful past actions, and since it is compassion that never fails to make us develop the extraordinary bodhicitta, we should persevere in meditating upon it.

The image given for meditating on compassion is that of a mother with no arms, whose child is being swept away by a river. How unbearable the anguish of such a mother would be. Her love for her child is so intense, but as she cannot use her arms she cannot catch hold of him.

"What can I do now? What can I do?" she asks herself. Her only thought is to find some means of saving him. Her heart breaking, she runs along after him, weeping.

In exactly the same way, all beings of the three worlds are being carried away by the river of suffering to drown in the ocean of saṁsāra. However unbearable the compassion we feel, we have no means of saving them from their suffering. Meditate on this, thinking, "What can I do now?" and call on your teacher and the Three Jewels from the very depth of your heart.

4. Meditation on sympathetic joy

Imagine someone of noble birth, strong, prosperous and powerful, someone who lives in the higher realms experiencing comfort, happiness and a long life, surrounded by many attendants and in great wealth. Without any feeling of jealousy or rivalry, make the wish that they might become even more glorious, enjoy still more of the prosperity of the higher realms, be free of all danger, and develop ever more intelligence and other perfect talents. Then tell yourself again and again how wonderful it would be if all other beings could live at such a level too.

Begin your meditation by thinking about a person who easily arouses positive feelings—like a relative, a close friend or someone you love—who is successful, contented and at peace, and feel happy that this is so. When you have established that feeling of happiness, try to cultivate the same feeling toward those about whom you feel indifferent. Then focus on all kinds of enemies who have harmed you, and especially anybody of whom you feel jealous. Uproot the evil mentality that finds it unbearable that someone else should have such perfect plenty, and cultivate a particular feeling of delight for each kind of happiness that they might enjoy. Conclude by resting in the state without any conceptualization.

The meaning of sympathetic joy is to have a mind free of jealousy. You should therefore try to train your mind with all sorts of methods to prevent those harmful jealous thoughts from arising. Specifically, a Bodhisattva, who has given rise to bodhicitta for the benefit of all beings, should be trying to establish all those beings in the everlasting happiness of Buddhahood, and temporarily in the happiness of the realms of gods and men. So how could such a Bodhisattva ever be displeased instead when some beings, through the force of their own past actions, possess some distinction or wealth?

Once people have been corrupted by jealousy, they no longer see the good in others, and their own negative actions increase alarmingly.

When the glory and activity of Jetsun Milarepa were spreading, a certain professor of logic named Tarlo became jealous and started to attack him. In spite of every example of clairvoyance and miraculous power that the Jetsun showed him, Tarlo had no faith in him, and only reacted with wrong views and criticism. He was later reborn as a great demon.

There are many other examples of what can happen under the power of jealousy, like how the logician, Geshe Tsakpuwa, tried to poison Jetsun Mila.

Even if the Buddha himself were present in person, there would be nothing he could do to guide a jealous person. A mind tainted with jealousy cannot see anything good in others. Being unable to see anything good in them, it cannot give rise to even the faintest glimmer of faith. Without faith one can receive neither compassion nor blessings. Devadatta and Sunakṣatra were the Buddha's cousins. Both were tormented by jealousy and refused to have the slightest faith in him. Although they spent their entire lives in his company, he could not transform their minds at all.*

Moreover, even when evil thoughts about others do not materialize as actual physical harm, they still create prodigious negative effects for the person who has the thought. There were once two famous geshes who were rivals. One day, one of them learned that the other had a mistress.

The geshe told his servant, "Prepare some good tea, because I have some interesting news."

The servant made tea, and when he had served it he asked, "And what is the news?"

"They say," replied the geshe, "that our rival has a mistress!"

When Kunpang Trakgyal heard this tale, it is said that his face darkened and he asked, "Which of the two geshes committed the worse action?"

Constantly dwelling on such feelings as jealousy and competitiveness neither furthers one's own cause nor harms that of one's rivals. It leads to a pointless accumulation of negativity. Give up vile attitudes of this kind. Always sincerely rejoice in the achievements and favourable circumstances of others, whether it be their social position, physique, wealth, learning or whatever else. Think over and over again how truly glad you are that they are such excellent people, so successful and fortunate. Think how wonderful it would be if they became even better off than they are now, and acquired all the strength, wealth, learning and good qualities

* See pages 189 and 147.

that they could possibly ever get. Meditate on this from the depth of your heart.

The image given for boundless sympathetic joy is that of a mother camel finding her lost calf. Of all animals, camels are considered the most affectionate mothers. If a mother camel loses her calf her sorrow is correspondingly intense. But should she find it again her joy knows no bounds. That is the kind of sympathetic joy that you should try to develop.

The four boundless qualities cannot fail to cause us to develop genuine bodhicitta. It is therefore vital to cultivate them until they have truly taken root in us.

To make things as easy as possible to understand, we can summarize the four boundless qualities in the single phrase "a kind heart." Just train yourself to have a kind heart always and in all situations.

One day, Lord Atīśa's hand was hurting, and so he laid it in Drom Tönpa's lap and said, "You who are so kind-hearted, bless my hand!"*

Atīśa always placed a unique emphasis on the importance of a kind heart, and rather than ask people, "How are you?," he would say, "Has your heart been kind?"

Whenever he taught he would add, "Have a kind heart!"

It is the power of kind or unkind intentions that makes an action positive or negative, strong or weak. When the intention behind them is good, all physical or verbal actions are positive, as was illustrated by the story of the man who put the leather sole over the *tsa-tsa*. When the intention behind it is bad, any action, however positive it looks, will in fact be negative. So learn to have kind intentions all the time, no matter what the circumstances. It is said:

> If the intention is good, the levels and paths are good.
> If the intention is bad, the levels and paths are bad.[133]
> Since everything depends on intentions,
> Always make sure they are positive.

How is it that the paths and levels are good if the intentions are good?

Once an old woman was crossing a wide river with her daughter, holding her hand, when both of them were swept away by the current.

The mother thought: "It's not that important if I am carried away by the water, as long as my daughter is saved!"

At the same time, the young girl was thinking, "It doesn't matter much

* It is customary to ask realized lamas to blow on a wound in order to cure it.

if I get swept away, as long as my mother isn't drowned!"

They both perished in the water, and as a result of those positive thoughts for each other, they were both reborn in the celestial realm of Brahmā.

On another occasion, six monks and a messenger boarded a ferryboat to cross the river Jasako. The boat set off from the bank.

About a quarter of the way across, the boatman said, "We're too heavy. If anybody knows how to swim, please jump in the water. If not, I'll jump in myself and one of you can take the oars."

None of them knew how to swim; but none of them knew how to row either.

So the messenger jumped out of the boat, crying, "It is better for me to die alone than for everybody to die!"

Immediately a rainbow appeared and a rain of flowers fell. Even though the messenger did not know how to swim, he was carried safely to the shore. He had never practised Dharma. This was the immediate benefit coming from a single good thought.

How is it that the paths and levels are bad if the thoughts are bad?

There was once a beggar who, as he was lying in the gateway of the royal palace, was thinking, "I wish that the king would have his head cut off and I could take his place!"

This thought was continually going round in his mind all night long. Towards morning he fell asleep and while he was sleeping the king drove out in his carriage. One of the wheels rolled over the beggar's neck and cut off his head.

Unless you remember the purpose of your quest for Dharma with mindfulness and vigilance, and watch your mind all the time, violent feelings of attachment and hatred can easily lead to the accumulation of very serious negative effects. Although the old beggar's wishes could never come true, the result of his thoughts materialized right away. Was it likely that the king, sleeping comfortably on his jewelled bed in the palace, would lose his head? Even if he were to be beheaded, would it not be more plausible that the crown prince would take over the kingdom? Even if somehow he did not, was there any chance that in spite of all the ministers, who were like tigers, leopards and bears, a scabrous old beggar would take over the throne? Unless you check yourself carefully, however, even such ludicrous negative thoughts as this can arise. So, as Geshe Shawopa says:

> Do not rule over imaginary kingdoms of endlessly proliferating possibilities!

One day the Buddha and his monks were invited to receive alms at the home of a benefactor. There were also two beggars there, one a young kṣatriya and the other a young brahmin. The brahmin went in to beg before the Buddha and the monks had been served, and received nothing. The kṣatriya waited until everybody else had been served, and received plenty of the good food left over from their begging bowls.[134] That afternoon, on the road, the two of them spoke their thoughts to each other.

"If I were rich," said the young kṣatriya, "I would offer clothes and alms to the Buddha and his monks for the rest of my life. I would honour them by offering everything I had."

"And if I were a powerful king," said the young brahmin, "I'd have that shaven-headed bigot's head cut off, and his whole band executed with him!"

The kṣatriya went to another country and installed himself in the shadow of a great tree. As the shadows of the other trees moved, the shadow of this particular tree stayed still. Now, the king of that country had just died, and since he had no heir the people had decided that the most meritorious and powerful person in the land would be installed as their king. Going off in search of their new sovereign, they came upon the young kṣatriya sleeping under his tree, still in the shade although midday had long since passed. They woke him up and made him king. Thereafter, he paid honour to the Buddha and his disciples as he had wished.

As for the young brahmin, the story goes that he lay down at a crossroads to rest and his head was cut off by the wheel of a passing wagon.

If you learn to always have only kind thoughts, all your wishes for this lifetime will come true. The benevolent gods will protect you and you will receive the blessings of all the Buddhas and Bodhisattvas. Everything you do will be positive, and at the moment of death you will not suffer. In future lives you will always be reborn in celestial or human realms until finally you attain the level of perfect Buddhahood.

Do not just rush off, without examining your thoughts and feelings, and perform a great show of virtuous activities—prostrations, circumambulations, prayers, recitation of mantras and so on. Instead, it is important to check your attitude all the time and to cultivate a kind heart.

II. AROUSING BODHICITTA[135]

1. Classification based on the three degrees of courage

1.1 THE COURAGE OF A KING

A king's first priority is to overcome all his rivals, promote those who support him and proclaim himself sovereign. Only after that does his wish to take care of his subjects come into effect. Similarly, the wish first to attain Buddhahood for oneself and then to bring others to Buddhahood is called the king's way of arousing bodhicitta.

1.2 THE COURAGE OF A BOATMAN

A boatman aims to arrive on the other shore together with all his passengers. Likewise, the wish to achieve Buddhahood for oneself and all beings at the same time is called the boatman's way of arousing bodhicitta.

1.3 THE COURAGE OF A SHEPHERD

Shepherds drive their sheep in front of them, making sure that they find grass and water and are not attacked by wolves, jackals or other wild beasts. They themselves follow behind. In the same way, the attitude of those who wish to establish all beings of the three worlds in perfect Buddhahood before achieving it for themselves is called the shepherd's way of arousing bodhicitta.

The king's way, called "arousing bodhicitta with the great wish," is the least courageous of the three. The boatman's way, called "arousing bodhicitta with sacred wisdom," is more courageous. It is said that Lord Maitreya aroused bodhicitta in this way. The shepherd's way, called "the arousing of bodhicitta beyond compare," is the most courageous of all. It is said to be the way Lord Mañjuśrī aroused bodhicitta.

2. Classification according to the Bodhisattva levels

On the paths of accumulating and joining, arousing bodhicitta is called "arousing bodhicitta by practising with aspiration." From the first to the seventh Bodhisattva level, it is called "arousing bodhicitta through excellent and perfectly pure intention. " On the three pure levels, it is called "arousing fully matured bodhicitta," and at the level of Buddhahood, "arousing bodhicitta free from all obscurations."

3. Classification according to the nature of bodhicitta

There are two types of bodhicitta: relative and absolute.

3.1 RELATIVE BODHICITTA

Relative bodhicitta has two aspects: intention and application.

3.1.1 Intention

In *The Way of the Bodhisattva*, Śāntideva says of these two aspects of bodhicitta:

> Wishing to depart and setting out upon the road,
> This is how the difference is conceived.
> The wise and learned thus should understand
> This difference, which is ordered and progressive.

Take the example of a journey to Lhasa. The first step is the intention, "I am going to go to Lhasa." The corresponding initial thought, "I am going to do whatever will ensure that all beings attain the state of total Buddhahood," is the intention aspect of arousing bodhicitta.[136]

3.1.2 Application

You then prepare the necessary supplies and horses, set out on the road and actually travel to Lhasa. Similarly, you decide to practise generosity, preserve discipline, cultivate tolerance, apply diligence, remain in meditative absorption, and train your mind in discriminating wisdom in order to establish all beings on the level of perfect Buddhahood, and you actually put this path of the six transcendent perfections into practice. This corresponds to the actual journey, and is the application aspect of bodhicitta.[137]

3.2 ABSOLUTE BODHICITTA

Both the intention and application aspects are relative bodhicitta.[138] Through training for a long time in relative bodhicitta on the paths of accumulating and joining, you come at last to the path of seeing, where you have the real experience of thusness, the natural state of all things. This is the wisdom beyond all elaboration, the truth of emptiness. At that time you arouse absolute bodhicitta.[139]

4. Taking the vow of bodhicitta[140]

True absolute bodhicitta is attained by the power of meditation and does not depend on rituals. To generate relative bodhicitta, however, as beginners we need some procedure to follow, a ritual through which we can take the vow in the presence of a spiritual teacher. We then need to constantly renew that vow, in the same way, over and over again, so that the bodhicitta we have aroused does not decline but becomes more and more powerful.

Visualize all the Buddhas, Bodhisattvas and other deities in the sky before you, as for the refuge practice. Take them as witnesses of your generating bodhicitta and think like this:

"Of all the countless living creatures throughout the vast reaches of the universe, there is not one who has not been my parent in the course of our succession of lives without beginning. I can be certain that, as my parents, they have all looked after me with every possible tenderness, given me the very best of their own food and clothing and nurtured me with all their love, just as my present parents have done. Now all these kind parents are foundering in the waves of saṁsāra's great ocean of suffering. They have been plunged into the deepest darkness of confusion. They have no idea of the true path to be practised, nor of the false path to be avoided. They have no authentic spiritual friend to guide them. They have no refuge or protection, no leader or companion, no hope and nobody to turn to, as lost as a blind man wandering friendless in the middle of a deserted plain. My old mothers, how could I ever liberate myself alone and leave you all behind here in saṁsāra? For the sake of all beings, I shall awaken the sublime bodhicitta. Learning to emulate the mighty deeds of the Bodhisattvas of the past, I shall make whatever efforts are necessary, till there is not one being left in saṁsāra!"

With this attitude, recite the following verse as many times as possible:

Ho! Led astray by myriad appearances like reflections of the moon in water,
Beings wander in the endless chain of saṁsāra;
To bring them rest in the radiant space of awareness,
With the four boundless qualities I arouse bodhicitta.[141]

At the close of the session visualize that, by the power of your yearning devotion towards the deities of the field of merit, the whole assembly melts into light, starting from the outside, and finally dissolves into the teacher, union of all three refuges, in the centre. The teacher in turn melts into light and dissolves into you, causing the absolute bodhicitta present in the mind of the refuge deities to arise clearly in your own mind. Make this wishing prayer:

May bodhicitta, precious and sublime,
Arise where it has not yet come to be;
And where it has arisen may it never fail
But grow and flourish ever more and more.

Then dedicate the merit with the lines:

Emulating the hero Mañjuśrī,
Samantabhadra and all those with knowledge,
I too make a perfect dedication
Of all actions that are positive.

This arousing of bodhicitta is the quintessence of the eighty-four thousand methods taught by the Conqueror. It is the instruction to have which is enough by itself, but to lack which renders anything else futile. It is a panacea, the medicine for a hundred ills. All other Dharma paths, such as the two accumulations, the purification of defilements, meditation on deities and recitation of mantras, are simply methods to make this wish-granting gem, bodhicitta, take birth in the mind. Without bodhicitta, none of them can lead you to the level of perfect Buddhahood on their own.[142] But once bodhicitta has been aroused in you, whatever Dharma practices you do will lead to the attainment of perfect Buddhahood. Learn always to use whatever means you can to make even the slightest spark of bodhicitta arise in you.[143]

The teacher who gives you the pith instructions on arousing bodhicitta is setting you on the path of the Great Vehicle, so his kindness is greater than that of teachers who give you any other instructions. When Atīśa mentioned the names of his teachers, he used to join his hands before his heart. But when he spoke of Lord Suvarṇadvīpa, he would join his hands above his head and his eyes would fill with tears. His disciples asked him why he made such a distinction.

"Is there really a difference in the spiritual qualities or kindness of these masters?" they asked.

"All my teachers were truly accomplished beings," Atīśa replied, "and in this their qualities are identical. But there is some difference in their kindness. The little bit of bodhicitta that I have comes from the kindness of Lord Suvarṇadvīpa. That is why I feel the greatest gratitude toward him."

It is said that the most important thing about bodhicitta is not arousing it, but rather that it has actually arisen. The love and compassion of bodhicitta must really be alive in us. To recite the formula many hundreds of thousands of times without taking the meaning to heart, therefore, is utterly pointless. To take the bodhicitta vow in the presence of the Buddhas and Bodhisattvas, and then not to keep it, would just be to swindle them. There is no worse fault than that. So do not cheat sentient beings either—try to cultivate bodhicitta all the time.

III. TRAINING IN THE BODHICITTA PRECEPTS

For the bodhicitta of intention, the training has three stages: considering others as equal to oneself, exchanging oneself and others and taking others as more important than oneself. For the bodhicitta of application, the training consists of practising the six transcendent perfections.

1. Training in the precepts of the bodhicitta of aspiration

1.1 CONSIDERING OTHERS AS EQUAL TO ONESELF

The reason we have been wandering in saṁsāra's ocean of suffering from time without beginning is that we believe in an "I" where there is no I, in a "self" where there is no self, and that we make that self the sole object of our affection. Instead, reflect as follows.

We want to be happy constantly and never to have any kind of suffering. The moment anything unpleasant happens to us we find it unbearable. Even a pinprick or the tiny burn of a spark makes us cry out in pain—we just cannot stand it. If a little louse should bite us on the back we fly into a rage. We catch that louse, put it on one of our thumbnails and crush it hard with the other, and long after we have already killed it we go on and on grinding our nails together in anger. Most people these days see no harm in killing a louse. But since it is invariably done out of anger, it is a sure cause for rebirth in the Rounding-Up and Crushing Hell. We should be ashamed to find such small discomforts so hard to bear and to react in a way that causes so much pain to another being.

Just like us, all beings of the three worlds want to be happy and to escape any kind of suffering, too. But although they want to be happy, they have no idea that happiness comes only from practising the ten positive actions. Although they do not want to suffer, they devote all their efforts to the ten harmful actions which bring about suffering. What they wish for and their attempts to attain it are therefore completely at odds, and they suffer all the time. Of all those beings, there is not a single one who has not, at some moment throughout time without beginning, been a parent to us. Now that we have been accepted as disciples by an authentic spiritual teacher, now that we have taken up the true Dharma and can distinguish what is profitable from what is detrimental, we ought to be caring lovingly for all our old mothers so enslaved by their own confusion, and should stop seeing any difference between them and ourselves. Putting up with their ingratitude and prejudices, we should meditate on the absence of any difference between friends and enemies.

Keeping all this in mind, meditate on it over and over again.

Whatever good or useful things you want for yourself, others want them just as much. So just as you work hard at bringing about your own happiness and comfort, always work hard for others' happiness and comfort, too. Just as you would try to avoid even the slightest suffering for yourself, strive too to prevent others having to suffer even the slightest harm. Just as you would feel pleased about your own well-being and prosperity, rejoice from your heart when others are well and prosperous, too. In short, seeing no distinction between yourself and all living creatures of the three worlds, make it your sole mission to find ways of making every one of them happy, now and for all time.

When Trungpa Sinachen asked him for a complete instruction in a single sentence, Padampa Sangye replied, "Whatever you want, others all want as much; so act on that!"

Completely eradicate all those wrong attitudes based on attachment and aversion which make you reject others and care only about yourself, and think of yourself and others as being entirely equal.

1.2 EXCHANGING ONESELF AND OTHERS

Look at a person actually suffering from sickness, hunger, thirst or some other affliction. Or, if that is not possible, imagine that such a person is in front of you. As you breathe out, imagine that you are giving that person all your happiness and the best of everything you have, your body, your wealth and your sources of merit, just as if you were taking off your own clothes and dressing the other person in them. Then, as you breathe in, imagine that you are taking into yourself all the other person's sufferings and that, as a result, he or she becomes happy and free from every affliction. Start this meditation on giving happiness and taking suffering with one individual, and then gradually extend it to include all living creatures.

Whenever anything undesirable or painful happens to you, generate heartfelt, overwhelming pity for all the many beings in the three worlds of saṁsāra who are now undergoing such pain as yours. Make the strong wish that all their suffering may ripen in you instead, and that they may all be freed from suffering and be happy. Whenever you are happy or feel good, generate the wish that your happiness might extend to bring happiness to all beings.

This bodhicitta practice of exchanging oneself and others is the ultimate and unfailing quintessential meditation for all those who have set out on the path of the Mahāyāna teachings. If you really experience that exchange happening even once, it will purify the negative actions and obscurations of many kalpas and create an immense accumulation of merit and wisdom. It will save you from the lower realms and from any rebirths that might lead to them.

In a previous life, the Buddha was born in a hell where the inhabitants were forced to pull wagons. He was harnessed to a wagon with another person called Kāmarupa, but the two of them were too weak to get their vehicle to move. The guards goaded them on and beat them with red-hot weapons, causing them incredible suffering.

The future Buddha thought, "Even with two of us together we can't get the wagon to move, and each of us is suffering as much as the other. I'll pull it and suffer alone, so that Kamarūpa can be relieved."

He said to the guards, "Put his harness over my shoulders, I'm going to pull the cart on my own."

But the guards just got angry. "Who can do anything to prevent others from experiencing the effects of their own actions?" they said, and beat him about the head with their clubs.

Because of this good thought, however, the Buddha immediately left that life in hell and was reborn in a celestial realm. It is said that this was how he first began to benefit others.

Another story tells how the Buddha, in a previous rebirth as the "daughter" of the sea-captain Vallabha, was once again freed from the lower realms as soon as he really experienced this exchanging of himself with others. There was once a householder called Vallabha, all of whose sons had died. So, when another son was born, he decided to name him Daughter in the hope that this would keep him alive. Vallabha then went to sea in search of precious gems, but his ship sank and he perished.

When the son grew up, he asked his mother what his father's caste occupation had been. His mother, fearing that were she to tell him the truth he too might go to sea, told him that his father had belonged to the caste of grain merchants. So Daughter became a grain merchant and looked after his mother with the four coins of one *karṣa* he earned each day. But soon the other grain merchants told him that he was not a member of their caste and that, consequently, it was not proper for him to practise their trade. He was forced to stop.

He went back to his mother and questioned her again. This time she told him that his father had been an incense seller. He started selling incense, and with the eight *karṣa* he earned each day, he took care of his mother.

But Daughter was stopped once again, and this time his mother told him that his father had sold clothes. He set up as a clothing merchant, and was soon able to give his mother sixteen *karṣa* a day. But yet again he was forced out of business by the other clothing merchants.

When he was told that he was of the jewellers' caste, he started to sell jewels and brought home thirty-two *karṣa* a day to give to his mother. It was then that the other jewellers told him that he belonged to the caste of those who brought back jewels from ocean voyages and that this was the work he was born to do.

When he got home that day, he said to his mother, "I belong to the caste of those who search for jewels. So I'm going to sail across the great ocean to carry on my own trade!"

"It is true that you are of the jewel hunters' caste," said she, "but your father and all your ancestors have died at sea in their quest for jewels. If you go you'll die too. Please don't go! Stay at home and trade here."

But Daughter could not obey her. He prepared everything he needed for his journey. As he was setting out, his mother, unable to let him go, caught hold of the hem of his garment and wept. He was furious.

Crying, "Your tears will bring me bad luck on the journey across the ocean!" he kicked her in the head and left.

During the voyage, his ship was wrecked and almost the entire crew was drowned, but Daughter held fast to a plank and was washed ashore on an island. He came to a town called Joy. In a beautiful house made of precious metals and jewels, four beautiful goddesses piled up silken cushions for him to sit on and offered him the three white and three sweet foods.

As he prepared to leave, they warned him, "Do not travel toward the south. Great misfortune will befall you if you do!" But Daughter did not listen and took to the road.

He came to a town called Joyous, even more beautiful than the one before. Here eight beautiful women placed themselves at his service. As before, they warned him of great misfortune threatening him if he went towards the south, but he took no notice and set off yet again.

In a town called Intoxication, still more perfect than the others, he was welcomed by sixteen exquisite goddesses who also served him and warned him as before, but once again it was to no avail.

He continued on his journey and came upon a white fortress whose top touched the very skies. It was called Guru Brahmā's Castle, and here thirty-two ravishingly beautiful goddesses invited him in. They prepared him a couch of silken cushions, served him with the three white and three sweet foods and begged him to stay. But he wanted to leave.

As he was setting off again, they said to him, "Wherever you are going, please avoid the south! Evil will befall you!" But he felt an urge to go south, and south he went.

Soon a fortress of iron rose before him, its towers soaring up to the skies. At the gate, he saw a black man with terrifying red eyes and a long iron bar in his fist. Daughter asked him what was inside the building, but the man remained silent. As he came closer, Daughter looked in and saw many more men like the first. A feeling of terror gripped his whole body, making his hair stand on end.

He said to himself, "The danger! This must be the danger they warned me about."

He went inside. There he saw a man whose brains were being pulverized by a steel wheel revolving on his head.

"What did you do to deserve this?" asked Daughter.

"I kicked my mother in the head and this is the fully ripened effect. But what about you? Why didn't you take advantage of the happiness they were offering you at Guru Brahmā's Castle? Why did you come looking for suffering here?"

"I suppose I was pushed here by my karma, too," thought Daughter.

At that moment a voice from the sky called out, "Let those who are bound be freed, and those who are free be bound!"

The steel wheel was suddenly spinning on Daughter's head. Like the other man's, his brain was smashed to a pulp and he experienced the most unbearable pain and suffering. That pain awakened in him a feeling of intense compassion for all those in the same state as himself.

He thought, "In the realms of saṁsāra there are other beings suffering like me for kicking their mothers in the head. May all their suffering ripen in me and may I alone bear it for all of them. May none of the others ever again experience such pain in any of their successive rebirths."

Immediately, the wheel flew up into the air, his agony ceased and he soared up to the height of seven palm trees in a state of bliss.

The bodhicitta practice of exchanging oneself with others is the ultimate, indispensable method for attaining enlightenment. Indeed, the

Kadampa Masters of the past used to make it their main practice. Once, Geshe Chekawa, who knew many teachings of both the New and the Ancient Traditions and who knew many texts on logic by heart, went to see Geshe Chakshingwa. On his pillow he saw a small text, and when he opened it he came across this sentence:

> Offer gain and victory to others.
> Take loss and defeat for yourself.

"What a wonderful teaching!" Chekawa thought, and he asked Chakshingwa what the teaching was called.

"It's *The Eight Verses of Langri Thangpa*," said Chakshingwa.

"Who holds these instructions?"

"Geshe Langri Thangpa himself."

Chekawa was determined to receive these teachings. First he went to Lhasa and spent some days circumambulating the sacred places. One evening, a leper from Langthang told him that Langri Thangpa had passed away. Chekawa asked who was the successor of the lineage and was told that there were two potential successors, Shangshungpa and Dodepa, but that they could not agree on the matter. However, they were not arguing out of competitiveness.

Shangshungpa would tell Dodepa, "You are the older; you take the succession. I will serve you as though you were Langri Thangpa himself."

But Dodepa would answer, "You are more learned. You be the successor!"

In spite of the pure perception they both had of each other, Chekawa interpreted their failure to agree about the succession as a shortcoming and considered neither of them to be the holder of Langri Thangpa's teaching. He tried to find out who was its best holder, and everybody told him that it was Sharawa.

Sharawa was giving a teaching of many volumes to some thousand members of the Saṅgha. Chekawa listened to him for a few days, but did not hear him say a word about the teaching he sought.

"He seems not to have it either," he thought, "but I'll ask him. If he has this teaching, I'll stay. Otherwise I'd better move on."

So Chekawa went to see Sharawa, who was circumambulating a stūpa. He spread out a cloth on the ground and invited Sharawa to sit down for a moment saying, "I have something to ask you."

"Venerable Monk," said Sharawa, "what is your problem? Personally, I've always found all my answers on my meditation cushion."

"I read these words in a text: 'Offer gain and victory to others. Take loss and defeat for yourself.' I liked them very much. Is this a profound teaching or not?"

"Venerable monk," Sharawa replied, "whether or not you like this teaching, it is one you can only dispense with if you don't want to attain Buddhahood."

"Do you hold this teaching?"

"Yes. It's my main practice," Sharawa replied.

"Then I beg you, teach it to me," said Chekawa.

"Can you stay with me for a long time?" Sharawa asked. "If you can, I will teach it to you."

From him, Chekawa received guidance according to his experience[144] in a continuous course of mind training that lasted six years. Through practising it he was able to rid himself completely of every trace of selfishness.

There is no better instruction for dispelling the sickness and sufferings of this life and for subjugating spirits, negative forces and obstacle makers than this bodhicitta meditation of exchanging oneself and others. Meditate on it with perseverance, always rejecting like poison the negative mentality which gives so much importance to yourself.

1.3 CONSIDERING OTHERS MORE IMPORTANT THAN ONESELF

"I may be in saṁsāra, I may be reborn in hell, I may be ill, feverish, or suffering from any other misfortune, but I will bear it all. May the sufferings of others ripen in me! May other beings have all my happiness and all the effects of my good actions!"

Arouse this thought in the depth of your being and actually put it into practice, following the examples of Atīśa's teachers, Maitrīyogī and Dharmarakṣita, and of our Teacher Śākyamuni in his rebirths as King Padma, as a turtle and as King Maṇicūḍa.

Once, Maitrīyogī, Atīśa's teacher, was expounding the Dharma, when a man nearby threw a stone at a dog. The Master yelled with pain and fell from his throne. The other people present, seeing nothing the matter with the dog, thought that Maitrīyogī must be pretending. But Maitrīyogī, who knew what they were thinking, showed them his back on which the welt of the stone that had been thrown at the dog was clearly visible. Everyone there was convinced by the evidence: he had physically taken upon himself the pain caused by the stone hitting the dog.

The Master Dharmarakṣita started out as a Śrāvaka paṇḍita of the Vaibhāṣika school. Although in the earlier part of his life he had never heard the teachings of the Great Vehicle, his natural affinity was to the

Atīśa (982-1054)

The great Indian scholar from the university of Vikramaśīla who spent the last ten years of his life in Tibet, where his teachings emphasized the basic practices of taking refuge and training the mind in love and compassion.

Great Vehicle tradition, and without any deliberate effort he was filled with great compassion.

Once, someone in the region where he lived was attacked by a violent illness which the doctor declared could only be healed with one medicine—the flesh of a live human being. If that could not be found, there would be no hope.

"If it helps, I'll give him mine," said Dharmarakṣita and, cutting some flesh from his own thigh, he gave it to the sick person, who ate it and was cured.

Dharmarakṣita, who had not yet realized emptiness, suffered enormous pain as a result of what he had done, but his great compassion prevented him from feeling any regret.

"Are you feeling better?" he asked the invalid.

"Yes, I am fine, but look at the difficulties I've brought upon you!"

"I would even bear death if it could bring you happiness," said Dharmarakṣita.

He was in such pain, however, that he could not sleep at all. Finally, at some time in the small hours, he dozed off and had a dream.

A man, all white, appeared to him and said, "Whoever wants to attain enlightenment must pass through such trials as yours. Well done! Well done!" The man spat on the wound and rubbed it with his hand. The wound disappeared, leaving no scar at all.

When Dharmarakṣita awoke from his dream, he saw that his wound really had been healed. The white man had been the Great Compassionate One[145] himself. The authentic realization of the natural state then dawned in Dharmarakṣita's mind and the words of Nāgārjuna's *Five Treatises on the Middle Way* were ceaselessly on his lips.

In ancient times, when Śākyamuni in a previous life was a king called Padma, a serious epidemic broke out amongst his subjects and many of them died. The king called the doctors and asked how the disease should be treated.

"This sickness can be cured with the flesh of the *rohita* fish," they said. "But the disease has so obscured our minds that we can think of no other remedy."

On the morning of an auspicious day the king bathed, donned new clothing and performed a ceremony of confession and purification. He made great offerings to the Three Jewels and prayed fervently, saying, "As soon as I die, may I immediately be reborn as a *rohita* fish in the Nivrītta river!"

He then cast himself down from the heights of his palace—one thousand cubits—and was immediately reborn as a fish, crying out in human speech, "I am a *rohita* fish, take my flesh and eat it!"

Everyone came to eat it. As soon as one side was eaten, the fish turned over and offered them the other side. While they were cutting off the flesh, the first side became whole again. In this way, by eating each side alternately, everybody who was ill could be cured. Then the fish spoke to them all.

"I am Padma, your king. I gave up my life and took birth as a *rohita* fish to save you from the epidemic. As an expression of your gratitude, give up doing evil and do all the good you can."

They all obeyed him and thenceforth never again fell into evil rebirths.

Another time Śākyamuni had been reborn as a giant turtle, when a boat transporting five hundred merchants was wrecked at sea.

They were all about to drown, but the turtle called out to them in human speech: "Get up on my back! I will carry you all to safety!"

The turtle carried all the merchants to dry land, and then collapsed exhausted by the water's edge, and fell asleep. But as it slept, a cloud of eighty thousand ketaka flies began to suck its blood. Waking up, it saw how many they were and realized that to go back into the water or roll on the ground would kill all the insects. So it just lay where it was, giving them its life.

Later, when the turtle became the Buddha, the flies were the eighty thousand gods who listened to his teachings and perceived the truth.

On another occasion, the Buddha was reborn in the land of Sāketa as the son of the king Golden Crest and the queen Joyous Beauty. On top of his head there was a protuberance[146] consisting of a precious jewel, from which came a nectar with the power to turn iron into gold. For this reason he was called Maṇicūḍa, "Jewel Crest." At the moment of his birth there had been a rain of all kinds of precious substances. He had in his possession a magnificent elephant named Excellent Mountain. As king, he conducted his worldly affairs according to the Dharma, always distributing largesse to the poor, thus putting an end to poverty and begging.

A ṛiṣi called Bṛighu gave him his daughter's hand in marriage. She had been born from a lotus and possessed all the propitious signs. From their union, a son just like his father was born, and they called him Lotus Crest.

One day the king decided to organize a huge offering and invited many guests, among them, the ṛiṣi Bṛighu and a king called Duṣyanta, Hard-to-Endure. Now Indra, wishing to test the intentions of the king, took the form of a *rākṣasa*. He sprang out of the oblation fire and, marching up to the king, demanded food and drink. The king offered him all sorts of dishes and drinks, but he refused them all.

"All I need," he said with the faintest of smiles, "is the warm flesh and blood of a freshly killed being!"

The king was somewhat shaken. "I can't obtain such a thing without harming others," he thought. "Even if he kills me, I will never hurt other beings. However, unless I give him what he needs, all his hopes will be dashed. What shall I do?"

He decided that the moment had come to make an offering of his own flesh and blood and said: "I will give you my own!"

Panic swept the assembly and they tried to dissuade him, but to no avail. The king opened his jugular vein and offered his blood to drink. The rākṣasa drank his fill. Then he cut off pieces of his flesh and the demon ate it to the bone. The retinue were smitten with grief. The queen fell unconscious to the ground. But the king remained in control of his faculties and Indra became extremely joyful.

"I am Indra," he said. "I have no need of flesh and blood so you can stop your act of charity." He applied divine nectar to the wounds on the king's body, which was restored to its former condition again.

Later, Jewel Crest gave the elephant Excellent Mountain to his minister, Chariot of Brahmā. At that time one of the ṛiṣi Marīcī's disciples, who was accomplished in concentration, arrived. The king received him with deep homage and asked him what he wanted.

"In gratitude to the teacher who taught me the Vedas, I would like to offer him a servant, since he is now old and has none. I have come to ask you for your wife and son."

So the king let them go. The disciple left with them and offered them to his teacher.

King Hard-to-Endure, meanwhile, had been coveting the elephant. Arriving back in his own kingdom, he sent a message demanding that the elephant be presented to him. He was duly informed that the elephant had already been given away to a brahmin. But he refused to listen and threatened war if the elephant was not handed over. As the enemy troops advanced, King Jewel Crest felt a profound sadness within him.

"How sad that greed can turn one's closest friend into one's most bitter enemy in an instant!" he thought. "If I were to prepare to fight, I could easily defeat him. But many beings would suffer, so I must flee!"

Four pratyekabuddhas appeared and said, "Great King, the time has come for you to go into the forest."

So he left for the Forest of Others' Enchantment, while his ministers went to Marīcī and asked for the young prince who had been given to him. Marīcī returned the prince, and the prince then took command of the army and did battle. Hard-to-Endure was defeated and forced to retreat, and his evil thoughts and activities brought disease and famine upon his own kingdom.

When Hard-to-Endure asked his brahmins what could bring these afflictions to an end, they said, "The remedy would be King Jewel Crest's jewel. You should ask him for it."

"But he will probably refuse," said King Hard-to-Endure.

The brahmins insisted, however, that Jewel Crest would give it—for was he not famous for never having refused a request? One brahmin was sent to ask him.

King Jewel Crest was walking through the forest, looking around, and had arrived in the vicinity of Marīcī's hermitage at the same moment that the queen—his wife—in search of roots and leaves in the woods not far away, was attacked by a hunter.

"King Jewel Crest, save me!" she cried.

Her distant wails came to the ears of Jewel Crest, who wondered what could be happening and went to investigate. The hunter, seeing him approach, thought it was the ṛiṣi. Fearing a curse, he fled. The queen, who before had enjoyed the immense comfort of the royal court, was in such distress that when Jewel Crest saw her he was overwhelmed.

"How sad!" he thought. "All compounded things are unreliable."

It was at that moment that the brahmin sent by Hard-to-Endure arrived. He told the king his story and asked him for the protuberance on his head.

"Cut it off and take it," said the king.

The brahmin did so and left. In Hard-to-Endure's kingdom, all disease and famine came to an end.

As the king experienced the pain caused by his wound, it aroused in him great compassion for all the beings living in the hot hells. Then he fell unconscious.

Meanwhile, prompted by the good omens that had appeared, numerous members of the court arrived, as well as many gods.

"O King," they said, "what happened?"

The king sat up and wiped away some of the blood that stained his face.

"Hard-to-Endure sent someone to ask me for the crest on my head, so I gave it to him," he answered.

"What made you do that?" they asked.

"I wasn't trying to get anything for myself. My only wish was that Hard-to-Endure's kingdom should be saved from disease and famine. But there is still one thing that I want..."

"What is that?" they asked

"To be able to protect all beings," he replied

"But don't you feel any regret?" they asked.

"No. None at all," said the king.

"Seeing the pain in your face, it's hard to believe what you say."

"Well," said the king, "if I really have no regrets about having given my crown protuberance to Hard-to-Endure and his followers, may my body become exactly as it was before!"

And that is what happened. His followers then begged him to return to the palace, but he refused. At that point, the four pratyekabuddhas reappeared.

"Since you help your enemies so much, why not help your friends too?" they said. "Now you should go back to your palace."

He returned to the palace, and brought benefit and happiness to his subjects.

2. Training in the precepts of the bodhicitta of application: the six transcendent perfections

The first five of the six transcendent perfections—generosity, discipline, patience, diligence and concentration—are all aspects of the practice of skilful means. The sixth, wisdom, belongs to the accumulation of primal wisdom.[147]

2.1 TRANSCENDENT GENEROSITY

Generosity can take three forms: material giving, giving Dharma and giving protection from fear.

2.1.1 Material giving

There are three kinds of material giving: ordinary giving, great giving and exceptionally great giving.

Ordinary giving. This refers to the giving of anything material, even if it is no more than a pinch of tea-leaves or a bowl of barley. If it is given with a perfectly pure intention, the amount is not important. The *Confession of Downfalls* speaks of "the positive effect for the future of giving a mere mouthful of food to a being born in the animal realm." The Conquerors, with their masterful skill in means and great compassion, are said to be able to help pretas as numerous as the sands of the Ganges with a single drop of water or grain of barley by using the power of dhāraṇis,* mantras and other techniques.

The white and the red burnt offerings bring great benefit to pretas that move through space. Spirits that otherwise feed on the lives of others can be temporarily satisfied by the smell of the burnt food offering, and their minds are liberated by the gift of Dharma.** As a result they no longer harm others, and many beings are thus protected from the danger of death. This constitutes giving protection from fear, so the burnt offering practice includes all three kinds of generosity.

Since water tormas and burnt offerings are both easy to perform and very effective, try to practise them regularly and without interruption. It is good to offer a hundred thousand water tormas every year.

When people get hold of a few supplies or a little money, they hold tight to them with a dying man's grip, and use them neither for this life nor for lives to come. No matter how much they have, they still think they have nothing, and moan as if they were on the point of starvation. Such behaviour can create right now an experience like that of the preta-realm, through the effect similar to the cause.†

Avoid such attitudes and try to be generous, through such activities as making offerings to the Three Jewels and giving to beggars. As Jetsun Mila says:

> Dig out food from your own mouth and give it as alms.

Otherwise, if you let yourself be a slave to your selfish attachment, the point might come where even if you had all the wealth in the world it would still not seem enough for one person; and, not daring to break into what you already have, you will tell yourself that anything you are going to use for offerings or give to the needy will still have to be found, later or from somewhere else.

Generally speaking, the Buddha taught material giving and other practices involving material possessions mainly for lay Bodhisattvas. If you are a monk or nun, the important thing is simply to reduce your desires, to learn to be content with whatever you have, and to practise the threefold training of the higher path with determination in mountain hermitages and solitary places, gladly accepting all hardships.

* A type of long mantra found in the sūtras.

** During the ritual of a burnt offering (see glossary), the "giving of Dharma" is usually included in the form of the verse summarizing the Buddha's teaching, "Abandon evil-doing...," quoted below on page 238.

† see pages 113-114.

Some practitioners abandon their spiritual practice to involve themselves in trade, agriculture or other means of livelihood, and pile up wealth through cunning and trickery. They maintain that they are practising Dharma through the offerings and charitable gifts they make with what they have gained. But it is of such people that it is said:

> When Dharma is not practised according to Dharma, Dharma itself can cause evil rebirth.

Their approach is absolutely worthless. It is most important, therefore, to be always satisfied with what one has.

Great giving. This means to give to others something rare or very precious to you personally, such as your own horse or elephant, or even your own son or daughter.

Exceptionally great giving. This refers to making a gift of your own limbs, body or life. Examples are Prince Great Courage giving his body to a starving tigress, Nāgārjuna giving his head to the son of King Surabhībhadra,* and Princess Mandabhadrī also feeding a tigress with her own body. However this sort of generosity should be practised only by a being who has attained one of the Bodhisattva levels. Ordinary beings are incapable of it.[148] For the moment, mentally dedicate your body, life and wealth to the benefit of others without attachment, praying that one day you will be capable of actually giving them away.

2.1.2 Giving Dharma

This means leading others to spiritual practice by giving empowerments, explaining the Dharma, transmitting texts and so forth. However, to work for the good of others when one's own selfish desires have not yet disappeared would be nothing but a show.

Atīśa's disciples asked him when they might be able to teach others, work for others' benefit or perform the transference of consciousness for those who had just died. His reply was this:

> You may guide others once you have realized emptiness and developed clairvoyance.
> You may work for their benefit once for your own benefit[149] there is no more left to do.
> You may perform the transference for the dead once you have entered the path of seeing.

* See page 122.

He also said:

> This degenerate time is no time for boasting;
> It is a time for arousing determination.
> This is no time for holding high positions;
> It is a time for keeping to a humble place.
> This is no time for having servants and disciples;
> It is a time for living in solitude.
> This is no time for taking care of disciples;
> It is a time for taking care of yourself.
> This is no time for analyzing the words;
> It is a time for reflecting on the meaning.
> This is no time for being out and about;
> It is a time for staying in one place.

The Three Brothers asked Geshe Tönpa whether it was more important to practise in solitude or to help others through the Dharma. Geshe Tönpa replied:

> It is useless for a beginner with neither experience nor realization to try to help others with the Dharma. No blessings can be obtained from him, just as nothing can be poured out of an empty vessel. His instructions are insipid and without substance, like beer brewed without pressing the grains.
>
> Someone at the aspiration stage who has the warmth[150] of the practice, but has not yet established a firm stability in it, cannot work for the benefit of beings. His blessings are like something poured from one vessel into another: he can only fill others by emptying himself. His instructions are like a lamp passed from hand to hand: if he gives light to others, he is left in the dark.
>
> But someone who has attained one of the Bodhisattva levels is ready to work for others' benefit. His blessings are like the powers of a wish-granting vessel: he can bring all beings to maturity without ever running dry. His instructions are like a central lamp from which others can take light without it ever being dimmed.
>
> This decadent age is therefore not a time for ordinary beings to help others externally, but rather a time for them to live in solitary places and train their own minds in the love and compassion of bodhicitta. It is a time to keep away from negative emotions. While a precious medicinal tree[151] is still just a shoot it is not yet time to pick it, it is the time to protect it.

For these reasons it is quite difficult to really make the gift of Dharma to others. To expound a teaching to others without having experienced it oneself will not help them at all. As for acquiring offerings and wealth by teaching Dharma, that is what Padampa Sangye called "using the Dharma as merchandise to get rich."

Until you have overcome wanting anything for yourself, it would be better not to rush into altruistic activities. Instead, pray that the minds of positively inclined spirits may be liberated when they hear you praying, reciting mantras or reading the scriptures. Consider it enough to recite the prayers for giving the Dharma that are found at the end of the ritual texts for water tormas or offering the body,[152] such as:

> Abandon evil-doing.
> Practise virtue well.
> Master your own mind.
> This is the Buddha's teaching.

When your own selfish desires have been exhausted, the time will have come to devote yourself entirely to others, without concern for your own peace and happiness and without relaxing your efforts for an instant.

2.1.3 Giving protection from fear

This means actually doing whatever you can to help others in difficulty. It includes, for instance, providing a refuge for those without any place of safety, giving protection to those without any protector, and being with those who have no other companion. It refers particularly to such actions as forbidding hunting and fishing wherever you have the power to do so, buying back sheep on the way to slaughter, and saving the lives of dying fish, worms, flies and other creatures. For the Buddha taught that, of all relative good actions, saving beings' lives is the most beneficial.

Taken together, the different kinds of generosity constitute a most essential point of the Tantric samayas. In *The Vows of the Five Families* it says:

> As the samaya of the Jewel Family,
> Always practise the four kinds of generosity.

2.2 TRANSCENDENT DISCIPLINE

Transcendent discipline consists of avoiding negative actions, undertaking positive actions, and bringing benefit to others.

2.2.1 Avoiding negative actions

This means rejecting like poison all ten negative actions of body, speech and mind that are not directed towards the benefit of others.[153]

2.2.2 Undertaking positive actions

This means always creating as many sources of good for the future as possible by always doing whatever positive actions you can, regardless of how insignificant they may seem.

As the common saying goes: "Positive actions just happen while our mouths or hands are free, negative actions while we move around or sit." Only by always checking with great mindfulness, vigilance and care, and by trying hard to do good and refrain from evil, can you avoid committing many serious negative actions—even while simply amusing yourself.

> Do not take lightly small misdeeds,
> Believing they can do no harm:
> Even a tiny spark of fire
> Can set alight a mountain of hay.

Always put this advice into practice, applying constant mindfulness and vigilance, and you will eventually acquire an unimaginable store of positive actions in the course of your everyday activities. Simply showing respect when you come across a pile of *maṇi* stones by taking off your hat and walking round it, keeping it on your right, and applying the three supreme methods, can lead unerringly to perfect enlightenment. It is said:

> Do not take lightly small good deeds,
> Believing they can hardly help:
> For drops of water one by one
> In time can fill a giant pot.

There is the story of a pig that was chased around a stūpa by a dog, and another of seven caterpillars who fell off their leaf into a stream and were carried around a stūpa by the current: such occurrences were enough to bring those beings eventually to liberation.

Always, therefore, renounce the smallest harmful act; do whatever good you can and dedicate all the merit to the benefit of beings. This includes all the precepts of the Bodhisattva vows.

2.2.3 Bringing benefit to others

As we have already seen, when you are totally free of wanting anything for yourself, the time will have come for you to work directly for the benefit of others, using the four ways of attracting beings. But as a beginner, the way to bring benefit to others is to dedicate to the benefit of all beings all the practice you do while training in undertaking positive actions and avoiding negative ones. All this is to be done applying the three supreme methods.

2.3 TRANSCENDENT PATIENCE

Patience includes three aspects: patience when wronged, patience to bear hardships for the Dharma, and patience to face the profound truth without fear.

2.3.1 Patience when wronged

This type of patience should apply whenever you are attacked, robbed or defeated, insulted to your face or slandered behind your back. Instead of getting annoyed and reacting angrily, you should respond positively, with loving kindness and compassion. If you lose patience and give way to anger, a single fit of rage can destroy the effects of the good actions you have accumulated over a thousand kalpas, as is mentioned in *The Way of the Bodhisattva*:

> Good works gathered in a thousand ages,
> Such as deeds of generosity,
> Or offerings to those gone to bliss:
> A single flash of anger shatters them.[154]

And again:

> No evil is there similar to hatred,
> Nor austerity to be compared with patience.[155]
> Steep yourself, therefore, in patience—
> In all ways, urgently, with zeal.

Remembering the ills that anger brings, strive to cultivate patience in all circumstances. Padampa Sangye says:

> To hate enemies is a delusion caused by karma.
> Transform your vicious thoughts of hatred, people of Tingri!

And Atīśa says:

> Do not get angry with those who harm you.
> If you get angry with those who harm you,

When are you going to cultivate patience?

Whenever someone hurts you, insults you or accuses you unjustly, the effect—as long as you do not lose your temper with that person or bear a grudge—will be to exhaust many of your past negative actions and obscurations. By developing patience in such situations you can accumulate abundant merit. Consider all who wrong you, therefore, as your teachers. As it is said,

> If there were no-one with whom to get angry, with whom could you cultivate patience?

Nowadays we often hear that someone is a really good lama or monk but has a terrible temper. But there is no worse fault in the world than anger—so how could anyone be so good and at the same time have a terrible temper? Padampa Sangye says:

> You don't understand that a moment's action arising from anger is worse than a hundred actions arising from desire.

If you have really assimilated the teachings properly, everything you do, say and think should be as soft as stepping on cotton wool and as mild as *tsampa* soup laced with butter. But it may well be the contrary, and the slightest virtuous practice you do, or vow you keep, makes you feel very pleased with yourself and puffs you up with pride. Or every time anyone says a single word you are extremely sensitive to the way they speak, and boil with anger whenever you think you are being humiliated or criticized. That sort of touchiness is a sign that your mind and the Dharma have gone separate ways and that the Dharma has not changed your mind in the least. Geshe Chengawa says:

> If, as we study, reflect and meditate, our ego grows bigger and bigger, our patience becomes more fragile than a baby's skin, and we feel even more irritable than the demon Tsang Tsen, these are sure signs that our study, meditation and reflection have taken the wrong direction.

Always be humble, dress modestly, and treat everyone, whether good, bad or mediocre, with respect. Tame your mind with the Dharma, taking the love and compassion of bodhicitta as your basis. Without any doubt, this is the most essential point of all practices. It is better than a thousand "most sublime" views or "most profound" meditations which do no good to the mind.

2.3.2 Patience to bear hardships for the Dharma

For the sake of practising Dharma you should ignore heat, cold and all other difficulties. The tantras say:

> Even through flaming infernos or seas of razor-sharp blades,
> Search for the Dharma until you die.

The ancient Kadampas had these four goals:

> Base your mind on the Dharma,
> Base your Dharma on a humble life,
> Base your humble life on the thought of death,
> Base your death on an empty, barren hollow.

Nowadays we think we can practise Dharma alongside our worldly activities, without the slightest need for determination* or for hardship, all the while enjoying comfort, well-being and popularity. "Other people manage to do it," we insist, and say admiringly, "Now, that's a good lama, he knows how to combine Dharma and worldly life."

But how could there be a way to marry Dharma with worldly life? Those who claim to be doing so are likely to be leading a good worldly life, but you may be sure that they are not practising pure Dharma. To claim that you can practise Dharma and worldly life at the same time is like saying that you can sew with a double-pointed needle, put fire and water in the same container or ride two horses in opposite directions. All these things are simply impossible.

Could any ordinary person ever surpass Buddha Śākyamuni? Yet even he found no way of practising the Dharma and worldly life side by side. Instead, he left his kingdom behind like spit in the dust, and went to live on the banks of the River Nairañjanā, where he practised asceticism for six years, nourishing himself on only a single drop of water and a single grain of barley every year.

What about Jetsun Milarepa? While he was doing his practice, he had neither food nor clothing. He ate nothing but nettles, and his whole body became like a skeleton covered in greenish hair. Those who saw him had no idea whether he was a man or a demon. The fact that he practised Dharma to that point, so tenaciously and accepting hardship so willingly, surely proves that it is impossible to follow the Dharma and worldly life

* *snying rus*, lit. "a bone in the heart," means a bold determination and courage which never gives up.

at the same time. Could Milarepa really have been too hopeless to know how to combine the two?

The great siddha Melong Dorje attained accomplishment after practising for nine years, eating nothing but the bark of the *lakhe* tree. Longchen Rabjam, the Omniscient Sovereign of the Dharma, lived only on twenty-one pills of mercury* for many months. When it snowed, he used to get into a rough sack that served him as both bed and clothing.

All the siddhas of the past attained accomplishment only by practising with determination, willingly accepting all hardships, having cast aside every worldly activity. Not one of them attained realization by practising alongside the usual activities of everyday life, enjoying comfort, well-being and fame. Rigdzin Jigme Lingpa says:

> By the time you have set yourself up with a comfortable place to stay, plenty of food, warm clothes and a generous benefactor, you have completely cultivated the demon before even starting to cultivate the Dharma.

Geshe Shawopa says:

> To practise Dharma with sincerity your ambition in life should be poverty. At the end of a life of poverty, you should be able to deal with your death. If you have this attitude, you can be sure that no god, demon or human being will ever be able to make difficulties for you.

Jetsun Mila sang:

> No-one to ask me if I'm sick,
> No-one to mourn me when I die:
> To die here alone in this hermitage
> Is everything a yogī could wish for.
>
> No trace of feet outside my door,
> No trace of blood within:**
> To die here alone in this hermitage
> Is everything a yogī could wish for.

* Mercury is used in the practice of *bcud len* (extracting the essence). Its toxicity is neutralized and pills are made from it on which meditators live without having to eat ordinary food.

** This may mean that there is no doctor to practise bloodletting or simply that there is no meat in Milarepa's frugal fare.

No-one to wonder where I've gone,
No particular place to go.
To die here alone in this hermitage
Is everything a yogī could wish for.

My corpse can rot and be eaten by worms,
My gristle and bone be sucked dry by flies;
To die here alone in this hermitage
Is everything a yogī could wish for.

It is therefore of fundamental importance to cast to the winds all the cravings of ordinary life and to practise without caring about heat, cold or any other difficulties.

2.3.3 Patience to face the profound truth without fear

Should you receive teachings on the natural state of profound emptiness or, more particularly, on the key points of the Natural Great Perfection beyond all activity and effort, or on the *Twelve Vajra Laughs* beyond the effects of good and bad actions, or on the *Eight Great Marvellous Verses*, try to grasp their true meaning without giving rise to negative views.

To have wrong views about these teachings or to criticize them is what is called "the harmful act of rejecting the Dharma." It can cast one into the depths of hell for innumerable kalpas. As one confession text says:

I confess all the times I have committed an act even more pernicious
Than the five acts with immediate retribution: that of rejecting the Dharma.

One day, two Indian monks who had the twelve qualities of full training presented themselves before Atīśa. When Atīśa explained to them that the ego has no intrinsic existence, they were pleased.

But when he explained that phenomena have no intrinsic existence either,[156] they exclaimed, "That's terrifying! Don't say such things!" and when he read the Heart Sūtra, they blocked their ears.

Atīśa, sick at heart, told them, "Unless you train yourselves in the love and compassion of bodhicitta and then develop confidence in the profound teachings, your pure vows alone will lead you nowhere."[157]

There were said to be many grossly arrogant monks at the time of the Buddha who, when they heard him teach on profound emptiness, vomited blood and died, and were reborn in the hells. A number of other stories recount similar happenings.

It is important to have a heartfelt and respectful interest in the profound teachings and those who teach them. At the very least, even if the limitations of your own mind make you indifferent to them, never criticize them.

2.4 TRANSCENDENT DILIGENCE

There are three kinds of diligence: armour-like diligence, diligence in action and diligence that cannot be stopped.[158]

2.4.1 Armour-like diligence

When you hear the stories of the lives of the great teachers, Buddhas and Bodhisattvas, of the deeds they did and the trials they went through for the Dharma, do not be discouraged. Never think that they were only capable of achieving all they did because they were Buddhas and Bodhisattvas, and that you could never do the same. Instead, remember that it was simply by acting in this way that they all became so accomplished. Since you are their disciple, even though you might not do better, you have no choice but to follow in their footsteps.

If so much perseverance and hardship was necessary for them, how could such things not be imperative for us, lacking as we do their continuous training in Dharma from time without beginning, and weighed down as we are by our past negative actions?

We have all the freedoms and advantages of a human existence. We have met an authentic spiritual teacher and are receiving the profound instructions. Now that we have this opportunity to practise the true Dharma properly, we should vow from the bottom of our hearts to do so, and be prepared to accept hardhips, take on heavy burdens, and risk life and limb without a care for our flesh and our blood. That is what is meant by armour-like diligence.*

2.4.2 Diligence in action

While having every intention of studying and practising Dharma, you may well keep putting it off until tomorrow or the next day, day by day all your life. You must avoid wasting a whole human lifetime forever planning to practise. Druk Pema Karpo said:

> Human life is like being in the slaughterer's pen:

* "The essence of diligence is to take joy in doing positive actions." NT

> Death comes closer with every second.
> If you unhurriedly put off today until tomorrow,
> Beware of tears and regret upon your deathbed!

Do not wait another second to practise. Do something about it immediately, like a coward finding a snake in his lap or a dancing-girl whose hair has just caught fire. Totally abandon worldly activities and devote yourself to the practice of the Dharma right now. Otherwise you will never find the time—one worldly activity will follow another, endlessly like ripples on water. They will only stop when you decide once and for all to put an end to them. As the Omniscient Longchenpa says:

> Worldly preoccupations never end until the moment we die.
> But they end when we drop them—such is their nature.

and:

> Our activities are like children's games:
> They go on as long as we continue, they stop as soon as we stop them.

Once you feel the wish to practise Dharma, do not let laziness or procrastination take over even for a moment. Set to work immediately, spurred on by the thought of impermanence. That is what is called diligence in action.

2.4.3 Diligence that cannot be stopped

Do not feel satisfied just at having done a little retreat, or some approach and accomplishment practices, a few prayers or one or two good works. Vow to practise for as long as you live, and determine to keep your efforts going, with all the constant power of a great river, until you have attained perfect Buddhahood.

The supreme beings of the past said that one should practise like a hungry yak grazing. As a yak tugs at one clump of grass, its eye is already fixed on the next. In the same way, before you finish one Dharma practice, tell yourself that as soon as you have finished your present practice you will start this or that new practice.

Try to make greater and greater efforts each day, all the time, without ever letting your body, speech or mind slip into idleness or separate from the Dharma even for an instant. Rigdzin Jigme Lingpa says:

> To practise with greater tenacity the closer one gets to death is the mark of a Dharma practitioner who has not been caught by the

> frost.*

These days, those who are reputed to be great meditators or good lamas are often told by people, "Now you no longer need to do prostrations, recite prayers, accumulate merit and wisdom, purify obscurations, and all that."

They soon start to believe it themselves, and think of themselves as being very important and no longer in need of these things. But, as the peerless Dagpo Rinpoche said,

> Thinking that one does not need such things proves that one needs them more than ever.

Every day the great Indian master Dīpaṁkara** would set to work making *tsa-tsas*. His hands would soon be covered in clay.

His followers said, "People are talking because a great teacher like you is handling mud. What's more, you're tiring yourself out. Why not let us do it for you?"

"What are you saying?" said Dīpaṁkara. "Are you soon going to start eating my food for me, too?"

Until you attain perfect Buddhahood, you will still have past actions and tendencies to remove, and will still need to attain more and more spiritual qualities. So do not fall into indolent and sporadic practice. Practise Dharma with diligence from the depth of your heart, without ever feeling that you have done enough.

Generally speaking, whether you attain Buddhahood or not depends solely on your diligence. So make every effort to practise the three kinds of diligence. Someone with exceptional intelligence but only a little diligence will only be an inferior practitioner. But someone with little intelligence and extraordinary diligence will become a superior practitioner. With no diligence whatsoever, all other good qualities would be useless. The Omniscient Jigme Lingpa said:

> No intelligence, no power,
> No wealth or strength can help
> Someone without diligence—
> He is like a boatman whose boat
> Has everything but oars.

* Frost, which destroys one's crop of fruit, symbolizes the obstacles which prevent us from attaining our goal.

** Another name for Atīśa.

Always moderate your eating. Arrive at a balanced amount of sleep. Make your efforts steady and constant. Make your mind like a good bowstring, neither too loose nor too tight. It will get you nowhere to practise sporadically, only when you have time.

2.5 TRANSCENDENT CONCENTRATION

It is impossible to develop concentration without first renouncing excitement and distracting preoccupations, and going to stay in a solitary place. So to start with, it is important to give up distractions.

2.5.1 Giving up distractions

Whatever is brought together will fall apart. Parents, brothers and sisters, spouses, friends and relatives—even the flesh and bones of the body that we received at birth—are all destined to separate. Understand the futility of becoming attached to ephemeral loved ones and friends, and always remain in solitude. Repa Shiwa Ö says:

> Buddhahood is within ourselves alone.
> Although spiritual companions support our practice,
> Having more than three or four together brings up hatred and attachment.
> So I for one shall stay alone.

Wanting things is what causes all of our troubles. We are never satisfied with what we have, and the wealthier we get the more our avarice grows. As the saying goes, "Being rich means being miserly." Or again, "Like the rich, the more you get, the more you need," and, "To lose your enemies, lose your money." The more resources, money and property you own, the more danger you face from enemies, robbers and so on. You can spend your entire life acquiring, protecting and increasing your wealth. This can only lead to suffering and negative actions. The sublime Nāgārjuna said:

> Amassing wealth, guarding it and making it grow will wear you out;
> Understand that riches bring unending ruin and destruction.

Even if one man were to own all the wealth and possessions in the whole world, it would not change the fact that he would still only need enough food and clothing for one person. But however rich they may be, people can still hardly bear to eat a mouthful of food themselves, or use enough clothing to cover their own backs. Heedless of wrongdoing or suffering, ignoring all criticism, they risk their present lives and throw future lives to the winds; for the most trifling material possession, they disregard any sense of shame and honesty, all prudence and wise forethought, and any consideration of Dharma or of their samayas. Spending all their time running after food, profit and social standing, like roving spirits hunting for tormas, they waste their whole lives without ever experiencing even a single day of freedom, well-being or happiness. Finally, having piled up all that wealth, they may well pay for it with their lives and get stabbed or shot just for their money. Then everything they have amassed over a whole lifetime gets spent by their enemies and other people. It is all squandered. But the pile of evil deeds as high as Mount Meru that they built up to get rich remains exclusively theirs, and will cause them to wander in the unbearable depths of the lower realms, never to be free. So while you still have the chance, use the few possessions you may have in this life to provide for future lives. Be content with a meagre amount of food and just enough clothing to keep out the wind.

Those whose ambitions are limited to this present life are known in the texts as "childish friends." They are not at all grateful for any help you may extend to them, and in return may well do you harm. No matter what you do for them, it is never right. They are very hard to please. If you have more than they do, they are jealous; if you have less, they look down on you. The more time you spend with them, the more your negative actions multiply and your positive ones dwindle. Renounce such friends and keep well away from them.

Occupations such as commerce, agriculture, industry and academia involve you in numerous activities and provide endless sources of distraction. These trivial pursuits keep you constantly busy for inconsequential goals. However much effort you make, none of it has any meaning. There is no end to the process of overcoming rivals and favouring friends.

Abandon all these endless activities and distractions like so much spit in the dust. Leave your homeland behind and head for unknown lands. Dwell at the foot of rocky cliffs with only wild animals for companions. Settle your body and mind down in a state of ease.[159] Stop caring about food, clothing or what people say. Live out your life in deserted places where there are no other human beings. Jetsun Milarepa said:

> In a rocky cave in a deserted land
> My sorrow is unrelenting.
> My teacher, Buddha of the three times,
> I yearn for you unceasingly.

If you do as he did, you will find that, as the saying goes, "in places where you feel lonely, concentration arises." There, all the good qualities of the path—disenchantment with saṁsāra, determination to free oneself from it, faith, purity of perception, concentration and absorption—arise naturally. Do whatever you can to live like that.

In secluded forests, those places where the Buddhas and Bodhisattvas of the past found tranquillity, there is nothing to make you busy, no distractions, no commerce, no fields to be worked, no childish friends. Birds and wild deer are easy companions; spring water and leaves provide good ascetic fare. Awareness is naturally clear and concentration develops by itself. Without enemies, without friends, you can be free from the chains of attachment and hatred. Such places have every advantage. In *The Moon Lamp Sūtra* and other sūtras, Lord Buddha says that simply having the wish to go to solitary places and taking seven steps in their direction is worth more than making offerings to all the Buddhas in the ten directions for as many kalpas as there are grains of sand in the Ganges. How much more so if you actually go to live in such places. It is also said:

> In the perfect secluded place, deep in the mountains,
> Everything one does is good.

Even without your making any diligent efforts to practice, in such places disillusionment with saṁsāra, determination to be free from it, love, compassion and all the other excellent qualities of the path will arise spontaneously. As a result, your whole way of life can only become wholesome. Attachment, hatred and all the negative emotions that you had tried in vain to control in places bustling with activity will diminish by themselves, simply because you are now in solitude. It will be easy to develop all the qualities of the path.

These points are the preliminaries for concentration, and are of vital importance. They cannot be dispensed with.

2.5.2 Actual concentration

Concentration is of three kinds: the concentration practised by ordinary beings, concentration which clearly discerns and the excellent concentration of the Tathāgatas.

The concentration practised by ordinary beings. When you are attached to the experiences of bliss, clarity and absence of thought in meditation and intentionally seek them, or your practice is coloured by any affinity for experiences, that is called the concentration practised by ordinary beings.[160]

Clearly discerning concentration. When you are free from any attachment to meditative experiences and are no longer fascinated by concentration, but still cling to emptiness as an antidote, that is called clearly discerning concentration.

The excellent concentration of the Tathāgatas. When you no longer have any concept of emptiness as an antidote, but remain in a concept-free concentration on the nature of reality, that is called the excellent concentration of the Tathāgatas.

Whenever you practise concentration, it is important to sit in the "seven point posture of Vairocana"[161] with your eyes maintaining the appropriate gaze. It is said:

> When the body is straight, the channels are straight;
> When the channels are straight the energies are straight;
> When the energies are straight the mind is straight.[162]

Do not lie down or lean against anything, but sit straight upright, your mind free from any thought, and rest in equanimity in a state where there is no grasping to anything. That is the essence of transcendent concentration.

2.6 TRANSCENDENT WISDOM

Transcendent wisdom has three aspects: wisdom that comes through hearing, wisdom that comes through reflection and wisdom that comes through meditation.

2.6.1 Wisdom through hearing

This means listening to all the words and meaning of the Dharma spoken by a spiritual teacher, and understanding the meaning of those words as they are spoken.

2.6.2 Wisdom through reflection

This means not only listening to what the teacher has taught and understanding it, but subsequently reviewing it in your mind and clearly establishing the meaning through reflection, examination and analysis, and asking questions about what you do not understand. It is not enough just to suppose that you know or understand some particular subject. You should make absolutely sure that when the time comes to practise in solitude you will be able to manage on your own, without needing to ask anyone to clarify certain points.

2.6.3 Wisdom through meditation

Through meditation, as you gain practical experience of what you have understood intellectually, the true realization of the natural state develops in you without any mistake. Certainty is born from within. Liberated from confining doubts and hesitations, you see the very face of the natural state.

Having first eliminated all your doubts through hearing and reflection, you come to the practical experience of meditation, and see everything as empty forms without any substantiality, as in the eight similes of illusion:

As in a dream, all the external objects perceived with the five senses are not there, but appear through delusion.

As in a magic show, things are made to appear by a temporary conjunction of causes, circumstances and connections.

As in a visual aberration, things appear to be there, yet there is nothing.

As in a mirage, things appear but are not real.

As in an echo, things can be perceived but there is nothing there, either outside or inside.

As in a city of gandharvas, there is neither a dwelling nor anyone to dwell.

As in a reflection, things appear but have no reality of their own.

As in a city created by magic, there are all sorts of appearances but they are not really there.

Seeing all the objects of your perception in this way, you come to understand that all these appearances are false by their very nature. When you look into the nature of the subject that perceives them—the mind—those objects that appear to it do not stop appearing, but the concepts that take them as having any true existence subside. To leave the mind in the realization of the nature of reality, empty yet clear like the sky, is transcendent wisdom.

To explain the six transcendent perfections in detail, each one is divided into three, making a total of eighteen sections. The category of material generosity has three sections of its own, making twenty sections altogether. If we add transcendent means, that makes twenty-one; transcendent strength, twenty-two; transcendent aspiration, twenty-three and transcendent primal wisdom, twenty-four.[163]

Going into even more detail, each of the six transcendent perfections can be divided into six, making thirty-six sections. We can see how this works by examining the section on the giving of Dharma in transcendent generosity.

When the teacher who teaches, the Dharma to be taught and the disciple to whom the teaching is to be transmitted come together, explaining the teaching is transcendent *generosity*. That the teacher does not seek gain or honour for teaching the Dharma, and does not contaminate what he is doing either with self-aggrandizement, resentment of the position of others, or any other negative emotion, is transcendent *discipline*. That he repeats the meaning of a phrase over and over again and ignores all difficulty and fatigue is transcendent *patience*. That he teaches at the appointed time without giving way to laziness and procrastination is transcendent *diligence*. That he explains his subject without letting his mind get distracted from the words and their meaning, without making any errors and without adding or omitting anything is transcendent *concentration*. That while teaching he remains imbued with wisdom free of all concepts of subject, object and action is transcendent *wisdom*. All of the transcendent perfections are therefore present.

Now look at material giving—offering food or drink to a beggar, for example. When the gift, the giver and the recipient are all brought together and the action is actually accomplished, that is *generosity*. Giving from what you would eat or drink yourself, rather than giving bad or spoilt food, is *discipline*. Never getting irritated, even when asked over and over again for alms, is *patience*. Giving readily, without ever thinking how tiring or difficult it is, is *diligence*. Not letting yourself be distracted by other thoughts is *concentration*. Knowing that the three elements of subject, object and action have no intrinsic reality is *wisdom*. Here again all the six transcendent perfections are included. The same subdivisions can be defined for discipline, patience, and so on.

Summing up the essence of the transcendent perfections, Jetsun Mila says:

> Perfectly give up belief in any true existence,
> There is no other generosity than this.
> Perfectly give up guile and deceit,
> There is no other discipline.
> Perfectly transcend all fear of the true meaning,
> There is no other patience.
> Perfectly remain inseparable from the practice,
> There is no other diligence.
> Perfectly stay in the natural flow,
> There is no other concentration.
> Perfectly realize the natural state,
> There is no other wisdom.
> Perfectly practise Dharma in everything you do,

There are no other means.
Perfectly conquer the four demons,
There is no other strength.
Perfectly accomplish the twofold goal,
There is no further aspiration.
Recognize the very source of negative emotions,
There is no other primal wisdom.

When Khu, Ngok and Drom* once asked him what were the best of all the elements of the path, Atīśa replied:

The best scholar is one who has realized the meaning of the absence of any true existence.
The best monk is one who has tamed his own mind.
The best quality is a great desire to benefit others.
The best instruction is always to watch the mind.
The best remedy is to know that nothing has any inherent reality.
The best way of life is one that does not fit with worldly ways.
The best accomplishment is a steady lessening of negative emotions.
The best sign of practice is a steady decrease of desires.
The best generosity is non-attachment.
The best discipline is to pacify the mind.
The best patience is to keep a humble position.
The best diligence is to give up activities.
The best concentration is not to alter the mind.[164]
The best wisdom is not to take anything at all as truly existing.

And Rigdzin Jigme Lingpa says:

Transcendent generosity is found in contentment;
Its essence is simply letting go.
Discipline is not to displease the Three Jewels.[165]
The best patience is unfailing mindfulness and awareness.
Diligence is needed to sustain all the other perfections.
Concentration is to experience as deities all the appearances to which one clings.[166]
Wisdom is the self-liberation of grasping and clinging;
In it there is neither thinking nor a thinker.
It is not ordinary. It is free from fixed convictions.[167]
It is beyond suffering. It is supreme peace.

* Atīśa's three main disciples (see glossary).

Do not tell this to everyone—
Keep it sacred within your own mind.

To put in a nutshell the whole vast path of the Bodhisattva teachings, including the six transcendent perfections, it could be summarized in its entirety as "emptiness of which compassion is the very essence." Saraha says in his *Dohās*:

Without compassion, the view of emptiness
Will never lead you to the sublime path.
Yet meditating solely on compassion, you remain
Within saṁsāra; so how could you be free?
But he who comes to possess both of these
Will neither in saṁsāra nor in nirvāṇa dwell.

To dwell neither in saṁsāra nor in nirvāṇa is the "non-dwelling nirvāṇa" of the level of total Buddhahood. As Lord Nāgārjuna says:

Emptiness of which compassion is the very essence
Is only for those who want enlightenment.

Drom Tönpa once asked Atīśa what was the ultimate of all teachings.

"Of all teachings, the ultimate is emptiness of which compassion is the very essence," replied the Master. "It is like a very powerful medicine, a panacea which can cure every disease in the world. And just like that very powerful medicine, realization of the truth of emptiness, the nature of reality, is the remedy for all the different negative emotions."

"Why is it, then," Drom Tönpa went on, "that so many people who claim to have realized emptiness have no less attachment and hatred?"

"Because their realization is only words," Atīśa replied. "Had they really grasped the true meaning of emptiness, their thoughts, words and deeds would be as soft as stepping on cotton wool or as *tsampa* soup laced with butter. The Master Āryadeva said that even to wonder whether or not all things were empty by nature would make saṁsāra fall apart.[168] True realization of emptiness, therefore, is the ultimate panacea which includes all the elements of the path."

"How can every element of the path be included within the realization of emptiness?" Drom Tönpa asked.

"All the elements of the path are contained in the six transcendent perfections. Now, if you truly realize emptiness, you become free from attachment. As you feel no craving, grasping or desire for anything within or without, you always have transcendent generosity. Being free from grasping and attachment, you are never defiled by negative actions, so you always have transcendent discipline. Without any concepts of 'I' and 'mine' you have no anger, so you always have transcendent patience. Your mind made truly joyful by the realization of emptiness, you always have transcendent diligence. Being free from distraction, which comes from grasping at things as solid, you always have transcendent concentration. As you do not conceptualize anything whatsoever in terms of subject, object and action, you always have transcendent wisdom."

"Do those who have realized the truth become Buddhas simply through the view of emptiness and meditation?" Drom Tönpa asked.

"Of all that we perceive as forms and sounds there is nothing that does not arise from the mind. To realize that the mind is awareness indivisible from emptiness is the *view*. Keeping this realization in mind at all times, and never being distracted from it, is *meditation*. To practise the two accumulations as a magical illusion from within that state is *action*. If you make a living experience of this practice, it will continue in your dreams. If it comes in the dream state, it will come at the moment of death. And if it comes at the moment of death it will come in the intermediate state. If it is present in the intermediate state you may be certain of attaining supreme accomplishment."

The eighty-four thousand doors to the Dharma that the Conqueror taught are thus all skilful means to cause the bodhicitta—emptiness of which compassion is the very essence—to arise in us.

Without bodhicitta, teachings on the view and meditation, however profound they may seem, will be no use at all for attaining perfect Buddhahood. Tantric practices like the generation phase, the perfection phase and so on, practised within the context of bodhicitta, lead to complete Buddhahood in one lifetime. But without bodhicitta they are no different from the methods of the tīrthikas. Tīrthikas also have many practices involving meditating on deities, reciting mantras and working with the channels and energies; they too behave in accordance with the principle of cause and effect. But it is solely because they do not take refuge or arouse bodhicitta that they are unable to achieve liberation from the realms of saṁsāra. This is why Geshe Kharak Gomchung said:

> It is no use taking all the vows, from those of refuge up to the tantric samayas, unless you turn your mind away from the things of this world.
>
> It is no use constantly preaching the Dharma to others unless you can pacify your own pride.
>
> It is no use making progress if you relegate the refuge precepts to the last place.

> It is no use practising day and night unless you combine this with bodhicitta.

Unless you first create the proper foundation with the refuge and bodhicitta, however intensively you might seem to be studying, reflecting and meditating, it will all be no more use than building a nine-storey mansion on a frozen lake in winter, and painting frescoes on its plastered walls. Ultimately it makes no sense at all.

Never undervalue the refuge and bodhicitta practices, assuming that they are inferior or just for beginners. Complete them in full, within the framework of preparation, main practice and conclusion that applies to any path. It is most important for everyone, good or bad, high or low, to concentrate their sincerest efforts on these practices.

In the particular case of lamas and monks who take donations from the faithful, who receive funds on behalf of the dead, or who do ceremonies to guide the dead, it is absolutely indispensable that they have sincere bodhicitta. Without it, none of their rituals and purifications will be of the slightest use to either the living or the dead. For others, they might appear to be helping, but deep down that help will always be mixed with selfish motives. For themselves, they will be defiled by accepting those offerings, and will engender endless faults that can only lead them to lower realms in their next life.

Even someone who can fly like a bird, travel under the earth like a mouse, pass through rocks unimpeded, leave imprints of his hands and feet on rocks, someone who has unlimited clairvoyance and can perform all kinds of miracles—if such a person has no bodhicitta, he can only be a tīrthika or possessed by some powerful demon. He might, at first, attract some naive innocents who will be impressed and bring offerings. But in the long run he will only bring ruin upon himself and others. On the other hand, a person who possesses true bodhicitta, even without having any other quality, will benefit whoever comes into contact with him or her.

You never know where there might be a Bodhisattva. It is said that many Bodhisattvas, using their skilful methods, are to be found even among slaughterers of animals and prostitutes. It is difficult to tell whether someone has bodhicitta or not. The Buddha said:

> Apart from myself and those like me, no one can judge another person.

So just consider anyone who arouses bodhicitta in you as being a real Buddha, whether a deity, teacher, spiritual companion or anyone else.

Whenever you feel that you have acquired certain qualities as signs of progress on the path, whatever they may be—realization of the natural state, clairvoyance, concentration, visions of the yidam and so on—you can be certain that they really are true qualities if, as a result, the love and compassion of bodhicitta steadily continue to increase. However, if the effect of such experiences is only to decrease the love and compassion of bodhicitta, you can be equally sure that what looks like a sign of success on the path is in fact either a demonic obstacle, or an indication that you are following the wrong path.

In particular, the authentic realization of the natural state cannot but be accompanied by extraordinary faith and pure perception toward those spiritually more mature than yourself, and extraordinary love and compassion for those who are less so.

The peerless Dagpo Rinpoche once asked Jetsun Mila, "When will I be ready to guide others?"

"One day," the Jetsun replied, "you will have an extraordinarily clear vision of the nature of your mind, quite different from the one you have now, and free from any kind of doubt. At that time, in a way that is not at all ordinary, you will perceive me, your old father, as a real Buddha, and you will inevitably feel natural love and compassion for all beings. That is when you should start to teach."

Study, reflect and meditate on the Dharma, therefore, without dissociating one from the other, on the firm basis of the love and compassion of bodhicitta. Without first eliminating doubts through study, you will never be able to practise. It is said:

> To meditate without having studied
> Is like climbing a rock when you have no arms.

Eliminating doubts through study does not mean that you have to know all the vast and innumerable subjects that there are to be known. In this degenerate era, that would never be possible within a short lifetime. What it does mean is that whatever teachings you are going to put into practice, you should know exactly how to do so from beginning to end without a single mistake. Any hesitations you might have, you should clear away by reflecting on those teachings.

When Atīśa was at Nyethang, Nachung Tönpa of Shang, Kyung Tönpa, and Lhangtsang Tönpa asked him to teach them about the different systems of logic.

Atīśa replied, "The non-Buddhist tīrthikas and the Buddhists themselves have many systems, but they are all just chains of discursive thought. There is no need for all those innumerable ideas: life is too short to go through them all. Now is the time to reduce these things to their essence."

"How does one reduce them to their essence?" Nachung Tönpa of Shang asked.

"By training in bodhicitta with love and compassion for all living creatures throughout space. By making strenuous efforts in the two accumulations for the benefit of all those beings. By dedicating all the sources of future good thus created to the perfect enlightenment of each and every being. And, finally, by recognizing that all these things are empty by nature, like dreams or magical illusions."

If you do not know how to reduce any practice to its essence, no amount of information, knowledge and intellectual understanding will be of any use to you at all.

When Atīśa came to Tibet, he was invited to visit the great translator Rinchen Zangpo. He questioned the translator about which teachings he knew, naming a long list, one after another. It turned out that there were none that Rinchen Zangpo did not know. Atīśa was extremely pleased.

"Wonderful!" he said. "The fact that someone as learned as yourself already lives in Tibet means my visit is quite superfluous. And how do you combine all these teachings when you sit down to practise?"

"I practise each one as it is explained in its own text," said Rinchen Zangpo.

"Rotten translator!" cried Atīśa in disappointment. "Then my coming to Tibet was necessary after all!"

"But what should I do instead?" asked the translator.

"You should find the essential point common to all the teachings and practise that way," Atīśa told him.

It is indispensable to seek the vital point of the practice, based on the teacher's pith instructions. Once you know the essential point, you must put it into practice, or it will be utterly useless. Jetsun Mila said:

> The hungry are not satisfied by hearing about food; what they need is to eat. In the same way, just to know about Dharma is useless; it has to be practised.

The purpose of practice is to be an antidote for negative emotions and ego-clinging. Jetsun Mila again:

> It is said that you can tell whether someone has just eaten by how red his face is. Similarly, you can tell whether people know and practise the Dharma by whether it works as a remedy for their negative emotions and ego-clinging.

Potowa asked Geshe Tönpa what was the dividing line between Dharma and non-Dharma. The geshe answered:

> If it counteracts negative emotions it is Dharma. If it doesn't, it is non-Dharma.
> If it doesn't fit with worldly ways it is Dharma. If it fits, it is non-Dharma.
> If it fits with the scriptures and your instructions it is Dharma. If it doesn't fit, it is non-Dharma.
> If it leaves a positive imprint it is Dharma. If it leaves a negative imprint it is non-Dharma.

Master Chegom says:

> To believe in the effects of actions is the right view for those of ordinary faculties. To realize all inner and outer phenomena as the union both of appearance and emptiness, and of awareness and emptiness, is the right view for those of higher faculties. To realize that the view, the one who holds it and realization itself are indivisible[169] is the right view for those of the highest faculties.
>
> To keep the mind totally concentrated on its object is the correct meditation for those of ordinary faculties. To rest concentrated on the four unions[170] is the right meditation for those of higher faculties. A state of non-conceptualization in which there is no object of meditation, no meditator and no meditative experience is the right meditation for those of the highest faculties.
>
> To be as wary about the effects of actions as one is careful to protect one's eyes is the right action for those of ordinary faculties. To act while experiencing everything as a dream and an illusion is the right action for those of higher faculties. Total non-action[171] is the right action for those of the highest faculties.
>
> The progressive diminution of ego-clinging, negative emotions and thoughts is the sign of "warmth"* for all practitioners, be they of ordinary, higher or the highest faculties.

Similar words are to be found in *The Precious Supreme Path* by the peerless Dagpo.

When studying Dharma, therefore, you should know how to get at the essence of it. The great Longchenpa says:

* *drod* (see glossary).

> Knowledge is as infinite as the stars in the sky;
> There is no end to all the subjects one could study.
> It is better to grasp straight away their very essence—
> The unchanging fortress of the dharmakāya.

Then, as you reflect on Dharma, you should rid yourself of any doubts. Padampa Sangye says:

> Seek the teacher's instructions like a mother falcon seeking her prey.
> Listen to the teachings like a deer listening to music;
> Meditate on them like a dumb person savouring food;
> Contemplate them like a northern nomad shearing sheep;
> Reach their result, like the sun coming out from behind the clouds.

Hearing the Dharma, reflecting on it and meditating upon it should go hand in hand. The peerless Dagpo says:

> To churn together study, reflection and meditation on the Dharma is an infallible essential point.

The result of study, reflection and meditation should be a steady and real increase in the love and compassion of bodhicitta, together with a steady and real diminution of ego-clinging and negative emotions.

This instruction on how to arouse bodhicitta is the quintessence of all Dharma teachings and the essential element of all paths. It is the indispensable teaching, to have which is definitely enough by itself but to lack which is sure to render everything else futile. Do not to be content just with hearing and understanding it. Put it into practice from the very depth of your heart!

> *I claim to be arousing bodhicitta, but still it has not arisen in me.*
> *I have trained in the path of the six perfections, but have remained selfish.*
> *Bless me and small-minded beings like me,*
> *That we may train in the sublime bodhicitta.*

Vajrasattva

CHAPTER THREE

Meditating and reciting on the teacher as Vajrasattva to cleanse all obscurations[172]

Beyond being defiled by the two obscurations, you purport to still be purifying them.*
Having certainly reached the sublime path's very end, you profess to still be learning.
Beyond the extremes of saṁsāra and nirvāṇa, you manifest still in saṁsāra.
Peerless Teacher, at your feet I bow.

Listen to this chapter with the same attitude as before.

I. HOW OBSCURATIONS CAN BE PURIFIED THROUGH CONFESSION

The main obstacles that prevent all the extraordinary experiences and realizations of the profound path from arising are negative actions, obscurations and habitual tendencies.** Just as it is important to clean the surface of a mirror if forms are to be reflected in it, so too it is

* The obscurations of negative emotions and conceptual obscurations. "Obscurations" means factors that cover and obscure our Buddha nature (see glossary).
** Habitual patterns created by past actions.

important to eliminate our obscurations so that realization can appear like a reflection in the mirror of the Ground of All.* The Conqueror taught countless methods of purification for this purpose, but the best of them all is meditation and recitation related to the teacher as Vajrasattva.[173]

There is no harmful act that cannot be purified by confession. As the great teachers of ancient times affirmed:

> There is nothing good about negative actions—except that they can be purified through confession.

Of all negative actions—be they external breaches of the prātimokṣa vows, inner transgressions of the bodhicitta training, or secret violations of the tantric samayas—there is not one, however serious, that cannot be purified by confession.

In the sūtras, the Buddha tells several stories illustrating this point. For instance, there is the tale of the brahmin Atapa, who was known as Aṅgulimāla, "Garland of Fingers." Aṅgulimāla killed nine hundred and ninety-nine people,[174] but then cleansed himself of those actions through confession and attained the state of Arhat in that very lifetime. There is also the case of King Ajātaśatru, who killed his father, but later repaired his crime through confession and attained liberation, having experienced the sufferings of hell only for the time it takes a ball to bounce once. The protector Nāgārjuna says:

> Someone who has acted carelessly
> But later becomes careful and attentive
> Is as beautiful as the bright moon emerging from the clouds,
> Like Nanda, Aṅgulimāla, Darśaka and Śaṅkara.[175]

However, purification only takes place when you confess sincerely in the right way, using the four powers as antidotes. The purification process will never work if your eyes and mouth are otherwise occupied, or if you are just mouthing the words, "I admit... I confess..." while your mind is busy pursuing other thoughts. And to think, "In future, even if I do wrong it won't matter because I can just confess afterwards," will stop the purification from working at all, even if you do confess.

Jetsun Mila says:

> You may doubt that confession can really purify negative actions,

* Skt. *ālaya*. The underlying consciousness in which karmic impressions are stored. See glossary.

> But if your thoughts have become positive, you are purified.

It is absolutely fundamental that any confession should include as antidotes all of the four powers.

II. THE FOUR POWERS

The four powers are the power of support, the power of regretting having done wrong, the power of resolution and the power of action as an antidote.

1. The power of support

In this context, the support is provided by taking refuge in Vajrasattva and cultivating the intention and application aspects of bodhicitta. In other cases, the support would be the particular object to which you address your confession. When you recite the confession of the *Sūtra in Three Parts*, for example, the power of support is provided by the Thirty-five Buddhas. It could also be a teacher, or a representation of the body, speech or mind of the Buddhas—in short, anyone or anything in whose presence you confess.[176]

Before any confession, arousing the bodhicitta of intention and application is indispensable. The Buddha taught that confessing your evil deeds and downfalls without arousing bodhicitta, even though you might apply the four powers, will reduce your faults but not purify them altogether. Sincerely giving rise to bodhicitta, however, will of itself purify all past misdeeds, whatever they might be.[177] In *The Way of the Bodhisattva*, Śāntideva says of bodhicitta:

> As though they pass through perils guarded by a hero,
> Even those weighed down with dreadful wickedness
> Will instantly be freed through having bodhicitta.
> Who then would not place his trust in it?
> Just as by the fires at the end of time
> Great sins are utterly consumed by bodhicitta.

2. The power of regretting having done wrong

The power of regretting having done wrong comes from a feeling of remorse for all the negative actions you have done in the past. There can be no purification if you do not see your misdeeds as something wrong and confess them with fierce regret, without concealing anything.[178] We recite in the *Sūtra in Three Parts*:

> I confess them all, without hiding or holding back anything.

The learned and accomplished Karma Chagme said:

> Confessing them without regret cannot purify them,
> For past misdeeds are like a poison within;
> So confess them with shame, trepidation and great remorse.

3. The power of resolution

The power of resolution means to remember the faults you have committed and to resolve never to commit them again from this very day on, even at the cost of your dear life. In the *Sūtra in Three Parts* we recite:

> I vow to stop from now on.

And the *Prayer of Sukhāvatī* says:

> Without a vow for the future from now on, there is no purification,
> So I make the vow for the future from now on
> That even at the cost of my life I will do no negative action.

4. The power of action as an antidote

This power involves accomplishing as many positive actions as you can, as an antidote to your past negative actions. It refers particularly to activities such as prostrating to the Buddhas and Bodhisattvas, rejoicing in the merit of others, dedicating your sources of future good to enlightenment, cultivating the bodhicitta of intention and application and staying in the essence of the unaltered natural state.

One day a meditator, a disciple of the peerless Dagpo Rinpoche, told his teacher that he felt regret when he remembered that he had once made his living from the sale of sacred books.

"Print books, then," the Master told him.[179]

So he set to work, but found that this work got him involved in many distractions. Disillusioned, he went back to see his teacher.

"Printing these texts brings up too many distractions," he said. "Is it not true that no method of confession is more profound than remaining in the essential nature?"*

Dagpo Rinpoche was delighted and told him that he was perfectly right.

"Even if you have committed negative actions as colossal as Mount

* Remaining in a state of recognition of the nature of the mind.

Meru itself," he said, "they are purified in one instant of seeing that nature."

There is indeed no deeper way to cleanse oneself of past misdeeds than to meditate on bodhicitta and to maintain the flow of the unaltered natural state. Keep these two things in mind as you go through the details of the meditation on Vajrasattva—purification by the stream of nectar, recitation of the hundred syllable mantra, and so on.

To practise the actual meditation and recitation, proceed as follows, remembering all the time the specific pure meaning[180] of each element in the context of the four powers as antidotes.

III. THE ACTUAL MEDITATION ON VAJRASATTVA

For the visualization that follows, see yourself as staying in your ordinary form.[181] Suspended in space an arrow's length above your head, visualize an open white lotus with a thousand petals, and upon it the disc of a full moon. We say "a full moon" here not to indicate how big the disc should be, but to signify that it is perfectly round and regular and looks like the completely full moon on the fifteenth day of the lunar month. Upon this lunar disc, visualize a brilliant white syllable *hūṁ*.* In other traditions the syllable emanates and reabsorbs rays of light, but that is not the case here.

In an instant the *hūṁ* is transformed into your glorious root teacher, that incomparable mine of compassion who in essence is the nature of all the Buddhas of past, present and future in one. He appears in the form of the sambhogakāya Buddha,[182] Vajrasattva, white in colour, like a snow peak lit up by a hundred thousand suns.

He has one face and two arms. With his right hand, he holds before his heart the five-pronged vajra of awareness and emptiness. With his left, he rests the bell of appearance and emptiness at his left hip.[183] His two legs are crossed in the vajra posture and he is adorned with the thirteen ornaments of the sambhogakāya—the five silken garments and eight jewels.

The five silken garments are: 1) a headband, 2) an upper garment, 3) a long scarf, 4) a belt and 5) a lower garment.

The eight jewels are: 1) a crown, 2) earrings, 3) a short necklace, 4) armlets on each arm, 5) two long necklaces, one longer than the other,[184] 6) a bracelet on each wrist, 7) a ring on each hand and 8) an anklet on

* The Tibetan syllable *hūṁ* is shown on page 272.

each foot.

Vajrasattva is seated above your head, facing in the same direction as you. He embraces in inseparable union[185] his consort, Vajratopa, who is also white. Their bodies are empty appearance, vividly present but without any substance of their own, like reflections of the moon in water or forms reflected in a mirror.

This visualization provides the power of support. It is not a flat image like a *tangka* or a fresco. Nor is it inert and inanimate like a clay or gold statue, which is solid and material. It appears: every detail appears clearly and distinctly, even the pupils and whites of the eyes. Yet it is empty: there is not one atom of solid substance to it, no flesh, no blood, no internal organs. It is like a rainbow appearing in space or an immaculate crystal vase. And it is imbued with wisdom: Lord Vajrasattva is identical in nature with your own compassionate root teacher, and his mind reaches out to you and to all beings with great love.

As the power of regret, in his presence call to mind all the negative actions you can think of that you have accumulated until now, in one samsaric existence after another since time without beginning: the ten negative actions of body, speech and mind, the five crimes with immediate retribution, the four serious faults, the eight perverse acts, all transgressions of the external vows of prātimokṣa, the inner Bodhisattva precepts or the secret tantric samayas of the vidyādharas, all the ordinary promises that you have not kept, all the lies you have told and everything you have done that is shameful or dishonourable. Feel that you are confessing them all in the teacher Vajrasattva's presence, your whole body breaking out in gooseflesh with shame, fear and remorse. You can be sure that during all those infinite lives in saṁsāra you have done many negative actions that you cannot remember, so confess them all too, saying:

"I am keeping nothing secret. I am hiding nothing. I confess openly and ask for forgiveness. Have compassion on me! Right away, at this very moment and in this very place, cleanse and purify me of all my negative actions and obscurations, so that not a single one remains!"

As the power of resolve, think, "Until now I have accumulated those harmful negative actions because of my ignorance and confusion. But now, thanks to the compassion of my kind teacher, I know what is beneficial and what is harmful, and I will never commit them again, even if it costs me my life."

Keeping in mind the pure meaning of the visualization,[180] recite the root text, starting from:

Ah! I am in my ordinary form, and above my head ...

down as far as the words:

> ... *Purify me until not a single one remains!*

Then, in the heart of Vajrasattva, who is indivisibly united with his consort, visualize a lunar disc no bigger than a flattened mustard seed, and upon it a white *hūṁ*, as fine as if it had been drawn with a single hair. As you recite the hundred syllable mantra once, "Oṁ Vajrasattva Samaya..." and so on, visualize its syllables arranged around the *hūṁ* in a circle. None of them touch each other, like the horns of cattle when they stand close together.* Then recite the hundred syllables as a prayer, imagining at the same time that a nectar of compassion and wisdom drips down from each of the syllables, one glistening drop after another, like water dripping down from ice as it melts near a fire. Pouring down through the body of Vajrasattva, the nectar emerges from the point of union of the deity and consort, and, passing through the crown of your head, flows into you, and into all other sentient beings too.

Like particles of earth being washed away by a powerful stream, all your physical illnesses are flushed out in the form of rotten blood and pus. All negative forces are expelled in the form of spiders, scorpions, toads, fish, snakes, tadpoles, lice and the like, and all harmful actions and obscurations as black liquid, dust, smoke, clouds and vapours. All this is carried away by the irresistible flood of nectar and pours out of your body as a black shower through the lower orifices, the soles of your feet and all the pores of your skin. The earth beneath you opens up and in the depths appears Death, personification of your past actions, surrounded by all the male and female beings to whom you owe karmic debts and all those who seek to venge themselves on your flesh. While you recite the hundred syllable mantra, visualize all those impurities pouring down into their open mouths and into the hands and arms they raise expectantly toward you.

If you can, visualize the whole process simultaneously. Otherwise, you can alternate. As you recite the mantra, sometimes concentrate on the body of Vajrasattva, his face, hands and so on; sometimes on his ornaments and clothing; sometimes on the flow of nectar purifying illnesses, negative forces, evil actions and obscurations; and sometimes on your regret for what you have done and your resolve never to repeat it.

At the end, imagine that Death, the embodiment of past actions, and all the others below the earth—every kind of karmic creditor and all those who seek vengeance on your flesh—are appeased and satisfied. Past scores

* That is, close together without becoming entangled.

have been settled, debts have been repaid and vengeance has been appeased. You are cleansed of all past negative actions and obscurations. Death closes his mouth and hands and lowers his arms. The earth closes again.

Imagine that your body has now become transparent inside and out, a body of light. Running vertically down inside it, visualize the central channel, at four points along whose length are the four wheels* where channels[186] branch out radially like the spokes of an umbrella. At the level of your navel is the wheel of manifestation, with sixty-four radial channels turning upwards. At the level of your heart is the wheel of Dharma, with eight radial channels turning downwards. In your throat is the wheel of enjoyment, with sixteen radial channels turning upwards. In the crown of your head is the wheel of great bliss, with thirty-two radial channels turning downwards.

The nectar then starts to flow down again as before. Beginning with the wheel of great bliss at the crown of your head, it completely fills the central channel and each of the four wheels and then spreads outward, filling your entire body to the tips of your fingers and toes. Brimming with white nectar, you are like a crystal vase filled with milk.

Think that you are receiving the four empowerments:[187] the vase empowerment, the secret empowerment, the wisdom empowerment and the precious word empowerment. You are also purified of the four kinds of obscurations: karmic obscurations, obscurations of negative emotions, conceptual obscurations and obscurations of habitual tendencies. The wisdom of the four joys arises in you: joy, supreme joy, extraordinary joy and innate joy. The levels of the four kāyas are established in you: the nirmāṇakāya, the sambhogakāya, the dharmakāya and the svābhāvikakāya.

Then recite the prayer beginning:

> *O Protector, in ignorance and confusion ...*

and ending:

> *... I beg you, cleanse and purify me!*

Imagine that the moment you recite these lines the teacher Vajrasattva is delighted, and smilingly grants your prayer with these words:

> *Fortunate one, all your negative actions, obscurations, violations and breaches are purified.*

* Skt. *cakra*

He then melts into light and dissolves into you, so that you yourself are now transformed into Vajrasattva, just as you visualized him before.

Visualize in his heart a moon disc the size of a flattened mustard seed. In its centre stands a blue *hūṁ*. In front of the *hūṁ* is a white syllable *oṁ*; to its left is the word *vajra* in yellow; behind is *sa* in red; and to its right is *tva* in green:

	ས	
ཏྭ	ཧཱུྃ	བཛྲ
	ཨོཾ	

	sa	
tva	*hūṁ*	*vajra*
	oṁ	

As you recite "Oṁ Vajra Sattva Hūṁ," five rays of light, white, yellow, red, green, and blue, emanate from the respective syllables in an upward direction. At the end of these rays are the Lady of Beauty and the other offering goddesses. From their hands emanate innumerable offerings, such as the eight auspicious symbols and the seven royal attributes, fringed parasols, victory banners, canopies, thousand-spoked golden wheels, white conch shells spiralling to the right and so on. These offerings delight all the Buddhas and Bodhisattvas in the inconceivable, infinite pure fields of the ten directions, completing the accumulations and purifying your obscurations. All the Buddhas' compassion and blessings come streaming back in the form of light-rays of different colours which dissolve into you. Think that as a result you attain the supreme and common accomplishments; the four levels of vidyādhara related to the path; and the ultimate result—the state beyond learning.[188] This visualization establishes the connections through which you will realize the dharmakāya and benefit yourself.

Then, visualize that innumerable hundreds of thousands of multi-coloured light-rays shoot out downwards from the five syllables, touching all living beings dwelling in the six realms of the three worlds, and purifying all their negative actions, obscurations, sufferings and habitual tendencies just like the light of the rising sun dispelling darkness. The whole universe becomes the Buddhafield of Manifest Joy. All beings within it are transformed into white, yellow, red, green and blue Vajrasattvas.[189] Recite the mantra, imagining that all of them are pronouncing the mantra "Oṁ Vajra Sattva Hūṁ" too with an immense humming sound. This visualization establishes the connections through which you will attain the rūpakāya* and benefit others.

Concerning this type of visualization, *The Dharma Practice that Spontaneously Liberates Habitual Clingings* says:

> Bringing benefit to oneself and others by emanating and reabsorbing light, one is cleansed of conceptual obscurations.

Using such visualization practices, the skilful means of the Secret Mantra Vajrayāna enables one to accumulate inconceivable amounts of merit and wisdom in an instant, while simultaneously benefiting all living creatures throughout the universe.

Recite the mantra as many times as you can, and when the time comes to conclude the session visualize that the whole universe, which you have been perceiving as the Buddhafield of Manifest Joy, dissolves into the beings dwelling in it, the Vajrasattvas of the five families. These deities themselves then gradually melt into light and dissolve into you. Then you yourself melt into light from the outside inwards, and that light dissolves into the *oṁ* in your heart. The *oṁ* dissolves into the *vajra*, the *vajra* into the *sa*, the *sa* into the *tva*, the *tva* into the *shapkyu* of the *hūṁ*, the *shapkyu* into the small *a*, the small *a* into the body of the *ha*, the body into the head, the head into the crescent moon, the crescent into the *bindu* and the *bindu* into the *nāda*.

hūṁ

its parts:

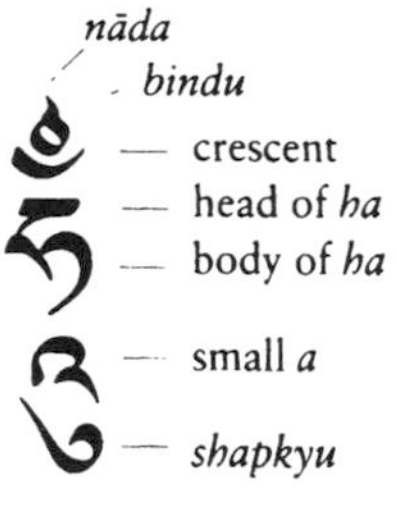

The *nāda*, in turn, like a rainbow vanishing into space, dissolves into simplicity free from any concepts and elaborations. Remain relaxed in that state for a while.

When thoughts start to arise, see clearly the whole universe and the

* Rūpakāya, *gzugs sku*: the body of form (see Glossary)

beings it contains as the Buddhafield of Vajrasattva.

Dedicate the merit with the words:

By the merit of this practice may I quickly attain
The level of Vajrasattva ...

and so on, and say other prayers of aspiration.

While practising any meditation and recitation, including this one on Vajrasattva, it is imperative not to let your mind be distracted from concentration on the practice, and not to interrupt the recitation with ordinary speech. It is said in the tantras:

Reciting without concentration
Is like soaking a rock in the depths of the sea;
Even for a whole kalpa it will bring no result.*

and also:

Purity is a thousand times better than impurity,[190]
Concentration is a hundred thousand times better than no concentration.

Gold or silver, if they contain even small quantities of brass or copper, are considered "not real gold" or "false silver." Likewise, mixing ordinary gossip with the recitation of mantras or the approach practice renders the mantra impure. That is why the Great Master of Oḍḍiyāna said:

A month's recitation with no other speech
Is better than a year of defiled recitation.

This being so, it is of primary importance that those who perform ceremonies in villages refrain from chatting within the ranks of the assembly while they are saying prayers and mantras. If such recitations are mixed with ordinary speech they lose all their meaning. In particular, when a ceremony is being performed for someone who has died, that being, in all the terror and suffering of the intermediate state, will rush to the sponsor, the invited monks and the officiating lama in the hope of obtaining help. Beings in the intermediate state know what is happening in others' minds. If the people doing the ceremony are not clearly concentrated, if they have not kept their vows and samayas, or if what they say and think arises from attachment and hostility, the being in the intermediate state will feel hatred towards them or have negative views

* However long the rock stays there, the water will never penetrate it.

about them, and as a result will fall into lower realms. One would be better off without the services of such officiants as these.

It is said of the rituals of the Secret Mantra Vajrayāna that "to recite the visualization texts of the generation phase is to use words as a means of access." The words of the visualization are there to call to mind the details of the generation phase.[191] But for people performing such ceremonies the proper subject of the visualization, which is the meaning of the generation and perfection phases, does not even cross their minds. They unthinkingly mouth the words of the ritual, like "visualize," "meditate" and "concentrate," using all sorts of ornate intonations, blaring their trumpets and banging away at their cymbals and drums. Finally the moment comes for what should be the most essential point, the approach practice, where the mantra is recited—at which point they just feel released of their duties. They no longer even make the effort to sit up straight. They start smoking tobacco, the source of hundreds of wrong actions,[192] and let loose a rich store of useless chatter, endlessly discussing all the local goings-on from the mountain tops to the valley floor, from the passes to the lowlands. Meanwhile they spend the time pushing the rosary through their fingers at top speed, as if they were making sausages. Towards evening, they glance up at the sky and, seeing the sun's position, with a huge clattering of cymbals start chanting, "Vajra puṣpe dhūpe ..."[193] and so on. This is not even a pale reflection of a proper ritual, nor even the reflection of a reflection. There can be little doubt that just reciting the *Confession of Downfalls* or the *Prayer of Good Actions* once, with perfectly pure motivation, would be far more worthwhile.

Lamas like these, whose impure recitation and travesties of rituals send the dead off to lower rebirths, will likewise do far more harm than good with their rituals for the living. Moreover, abusing people's offerings in this way is exactly what is meant by "swallowing red hot metal balls."[194]

Lamas and monks who profit from the offerings of the faithful and the possessions of the dead should have as the very soul of their practice something more than an evaluation of the quantity of meat, the thickness of cheese, and the quality of the offerings they are getting. Whether they are working for those who are sick or those already dead, the moment is crucial for those beings. For the latter have no refuge from their suffering. They need to be caught and secured by the love and compassion of the lamas' bodhicitta, and the sincere desire to help. The lamas should make every effort to practise whatever they may know of the generation and perfection phases, sincerely and without any distraction. If they know nothing at all of these subjects, they should simply try to think of the meaning of the words they are saying. At the very least, they should focus their body, speech and mind on love and compassion for the suffering being and confident faith in the unfailing power of the Three Jewels. If they also make sure that they perform the ritual properly by correctly reciting the different texts and mantras, there is no doubt that through the compassion of the refuge, the Three Jewels, through the infallible power of the effect of actions and through the immeasurable benefits of bodhicitta, they can really help the sick or the dead. This is what they should make every effort to do, and as in the expression "dissolving your own obscurations on someone else's cushion,"* they will complete the twofold accumulation both for themselves and for others at the same time. They will also establish all those who have contact with them on the path to liberation.

These days, lamas and monks whom one might expect to be a little better than others, and who know about the principle of cause and effect, are so afraid of the defilements attached to offerings that they refuse even to give blessings or say dedication prayers for suffering beings who are sick or dead. In so doing they cut off the love and compassion of bodhicitta at the very root.

The majority are extremely selfish. They take part in ceremonies at the request of their benefactors. But, instead of reciting what the families in question need, they pull out their own prayer-books, grimy and worn out from long use, and with the excuse that they must not interrupt the continuity of their own personal practice, they recite from that while everyone else is reciting the prayers.[195] Whenever they are reciting the least prayer for their own good, they are all extremely scrupulous and claim to be purifying their own obscurations or their abuse of offerings. But they treat prayers in large assemblies for the benefit of patrons as a tiresome chore. They look around all the time, say whatever they want, and never even give a thought for the dead or living person that they are supposed to be protecting. This cuts off the love and compassion of bodhicitta at the very root. Later on, should they ever try to purify themselves of this abuse of offerings, their evil and selfish attitude will make it very difficult to do so successfully.

Instead, take the love and compassion of bodhicitta as your basis from the very start. Never give up your wish to help others. Make a sincere effort to put everything you know about the generation and perfection

* This means that any practice that is performed with the intention of helping another being will benefit not only that being but also the person doing the practice.

phases into practice to the best of your ability. To meditate on the generation and perfection phases and recite mantras in other people's houses will then be no different from doing it in your own. In either case, the need to be free of selfish thoughts and to care about helping others is the same. For these two attitudes are both indispensable.

If you stay undistracted and do not mix your recitation with ordinary speech, to say the hundred syllable mantra one hundred and eight times without interruption will undoubtedly purify all your evil actions and obscurations, and all violations and breaches of vows and samayas. Such is Vajrasattva's promise. The *Tantra of Immaculate Confession* says:

> The hundred syllable mantra is the quintessence of the mind of all the Sugatas. It purifies all violations, all breaches, all conceptual obscurations.
> It is the supreme confession, and to recite it one hundred and eight times without interruption repairs all violations and breaches and will save one from tumbling into the three lower realms.
> The Buddhas of past, present and future will look on the yogī who recites it as a daily practice as their most excellent child, even in this very lifetime, and will watch over and protect him.
> At his death he will undoubtedly become the finest of all the Buddhas' heirs.

Whatever violations and breaches of the root and branch samayas you may commit after setting out on the path of Secret Mantra Vajrayāna, the daily repetition of the hundred syllable mantra twenty-one times every day while meditating on Vajrasattva constitutes what is called "the blessing of downfalls." It will prevent the effects of those downfalls from developing or increasing. One hundred thousand recitations will completely purify all your downfalls. According to *The Essential Ornament*:

> To recite correctly twenty-one times
> The hundred syllable mantra,
> While clearly visualizing Vajrasattva
> Seated on a white lotus and moon,
> Constitutes the blessing of the downfalls,
> Which are thus kept from increasing.
> Thus the great siddhas have taught.
> So practise it always.
> If you recite it a hundred thousand times,
> You will become the very embodiment of utter purity.

In Tibet these days there cannot be a single lama, monk, layman or laywoman who has never received an empowerment and who has therefore not taken up the Secret Mantrayāna. Now, once you have entered the Secret Mantrayāna, if you fail to keep the samayas you go to hell, and if you keep them you attain perfect Buddhahood. There is no third alternative. Just as for a snake that has crawled inside a length of bamboo, it is said, there are only two ways out—straight up or straight down. *The Treasury of Precious Qualities* says:

> Once in the Secret Mantrayāna, you can only go to lower realms
> Or attain Buddhahood; there is no third direction.

The tantric samayas are subtle, numerous and difficult to keep. Even a great master like Atīśa said that, having taken up the path of the tantras, he committed fault after fault in rapid succession. As for us nowadays, the antidotes we have are few. Our mindfulness is weak and our vigilance is non-existent. We are not even really sure what the various downfalls are. Since there can be no doubt that those downfalls must be pouring down on us all the time like rain, it is vital that by way of remedy we make the meditation and recitation of Vajrasattva our daily practice, or at least recite the mantra twenty-one times a day without fail.

Even for an expert in all the essential points of the generation and perfection phases who, through mindfulness, vigilance and so on, has avoided committing the fault of violating the samayas, it is still necessary to persevere in confession and purification. For in fact, any contact through word or deed with someone who has violated the root samayas—even just drinking the water of the same valley—is enough to engender the faults known as "violation through contact" or "occasional violation." The tantras say:

> Having associated with transgressors or gratified their wishes,
> Having explained the Dharma to them or to those unfit to hear it,
> Having not avoided all transgressors, we know we too have been contaminated
> By the obscurations of those transgressions,
> Bringing adversity in this life and obscurations in the next.
> Full of regret, all these mistakes we expose and confess.

If just one person in an assembly has violated the samayas, the other hundred or thousand people who have all kept their own commitments will be contaminated to the point that they will receive no benefit from their practice. It is like a single drop of sour milk turning a whole pot of fresh milk sour, or one frog infested with sores infecting all the others around. As it is said:

> One drop of sour milk
> Turns all the milk sour.
> One degenerate yogī
> Spoils all the other yogīs.

What is more, there is not a single teacher, even if he is a great lama or a siddha, who can escape this sort of contamination by samaya violations. The story of the great teacher Lingje Repa bears this out. While he was in the sacred place of Tsari, the ḍākinī Shingkyong started to create obstacles for him. In the middle of the day, she brought down a darkness so profound that the stars came out and shone brightly in the sky. Yet nothing could stop him reaching the banks of the Dark Red Blood Lake, where he danced to a vajra song, leaving footprints in the solid rock that can still be seen today. Nonetheless, later in his life he was visited by a disciple who had broken the samaya—and even such an accomplished master could still be contaminated. He became delirious and lost the power of his speech.

Likewise we find in the vajra songs of the Siddha Urgyenpa:

> I, Rinchen Pel, the beggar from the Land of the Snows,
> Was defeated by no other enemy than contamination by samaya violation
> And was protected by no other friend than my teacher.

To break the samayas of the Vajrayāna is a great fault, but to keep them is extremely difficult. It would be totally wrong to suppose, without checking carefully, that you are keeping them faithfully, and to feel proud about it.

The tantras explain that to forget for a single instant to identify your body, speech and mind with the three maṇḍalas[196] is to transgress the tantric samayas. Hence the difficulty of keeping them. In detail, there are said to be one hundred thousand samayas—a very large number. According to the tantras, to break them will bring the following evils upon us:

> The Vajra Ogre will drink your heart blood,[197]
> Your life will be short and diseased, your wealth will vanish, enemies will terrify you,
> In the extremely frightening Hell of Ultimate Torment
> You will undergo long and unbearable sufferings.

To remedy all your visible and hidden violations, breaches, faults and downfalls, therefore, always do everything you can to practise the meditation and recitation of Vajrasattva and confess those faults with the hundred syllables. As the great teachers of old used to say:

> The best is not to be sullied by evil actions in the first place, but if it happens, it is important to confess.

Violations of the tantric samayas are easy to repair, since they can be purified by confession. In the śrāvakas' tradition, to commit one complete root downfall[198] is like smashing an earthenware pot: there is simply no way to repair it. To break the Bodhisattva vows is more like breaking an object made of precious metal. Such an object can be repaired if entrusted to a skilful goldsmith. Likewise, the broken vow can be purified with the help of a spiritual friend. As for the tantric vows, committing downfalls is like slightly denting something made of precious metal. It is said that you can completely purify it yourself, simply by confessing it, using the support of the deity, the mantra and concentration. If the fault is confessed immediately, purification is easy. The longer you wait, however, the more powerful the fault grows, and the more difficult confession becomes. If you wait more than three years, the downfall is said to be beyond confession. Even if you confess it, no purification will take place.

There are some gifted people who can use the power and blessing of their speech to work both for their own and others' benefit by providing protection, stopping frosts, preventing hail, halting epidemics, curing sick adults and children and so on. But even such people, to maintain that ability and those blessings, need to purify the obscurations of speech. There is no better means of doing so than reciting the hundred syllable mantra. It is important to recite it earnestly and unremittingly.

My venerable teacher used to joke that those who protect others and make use of offerings should most definitely start to purify their obscurations of speech by completing ten million repetitions of the hundred syllables. In fact, many of his disciples actually recited it ten or even twenty million times, and there was not one of them who did not complete at least two or three hundred thousand recitations.

The teacher Vajrasattva embodies the hundred deities in one. He is called "Vajrasattva, the single deity of the great secret." Of the whole inconceivable infinity of peaceful and wrathful yidam deities, there is not one whom he does not embody. While you meditate on him, consider him as being one in essence with your own root teacher. This is the practice of Guru Yoga "in the manner of the jewel which includes all."[199]

It is the ultimate, the most profound of all methods. Since, as I have already said, the hundred syllable mantra is superior to all other mantras, you must know that there is no more profound practice than this.

I have heard the beneficial instructions, but have left them as words.
I have practised them a little, but have been fooled by distraction.
Bless me and all phantom beings like me
That we may extract the essence of the generation and perfection phases.

ཨོཾ
ཨཱཿ
ཧཱུྃ

The Maṇḍala of the Universe

A three-dimensional representation of the ancient Indian cosmos as visualized in the maṇḍala offering. The square Mount Meru, broader at the summit than at the base, is topped by the palace of Indra and surrounded by the four continents and their subcontinents. Above it are all the different realms of the gods of form and formlessness.

CHAPTER FOUR

Offering the maṇḍala to accumulate merit and wisdom

You know the relative to be a lie, yet still you practise the two accumulations.
You realize that in the absolute there is nothing to be meditated on, yet still you practise meditation.
You see relative and absolute as one, yet still you diligently practise.*
Peerless Teacher, at your feet I bow.

I. THE NEED FOR THE TWO ACCUMULATIONS

It is impossible to attain the twofold purity[200] of Buddhahood or to realize fully the truth of emptiness without completing the two accumulations of merit and wisdom. As it says in the sūtras:

> Until one has completed the two sacred accumulations,
> One will never realize sacred emptiness.

And:

> Innate absolute wisdom can only come

* Lit. "You have actualized the state of inseparable union."

> As the mark of having accumulated merit and purified obscurations
> And through the blessings of a realized teacher.
> Know that to rely on any other means is foolish.

Even those who have truly realized emptiness need to maintain their progress along the path until they attain perfect Buddhahood, so they still need to make efforts to accumulate merit and wisdom. Tilopa, the Lord of Yogīs, said to Nāropa:

> Nāropa, my son, until you realize
> That all these appearances which arise interdependently
> In reality have never arisen, never part
> From the two wheels of your chariot, the two accumulations.

The great yogī Virūpa says in his *Dohās*:

> You may have the great confidence of not hoping for relative Buddhahood,*
> But never give up the great accumulation of merit; endeavour as much as you can.

And the peerless Dagpo Rinpoche says:

> Even when your realization transcends the very notions of there being anything to accumulate or purify,[201] continue still to accumulate even the smallest amounts of merit.

The Conqueror, in his great compassion and with all his skill in means, taught innumerable methods by which the two accumulations can be performed. The best of all these methods is the offering of the maṇḍala. A tantra says:

> To offer to the Buddhas in all Buddhafields
> The entire cosmos of a billion worlds,
> Replete with everything that could be desired,
> Will perfect the primal wisdom of the Buddhas.**

* This refers to a state of realization where one has unshakeable confidence in the Buddha nature already present in one's own mind.

** Meaning that the accumulation of merit through this practice will allow the perfect wisdom of one's Buddha nature to manifest.

In this tradition, when making such an offering, we use two separate maṇḍalas: the *accomplishment maṇḍala* and the *offering maṇḍala*.

The material out of which the maṇḍala should be made depends on your means. The best kind of maṇḍala base would be made of precious substances such as gold and silver. A medium quality one would be made of bell-metal or some other fine material. At worst, you could even use a smooth flat stone or a piece of wood.

The offering piles placed on the maṇḍala base would ideally consist of precious stones: turquoises, coral, sapphires, pearls and the like. Second best would be medicinal fruits such as *arura* and *kyurura*. Ordinarily they would consist of grains such as barley, wheat, rice or pulses, but at the very worst you could also just use pebbles, gravel, sand and so on, simply as a support for your visualization.

Whatever material your maṇḍala base is made of, clean it with great care.

II. THE ACCOMPLISHMENT MAṆḌALA[202]

Begin by arranging five piles on the accomplishment maṇḍala.[203]

Put one small pile in the centre to represent the Buddha Vairocana surrounded by the deities of the Buddha Family. Put another one in the eastern direction—meaning towards yourself[204]—to represent the Buddha Vajra Akṣobhya surrounded by the deities of the Vajra Family. Then one in the south for the Buddha Ratnasambhava surrounded by the deities of the Jewel Family, one in the west for the Buddha Amitābha surrounded by the deities of the Lotus Family, and one in the north for the Buddha Amoghasiddhi surrounded by the deities of the Action Family.

Another possibility is to visualize the field of merit as in the refuge practice.* The central pile would then represent the Great Master of Oḍḍiyāna, inseparable from your own root teacher, with all the teachers of the Great Perfection lineage above him, arranged in order, one above the other. The front pile would represent the Buddha Śākyamuni, surrounded by the thousand and two Buddhas of this Good Kalpa. The pile on the right would represent his eight great Close Sons surrounded by the noble saṅgha of Bodhisattvas, and the pile on the left would represent the Two Principal Śrāvakas, surrounded by the noble saṅgha of Śrāvakas and Pratyekabuddhas. The pile at the back would be the Jewel of the Dharma, in the form of stacked-up books encased in a lattice of light rays.

* See page 179.

Whichever is the case, place this accomplishment maṇḍala on your altar or another suitable support. If you have them, surround it with the five offerings,* and place it in front of representations of the Buddha's body, speech and mind. If this is not feasible, it is also possible to dispense with the accomplishment maṇḍala altogether, and simply to visualize the field of merit.

III. THE OFFERING MAṆḌALA

Holding the offering maṇḍala base with your left hand, wipe it for a long time with the underside of your right wrist while you recite the Seven Branches and other prayers, without ever being distracted from what you are visualizing.

This wiping of the base is not only to clean away any dirt on the maṇḍala base. It is also a way of using the effort we put into this task to rid ourselves of the two obscurations which veil our minds. The story goes that the great Kadampas of old cleaned their maṇḍalas with the undersides of their wrists until the skin was worn through and sores started to form. They still carried on, using the edge of their wrists. When sores formed there, they used the back of their wrists instead. So when you clean the maṇḍala base, do not use a woollen or cotton cloth but only your wrist, like the great Kadampas of the past.

As you arrange the offering piles on the base, follow the prayer known as *The Thirty-seven Element Maṇḍala*, which was composed by Chögyal Pakpa, the Protector of Beings of the Sakya school. This method is easy to practice, and has therefore been adopted by all traditions both old and new without distinction. Here we start by offering the maṇḍala in this way because that is our tradition too.

Both the old and the new traditions have several other methods, each according to its own customs. Indeed, each spiritual treasure of the Nyingma tradition has its own maṇḍala offering. In this particular tradition of ours there are several detailed offering prayers for the maṇḍala of the three kāyas taught by the Omniscient Longchenpa in the various *Heart-essences*.[205] Any of these can be chosen.

1. The thirty-seven element maṇḍala offering

Start by saying the mantra:

* The five offerings are flowers, incense, lamps, perfume and food.

Oṁ Vajra Bhūmi Ah Hūṁ,

at the same time holding the maṇḍala in your left hand and with your right sprinkling it with perfumed water containing *bajung.** Then, with your right thumb and ring finger, take a small pinch of grain. Saying:

Oṁ Vajra Rekhe Ah Hūṁ,

circle your hand clockwise on the maṇḍala base and then place the pinch of grains in the middle. If you have a ready-made "fence of iron mountains,"[206] now is the time to place it on the maṇḍala. Reciting:

Mount Meru, King of Mountains,

place a larger pile in the centre. To lay out the four continents, recite:

To the East, Pūrvavideha ...,

and place a small pile in the east, which can be either on the side towards you or on the opposite side, facing those to whom you are making the offering.[207] Then put three piles for the other continents, going round in a clockwise direction from the east.

For the subcontinents, Deha, Videha and so on, place a pile on either side of each continent in turn.

Next, place the Precious Mountain in the east, the Wish-fulfilling Tree in the south, the Inexhaustibly Bountiful Cow in the west and the Spontaneous Harvest in the north.

Then come the Seven Attributes of Royalty plus the Vase of Great Treasure, which are placed one after another in the four cardinal and four intermediate directions.

Next, place the four outer goddesses in each of the four cardinal directions, beginning with the Lady of Beauty; and the four inner goddesses in the four intermediate directions, beginning with the Lady of Flowers.

Place the Sun in the east and the Moon in the west. Place the Precious Umbrella in the south and the Banner Victorious in All Directions in the north.

As you recite,

All the wealth of gods and men, leaving out nothing ...

* *ba byung,* a ritual preparation made from five different substances collected from a cow.

pile more grains on top of the rest so that no space is left unfilled. If you have an ornament for the summit, place it on top now. Recite:

> *I offer this maṇḍala to all the glorious and sublime root and lineage teachers and to all the Buddhas and Bodhisattvas.*

At this point some people add the words, "... pleasant and complete in all its parts, lacking nothing," but according to my teacher, that is an addition not found in the original text.

As to what should be visualized for each of these points, my teacher did not say any more than this when he gave the teaching, so I shall write nothing more here myself. However, those who wish to know the details should consult the *Detailed Commentary on the Condensed Meaning*, as suggested in the basic explanatory text for these preliminary practices.[208]

2. The maṇḍala offering of the three kāyas according to this text

2.1 THE ORDINARY MAṆḌALA[209] OF THE NIRMĀṆAKĀYA

The four continents mentioned above in the arrangement of the piles of offering substances, with Mount Meru in the centre and the realms of the Brahmā heavens above it, make up one world. One thousand of those worlds make up what is called "a first-order universe of one thousand worlds." Taking such a universe consisting of a thousand worlds, each with four continents, and multiplying it a thousand times, we get what is called "a second-order intermediate universe of one thousand times one thousand worlds," or a universe of a million worlds. Taking such a millionfold universe and again multiplying that a thousand times gives us "a third-order great universal system of one thousand million worlds," or a cosmos of a billion universes. A universe of this order, made up of one thousand million worlds of four continents each, is the dominion of a single manifest Buddha—Śākyamuni, for example, whose Buddhafield is called The Universe of Endurance.[210]

Imagine, throughout all of these innumerable and inconceivable worlds, all the most exquisite treasures to be found in human or celestial realms, such as the seven attributes of royalty and so on, whether owned by anyone or not. To all that add your own body, your wealth, life, good fortune, power and strength, as well as all the sources of merit that you have accumulated throughout all time and will accumulate in future, together with everything that could ever bring pleasure and happiness. Pile up everything that is best and most desirable and, without even as much as a sesame seed of desire or attachment, offer it all to your teacher and the deities of the nirmāṇakāya, complete and lacking nothing. This is the offering of the ordinary maṇḍala of the nirmāṇakāya.

2.2 THE EXTRAORDINARY MAṆḌALA OF THE SAMBHOGAKĀYA

Above all that, create in your imagination an infinity of heavenly realms and inconceivable palaces in the five great Buddhafields,[211] all graced by the Lady of Beauty and the other goddesses offering the delights of the senses, multiplied infinitely. Offer all of this to your teacher and the deities of the sambhogakāya. This is the offering of the extraordinary maṇḍala of the sambhogakāya.

2.3 THE SPECIAL MAṆḌALA OF THE DHARMAKĀYA

Upon the maṇḍala base representing unborn absolute space, place piles representing the four visions and whatever thoughts arise. Offer them to your teacher and the deities of the dharmakāya. This is the offering of the special maṇḍala of the dharmakāya.

For this maṇḍala offering of the three kāyas, maintain a clear idea of all these instructions for the practice and repeat with devotion the prayer beginning:

> *Oṁ Ah Hūṁ. The cosmos of a billion universes, the field of one thousand million worlds ...*

While you are counting the number of offerings you make, hold the maṇḍala base in your left hand, leaving the offerings you made the first time still on it, and for each recitation of the text add one pile with your right hand. Practise with perseverance, holding up the maṇḍala base until your arms ache so much that they can no longer keep it up. "To bear hardships and persevere courageously for the sake of the Dharma" means more than just going without food.[212] It means always being determined to complete any practice that is difficult to do, whatever the circumstances. Practise like this, and in doing so you will acquire a tremendous amount of merit through your patience and effort.

When you can truly hold the maṇḍala no longer, put it down on the table in front of you and continue piling on the heaps of offering and counting the number of times. When you take a break, for tea for instance, collect up everything you have offered, and when you start again begin with the thirty-seven element maṇḍala before continuing as before.

Be sure to make at least one hundred thousand maṇḍala offerings in this way. If you cannot manage that number using the detailed maṇḍala of the three kāyas, it is acceptable instead to recite the verse beginning:

The ground is purified with perfumed water ...

while offering the seven-element maṇḍala.[213]

Whatever form the offering takes, it is important—as with every practice you do—to apply the three supreme methods. Start by arousing bodhicitta, do the practice itself without any concepts, and seal the practice perfectly at the end with the dedication of merit.

If it is barley, wheat, or another grain that you are using for the maṇḍala offering, as long as you can afford the expense, always offer fresh grain and do not use the same grain twice. What has already been offered you can give to the birds, distribute to beggars, or pile up in front of a representation of the Three Jewels. But never think of it as your own or use it for yourself. Should you lack the resources to renew the offerings every time, do so as often as your means allow. If you are very poor, you can use the same measure of grain over and over again.

However often you change the grain, clean it before offering it by picking out all foreign bodies, dust, chaff, straw, bird droppings and the like, and saturate it with saffron or other scented water.

Although the teachings do permit the offering of earth and stones, this is for the benefit of those so poor that they have no possessions at all, or for those with such superior faculties that their minds can create, on a single speck of dust, Buddhafields as numerous as all the particles of earth in the whole world. You may actually have what is necessary but, unable to let go and generously offer it, you may claim with all sorts of considered and highly plausible reasons—and even convince yourself—that you are making offerings using mantras and visualization. But you will only be fooling yourself.

Moreover, all the tantras and pith instructions speak of "clean offerings, cleanly prepared" or "these cleanly prepared objects of offering." They never recommend "dirty offerings, dirtily prepared." So never offer left-overs or food that is contaminated with stinginess or dirty. Do not take the best of the barley for your own consumption and leave the rest for offerings or to make tsampa for tormas. The ancient Kadampas used to say:

> To keep the best for yourself and offer mouldy cheese and withered vegetables to the Three Jewels will not do.

Do not make tormas or lamp-offerings with rancid or rotten ingredients, keeping for your own use whatever is not spoiled. That sort of conduct will deplete your merit.

When making *shelze*[214] or tormas, prepare the dough with the consistency that you yourself would like. It is wrong to add a lot of water to the dough just because it makes it easier to work.

Atīśa used to say: "These Tibetans will never be rich, they make their torma-dough too thin!"

He also said: "In Tibet, just to offer water is enough to accumulate merit. In India it is too hot, and the water is never as pure as here in Tibet."

As a way of accumulating merit, offering clean water is extremely effective if you can do it diligently. Clean the seven offering bowls or other recipients and lay them out side by side, not too close together and not too far apart. They should all be straight, with none of them out of line. The water should be clear with no grains, hair, dust or insects floating in it. The bowls should be filled with care, full but not quite to the brim, without spilling any water on the offering table. This is the way to make beautiful and pleasing water offerings.

The Prayer of Good Actions speaks of offerings "arranged perfectly, distinctively and sublimely ..." Whatever form of offering you make, if you make it beautiful and pleasing, even in the way it is set out, the respect you show to the Buddhas and Bodhisattvas in so doing will bring a vast amount of merit. So make the effort to arrange your offerings well.

If you lack resources or are otherwise unable to make offerings, there is nothing wrong with offering even something dirty or unpleasant, as long as your intention is perfectly pure. The Buddhas and Bodhisattvas have no concepts of clean or dirty. There are examples of such offerings in stories, like the one about a poor woman known as Town Scavenger offering the Buddha a butter lamp. And there is the story of the leper-woman who offered to Mahākāśyapa a bowl of rice-gruel she had received on her begging round. As she was offering it to Mahākāśyapa, a fly fell in. When she tried to fish out the fly her finger fell in too. Mahākāśyapa drank it anyway in order to fulfil her good intention, and as her offering had provided him with a whole day's food, the leper-woman was filled with joy. She was reborn in the Heaven of the Thirty-three.

In short, when you offer the maṇḍala, whatever you use should be clean, it should be offered in a pleasing way, and your intention should be utterly pure.

At no stage of the path should you stop trying to perform practices for accumulating merit, such as the maṇḍala offering. As the tantras say:

> Without any merit there can be no accomplishment;
> One cannot make oil by pressing sand.

To hope for any accomplishments without accumulating merit is like trying to get vegetable oil by pressing sand from a river bank. No matter how many millions of sand grains you press, you will never get the tiniest drop of oil. But to seek accomplishments by accumulating merit is like trying to get oil by pressing sesame seeds. The more seeds you press, the more oil you will get. Even a single seed crushed on your fingernail will make the whole nail oily. There is another similar saying:

> Hoping for accomplishments without accumulating merit is like trying to make butter by churning water.
> Seeking accomplishments after accumulating merit is like making butter by churning milk.

There is no doubt that attaining the ultimate goal, supreme accomplishment, is also the fruit of completing the two accumulations. We have already discussed the impossibility of attaining the twofold purity of Buddhahood without having completed the accumulations of merit and wisdom. Lord Nāgārjuna says:

> By these positive actions may all beings
> Complete the accumulations of merit and wisdom
> And attain the two supreme kāyas
> Which come from merit and wisdom.

By completing the accumulation of merit, which involves concepts,[215] you attain the supreme rūpakāya. By completing the accumulation of wisdom, which is beyond concepts, you attain the supreme dharmakāya.

The temporary achievements of ordinary life are also made possible by accumulated merit. Without any merit, all our efforts, however great, will be in vain. Some people, for example, without ever having to make the slightest effort, are never short of food, money or possessions in the present because of the stock of merit they have accumulated in the past. Other people spend their whole lives rushing hither and thither trying to get rich through trade, farming and so on. But it does them not even the tiniest bit of good, and they end up dying of hunger. This is something that everyone can see for themselves.

The same applies even to propitiating wealth deities, Dharma protectors and so on in the hopes of obtaining a corresponding supernatural accomplishment. Such deities can grant us nothing unless we can draw on the fruit of our own past generosity.

There was once a hermit who had nothing to live on, so he started doing the practice of Damchen.* He became so expert in the practice that he could converse with the protector as if with another person, but he still achieved no accomplishment.

Damchen told him: "Even the faintest effects of any past generosity are lacking in you, so I cannot bring you any accomplishment."

One day the hermit lined up with some beggars and was given a full bowl of soup. When he got home, Damchen appeared and said to him; "Today I granted you some accomplishment. Did you notice?"

"But all the beggars got a bowl of soup, not only me," said the hermit. "I don't see how there was any accomplishment coming from you."

"When you got your soup," Damchen said, "a big lump of fat fell into your bowl, didn't it? That was the accomplishment from me!"

Poverty cannot be overcome through wealth practices and the like without some accumulation of merit in past lives. If such beings as the worldly gods of fortune were really able to bestow the supernatural accomplishment of wealth, the Buddhas and Bodhisattvas, whose power and ability to perform miracles are hundreds and thousands of times greater, and who devote themselves entirely to helping beings without even being asked, would certainly rain down such an abundance of wealth on this world that all poverty would be eliminated in an instant. But this has not happened.

Since whatever we have is only the result of the merit we have accumulated in the past, one spark of merit is worth more than a mountain of effort. These days when people see the slightest wealth or power in this barbaric land of ours, they are all amazed and exclaim, "My, my! How is it possible?" In fact this sort of thing does not require much in the way of accumulated merit at all. The effect of making an offering, when the intention of the one who offers and the object to which the offering is made are both pure, is exemplified by the tale of Māndhātri.** By offering seven beans he won sovereignty over everything up to the Heaven of the Thirty-three. Then there is the case of King Prasenajit, whose power was the result of offering a dish of hot food with no salt.

When Atīśa came to Tibet, the country was much richer and bigger

* Damchen Dorje Lekpa, Skt. Vajrasādhu, one of the principal Dharma protectors.
** See page 123.

than it is today. And yet he said, "Tibet is really a kingdom of preta cities. Here I see no-one reaping the fruit of having offered even a single measure of barley to a pure object!"

If people really find everyday possessions or a little power so wonderful and amazing, it is a sign, first of all, of how small-minded they are; secondly, of how strongly attached they are to ordinary appearances; and thirdly, of their failure to understand properly the proliferating effects of actions, as illustrated earlier by the seed of the *aśota* tree—or of the fact that they do not believe it, even if they do understand.

But anyone with sincere and heartfelt renunciation will know that of all the apparent perfections to be found in this world—even to be as rich as a nāga, to have a position as high as the sky, to be as powerful as a thunderbolt or as pretty as a rainbow—none of this has the tiniest speck of permanence, stability or substance. Such things should only arouse disgust, like a plate of greasy food offered to a person with jaundice.

To accumulate merit in the hopes of getting rich in this life is all very well for ordinary worldly people, but it is a far cry from the authentic Dharma, which is based on the determination to be free from saṁsāra. As I have already said over and over again, if you are looking for the real Dharma that leads to liberation, you must abandon all attachment to worldly life as if it were so much spittle in the dust. You must leave your homeland and head for unknown lands, staying always in solitary places. You must practise cheerfully in the face of sickness and happily confronting death.

A disciple of the peerless Dagpo Rinpoche once asked him: "In this degenerate age it is difficult to find food, clothing and other necessities in order to practise the true Dharma. So what should I do? Should I try to propitiate the wealth deities a little, or learn a good method to extract essences,[216] or resign myself to certain death?"

The master replied: "However hard you try, without any fruit of past generosity, propitiating the wealth deities will be difficult. Moreover, seeking wealth for this life conflicts with the sincere practice of Dharma. To practise extracting the essences of things is no longer what it used to be in the ascending kalpa,[217] before the essence of earth, stones, water, plants and so on had dissipated. These days it will never work. Resigning yourself to certain death is no good either. Later it could prove difficult to find another human life with all the freedoms and advantages that you have now. However, if you feel certain from the depth of your heart that you can practice without caring whether you die or not, you will never lack food and clothing."

There is no example of a practitioner ever dying of hunger. The Buddha declared that even during a famine so extreme that to buy a measure of flour would cost a measure of pearls, the disciples of the Buddha would never be without food and clothing.

All the practices that Bodhisattvas undertake to accumulate merit and wisdom, or to dissolve obscurations, have but one goal: the welfare of all living creatures throughout space. Any wish to attain perfect Buddhahood just for your own sake, let alone practice aimed at accomplishing the goals of this life, has nothing whatever to do with the Great Vehicle. Whatever practice you may do, whether accumulating merit and wisdom or purifying obscurations, do it for the benefit of the whole infinity of beings, and do not mix it with any self-centred desires. That way, as a secondary effect, even without your wishing it, your own interests, and comfort and happiness in this life will automatically be taken care of, just like smoke rising by itself when you blow on a fire, or barley shoots springing up as a matter of course when you sow grain. But abandon like poison any impulse to devote yourself to such things for their own sake.

Machik Labdrön (1031-1129)

The consort of Padampa Sangye and principal holder of his *Chö* lineage. She holds the large double drum used in this practice to summon all the guests to the symbolic feast.

CHAPTER FIVE

The kusāli's accumulation: destroying the four demons at a single stroke*

Now comes a brief offering of one's own body called the *kusāli's* accumulation. Since this practice is linked to the Guru Yoga in *Finding Rest in the Nature of Mind*, it is permissible to combine it with the Guru Yoga. Alternatively, and without any contradiction, it can also be practised as part of the accumulation of merit along with the maṇḍala offering. That is how it will be explained here, in accordance with an oral tradition that teaches it in that way.

I. THE BODY AS AN OFFERING

The word "kusāli" means a beggar. To accumulate merit and wisdom, yogīs who have renounced ordinary life—hermits who live in the mountains, for instance—use visualization to make offerings of their own bodies, having no other possessions to offer.

All the other material things that we gather around us with so much

* The name of the practice discussed here is *gcod*, pronounced "Chö." Its basic meaning is "to cut." In this chapter it is used constantly with the various meanings of destroy, cut, eradicate, cut through concepts. We have translated it in its verbal form in various ways according to the context. When it appears as the name of the practice, we have left it untranslated. The reader should appreciate the range of meaning implied.

effort and concern are for the care of our bodies, and compared to any other possession it is without doubt our bodies that we cherish most. To sever our infatuation with our own bodies and use them as an offering* is therefore far more beneficial than offering any other possession. It is said:

> Offering your horse or elephant is worth hundreds of other offerings;
> Offering your child or spouse is worth thousands;
> Offering your own body is worth hundreds of thousands.

Machik Labdrön says:

> Not knowing that to give away my body without attachment
> Was to accumulate merit and wisdom,
> I have clung to this dear body of mine.[218]
> This I confess to the nirmāṇakāya of the Mother.[219]

II. THE PRACTICE OF OFFERING THE BODY

First, if you are used to the visualization you may choose to shoot your consciousness directly into space and visualize it there instantaneously as the Wrathful Black True Mother.[220] If you are not, imagine in your heart the essence of your mental consciousness in the form of the Wrathful Mother. She is dancing and swaying, brandishing a curved knife high in the air with her right hand, and with her left holding a skull-cup full of blood at her heart. The squealing head of a black sow protrudes from behind her right ear. She is wearing the apparel of a wrathful goddess.

As you pronounce the syllable "P'et!"[221] the Wrathful Mother flies up through your central channel. At the exact instant that she shoots up out of the aperture of Brahmā on the top of your head, your body becomes a corpse and collapses in a heap. Here, do not think of your body as having its normal appearance. Instead, see it as fat, greasy and huge, as big as the entire cosmos of a billion worlds.

With a single blow of the curved knife in her right hand, the Wrathful Black Mother—the visualized form of your consciousness—instantly slices off the top of the inanimate body's skull at the level of the eyebrows to make a skull cup. Again, meditate that the skull cup is not life-size, but as big as the entire cosmos of a billion worlds. With her left hand the Wrathful Mother picks up the skull cup and places it, with the brow facing

* This is the basic practice of Chö.

her, on a tripod made of three human skulls, each as large as Mount Meru. Then with the hooked knife in her right hand, she lifts the whole corpse and puts it into the skull-cup.

Now visualize in space above the skull a white syllable *hang* with the nature of nectar, and beneath the skull the vertical stroke of a syllable *A*,[222] red, with the nature of fire:

hang  vertical stroke of *A* 

As you say "Oṁ Ah Hūṁ," fire blazes up from the stroke of the *A* and heats the skull-cup until the corpse sizzles and melts into nectar, which boils up and fills the whole skull. Everything foul and impure flows off in the form of a frothing scum. Steam rises from the nectar and touches the *hang*, heating it up by the contact. The *hang* exudes streams of red and white nectar, which drip down and blend together in an inseparable unity within the skull. The *hang* itself dissolves into light and melts into the nectar too. Visualizing all this, recite:

P'et! Ridding myself of infatuation with the body ...

and so on. Then, as you repeat "Oṁ Ah Hūṁ," visualize that the *oṁ* purifies the nectar of all imperfections of colour, smell, taste and so on; the *ah* makes it increase many times over; and the *hūṁ* transforms it into everything that could be wished for. It takes on the nature of the immaculate nectar[223] of primal wisdom, which manifests in clouds that billow out and satisfy all possible desires.

Visualize in the sky in front of you a throne piled with silken cushions, on which is seated your gracious root teacher in person. Above him are the lineage teachers, around him are all the yidams, and below in the space above the skull-cup are the Seventy-five Glorious Protectors[224] and all the hosts of other Dharma protectors, both the wisdom protectors and the protectors constrained by the effect of their past actions, along with the deities of the locality and owners of the ground.

Below the skull, visualize all beings of the six realms and the three worlds, among whom your principal guests are the eighty thousand types of obstacle makers, the fifteen great demons that prey on children, and, in short, all those who create obstacles and to whom you owe karmic debts, teeming like the countless specks of dust in a sunbeam.

1. The white feast for the guests above

Now visualize that your root teacher, the lineage teachers and all the assembled Buddhas and Bodhisattvas above his head all imbibe the nectar through their tongues, which have the form of hollow vajra tubes.[225] As a result, you complete the accumulations, you are freed of your obscurations, your violations and breaches of the samaya are purified and you attain both the common and supreme accomplishments.

The yidams and deities of the four and six classes of tantra surrounding the teacher also consume the nectar, absorbing it through hollow tongues whose shapes correspond to the symbol associated with each deity—a vajra, wheel, jewel, lotus, or crossed vajra.* As a result you complete the accumulations, clear away your obscurations, purify all violations and breaches of samaya, and attain the common and supreme accomplishments.

The ḍākas, ḍākinīs, Seventy-five Glorious Protectors and all the other Dharma protectors now also take their share of the nectar through the hollow sunbeams of their tongues. You complete the accumulations and are freed from all obscurations; all obstacles and circumstances unfavourable to the Dharma and the attainment of enlightenment are dispelled. All the favourable circumstances and good things that you seek are multiplied.

2. The white feast for the guests below

Next, if you are experienced in visualization, continue to visualize yourself as the Wrathful Black True Mother and from your heart send out swarms of activity-performing ḍākinīs—white, yellow, red, green and blue, like myriads of specks of dust dancing in the sun's rays. Imagine them appeasing and satisfying all beings throughout the six realms and the three worlds, as they offer to each a wisdom skull-cup filled with immaculate nectar.

If you are less experienced in visualization, imagine that you yourself—the Wrathful Black Mother—use the skull-cup in your left hand to scoop nectar out of the great skull and scatter it, so that it rains down everywhere in the six realms and the three worlds of existence. All beings drink it and are utterly satisfied.

* These are the symbols of the five Buddha families.

3. The variegated feast for the guests above

Again, steam rises from the boiling nectar, giving rise to inconceivable clouds of offerings. Offer them to the guests above: fresh water to drink and for their feet, flowers, incense, lamps, perfume, foodstuffs and music, the eight auspicious symbols and seven attributes of royalty, parasols, victory-banners, canopies, golden wheels with a thousand spokes, white conches spiralling to the right, and more. As a result, you and all beings complete the accumulations and are cleansed of all obscurations.

4. The variegated feast for the guests below

Now come the guests below, namely all the beings of the six realms of existence. Whatever each of them desires, whatever each of them wishes, it pours down on them like rain, satisfying them and filling them with joy.

Think particularly of those beings to whom you have been indebted in all your lives until now in saṁsāra without any beginning. We have all kinds of debts due to past actions: debts that shorten our lives because we have killed; debts that make us poor because we have robbed; debts that plague us with sickness because we have attacked and beaten others; debts for protection given by superiors, for services rendered by inferiors, and for friendship from equals; debts to overlords and underlings,[226] to loved ones, friends, subjects, children and livestock; debts for the food we have eaten and the clothes we have worn, for the money we have borrowed, for the milk we have milked, for the loads we have made others carry and for the fields we have ploughed, and for whatever else we may have used.

All of those karmic creditors, whether male and female, want to venge themselves on your flesh and bones, shorten your lifespan and snatch away your life-force. They gather round holding containers, running after you and demanding repayment. The offering is transformed into an inexhaustible treasury of everything desirable, which rains down upon them, bringing each of them whatever they most wish. It brings food for those who want food, clothing for those who want clothing, wealth for those who want wealth, gardens for those who want gardens, horses for those who want horses, houses to live in for those who want houses, and friends and loved ones for those who want friends and loved ones.

When each of them has enjoyed these things you are freed from your karmic obligations. Your debts are repaid. You are delivered from those deadly avengers and purified of all your harmful deeds and obscurations. Everyone is placated and satisfied.

Then imagine that for all those who may have been left behind—the lowly, the weak, the crippled, the blind, the deaf, the dumb and all beings in the six realms who are tortured and worn out by suffering—the offering becomes whatever they may need. It turns into a refuge for those with no refuge, a protector for those who have no protector, friendly assistance for those with no support, loved ones and friends for the lonely, a place in society for the deprived, medicines to cure the sick, life-restoring elixirs for the dying, miraculous legs for the crippled, eyes of wisdom for the blind, immaculate ears for the deaf, wisdom tongues for the dumb,[227] and so on. These beings all enjoy the gifts and are satisfied, delivered from all the effects of actions, sufferings and habitual tendencies of each of the six realms. All the males reach the level of sublime Avalokiteśvara, all the females reach the level of noble Tārā, and the three worlds of saṁsāra are liberated to their very depths.

Continue to recite "Oṁ Ah Hūṁ" until you have completed this whole visualization. Then recite the passage:

> *P'et! The guests of the offering above ...*

down to the words:

> *... uncontrived Great Perfection. Ah!*

Then rest in the state beyond any concept of an offering, an offerer or a recipient of the offerings.

In the Chö texts there are usually four great feasts: white, red, variegated and black. In this one there are the white and variegated, but no red or black feasts.

What today's so-called Chö practitioners mean by Chö is a grisly process of destroying malignant spirits by killing, slashing, chopping, beating or chasing them. Their idea of Chö involves being constantly full of anger. Their bravado is nothing more than hatred and pride. They imagine that they have to behave like the henchmen of the Lord of Death. For example, when they practise Chö for a sick person, they work themselves into a furious display of rage, staring with hate-filled eyes as large as saucers, clenching their fists, biting their lower lips, lashing out with blows and grabbing the invalid so hard that they tear the clothes off his back. They call this subduing spirits, but to practise Dharma like that is totally mistaken. Machik Labdrön says:

> Since time without beginning, harmful spirits have lived in a ceaseless whirl of hallucination and suffering, brought on by their own evil

> actions and by inauspicious circumstances which drive them like a wind. When they die they inevitably plunge to the very depths of the lower realms. With the hook of compassion I catch those evil spirits. Offering them my warm flesh and warm blood as food, through the kindness and compassion of bodhicitta I transform the way they see everything and make them my disciples. Those malignant spirits are for me the prize that I hold with the hook of compassion—but the great adepts of Chö of the future will boast of killing them, casting them out or beating them. That will be a sign that false doctrines of Chö, the teachings of demons, are spreading.

All the various false Chö practices that she predicted, such as the Ninefold Black Chö, are only the result of thinking that one can subjugate spirits through violence, without the love and compassion of bodhicitta.

A person who uses those practices might just be able to overcome one or two puny little elemental spirits, but if he encounters any really vicious ones, they will attack his life in retaliation—as has been seen to happen on many occasions.

It is particularly difficult for practitioners to tell whether signs of success which occur on the path—the subjugation of a demon, or the experience of some kind of blessing, for instance—are authentic signs of progress, or whether they are in fact obstacles created by demonic forces.

People possessed by malicious spirits usually seem to have clairvoyance and supernatural powers. But as time goes on they get further and further from the genuine Dharma, until not even the tiniest scrap of goodness is left in them. The mountains of offerings that might be heaped upon them are just karmic debts for the future, and even in this life do them no good. In the end they find it hard to scrape together enough to eat or wear. And what they do have, they cannot bear to use up. When they die, they are sure to be reborn in an ephemeral hell or some such realm, as we have already mentioned.[228]

III. THE MEANING OF CHÖ

The so-called spirits to be destroyed in Chö practice are not anywhere outside. They are within us. All the hallucinations that we perceive in the form of spirits outside ourselves arise because we have not eradicated the conceit[229] of believing in an "I" and a "self." As Machik says:

> The tangible demon, the intangible demon,
> The demon of exultation and the demon of conceit—
> All of them come down to the demon of conceit.[230]

This thing we call a spirit is in fact the demon of conceit, the belief in a self. Machik also says:

> "The many spirits" means concepts;
> "The powerful spirit" means belief in a self;
> "The wild spirits" means thoughts.
> To destroy these spirits is to be an adept of Chö.

Jetsun Mila's conversation with the Ogress of the Rock included these words:

> Belief in an "I" is more powerful than you are, demoness.
> Concepts are more numerous than you are, demoness.
> Thoughts are more spoilt by habits than you are, demoness.

He also classified the various kinds of Chö as follows:

> Outer Chö is to wander in fearsome places and mountain solitudes;
> Inner Chö is to cast away one's body as food;
> Absolute Chö is to sever the root once and for all.
> I am a yogī who possesses these three kinds of Chö.

All Chö practices are therefore to cut through the belief in a self, which is the root of all ignorance and deluded perceptions. This is what is meant by the line "absolute Chö is to sever the root once and for all." External demons are just deluded perceptions, and as long as you do not destroy your belief in a self, trying to kill them will not put them to death. Beating them will have no effect on them. Trampling them will not crush them. Chasing after them will not make them go away. Unless you sever the root, which is the conceit within you, you will no more be able to annihilate the illusory spirits which are its external manifestation than get rid of smoke without putting out the fire. The Ogress of the Rock told Jetsun Mila:

> If you don't know that demons come from your own mind,
> There'll be other demons besides myself!
> I'm not going to leave just because you tell me to go.

and Jetsun Mila said:

> Take a demon as a demon and it'll harm you;
> Know a demon's in your mind and you'll be free of it;
> Realize a demon to be empty and you'll annihilate it.

And again:

> You who appear as harmful spirits and yakṣas, male or female,
> Only when one has no understanding are you demons,
> Bringing all your mischief and your obstacles.
> But once one understands, even you demons are deities,
> And become the source of all accomplishments.

What is called Chö is to eradicate any belief in demons from within, not to kill them, thrash them, cast them out, crush and destroy them. We must understand that the thing to be destroyed is not outside; it is within us.

Generally speaking, most other religious traditions teach an aggressive approach to outer hostile forces and external creators of obstacles, using the sharpness, severity and power of violent methods, the points of arrows and spears, all directed outwards. But our tradition is as Jetsun Mila says:

> My system is to eradicate the belief in a self, to cast the eight ordinary concerns to the winds, and to make the four demons feel embarrassed.

Direct all your practice inwards and mobilize all your strength, skill and powers against the belief in a self that dwells within you. To say, "Eat me! Take me away!" once is a hundred times better than crying, "Protect me! Save me!" To offer yourself as food to a hundred spirits is better than calling on a hundred protection deities for help.

> We entrust the sick to the demons.
> We rely on our enemies to guide us.
> One "Devour me! Carry me off!"
> Is better than "Protect me! Save me!" hundreds of times.
> This is the venerable Mother's[231] tradition.

If you cut your belief in demons at the root from within, you will perceive everything as pure, and, as the saying goes:

> Demons become Dharma protectors, and those protectors' faces become the face of the nirmāṇakāya.

People today who claim to be practitioners of Chö do not understand any of this, and persist in thinking of spirits as something outside themselves. They believe in demons, and keep on perceiving them all the time; in everything that happens they see some ghost or *gyalgong*. They have no peace of mind themselves, and are always bewildering others with their lies, delivered with much assertive blustering:

"There's a ghost up there! And down there, too, a spirit! That's a ghost! That's a demon! That's a *tsen*! I can see it ... Ha!—I've got it, I've killed it! Watch out, there's one lying in wait for you! I've chased it away! There—it looked back!"

Spirits and pretas know what such people are up to, and follow them around wherever they go. They might take possession of women who fall easily into trances, for example, and make all sorts of insistent and plausible claims: "I am a god," "I am a ghost," "I am the person who died," "I am your old father," "I am your old mother," and so on. Sometimes they announce, "I am the deity, I am a Dharma protector. I am Damchen," and speak of supernatural visions or make false predictions.

Demons fool the lamas and the lamas fool their patrons, or, as the saying goes, "The son fools his father while enemies fool the son." These are manifest signs of the degenerate age, and show that the demons are taking over. As the Great Master of Oḍḍiyāna prophesied:

> In the decadent age, male spirits will enter men's hearts;
> Female spirits will enter women's hearts;
> Goblins will enter children's hearts;
> Samaya-breakers will enter the clergy's hearts.
> There will be a spirit in every single Tibetan's heart.

And:

> When goblins are taken for gods, a time of suffering will come upon Tibet.

These prophecies have come to pass.

Do not be taken in by that false perception that makes gods, spirits and obstacle-makers appear outside you; that would only reinforce it. Train yourself to see everything as a dream-like display or an illusion. The phenomena of spirits on the one hand and sick people on the other, appearing momentarily as aggressor and victim, both arise from the negative actions and distorted perceptions which link them together in that way. Do not take sides, do not love the one and hate the other. Generate the love and compassion of bodhicitta towards both. Sever at the root all your self-concern and belief in an "I," and give your body and life to the spirits as food without holding back. Pray from the depths of your heart that these beings may take an interest in the true Dharma and pacify their hatred and maliciousness, and then explain the teachings.[232]

When you finally cut through at its very root all belief in the duality of aggressor and victim, perceiving as deity and perceiving as demon, self and others—and all the resulting dualistic concepts of hope and fear, attachment and hatred, good and bad, pleasure and pain—you will find, as it is said:

> Neither deity, nor demon: the confidence of the view.
> Neither distraction, nor fixation: the vital point of the meditation.
> Neither acceptance, nor rejection: the vital point of the action.
> Neither hope, nor fear: the vital point of the result.

When all concepts of anything to be cut and anyone to do the cutting dissolve into the expanse of absolute reality where all things are equal, the inner harmful spirit of conceit is severed at the root. That is the sign that you have realized the absolute and ultimate Chö.

> *I understand that there is no self, but still have gross concepts of "I."*
> *I have decided to renounce duality, but am beset by hopes and fears.*
> *Bless me and all those like me who believe in a self*
> *That we may realize the natural state, the absence of self.*

Dudjom Rinpoche (1904-1987)

An outstanding scholar and master of the Great Perfection, he held all the major Nyingma transmissions, discovered numerous spiritual treasures and was a prolific author and compiler of teachings. He became the leader of the Nyingma school in exile, and taught extensively in the West and Far East as well as all over the Himalayan region. This photograph was taken in Tibet. He died at his home in the Dordogne, France, in 1987.

CHAPTER SIX

Guru Yoga,[233] entrance-way for blessings, the ultimate method for arousing the wisdom of realization

First you followed a supreme Master and obeyed him;
Then you practised, undertaking great hardships;
Finally, your mind and your teacher's became one, and you inherited the lineage.
Peerless Teacher, at your feet I bow.

I. THE REASON FOR GURU YOGA

In order to practise true Dharma, it is of great importance first to seek an authentic spiritual friend, a teacher who has all the necessary qualifications. Then you should obey his every instruction, praying to him from the very depths of your heart and considering him to be a real Buddha. As one of the sūtras says:

> It is through faith that absolute truth is realized.

Likewise, Atīśa says:

> Friends, until you attain enlightenment you need a teacher, so follow a supreme spiritual friend.
> Until you realize the natural state, you need to learn, so listen to his instructions.

> All happiness is the teacher's blessing, so always remember his kindness.

And Geshe Kharak Gomchung says:

> The teacher should be recognized as the source of all accomplishments, worldly and beyond the world.

and also:

> You may know the whole Tripiṭaka, but without devotion to your teacher that will be of no use to you.

Particularly in all the paths of the Secret Mantra Vajrayāna, the teacher has a unique and paramount importance. For this reason, all the tantras teach the practice of Guru Yoga, and say that it is superior to all the practices of the generation and perfection phases. In one tantra it says:

> Better than meditating on a hundred thousand deities
> For ten million kalpas
> Is to think of one's teacher for a single instant.

This is especially true in this particular vehicle, the heart essence of the natural Great Perfection, the vajra core-teaching. Here it is not taught that the profound truth should be established on the basis of analysis and logic, as is the practice in the lower vehicles.[234] Nor is it said that common accomplishments should be used in order to finally obtain supreme accomplishment, as in the lower tantras. The use of the illustrative primal wisdom of the third empowerment to introduce true primal wisdom is not stressed,[235] as it is in the other higher tantras. What is taught in this tradition is to pray with fervent devotion and complete faith to a supremely realized teacher whose lineage is like a golden chain untarnished by any variance with the samayas, to rely on him alone and to consider him to be a real Buddha;[236] in this way, your mind will merge completely with his. By the power of his blessings being transferred to you, realization will take birth.[237] As we have quoted before:

> Innate absolute wisdom can only come
> As the mark of having accumulated merit and purified obscurations
> And through the blessings of a realized teacher.
> Know that to rely on any other means is foolish.

And Saraha says:

> When the teacher's words enter your heart

It is like seeing you have a treasure in the palm of your hand.

Longchenpa, the Omniscient Dharma King, in his *Finding Rest from Illusion*,[238] wrote:

> In practices such as those of the generation and perfection phases, it is not the nature of those paths itself that brings liberation, for that depends on other factors, such as how one makes it a living experience and deepens one's practice. In Guru Yoga, however, the path—by its very nature alone—awakens the realization of the natural state within one and brings liberation. For that reason Guru Yoga is the most profound of all paths.[239]

The *Tantra of the Array of Samayas* says:

> Better than meditating for a hundred thousand kalpas
> On a deity with all the major and minor marks
> Is to think of one's teacher for an instant.
> Better than a million recitations of the approach and
> accomplishment practices
> Is a single prayer addressed to the teacher.

And the *Array of Ati*:

> Whoever meditates on his kind teacher
> Above the crown of his head,
> In the centre of his heart
> Or on the palm of his hand
> Will have a thousand Buddhas' accomplishments.

The venerable Gotsangpa said:

> To practise Guru Yoga
> Exhausts all defects and perfects all attainments.

and also:

> There are many practices of the generation phase,
> But not one of them surpasses meditation on the teacher.
> There are many practices of the perfection phase,
> But not one of them surpasses that total trust and surrender.

Drikung Kyobpa Rinpoche said:

> Unless the sun of devotion shines
> On the snow peak of the teacher's four kāyas,

> The stream of his blessings will never flow.
> So earnestly arouse devotion in your mind!

And Jetsun Rangrik Repa says:

> Wishing for primal wisdom beyond the intellect to dawn
> Without fervent trust in the teacher
> Is like waiting for sunshine in a north-facing cave.
> That way, appearances and mind will never merge.[240]

The devotional practice of Guru Yoga is the only way to awaken within you the realization of the uncontrived natural state. No other method can bring such realization.

Nāropa was a paṇḍita, highly learned in all three vehicles, and after vanquishing all the challenges of the tīrthikas, he was given the position of paṇḍita protector of the northern gate of Vikramaśīla.[100]

But one day a wisdom ḍākinī told him, "You are learned in words, but not in their meaning. You still need to follow a teacher."

Complying with her instructions, he followed Tilopa and endured numerous trials, until one day, Tilopa said to him, "In spite of everything I have taught you, you still haven't understood!" and hit him on the forehead with his sandal. At that instant, Nāropa realized the natural state and his wisdom became identical with his teacher's.*

It is also said that Nāgabodhi attained supreme accomplishment by snatching up and eating a piece of snot dropped by the noble master Nāgārjuna. And Rigdzin Jigme Lingpa says:

> When I saw the writings of that second Buddha, Longchenpa, it dawned on me that he was genuinely a Buddha, and I prayed to him with great fervour. He appeared to me in a vision and accepted me. Spontaneous realization was born within me and from that day forth, I have ben able to guide over a hundred disciples. The diligent ones would not have advanced beyond worldly concentrations, the intelligent ones would have strayed into intellectualization; they only realized the absolute truth because they were driven by the counterbalancing force of their devotion.

During the period of his exile in Gyalmo Tsawarong, the great translator Vairotsana taught the old man Pang Mipham Gönpo how to take the teacher's blessings as the path. Mipham Gönpo was eighty, and stiff with

* For more details, see pages 157-159.

old age, so Vairotsana tied his body upright with a meditation-band and made him rest his head on a meditation support.* Mipham Gönpo experienced realization of the primordial purity of *trekchö* without error. His body dissolved into infinitesimal particles and he attained Buddhahood.[241]

You can compare this teaching with any others from all the nine yānas, but you will never find a path better or more profound than this. It may be called a preliminary practice, but in fact this is the ultimate key point of all main practices. This alone, if you always and in every situation make it the heart of your practice, is enough—even if you practise nothing else. It is of the utmost importance, therefore, that you dedicate yourself to it from the very depths of your being.

II. HOW TO PRACTISE GURU YOGA

For the actual practice of this profound path of Guru Yoga there are three stages: visualizing the field of merit, offering the seven branches and praying with resolute trust.

1. Visualizing the field of merit

To transform your perception of the world requires a strong and open mind, so begin by visualizing everything, as far as you can see, as the Palace of Lotus Light, complete in all its features.

Visualize yourself at the centre of the palace, and think of yourself as having the nature of the ḍākinī Yeshe Tsogyal. This will ensure that you are a fit receptacle for the empowerments, arouse the primal wisdom of bliss and emptiness, and create a connection with the guidance she had from her teacher.[242] In form, however, visualize yourself as Vajrayoginī. She is red, with one face, two arms and three eyes. She is gazing longingly at the heart of the teacher—"longingly" here expressing a sense of impatience to be with the teacher, this being the only source of joy. With her right hand she is playing a small skull-drum held up in the air, awakening beings from the sleep of ignorance and confusion. Her left hand is resting on her hip, holding the curved knife that cuts the root of the three poisons. She is naked except for her bone ornaments and garlands of flowers. She is visible but insubstantial, like a rainbow shining

* The band is a long belt which helps the meditator to maintain a correct posture over a long period. The meditation support is a long stick cupped at one end which serves as a chin rest.

in the sky.

Suspended in space, an arrow's length above her head, is a lotus of many kinds of jewels with a hundred thousand petals, in full bloom. Upon it is a sun disc and upon that a moon disc. On this throne sits your glorious root teacher, that incomparable treasure of compassion, the embodiment of the Buddhas of past, present and future, in the form of the Great Guru of Oḍḍiyāna. His complexion is white, tinged with red. He has one face, two arms and two legs. He is seated in the royal posture and is wearing a brocade cape, a monk's robe, a long-sleeved blue gown and a lotus hat.

Three different hats are associated with Guru Rinpoche, who is also called the Second Buddha from Oḍḍiyāna. The first was offered to him by the ḍākinīs at the time of his birth. He was not conceived by a father or born from a mother, but was born in the south-west, on the Lake of Milk, in the heart of a lotus, the sudden, spontaneous birth of awareness, the realization that everything that exists arises from the primordial ground. The hat that the ḍākinīs offered him at that time, to crown him as the lord of their family, is called the *Lotus-bud.*

Later, when he practised extraordinary activity[243] in the Eight Great Charnel-grounds and went beyond all actions, good or bad, the ḍākinīs presented to him as a symbol of his greatness the hat called the *Deerskin Hat.*[244]

The third was offered to him by Ārṣadhara, King of Zahor. The king had tried to burn the Master alive, but discovered his vajra body, unharmed by the fire, sitting naked, perfectly cool and fresh, in the heart of a miraculous lotus. He was struck with wonder and faith arose in him.

"Open up my new store of silken garments," he ordered, "and bring all the hats and clothes to me."

The hat he offered at that time, not only along with all his other possessions, but also with his retinue, his kingdom and his subjects, is called *The Lotus which Liberates on Sight*, also known as *The Petalled Hat of the Five Families.* It is this particular hat that concerns us here. It has two layers, inner and outer, symbolizing the unity of the generation and perfection phases. It has three points, representing the three kāyas. Its five colours represent the five kāyas* working for the benefit of beings. It is emblazoned with a sun and moon symbolizing skilful means and wisdom. It has a blue border which symbolizes unlimited samaya. On top is a vajra, as a symbol of unshakeable concentration, and a vulture's feather, which symbolizes the realization of the highest view and the

* See glossary.

༄། ཀློང་ཆེན་སྙིང་ཐིག་ལ་བླ་བརྒྱུད་གོང་རིམ་རྒྱང་པ་བཞུགས་སོ།།

Guru Rinpoche and the lineage of the Heart-essence of the Vast Expanse

Jñānasūtra — Samantabhadra — Trisong Detsen

Vajrasattva — Garab Dorje

Śrī Siṁha — Mañjuśrīmitra

Yeshe Tsogyal — Guru Rinpoche — Vairotsana

Longchenpa — Vimalamitra — Jigme Lingpa

culmination of the practice.

With his right hand at his heart, he displays the threatening mudrā and holds a golden vajra. In his left hand, resting in his lap in the gesture of meditation, he holds a skull-cup. It is filled with the wisdom nectar of immortality and contains a long-life vase topped with a sprig from the wish-granting tree. In the crook of his left arm, the Master holds Mandāravā, queen of Ḍākinīs, in hidden form as his *khaṭvāṅga*.* The *khaṭvāṅga*'s three prongs symbolize the essential nature, natural expression, and compassion, and below them are three severed heads: a dried-up one, representing the dharmakāya, a rotten one, representing the sambhogakāya, and a fresh one, representing the nirmāṇakāya. The nine metal rings looped over its prongs represent the nine vehicles; its five-coloured silken pennants symbolize the five wisdoms. The *khaṭvāṅga* is also adorned with locks of hair from dead and living *mamos*** and ḍākinīs, as a sign that the Master subjugated them all during his practice of extraordinary activity in the Eight Great Charnel-grounds.[245]

All around him, within a luminous rainbow sphere encircled by a lattice of myriad five-coloured points of light, visualize the Eight Vidyādharas of India, the Twenty-five Disciples of Tibet and so on, as well as the infinite deities of the Three Roots and faithful protectors. They should have such presence that your ordinary thoughts automatically cease.

Broadly speaking, there are three different ways of visualizing the lineage. In the refuge practice, we visualized the lamas *one above the other*. All the lamas of the Great Perfection lineage appeared one above the other above the head of the Great Master of Oḍḍiyāna. The way we visualized for the meditation and recitation on Vajrasattva is known as *the jewel which includes everything*. All the root and lineage lamas are embodied by Vajrasattva alone. But now, as we meditate on the Guru Yoga, we visualize the lamas *as a crowd*. All the lamas of the Great Perfection Lineage, the ocean of the Three Roots and faithful protectors are gathered in a crowd around the Great Master of Oḍḍiyāna.

Recite the visualization text, paying attention to the meaning of the words:

> *Emaho!*[246] *Everything I perceive is the spontaneously formed, pure and infinite Buddhafield ...*

down to:

* A particular kind of trident.

** Skt. *māṭrikā*, a type of wrathful ḍākinī.

... visualized in the great evenness of inseparable clarity and emptiness.

Then with intense devotion recite the lines:

Hūṁ! On the north-west frontier of the land of Oḍḍiyāna ...

down to:

... Guru Padma Siddhi Hūṁ.[247]

As you say these lines, imagine that all the deities and the Palace of Lotus Light of the Glorious Copper-coloured Mountain come in reality and dissolve into the samaya deities and palace[248] that you have visualized, becoming one with them like water poured into water.

2. Offering the seven branches

The Vajrayāna path includes many methods and is without great hardships. It is intended for those with sharp faculties. If we constantly train ourselves to accumulate merit and wisdom with a strong mind, everything that would otherwise take a whole great kalpa to accumulate through the six pāramitās can be accomplished in an instant, and liberation can be attained in a single lifetime.

There can be no doubt that the single most excellent, secret and insurpassable field of merit is the vajra master.[249] That is why the practice of accumulating merit is combined with the Guru Yoga. The seven parts of the Offering of the Seven Branches include all the innumerable methods for the accumulation of merit and wisdom.

2.1 PROSTRATION,[250] THE ANTIDOTE TO PRIDE

For this practice, visualize that you are emanating a hundred, then a thousand, then innumerable bodies like your own, as numerous as the particles of dust in the universe. At the same time, visualize that all beings, as infinite as space itself, are prostrating with you. The words for this part are:

Hrīḥ! I prostrate, emanating as many bodies
As there are particles of dust in the whole universe.

In general, when you practise the entire "five hundred thousand preliminaries"[251] it is correct to combine prostrations with the refuge practice, and that tradition is often followed. But in the present teaching the actual explanation of prostration is given here, so to combine prostrations with the Guru Yoga is a perfect way to practise them.

An important point when doing prostrations is to link body, speech, and mind. As you physically prostrate with your body, recite the text of the prayer for the prostrations with your speech. With your mind, consider that you are doing prostrations in the company of all beings and practise with respect and devotion, relying entirely on the teacher and confidently surrendering yourself to him. Otherwise you will end up just saying whatever you like and looking around everywhere, while your mind chases after all sorts of external events. A passer-by or someone talking on your right will draw your eyes and your attention in that direction, and you will find your joined hands pressing against your left cheek. When someone comes along on your left, you will look round and listen on that side and your joined hands will end up touching your right cheek instead. You must understand that to make an outward show of doing prostrations like that, letting your mind be taken over by distractions while your body lurches up and down by itself, is just a physical ordeal that serves no purpose whatsoever.

When you prostrate, cup your hands together in the shape of a lotus-bud about to blossom, leaving a space in the middle. It is not right to press your palms tightly together leaving no space between them, nor to touch together only the tips of your fingers. The *Sūtra of Great Liberation* says:

> I join my hands above my head
> Like an opening lotus-bud,
> And with countless bodies amassed in clouds
> I prostrate to the Buddhas of the ten directions.

And *The Treasury of Precious Qualities* says:

> Make a sign of reverence at your heart,
> Your body bending low without distraction,
> Your hands as though they cupped a flower bud
> And held together like a relic case.

Put your hands together and place them on the crown of your head, then at your throat, and then at your heart, to purify the obscurations of body, speech and mind respectively. Then touch the floor with your body at five points, the forehead, the palms of the two hands and the two knees,[252] in order to purify the obscurations of the five poisons and obtain the blessings of body, speech, mind, qualities and activity. Then stand up straight, put your hands together again and continue the prostrations in the same way.

It is not right to wave your arms around without placing your hands together. Nor should you just bend forward without touching your knees and forehead to the ground. Nor should you stay bent over when you get up, without standing up straight again. To prostrate like that is disrespectful. It is said that the fully ripened effect of doing prostrations without standing up straight is to be reborn as a hunchback dwarf. We do prostrations in the hope of benefiting from them—so there is no point in doing them in a way that will only result in a deformed body.

Even if you cannot do many prostrations, make the effort to ensure that however many you can do, they are all done impeccably. It is meaningless to try to make prostrations easier by doing them on a slope, such as the side of a hill, or by any other such methods.

Moreover, nowadays when people pay their respects, visiting a lama for instance, they do one prostration that is almost correct and then follow it up with two more for which they just bend over. That, supposedly, is how important people do it—and most ignorant people follow their example. But it is an extremely vulgar way to do prostrations. The purpose of asking for teaching, even on such simple things as how to do prostrations, is to hear the teacher explain whatever it is one does not know, and then to put it into practice all the time without forgetting any of the details. If people cannot even put into practice something so simple to learn and so simple to do, studying the Dharma becomes completely meaningless and fruitless. Those who have studied the Dharma should be more proficient than those who have not, even in their manner of doing simple prostrations.

When Jetsun Mila went to ask Lama Ngokpa for teachings, he arrived while Lama Ngokpa was teaching the *Hevajra Tantra* to a large assembly of monks. Mila paid his respects by doing prostrations from afar. The Lama was delighted.

Taking off his head-dress, he prostrated to Mila in return, saying, "What an auspicious interruption! That person doing prostrations over there is doing it in the style of the disciples of Marpa of Lhodrak.* Ask him who he is."

Anyone who follows a teacher and receives his teachings ought to be like a piece of cloth being soaked in dye. As he learns to emulate the actions of his respected master, there should certainly be some noticeable change from how he was before. When a piece of cloth is dyed, it may

* Milarepa's root teacher, and Lama Ngokpa's also.

take the new colour more or less successfully—but how can it fail to change colour at all? Nowadays, there are people who have received the Dharma hundreds of times but who still fail to improve themselves in the least, and behave exactly like ordinary worldly people in all respects. All the Dharma has produced is impervious practitioners, violators of samaya. It is said:

> The Dharma can inspire evildoers to change, but it cannot inspire practitioners who have become impervious through Dharma—just as grease can soften stiff leather, but cannot soften the leather of a butter-bag.[253]

Once you have learned about the benefits of positive actions, the harmfulness of negative actions and the qualities of the Buddhas, merely to subscribe to those beliefs is not enough; you still have to arouse the sort of certainty and faith that can truly transform your outlook. Otherwise, even the perfectly enlightened Buddha in person would not be able to help you. The Great One of Oḍḍiyāna gives the following warning:

> Do not surround yourself with disciples who have strayed into just talking about the teaching, but whose minds have become impervious to it.
> Do not associate with companions who set limits to their samayas.

Even if you only understand one word of the teaching, you need to recognize how to mix it with your mind and put it into practice. The purpose of following a teacher is to observe his thoughts, words and deeds and learn to do as he does. As the proverb goes:

> All actions are only imitation:
> Those act best who imitate best.

In this way, you should let the teacher's outer, inner and secret qualities be imprinted on you, like a *tsa-tsa* coming out of its mould.

"Prostration" is a general term describing a gesture of homage and respect. There are many different ways to do prostrations, and customs vary from place to place. However, in this case your teacher has taught you how to do them according to the words of the Conqueror. So knowingly to prostrate in the wrong way, whether out of pride or in order to make it easier, is an act of disrespect and a demonstration of contempt. It should also be understood that to do prostrations as though paying a tax serves no purpose and will only bring the wrong results.

Proper prostrations, on the other hand, bring immeasurable benefits.

Once, when a monk was prostrating to a stūpa containing hair and nail clippings of the Buddha, Ānanda asked the Buddha what the benefits of such an act might be. The Buddha replied:

> A single prostration is so powerful that if, as a result, one were to become a universal emperor as many times as the number of grains of dust beneath one's body down to the lowest depths of the earth,[254] the benefits of that act would still not be exhausted.

And in the sūtras it says:

> The unfathomable crown protuberance on the Buddha's head comes from his having respectfully prostrated before his teachers.

Prostrations will finally lead us, too, to obtain the unfathomable *uṣṇīṣa* that crowns the heads of the perfect Buddhas.

2.2 OFFERING[255]

Set out as many offerings as your resources permit, as was explained in the chapter on the maṇḍala offering—that is to say, using clean and perfectly pure offerings, and without being ensnared by miserliness, hypocrisy or ostentation. These offerings are just the support for your concentration.

Then make a mental offering in the manner of the Bodhisattva Samantabhadra,[256] filling the entire world and the whole of space with all the offerings of the human and celestial realms: flowers, incense, lamps, perfumed water, nourishment, palaces, landscapes, mansions, pleasure-gardens, the seven attributes of royalty and the eight auspicious symbols, with the sixteen vajra goddesses dancing and singing, each one playing her own particular musical instrument.

By the power of his meditation, the Bodhisattva Samantabhadra emanated hundreds of millions of multicoloured light rays from his heart, as multitudinous as the particles of dust in innumerable Buddhafields. At the end of each ray of light, he projected a form identical to himself, also emanating identical light rays from its heart. At the end of each of those light rays, in turn, appeared even more Samantabhadras, and so it continued in an infinite progression, until the number of forms manifested was utterly inconceivable. Each of these was offering to the Buddhas and Bodhisattvas of the ten directions innumerable offerings of infinite variety. This is what is called "noble Samantabhadra's cloudbanks of offering." Make offerings by mentally creating as many emanations as you can in this way, as you say the corresponding words:

With both physically arranged and mentally created offerings
I offer everything in the universe as one vast gesture of offering.

Whatever we have the power to offer, the Buddhas and Bodhisattvas have the power to accept. So mentally take all the wealth that has no owner in all the human and celestial realms throughout the universe and make an offering of it. Then manifest as much wealth as you can with your imagination and offer that too. You can accumulate exactly the same merit in this way as you would if all those things were your own real possessions. You never need to think that you have nothing to offer. Whatever you or others have, and whatever you see, let your first thought always be to offer it to the Three Jewels and the root and lineage teachers. Mentally take whatever you find beautiful as you pass by, even pure flowing water or fields of flowers, and offer it all to the Three Jewels, thus perfecting the accumulation of merit and wisdom in the midst of your other activities.

2.3 CONFESSION OF HARMFUL ACTIONS[257]

Confess by first thinking, "With intense shame and regret, I openly confess all my downfalls and harmful deeds, those I remember and those I do not, all the unmentionably negative things I have done in all my lives in saṁsāra from time without beginning: the ten negative actions of body, speech and mind, the five crimes with immediate retribution and the five crimes which are almost as grave, the four serious faults, the eight perverse acts, the abuse of funds donated to the Three Jewels and so forth. From now on, I will never repeat those misdeeds."

With this thought, confess as explained in the chapter on Vajrasattva, keeping in mind the antidotes of the four powers. Then imagine that all your wrong actions and obstructions gather together in the form of a black heap on your tongue. Visualize rays of light pouring forth from the body, speech and mind* of the deities of the field of merit, touching the pile, and cleansing you of your defilements as if all the dirt were being washed away. Recite the words:

In the luminous dharmakāya
I confess all wrong thoughts, words and deeds.

* White light from the forehead centre, representing the body; red light from the throat centre, representing speech; blue light from the heart centre representing mind.

2.4 REJOICING, THE ANTIDOTE TO JEALOUSY

Rejoice profoundly and sincerely at the turning of the Great Wheel of the Dharma, set in motion by the Conquerors for the benefit of beings. Rejoice at the vast, powerful activities of the Bodhisattvas and the positive actions of beings, those that are meritorious and those that lead to liberation.[258] Rejoice at whatever good you yourself have done in the past, are doing at present and are certain that you will do in the future, saying:

I rejoice at all good actions
Included in the two truths.

We rejoice at all positive actions included within the two truths,[259] whether done by ourselves or others, whether tainted by emotions or perfectly pure, because there is not one teaching in all the nine vehicles which is not included in relative truth or absolute truth.

The benefits of rejoicing in this way are infinite. Once King Prasenajit invited the Buddha and his followers to take their daily meal at his palace for a period of four months, during which time he offered them all his possessions. An old beggar woman who came past was filled with joy at this action.

"King Prasenajit has acquired all this wealth through the merit he has accumulated in the past," she thought, "and now that he has met the Buddha, who is such an exceptional focus for his meritorious actions, his accumulation of merit will be truly immense. How wonderful!"

Through her sincere and perfect rejoicing, she created boundless merit. Lord Buddha was aware of this.

That evening, when it was time for the dedication of merit, he said to the king, "Would you like me to dedicate the source of merit that you have acquired to you, or shall I dedicate it to someone who is more worthy of it than you?"

The king replied, "Dedicate it to whoever has the greatest source of merit."

So the Buddha dedicated the merit in the name of the old beggar woman. This happened for three days in a row. Exasperated, the king consulted his ministers to find some way to put an end to the situation.

"What do you say to this?" they said. "Tomorrow, when we invite the Mighty One and his followers for the offering of alms, we'll spill a lot of food and drink around the pots. When the beggars come to get it, we'll beat them severely to stop them taking it."

And that is what they did. When the beggar woman who had rejoiced came to gather up the spilt food, they stopped her and beat her. She became angry, thus destroying the source of merit; that day, the merit was dedicated in the name of the king.

As I have repeated here many times, it is the intention of the doer alone that determines whether actions are positive or negative—not the actual physical or verbal execution of that intention. For this reason, in *The Sūtra of Instructions to the King*, the Buddha explains in detail that simply observing the good that others have done with a pure mind, sincerely rejoicing in it and dedicating its power to the complete enlightenment of all beings will bring more merit than ostentatious good deeds poisoned by the eight ordinary concerns, by ambitions for this life, by pride about good deeds, by the wish to compete with other people's virtue, and so on. Chagme Rinpoche said:

> When we hear about good done by others,
> If we cast out all negative thoughts of jealousy
> And really rejoice in the depth of our hearts,
> It is said that the merit we gain will be equal to theirs.

The *Condensed Transcendent Wisdom* says:

> The weight of all Mount Merus in a billion worlds could be calculated,
> But not the merit of rejoicing.

Always rejoice at the good done by others, since it is so easy to do and so beneficial.

2.5 EXHORTING THE BUDDHAS TO TURN THE WHEEL OF DHARMA[260]

Imagine that you are in the presence of the Buddhas and Bodhisattvas, teachers and all those who are able to assume the immense load of working for the benefit of other beings. Think that they have grown tired of the ungrateful and discouraging attitude of those beings and are intending to remain in the state of peace without teaching. Emanating hundreds and thousands of millions of bodies, offer wheels, jewels and other precious objects to them all, and exhort them to turn the wheel of the Dharma, with the words:

> *I entreat you to turn the wheel of the Dharma of the three vehicles.*

The Dharma is generally divided into three vehicles: the vehicle of the Śrāvakas, the vehicle of the Pratyekabuddhas, and the vehicle of the Bodhisattvas. Together they include the entire teaching of the Buddha.

But it may also be subdivided into nine: the three outer vehicles, those of the Śrāvakas, Pratyekabuddhas and Bodhisattvas, that liberate from the origin of suffering;* the three inner vehicles, Kriyā, Upayoga and Yoga, related to ascetic practices in the manner of the Vedic tradition;** and the three secret vehicles, Mahāyoga, Anuyoga and Atiyoga, teaching powerful methods of transmutation. When we request the turning of the wheel of Dharma, what we are requesting is this Dharma of three vehicles, further divided into nine, which can provide teachings suitable for every kind of follower.

2.6 REQUESTING THE BUDDHAS NOT TO ENTER NIRVĀṆA[261]

Address your request to the teachers, the Buddhas and the Bodhisattvas who have completed their work for the good of others, in this and other Buddhafields, and now wish to enter nirvāṇa. Entreat them, like the layman Cunda[262] did in the past, mentally producing many emanations of yourself. Say:

> *Until saṁsāra has been emptied*
> *Stay with us and do not pass into nirvāṇa!*

Then think that because of your prayer all the Buddhas stay to work for the good of beings until saṁsāra is emptied.

2.7 DEDICATION[263]

Follow the example of Mañjuśrī by dedicating to all beings whatever merit has been, is being and will be acquired by yourself and others, starting with the action you are doing now. Seal the dedication with the seal of non-conceptual wisdom. Say the lines:

> *All sources of merit accumulated throughout past, present and future,*
> *I dedicate as a cause of great enlightenment.*

Never forget to perform the dedication at the end of any meritorious act, great or small. Any source of merit not dedicated in this way will bear fruit only once and will then be exhausted. But whatever is dedicated to ultimate enlightenment will never be exhausted, even after bearing fruit a hundred times. Instead, it will increase and grow until perfect Buddha-

* Alternative interpretation: "that guide us taking the origin of suffering as the starting point."

** In which there is a great emphasis on ritual cleanliness and outer conduct.

hood is attained. In *The Sūtra Requested by Sāgaramati* it says:

> Just as a drop of water that falls into the ocean
> Will never disappear until the ocean runs dry,
> Merit totally dedicated to enlightenment
> Will never disappear until enlightenment is reached.

You may wish to attain the level of a śrāvaka or pratyekabuddha, or to achieve total enlightenment. You may just wish to be reborn in the higher realms, either as a god or as a human. Or you may only wish for a temporary result such as a long life or good health. But whatever end you have in view, when you do something meritorious, it is important to dedicate it to that end. Drikung Kyobpa Rinpoche says:

> Unless, by making wishing prayers,
> You rub the wish-granting gem of the two accumulations,
> The result you wish will never appear:
> So do the concluding dedication wholeheartedly.

It is the power of the dedication that determines whether positive actions lead to complete enlightenment or not. The conditioned positive actions you accumulate, immense though they may be, cannot lead to liberation unless you give them a direction by dedicating them. Geshe Khampa Lungpa says:

> No conditioned good actions have a direction of their own,[264]
> So make vast prayers of aspiration for the benefit of beings.

The same applies to a positive activity you might undertake on behalf of your father, mother or loved ones, or for the dead.[265] Without a dedication it will not work. But if you dedicate that activity, the people you have in mind will benefit accordingly.

Once the inhabitants of Vaiśālī came to invite the Buddha to a meal on the following day.

After they had left, five hundred pretas arrived and requested him, "Please dedicate to us the merit of the alms that the people of Vaiśālī are going to offer to you and your followers tomorrow."

"Who are you?" the Buddha asked, although he already knew the answer. "Why should the people of Vaiśālī's sources of merit be dedicated to you?"

"We are their parents," the pretas replied. "We were reborn as pretas as the effect of our miserly behaviour."

"In that case," said the Buddha, "come along at the time of the dedication and I shall do as you ask."

"That is impossible," they said. "We are too ashamed of our ugly bodies."

"You should have been ashamed when you were doing all those wrong deeds," the Lord replied. "What sense does it make to have felt no shame then, but to feel ashamed now, when you have already taken rebirth in this miserable form? If you do not come I shall not be able to dedicate the merit to you."

"In that case we will come," they said, and departed.

The following day, when the moment arrived, the pretas came to receive the dedication. The inhabitants of Vaiśālī were horrified and started to run away.

"There is no reason to be afraid," the Buddha reassured them. "These are your parents who have been reborn as pretas. They told me so themselves. Should I dedicate your sources of merit to them or not?"

"You certainly should!" they cried.

The Buddha said:

> May all the merit of this offering
> Go to these pretas.
> May they be rid of their ugly bodies
> And obtain the happiness of the higher worlds!

No sooner had he spoken than the pretas all died. The Buddha explained that they had been reborn in the Heaven of the Thirty-three.

Jetsun Mila says:

> Between the hermit meditating in the mountains
> And the donor who provides his sustenance
> There is a link that will lead them to enlightenment together.
> Dedication of merit is the very heart of that link.

For any dedication of merit to lead to perfect enlightenment, it must be accompanied by wisdom, freedom from the three concepts. Dedication sullied by clinging to those concepts as real is known as poisoned dedication. The *Condensed Transcendent Wisdom* says:

> The Conqueror has said that to do good with concepts
> Is like eating wholesome food mixed with poison.

The three concepts referred to here are the concepts of there being a source of merit to dedicate, someone for whom it is dedicated and a goal towards which the dedication is directed. If one could dedicate merit in the state of wisdom, fully realizing how those three things are without any true existence, that dedication would indeed be without poison. That may not be within the reach of ordinary people at our level. Nevertheless, simply to think that one is dedicating the merit in the very same way as the Buddhas and Bodhisattvas of the past will serve as a dedication totally free of the three concepts. The *Confession of Downfalls* says:

> Just as all the Bhagavān Buddhas of the past perfectly dedicated merit; just as all the Bhagavān Buddhas yet to come will perfectly dedicate merit; and just as all the Bhagavān Buddhas now present perfectly dedicate merit; so likewise I, too, perfectly dedicate all merit.

and the *Prayer of Good Actions*:

> Emulating the hero Mañjuśrī,
> Samantabhadra and all those with knowledge,
> I too make a perfect dedication
> Of all actions that are positive.

Always be sure to set the seal on your positive actions with a proper dedication, for that is the only infallible method of ensuring that the merit will lead to perfect enlightenment.

3. Praying[266] with resolute trust

This is to bring one's mind to accomplish the nature of the four vajras[267] by praying to the teacher with resolute trust.

Reflect that your revered teacher, your glorious protector, has perfect authority, as having the nature of the heruka[268] in every maṇḍala of deities. Simply seeing him, hearing him, touching him or thinking about him plants the seed of liberation. Since the activity he undertakes is the same as that of all the Buddhas, he is the fourth Jewel. For you, his kindness is greater by far than that of all the Buddhas, because he swiftly establishes you—in a single lifetime and in this very body—on the level of Vajradhara, just by means of the profound path that ripens and liberates and the blessing of his compassion. As for his qualities, his realization is as vast as the sky and his knowledge and love are as limitless as the ocean. His compassion is as powerful as a great river. His nature is as steadfast as Mount Meru. He is like a father or a mother to all beings, since his heart goes out equally to all. Every individual aspect of each of his qualities is immeasurable. He is like a wish-granting jewel. You need only trust in and pray to him, and whatever accomplishments you seek will arise without any effort.

With tears of devotion, thinking, "I rely entirely on you, I place all my hopes in you, I pledge myself to you alone!" recite the lines for the practice of receiving the accomplishments, from:

Precious Lord Guru,
Of all Buddhas, you are ...

as far as:

... I rely on you, great Lotus-born Lord!

Next, concentrate on reciting the Vajra Guru mantra, as an invocation prayer. After every hundred repetitions, say the prayer "Precious Lord Guru ..." again once. Halfway through the time you have set aside for recitation, proceed to the invocation of the accomplishments by saying, after each complete mala of recitations, the prayer beginning:

I have no other hope but you ...

and ending:

O Mighty One, purify me of the two obscurations!

4. Taking the four empowerments

When the time comes for requesting the accomplishments, receive the four empowerments by visualizing that the syllable *oṁ* between the Guru's eyebrows, shining like a moon-crystal, emanates rays of light which penetrate the crown of your head and purify you of the effects of the three harmful physical actions—taking life, taking what is not given and sexual misconduct—and purify of all obscurations your channels, from which the body develops.[269] Recite the lines beginning:

The blessings of the vajra body enter into me ...

and think that the potential to attain the level of the nirmāṇakāya has been established in you.

Then the syllable *ah*, blazing like a ruby in the Guru's throat, emanates rays of light which enter your throat, purifying you of the effects of the four harmful verbal actions—lying, sowing discord, harsh words and worthless chatter—and purifying of all obscurations your energies, from which speech develops. Recite the lines beginning:

The blessings of vajra speech enter into me ...

and think that the potential to attain the level of the sambhogakāya has been established in you.

Then the deep blue syllable *hūṁ* in the Guru's heart emanates rays of light which penetrate your heart, purifying you of the effects of the three harmful mental acts—covetousness, wishing harm on others and wrong views—and purifying of all obscurations your essence, from which mental processes develop. Recite the lines beginning:

The blessings of vajra mind enter into me ...

and think that the potential to attain the level of the dharmakāya has been established in you.

Then from the *hūṁ* in the teacher's heart a second *hūṁ*, like a shooting star, streaks down and mixes completely with your mind, purifying of all the karmic and conceptual obscurations the ground of all, which is what underlies body, speech and mind. Recite the lines beginning:

The blessings of vajra primal wisdom enter into me ...

and think that from that moment the potential to reach the ultimate fruit, the level of the svabhavikakāya, is established in you.

Finally, merge your own mind completely with the teacher's mind, and remain in that state. At the end of the session, recite with devotion and ardent longing the prayer beginning:

When my life comes to its end ...

and ending:

... grant my wishes, I pray.

Guru Rinpoche smiles, his eyes filled with compassion. From his heart, a ray of warm red light beams out. The moment it touches you—up to now you still visualize yourself as Vajrayoginī—you are transformed into a sphere of red light the size of a pea, which shoots up towards Guru Rinpoche like a crackling spark and dissolves into his heart. Rest in that state.

Then, seeing everything that exists as the manifestation of the teacher, conclude by reciting the dedication verse:

By the merit of this practice may I quickly attain
The level of the glorious teacher, my protector ...

as well as the *Prayer of the Copper-coloured Mountain*.

Whenever you are walking around, you can also practise Guru Yoga by visualizing your teacher in the sky above your right shoulder and imagining that you are circumambulating him. Whenever you are sitting down, visualize him above your head as the focus of your prayers. While eating and drinking, visualize him inside your throat and offer him the first part of your food or drink. As you go to sleep, visualize him in the centre of your heart: this is the essence of the sleep yoga technique of "putting everything that can be known into the vase".[270]

In short, arouse your devotion all the time, in every situation. Maintain the thought that wherever you are is really the Glorious Copper-coloured Mountain, and purify everything you perceive by seeing it as the teacher's form.

Whenever sickness, obstacles from negative forces or other unwanted circumstances arise, do not just try to be rid of them. Be glad, thinking that they have been provided by your teacher in his compassion as a way to exhaust your past negative actions. Whenever happiness, comfort and virtuous practice predominate, recognize this too as your teacher's compassion, and do not be proud or overexcited. During meditation, whenever such states of mind as discouragement, lassitude, torpor and mental agitation arise, merge your awareness inseparably with the teacher's mind. Rest in the view of the natural state, maintaining its innate brilliance. At the same time, say the Vajra Guru mantra as a prayer and a recitation. In this way, all appearances will arise as the teacher and deities. Everything you do will become positive. As Jetsun Mila says:

> As I walk, I take all perceptions as the path;
> That is how to walk, letting the six consciousnesses liberate themselves.[271]
> As I rest, I rest in unaltered naturalness;
> That is the essential and absolute way to rest.
> As I eat, I eat the food of emptiness;
> That is how to eat without any dualistic notions.
> As I drink, I drink the water of mindfulness and vigilance;
> That is how to drink unceasingly.

What is more, once you enter the Secret Mantra Vajrayāna, it is essential to receive empowerments, which mature and liberate.[272] They repair violated and broken samayas, and enable you to meditate on all the paths of the generation phase, the perfection phase, and the Great Perfection. They prevent obstacles and errors from arising, and allow all your attainments to develop more and more. It is said:

> In the Secret Mantra Vehicle, there can be no accomplishment without empowerment,

> For that would be like a boatman without oars.

and also:

> Without empowerment there's no accomplishment;
> You can't get oil from pressing sand.

The empowerment that we receive when we are first introduced into the maṇḍala by an authentic Vajra Master is the ground empowerment. The fourfold empowerment that we take by ourselves when we practise Guru Yoga, without depending on anyone or anything else, is the path empowerment. The empowerment that we obtain at the moment of the ultimate fruit, called the "great ray of light empowerment" or the "empowerment of indivisible profundity and radiance," is the fruit empowerment, perfect and total Buddhahood.[273]

These empowerments possess three inconceivably profound characteristics: they purify, perfect and mature.[274] Even when you are doing the main practice it is a mistake to dispense with any of the preliminaries. It is particularly important, when you are meditating on practices such as the generation or perfection phases, always to start each session with the path empowerment of Guru Yoga.

Anyone whose devotion and samaya are completely pure and who completes the path up to Guru Yoga, even without doing the main practice, will be reborn in the Glorious Mountain of the South Western Continent.[275] In that pure Buddhafield they will travel the path of the four Vidyādhara levels even more swiftly than the movements of the sun and moon and reach the level of Samantabhadra.

III. THE HISTORY OF THE ADVENT OF THE EARLY TRANSLATION DOCTRINE

At this point, for the enjoyment of the listeners and for other reasons, it is traditional to relate—neither too briefly nor in too much detail—the history of how the teachings in general, and the three inner yogas in particular, came into being. So I will now describe briefly how the three inner yogas of the Old Translations—known as Mahāyoga, Anuyoga and Atiyoga and corresponding to the generation, perfection and Great Perfection phases—came down to us today. There are three lineages of transmission: the mind lineage of the Conquerors, the symbol lineage of the Vidyādharas and the hearing lineage of ordinary beings.

1. The mind lineage of the Conquerors

The Buddha Samantabhadra* is enlightened from the very beginning. As the infinite, magical display of his compassion there appear the pure fields of all Buddhas, all the places where the teaching is given and the teachers of the four kāyas. His circle of disciples consists of the spontaneously accomplished Vidyādharas of the five kāyas and of inconceivable, infinite hosts of Conquerors; there is no distinction between them and himself. He teaches without teaching, transmitting all the doctrines without words or symbols, through the natural and effortless clarity of the great compassion that radiates spontaneously from primordial awareness. His disciples actualize in themselves the meaning of this absolute teaching without any mistake, and their qualities of freedom and realization[276] become one with his.

For those who do not have the good fortune to understand this first transmission there are the other vehicles that involve a progressive path. Samantabhadra taught these by manifesting countless forms in the inconceivably infinite worlds of the universe to benefit beings, guiding each one by the most appropriate means. The specific forms in which he trains the six classes of beings are the Six Munis. In this world of Jambudvīpa the Buddha Śākyamuni turned the wheel of Dharma on three different levels for gods and humans. He taught the causal vehicle of characteristics, comprising the Vinaya, the Sūtras and the Abhidharma, and the outer Mantrayāna—Kriyā Tantra, Upayoga Tantra, Yoga Tantra, and so on.

> As the antidote to the emotion of attachment
> The Buddha taught the twenty-one thousand sections of the Vinaya Piṭaka;
> As the antidote to the emotion of hatred
> He taught the twenty-one thousand sections of the Sūtra Piṭaka;
> As the antidote to the emotion of bewilderment
> He taught the twenty-one thousand sections of the Abhidharma Piṭaka.
> As the antidote that subdues all three poisons together
> He taught the twenty-one thousand sections of the Fourth Piṭaka.

2. The symbol lineage of the Vidyādharas

At the time of his passing away into nirvāṇa, the Buddha Śākyamuni

* Tib. *kun tu bzang po*, see Introduction: the Great Perfection.

himself predicted the coming of the unsurpassable Secret Mantra Doctrine:

Twenty-eight years
After I have ceased to appear in this world,
The sublime essence of the teaching,
Acclaimed throughout the three divine realms,
Will be taught in the east of Jambudvīpa
To one known as King Ja,
A noble and fortunate human being,
Preceded by auspicious omens.
And on the peak called Fearsome Mountain
Vajrapāṇi will teach it
To the Lord of Laṅkā
With companions of lesser rank, and others.

After making this prediction the Buddha displayed his passing into nirvāṇa.[277] The three yogas of the unsurpassable inner doctrine, the generation and perfection phases and the Great Perfection subsequently made their appearance just as he had predicted.

2.1 THE MAHĀYOGA TANTRAS

Twenty-eight years after the Buddha's departure, King Ja received seven omens in his dreams. Then, on the roof of his palace, he found a large number of precious golden volumes of the Secret Mantrayāna tantras, written with powdered lapis lazuli on sheets of gold, and a statue of Vajrapāṇi one cubit high. He prayed, and afterwards was able to understand the chapter known as *The Vision of Vajrasattva*. He practised for six months, using that chapter and the statue of Vajrapāṇi as the support for his meditation. He had a vision of Vajrasattva, who blessed him so that he understood perfectly the meaning of these volumes. From that time on the teachings gradually spread.

2.2 THE TRANSMISSION OF ANUYOGA

During the same period, on the summit of Mount Mālaya[278] the Five Excellent Ones of Sublime Nobility[279] concentrated their minds on all the Buddhas of the ten directions and recited a twenty-three verse lament, beginning:

Alas! Alas! Alas!
Now that the sun of the Buddha has disappeared,

Who will dispel the world's darkness?

All the Tathāgatas together invoked the Lord of Secrets, Vajrapāṇi:

Listen to us, Lord of Secrets, we pray!
Have you cast off the armour of your past resolve?
Do you not see the suffering of the world?
Have pity and descend to earth,
Dispel the torments of the world!

The Lord of Secrets consented:

Without beginning and without end
Never abandoning my pledge,
Responding whenever I am invoked
I unfold my miraculous display.

There and then, on that very peak of Mount Mālaya, he taught *The Sūtra of the Condensed Meaning*[280] and other teachings to those five noble ones. At Dhanakośa in the western land of Oḍḍiyāna, Vajrapāṇi taught *The Tantra of the Secret Essence*[281] along with its pith-instructions and the tantras of Kīla, Mamo and others to the nirmāṇakāya, Garab Dorje.[282] All of these transmissions were received by Padma Thötrengtsel of Oḍḍiyāna and then gradually spread.

2.3 THE PITH-INSTRUCTIONS OF ATIYOGA

Atiyoga was first taught amongst the gods. In the Heaven of the Thirty-three, there was a god named Devabhadrapala who had some five hundred sons, all born from his mind.* The eldest, Ānandagarbha by name, was more intelligent and physically gifted than his brothers. He liked to practise the vajra recitation, alone in a meditation hut. He became known as Devaputra Adhicitta, "the god's son of superior mind."

In the year of the female water ox, he had four symbolic dreams. In the first, all the Buddhas were emanating rays of light in the ten directions, and the forms of the Six Munis made of beams of light were circling round sentient beings before dissolving into him through the crown of his head. In the second, he swallowed Brahmā, Viṣṇu and Paśupati.** In the third, the sun and moon in the sky appeared in his hands and filled the whole universe with light. In the fourth, a rain of ambrosia fell from a jewel-col-

* They were born miraculously simply through his wish.
** The three principal Hindu gods. Paśupati is another name for Śiva.

oured cloud, and all at once there burst forth forests, precious plants, flowers, fruits and berries.

The following day he went to tell his dreams to Kauśika, king of the gods, who uttered this praise:

> Emaho!
> Now is the time for the effortless heart doctrine to appear!
> Emanation of the Buddhas, Bodhisattva of past, present and future,
> Lord of the tenth level—you will light up the whole world.
> What a wondrous adornment for the heavenly realms!

The first dream was a sign that he would assimilate the wisdom mind of all the Buddhas and become their representative. The second indicated that he would subjugate all demons and eradicate the three poisons. The third meant that he would disperse the darkness in the minds of beings and illuminate them with the teachings. The fourth symbolized the quelling of the feverish torment of negative emotions by the nectar of the naturally arising Ati teachings, and the effortless fruition of the spontaneously accomplished Ati vehicle.

Once again, all the Buddhas of past, present and future assembled and said:

> We invoke glorious Vajrasattva:
> You who possess the jewel of miraculous means,
> Open the gate to all that beings desire.
> Bestow on them this jewel free of all effort.

From Vajrasattva's heart appeared a glowing jewelled wheel, which he offered to Sattvavajra,* saying:

> Wisdom beyond duality, hidden reality,
> Primordially Buddha, with no effort and no action:
> This path is known as the Great Middle Way.
> Reveal it to the assembled disciples.

Sattvavajra promised to teach:

> Vajrasattva, vast as the sky,[283]
> That which is beyond the scope of words
> Is very hard for me to express.

* Another name for Vajrapāṇi

But for those who have not realized it I shall use words
To point out the meaning. So that they may realize it,
I shall use whatever means are needed to liberate practitioners.

In Vajrāloka, the eastern Buddhafield, Vajrapāṇi consulted the Buddha Vajraguhya and the Tathāgatas of the Vajra Family. In Ratnāloka, the southern Buddhafield, he consulted the Tathāgata Ratnapada and the Tathāgatas of the Jewel Family. In Padmakūṭa, the western Buddhafield, he consulted the Bhagavān Padmaprabha and all the innumerable Tathāgatas of the Lotus Family. In Viśuddhasiddha, the northern Buddhafield, he consulted the Tathāgata Siddhyāloka and the countless Tathāgatas of the Action Family. In Viyogānta, the central Buddhafield, he consulted the Tathāgata Śrī Vairocana and many other Conquerors of the Tathāgata Family.

Vajrapāṇi thus distilled the essence of all the Conquerors' wisdom and removed all misconceptions about each and every aspect of Atiyoga, the marvellous essence of the teaching, the spontaneous, effortless realization beyond cause and effect. He knew that Adhicitta, the god's son, possessed the right karma and good fortune, and that he was to be found in the Heaven of the Thirty-three, in the central chamber of the All-Victorious Palace, at the very summit of which was a tree of life, topped by a nine-pointed vajra. Vajrapāṇi went there to meet him and took his seat upon a dazzling jewel-encrusted throne on the very tip of this vajra.

Adhicitta spread out a canopy of various jewels and made offerings of many divine objects. Then Vajrapāṇi transmitted to him, by means of symbols, the entire direct empowerment through the "pouring of the conquerors' means."[284] He also conferred on him the ten transmissions of the miraculous pith instructions, the seven empowerments, the five pith instructions and a large number of other tantras and pith instructions, transmitting them in their entirety in a single instant. Vajrapāṇi empowered him as the foremost representative of the Buddhas and pronounced these words:

May this miraculous essence of the teachings
Become known in the three divine realms
And be propagated in the centre of Jambudvīpa
By a heart-son who is the emanation of an emanation.[285]

Thus it was that the doctrine spread throughout the three divine realms.

2.4 THE COMING OF ATIYOGA TO THE HUMAN REALM

To the west of India lies Oḍḍiyāna, the land of the ḍākinīs. There, in the region of Dhanakośa, was a lake called Kutra. On the bank of the lake, set in a pleasant grove full of beautiful flowers, was a cave called the Place of the Vajra, and there lived a young girl named Bright Flower, daughter of King Uparāja and Queen Ālokabhāsvatī. She bore every sign of perfection, was virtuous of heart and possessed immense bodhicitta. Renouncing hypocrisy and negligence, she had been ordained as a nun and kept all of her vows perfectly without fault. She had a following of five hundred other nuns.

During the year of the female wood ox, at the dawn of the eighth day of the second month of summer, she had a dream in which she saw all the Tathāgatas sending out rays of light that were transformed into a sun and a moon. The sun dissolved into her through the top of her head, moving downwards. The moon dissolved into her through the soles of her feet, moving upwards. In the morning, her realization increased, and she went to wash on the shore of Lake Kutra. Meanwhile, Vajrapāṇi had taken the form of a swan, the king of birds; he had turned Adhicitta into a syllable *hūṁ* and had then transformed himself into four swans. The four swans came down from the sky to bathe in the waters of the lake. Three of them then took off again into the sky, but one of these manifestations of the Lord of Secrets first touched the princess three times on the heart with its beak, and a shining *hūṁ* melted into her heart. Then it too flew away.

The astonished princess told her father and followers what had happened. Filled with wonder, her father the king rejoiced.

"Does this presage the coming of an emanation of the Buddha?" he asked.

The king proceeded to conduct many feasts and ceremonies. Although the princess had no visible signs of pregnancy, when she came to term a gleaming nine-pointed vajra sprang from her heart. It then vanished, leaving in its place a child bearing the major and minor marks of Buddhahood, holding a vajra in his right hand and a rod of precious material in his left. He was reciting the lines beginning, "Vajrasattva, vast as the sky..." Everyone rejoiced. They showed him to a brahmin versed in the art of reading signs. Marvelling greatly, the brahmin declared the child to be a nirmāṇakāya manifestation who would hold the teachings of the highest vehicle. As everyone was extremely happy and he was holding a vajra, they called him Garab Dorje, which means Vajra of Supreme Happiness. As everyone was joyful, they also called him Vajra of Joy. And as they were filled with laughter, they also called him Vajra of Laughter.

When Garab Dorje came to the throne, Vajrapāṇi appeared in person and conferred on him the complete direct empowerment by the pouring of the conquerors' means as well as other empowerments. In a single instant, he also transmitted to him all the tantras and pith-instructions, such as the twenty-thousand volumes of the Nine Expanses and so on, and empowered him as the holder of the teachings. He appointed the faithful protectors as his companions to protect the doctrine. Without effort, and in a single instant, Garab Dorje attained Buddhahood at the level of the Great Perfection.

At that time, in the noble land of India, the brahmin Sukhapāla and his wife Kuhanā had given birth to a son, an emanation of the noble Mañjuśrī. The brahmin child was called Sārasiddhi, and was also known as Saṁvarasāra. Later he became a monk and the chief of five hundred paṇḍitas and received the name Master Mañjuśrīmitra.

In a vision, the noble Mañjuśrī told him, "Go west to the land of Oḍḍiyāna. On the shores of Lake Kutra, there is a vast charnel ground called the Golden Place of Mahāhe. In the middle is a cave called the Place of the Vajra, and there lives the nirmāṇakāya manifestation called Garab Dorje. He is an emanation of Vajrasattva. He holds the effortless doctrine of all the Buddhas, and all the Buddhas have empowered him. Go to him and request the marvellous essence of the teachings, the Dharma known as Atiyoga which he holds, and through which Buddhahood can be attained without effort. You should be the compiler of his teaching."

Mañjuśrīmitra said to his fellow paṇḍitas, "In the west, in the land of Oḍḍiyāna, there is a master teaching a doctrine beyond the principle of cause and effect. We ought to go and demolish him with logic."

They discussed the matter and seven of them, including the elder Rājahasti, travelled the difficult road to Oḍḍiyāna. But no matter how hard they debated with Garab Dorje, whether on the teachings based on cause or on those based on result, the teachings of the Secret Mantrayāna, outer or inner, they could not defeat him.

Mañjuśrīmitra then asked the other paṇḍitas, "Shall we ask this nirmāṇakāya manifestation for his teaching beyond the principle of cause and effect?"

The elder Rājahasti wanted to request the teaching but declared, "I do not dare, because of the disrespect we have shown him."

Some of the others felt that they could ask for the teaching because they were now convinced. Together they decided to confess to the master.

Some began to do prostrations and circumambulate him. Others started to weep.

Mañjuśrīmitra prostrated before him, saying: "Nirmāṇakāya manifestation, by uttering such a stream of uncontrolled polemic, I have treated you with disrespect."

Intending to express his confession by cutting off his tongue, he started to look for a razor. But Garab Dorje read his mind.

"You will never purify your evil actions by cutting off your tongue!" he said. "Compose a teaching far surpassing those dependent on the principle of cause and effect. That will purify you."

All the paṇḍitas who lacked the necessary karma and good fortune returned home. But Mañjuśrīmitra assimilated the entire Dharma, obtaining instantaneous realization merely by seeing a gesture from the master. To make the teaching perfectly complete, Garab Dorje gave him the full direct empowerment by the pouring of the conquerors' means, and all the tantras and pith-instructions without exception, including the twenty thousand volumes of the Nine Expanses. It was at this time that he gave him the name Mañjuśrīmitra. The nirmāṇakāya manifestation Garab Dorje set down the meaning of these instructions in writing, and gave Mañjuśrīmitra the following teaching:

> Mind's nature is Buddha from the beginning.
> It has neither birth nor cessation, like space.
> When you realize the real meaning of the equal nature of all
> things,
> To remain in that state without searching[286] is meditation.

Mañjuśrīmitra understood perfectly what this meant and expressed his own realization as follows:

> I am Mañjuśrīmitra,
> I have attained the accomplishment of Yamāntaka.
> I have realized the great equality of saṁsāra and nirvāṇa;
> Omniscient primal wisdom has arisen.

He wrote the *Instructions on Bodhicitta Written in Gold on Stone*[287] as a confession, and compiled the teachings of Garab Dorje.

These teachings were next passed on to Śrī Siṁha, who was born in China in a place called Shosha to a father named Virtuous and a mother called Clear Perception. He became learned in the five sciences, in language, logic, astrology and so on, which he studied with the master Hastibhala. At the age of twenty-five he met Ācārya Mañjuśrīmitra, from whom he received the totality of the profound Atiyoga teaching, with its tantras, transmissions and pith-instructions, and he obtained the highest realization free from all mental fabrications.

From Śrī Siṁha, the teachings were transmitted to the Second Buddha from Oḍḍiyāna* and then to the scholar Jñānasūtra, the great paṇḍita Vimalamitra and the great translator Vairotsana. The lineage up to this point is the symbol lineage of the Vidyādharas.

IV. PROPAGATION OF THE ESSENCE-TEACHING IN TIBET, LAND OF SNOWS

During the time of the Buddha, Tibet had no human inhabitants. Later, it was populated by a human tribe descended from an ape—an emanation of the noble Avalokiteśvara—and a crag-demoness.** During this early period Tibet was in a state of chaos with no religion, no laws, and no ruler at its head.

Meanwhile, in India, a son was born to a king called Śatānīka. The child's hands and feet were webbed like a swan's and his eyelids closed upwards like a bird's. His father, thinking that the child must be of non-human origin, declared that he should be banished. As soon as he had grown up a little, the boy was sent away. Driven by his karma, he wandered off on foot and finally ended up in Tibet. There he came across some shepherds. When they asked him where he had come from and who he was, he pointed up at the sky. The shepherds assumed that he must be a god who had come down from the heavens, and made him their chief. They built him a throne with earth and stones that they carried on their shoulders, and so he came to be known as Nyatri Tsenpo the Ancient—Nyatri Tsenpo meaning "King of the Throne on the Shoulders." He was the first king,[288] and was a manifestation of the Bodhisattva Sarvanivāraṇaviṣkambhin.

Many generations later, during the reign of Lha-Thothori Nyentsen, who was an emanation of Bodhisattva Samantabhadra, there appeared on the roof of the Yumbu Lakhar Palace a number of sacred objects:[289] the image called the *Cintāmaṇi*,[290] representing the body of the Buddhas; the *Sūtra Designed like a Jewel Chest*[291] and the *Sūtra of a Hundred Invocations and Prostrations*,[292] representing their speech; and a cubit-high crystal stūpa, representing their mind. This was the beginning of

* Padmasambhava.

** It is said that the demoness was an emanation of Tārā.

Dharma in Tibet.

Five generations later came the reign of King Songtsen Gampo,[293] an emanation of Avalokiteśvara. He built all the Thadul and Yangdul temples and the central temple of Lhasa[294] and took in marriage the Chinese princess Kongjo—a manifestation of Tārā—and the Nepalese princess Tritsun—a manifestation of the goddess Bhṛikutī. Each brought with her, as part of her dowry, an image of the Buddha. These two statues came to be known as Jowo.[295]

For the first time a Tibetan alphabet was introduced by Thönmi Sambhota, who studied languages under the Indian paṇḍita Devavit Siṁha and then set about translating *The Cloud of Jewels* and other sūtras. The king manifested a monk named Akarmati from between his eyebrows, who went to convert the non-Buddhist kings in India, and found five spontaneously arisen statues of Avalokiteśvara called the Five Noble Brothers inside the trunk of a kind of sandalwood tree called "snake's essence," at the Place of Sands between India and Tamradvīpa. He also made the particularly sacred statue of eleven-headed Avalokiteśvara which is in Lhasa.[296] It was during this reign that the Dharma really took root in Tibet.

After five more generations, King Trisong Detsen,[297] an emanation of Noble Mañjuśrī, was born. When he was thirteen years old, his father died. First he subjugated a large number of countries by force of arms, taking his counsel from ministers such as Ngam Tara Lugong and Lhazang Lupel.

Then, at the age of seventeen, consulting his ancestors' archives, he became aware that the Dharma had first come to Tibet during the reign of Lha-Thothori Nyentsen and had been firmly established by Songtsen Gampo. Discovering how single-mindedly his forebears had worked for the Dharma, he felt that he too should concern himself wholly with spreading the doctrine. Consulting his minister of religious affairs, Go Pema Gungtsen, he skilfully requested the other ministers' opinions so that they all agreed to the construction of a temple. Looking for a priest to pacify the ground,[298] they consulted Nyang Tingdzin Zangpo, the teacher most venerated by the king, who resided at Samye Chimpu.

By insight gained in meditation, Tingdzin Zangpo knew that in Zahor, in eastern India, lived a great abbot called Śāntarakṣita, son of the religious king Gomadeviya. He imparted this information to the king, and the abbot was invited to Tibet.

Śāntarakṣita then tried to consecrate the temple site. But a nāga who lived in a place called Āryapālo, knowing that the thicket in which he lived was going to be cut down, called all the spirits to his aid. The twenty-one *genyen*, accompanied by humans and non-humans, gathered together in an army, and by night the spirits destroyed whatever had been built by men during the day, putting all the earth and stones back where they had come from.

The king went to the abbot and asked for an explanation. "Is it because my obscurations are too dense? Or have you not blessed the site? Must my plans remain unrealized?"

"I have mastered bodhicitta," the abbot replied, "but gods and demons cannot be subdued by such peaceful methods. Only wrathful methods will work. At this moment there is in Bodh Gaya, in India, a teacher known as the Lotus-Born of Oḍḍiyāna. He came into the world in a miraculous way. He has mastered the five sciences and harnessed the power of the absolute.[299] He has attained both the common and supreme accomplishments. He crushes demons, and binds the eight classes of spirits in servitude. He makes all gods and demons tremble, and subjugates the elemental spirits. If you invite him here, no spirit will be able to resist him and all your wishes will be realized."

"Will it not be impossible to invite someone like that?" asked the king.

"No," replied the abbot, "It will be possible because of prayers that were made in the past. Long ago in Nepal, a woman called Saṁvarī, daughter of Salé the chicken farmer, had four sons from unions with a horse-breeder, a swineherd, a poultryman and a dog-breeder ..." And he told him the story of how the stūpa of Jarung Khashor[300] had been built and the prayers that were made at that time.

The king sent Ba Trisher, Dorje Dudjom, Chim Śākyaprabha and Shübu Palgyi Senge to India, each of them carrying a measure of gold dust and a gold knot of eternity. They explained to the Master that he was needed in Tibet to bless the site of a temple.

The Master promised to come. He set off, stopping along the way to bind the twelve *tenma*, the twelve protectresses, the twenty-one *genyen* and all the gods and spirits of Tibet to firm oaths.

Finally he arrived at Trakmar to pacify the site, and the Spontaneously Arisen Temple of Samye was built. It had a three-storey central building, surrounded by buildings representing the four continents and the subcontinents. The two Yakṣa temples, upper and lower, represented the sun and moon. The entire complex was enclosed by a wall. The abbot Śāntarakṣita, the ācārya Padma and Vimalamitra threw flowers for its consecration three times and many marvellous signs and miracles were seen.[301]

Samye

The first monastery in Tibet, it was constructed at the beginning of the ninth century, its shape representing the universe of ancient Indian cosmology. It was severely damaged during the Cultural Revolution, but the central temple has since been carefully restored and was reconsecrated by Dilgo Khyentse Rinpoche in 1990.

3. The hearing lineage of ordinary beings*

The abbot Śāntarakṣita then taught the traditions of the Vinaya and the Sūtras, while Master Padma and Vimalamitra established the teachings of the Mantras. It was at this time that the Second Buddha from Oḍḍiyāna and the great paṇḍita Vimalamitra taught the three heart-disciples—the King, the Subject and the Friend**—as well as Nyangwen Tingdzin Zangpo and other fortunate disciples who were fit vessels for the teaching. For them they turned the Wheel of Dharma of the three inner yogas, including the Atiyoga of the Great Perfection, and clearly pointed out the three key points: distinguishing, clear decision and self-liberation.[302] The lineage of transmission from this point on is called "the hearing lineage of ordinary beings."

The Second Buddha of Oḍḍiyāna also conferred upon each of his twenty-five disciples,† who all had the requisite good fortune, whichever of the innumerable teachings of the Buddha was destined for them by their karma. The Tantric texts were then put into writing on "yellow scrolls"[303] and hidden as spiritual treasures.‡ The Master made prayers and concealed them as a legacy for the benefit of future disciples. Later, at the prophesied times, emanations of those accomplished practitioners, for whom the prayers had been made, took opportune birth to reveal these profound treasures. The many disciples with the appropriate karma who followed them and worked for the benefit of beings gave rise to the lineages known as those with the six or nine transmissions.[304]

Of the countless *tulkus* and treasure-discoverers, the one who concerns us here is Rigdzin Jigme Lingpa. He was truly Avalokiteśvara Resting in the Nature of Mind†† himself, and took on the form of a spiritual friend. He received the complete transmission of all three lineages together—the mind lineage, the symbol lineage and the hearing lineage—from the Second Buddha of Oḍḍiyāna, the great scholar Vimalamitra and the omniscient Longchen Rabjampa.[305] He was a completely perfect Buddha. He turned the Wheel of the complete Doctrine for beings with fortune and favourable karma. As the saying goes:

> His body is that of an ordinary god or man

* This heading has been inserted in the translation for the sake of clarity.

** Trisong Detsen, Yeshe Tsogyal and Vairotsana.

† *rje 'bangs*, literally "lord and subjects," the lord being King Trisong Detsen and the subjects being the other twenty-four disciples.

‡ See glossary: treasure.

†† *sems nyid ngal gso*: a form of Avalokiteśvara.

But his perfect mind is the true Buddha.

For this reason my venerable master* used to say: "For those who can practise and pray, my teacher, Vajradhara,[306] the lord and protector of beings, is really a perfect Buddha. I do not say so just because I want to praise or honour him. He really is the Great Perfect Vajradhara, come to benefit beings in an ordinary human form. Between him and yourselves in the lineage there is no-one but me. And as for me, ever since I first met him I have done everything he told me. I have served him in the three ways** and have never done anything to displease him or even to make him frown. So you can be sure that there has been absolutely no degradation of samaya to tarnish the golden chain of this lineage. The stream of its blessings is different from that of any other."

The *Tantra of the Union of Sun and Moon* says:

If you do not explain the history of its origins
People will commit the fault of not believing
In the profoundly secret true teaching.

It is because of this need to inspire the confidence of disciples, by explaining to them how their lineage can be traced back to its authentic source and recounting its history, that I have done so here in the context of the Guru Yoga.

It is of the utmost importance in Guru Yoga that the mantra be recited ten million times. Some people fail to recite it for that long, thinking that these preliminary practices are not very important. Or perhaps they are filled with high hopes after hearing how profound the teachings of the main practice are. But to imagine that they can do the generation and perfection phase practices without having taken the time to practise the preliminaries properly is like the common proverb:

Sticking your tongue out before the head is cooked,[307]
Stretching your legs out before the bed warms up.

To practise the preliminaries without going right through to the end makes no sense whatsoever. Even if some small momentary signs of "warmth" occur, they are unstable, like a building without foundations.

* Patrul Rinpoche's teacher, Jigme Gyalwai Nyugu, was one of Rigdzin Jigme Lingpa's principal disciples. See Introduction.
** See page 145.

Part of the same misunderstanding is to drop the preliminaries once you start the main practice, thinking that you have practised them properly already—with the idea that the preliminaries are preliminary and therefore no longer necessary. If you give up the preliminaries, the basis of the path, you cut off the very root of Dharma. It is like trying to paint a fresco where there is not even a wall. Always keep trying until you arouse genuine conviction in the preliminary practices. Concentrate particularly on Guru Yoga, the entrance-way for blessings, and make it the very foundation of your practice. That is the essential point.

I see that my kind teacher is a real Buddha,
But with my obstinate nature, I disobey his instructions.
I know that all beings of the three worlds have been my parents
But with my bad temper, I still abuse my Dharma-companions.
Bless me and those with evil karma like me,
That we may, in this life and all others,
With humble, steadfast discipline, flexible in mind and deed,
Follow our spiritual teacher.

Guru Rinpoche and his twelve manifestations

These different forms of Guru Rinpoche are depicted according to the cycle of 'Dispelling All Obstacles' (*Parché Kunsel*), a spiritual treasure rediscovered by Chogyur Dechen Lingpa and Jamyang Khyentse Wangpo, contemporaries of Patrul Rinpoche.

Part Three

THE SWIFT PATH OF TRANSFERENCE

Kangyur Rinpoche (1898-1975)

A great scholar and practitioner who, although he could have continued to hold high office in the great monastery of Riwoche in Eastern Tibet, chose to spend his life wandering from place to place to practise and teach, avoiding involvement in institutions. From his childhood onwards he had visions of Padmasambhava, and discovered a number of spiritual treasures in Tibet, Bhutan and India.

CHAPTER ONE

Transference of consciousness, the instructions for the dying: Buddhahood without meditation

Supreme is your compassionate action for confused beings.
Supreme is the way you embrace great evil-doers as your disciples.
Supreme are your skilful methods with the hard to tame.
Peerless Teacher, at your feet I bow.

I. THE FIVE KINDS OF TRANSFERENCE

There are five different kinds of transference of consciousness:

1. Superior transference to the dharmakāya through the seal of the view.

2. Middling transference to the sambhogakāya through the union of the generation and perfection phases.

3. Lower transference to the nirmāṇakāya through immeasurable compassion.

4. Ordinary transference using three metaphors.

5. Transference performed for the dead with the hook of compassion.

1. **Superior transference to the dharmakāya through the seal of the view**

   People who have developed and established familiarity with the unmistaken view of the unfabricated natural state during their lives can, at the moment of death, put into practice the essential point of space and awareness on the secret path of the primordial purity of *trekchö*, and transfer their consciousness into the expanse of the dharmakāya.[308]

2. **Middling transference to the sambhogakāya through the union of the generation and perfection phases**

   People well accustomed to practising the generation and perfection phases together as one indivisible yoga, and fully trained in seeing the form of the deity as being just like a magical display can, when the hallucinations of the intermediate state arise at the time of death, transfer their consciousness into the union wisdom kāya.[309]

3. **Lower transference to the nirmāṇakāya through immeasurable compassion**

   People who have received the ripening empowerments of the Secret Mantra Vehicle, who have faultless samaya, who have an inclination for the generation and perfection phases and who have received instructions on the intermediate state can, as it is said:

   > Interrupt the entry to the womb, remembering to turn back:*
   > This is a moment demanding determination and purity of vision.

   Those practising this transference must block any undesirable entry into an impure womb. Driven by great compassion and applying the practice of assuming rebirth as a nirmāṇakāya emanation, they then transfer their consciousness to a place of rebirth in one of the pure lands.[310]

4. **Ordinary transference using three metaphors**

   People practise this mode of transference by imagining the central channel as the route, the bindu of mind-consciousness as the traveller, and a pure land of great bliss as the destination.[311]

5. **Transference performed for the dead with the hook of compassion**

   This kind of transference is done either for a being on the point of dying,

* This means to turn back before the consciousness enters a womb.

or for one already in the intermediate state. It can be performed by a yogī with highly developed realization, mastery over mind and perceptions, and the ability to recognize the consciousness of a being in the intermediate state. Generally speaking, to perform transference for the dead one should have definitely attained the Path of Seeing. As Jetsun Mila says:

> Until you have perceived the truth of the path of seeing,
> Do not practice transference for the dead.

Nonetheless, anyone who really knows the right moment to perform it—which is when the outer breath has stopped but the inner breath is still continuing[312]—can perform it at that very moment if they have a little experience of the instructions on transference. It is extremely helpful for the dying person and, like a traveller being put on the right path by a friend, has the power to prevent rebirth in the lower realms.

Transference is more difficult once mind and body have become completely separated. It then requires a yogī with mastery over his own mind who can find the dead person in the intermediate state. It is easy to influence someone who no longer has a material body, and, performed by such a yogī, transference from the intermediate state itself has the power to send the being's consciousness to a pure land. It is quite meaningless, however, to claim that transference can be performed by summoning the consciousness back into the body after death.[313]

Many people nowadays, who are lamas or *tulkus** in name only, practise rituals of transference. If they perform them with the love and compassion of bodhicitta and have no selfish considerations at all, there is every chance that without obscuring their own minds they can really help those who have died. This is made possible only by the motivation of bodhicitta. But anyone who just does it for personal profit, knowing only how to recite the words, and then takes a horse or some other valuable as payment, is really despicable.

> To be the guide and teacher of others,
> Not having yourself reached liberation's shore,
> Is as contradictory as giving your hand to someone drowning
> While you yourself are being swept away by the flood.

* *sprul sku*, lit. nirmāṇakāya. An incarnate lama. Such lamas are usually considered to be manifestations of a great Bodhisattva. There are, however, many social influences on the selection of a *tulku*, and there are cases where the genuineness of the selection is questionable.

Once, when the great master Tendzin Chöpel was in Tsari, he had a vision of a person for whom he had once performed transference and accepted a horse in payment. All he could see was the person's head protruding from a lake of crimson blood. The apparition was calling Tendzin Chöpel by name and asking him what to do.

Tendzin Chöpel felt afraid. He replied, "I offer you my pilgrimage to Tsari,"* and the vision disappeared.

Even for a great teacher with a high degree of realization, to accept offerings made on behalf of a dead person without doing a ritual or the like for his benefit causes impediments on the path.

When the incarnate abbot of Dzogchen, Gyurme Thekchok Tendzin, passed away, Trime Shingkyong Gönpo was invited for the funeral ceremonies. For a whole day, he performed only rituals of purification and bringing back the consciousness, repeating the transference over and over again, just as he would after the death of an ordinary person. The monks asked him why.

"Long ago," he explained, "Dzogchen Rinpoche omitted to perform the rites and dedication prayers for someone on behalf of whom a black horse had been offered to him. That person had been a great evil-doer and because of this the levels and paths became slightly obscured for Rinpoche. Now he and I have combined forces and have solved the problem." It is said that the evil-doer in the story was called Golok Tendzin.

It is quite wrong for those in the position of great lamas or *tulkus* to accept offerings in the name of the deceased just thinking "I am the great so-and-so," and failing to apply bodhicitta or do the prayers, rituals and dedications properly and effectively. Important *tulkus* recognized as authentic incarnations of great teachers of the past still have to learn how to read again, and start with the alphabet just like ordinary people. Since they have forgotten the art of reading from their previous lives, there can be little doubt that they must have forgotten everything they ever knew about the yogas of the generation and perfection phases too. I wonder whether they would not do better to spend a little time training in bodhicitta and learning about practice and retreats, rather than going around looking for offerings as soon as they can ride a horse.

* That is, the merit of his pilgrimage.

II. ORDINARY TRANSFERENCE USING THREE METAPHORS

I will now describe the kind of transference called "ordinary transference using three metaphors" or "the transference of consciousness into the teacher." It also corresponds to what the *Tantra of Immaculate Confession* calls "transfer of the ball of light using sound at the moment of death." This kind of transference practice is unnecessary for those who already have a high degree of realization. For them, as the tantras say:

> What is called "death" is only a concept,
> Something that leads to the heavenly fields.[314]

And, again

> Death, or what we know as death,
> Is a small enlightenment for a yogī.

Those who have captured the stronghold of the absolute during their lifetime and have achieved mastery over birth and death still appear to die. But for them death is no different from moving from one place to another. Those with experience in the essential practices of the generation and perfection phases can, as we mentioned before, use one of the three practices for death, the intermediate state or rebirth to transfer their consciousness into one of the three kāyas.

On the other hand, as it is said:

> Those without sufficient training can be received through transference.

This technique is essential for practitioners who have not attained stability on the path, or who have committed numerous harmful actions. For anyone holding these special instructions, however serious his or her wrong actions, the gates of the lower realms are closed. Even those who have committed a crime with immediate retribution, and so would otherwise fall straight downwards, will definitely not be reborn in the lower realms if they use this teaching. The tantras say:

> You might have killed a brahmin every day
> Or committed the five acts with immediate retribution,
> But you will still be liberated by this path.
> None of those crimes will defile you.

And:

> Whoever practises the transference,
> Concentrating on the opening above the other nine*
> Will not be defiled by his negative acts,
> And will be reborn in a pure Buddhafield.

And again:

> At the feet of your father, the qualified teacher
> Enthroned on a sun and moon on the crown of your head,
> Follow the white silk pathway of your central channel,
> And you will be liberated, even if you've committed the five crimes with immediate retribution.

These instructions on the profound path of transference are therefore a way to Buddhahood without meditating, a secret path that forcefully liberates even great sinners. The Buddha Vajradhara said:

> You might have killed a brahmin every day
> Or committed the five acts with immediate retribution,
> But once you encounter these instructions
> You will, beyond any doubt, be liberated.

And the Great Guru of Oḍḍiyāna himself said:

> Everyone knows about Buddhahood through meditation
> But I know a path without meditation.

The great paṇḍita Nāropa said:

> The nine openings open on saṁsāra
> But one opening opens up to Mahāmudrā.
> Close the nine openings and open up the one;
> Do not doubt that it leads to liberation.

And Marpa, the translator from Lhodrak:

> Up to now I have practised transference,
> Training, training, and training again.
> I might die an ordinary death, but I need not worry;
> Familiarity has given me perfect confidence.

Jetsun Shepa Dorje said:

* The aperture of Brahmā (see glossary).

These instructions which blend, transfer and link,*
Are the essential guide to overcoming the intermediate state.
Is there anyone with such a path?
How happy the person whose life-energy enters the central
channel—
How wonderful! He arrives in absolute space!

The instructions are in two parts: first the training, and then the actual practice.

1. Training for transference

Using the explanations on transference that you have received, train yourself over and over again with diligence until the signs of success appear.

At the moment, while all your body's channels, energies and essences are intact and vigorous, you will find that actually to perform the transference is quite difficult. But once you arrive at your final hour, or in extreme old age, it becomes much easier. It is like fruit on a tree, hard to pluck in summer while it is still growing. But once it is ripe and ready to fall in autumn, the hem of your clothes only has to brush against it for it to fall from the branch.

2. Actual transference

The time to put transference into actual practice is after the signs of approaching death have already appeared, when you are sure that there is no turning back and that the process of dissolution has already begun. Do not do it at any other time. As it says in the tantras:

Perform transference when the right time comes.
Otherwise you will kill the deities.**

There are many stages in the process of dissolution, but to make it easy to understand, it can be divided into the dissolution of the five sense faculties, the dissolution of the four elements, and the phases of clarity, increase and attainment.

* Linking us with the pure lands through transference of consciousness by blending with the teacher.

** According to the Vajrayāna, the body is considered a sacred maṇḍala of deities. In this sense, to shorten one's life by performing transference prematurely would be to destroy that maṇḍala.

Dissolution of the five sense faculties has started when, for instance, the recitation of the monks gathered around your death-bed only sounds like a confused murmur. You can no longer distinguish the syllables. Or when you hear the sound of people's voices as though coming from very far away, and can no longer make out the words. That is your auditory consciousness coming to an end. Your visual consciousness is coming to an end when, instead of seeing forms as they are, you can only see a blur. As the experiences of smell, taste, and touch likewise come to an end and reach their final dissolution, that is the moment that the introducing instructions should be given. If there is someone present who is able to perform the transference of consciousness, that is definitely the right moment to do it.

Then, as the inner element of flesh dissolves into the outer element of earth,[315] you experience a sensation like falling down a hole. You feel heavy, as though being crushed under the weight of a mountain. Sometimes, the dying person asks to be pulled up or for his pillow to be raised. As the blood dissolves into the outer water element, you salivate and your nose runs. As the body's heat element dissolves into the outer fire element, your mouth and nostrils feel dry and, starting with the extremities, your body starts to lose its heat. In some cases vapour emerges from the top of the head at this stage. As the inner breath, or energy, element dissolves into the outer air element, your different energies—the ascending energy, the energy of evacuation, the fiery energy and the all-pervading energy—all dissolve into the life-supporting energy. Breathing in becomes difficult. Breathing out is a panting, pouring out of the lungs through the throat. Then all the blood in your body gathers together in the life-channel and three drops trickle into the centre of your heart, one after the other. With three long sighs, your outer breath suddenly stops.

At that moment the white element or "semen" that you received from your father moves swiftly downward from the top of your head. As the outward sign, you perceive a whiteness something like a cloudless sky lit up by moonlight. As the inward sign, you experience clarity in your consciousness and the thirty-three kinds of hostile thought cease. This state is called "clarity."

The red element or "blood" that you received from your mother moves swiftly upward from the region of your navel. As the outward sign, you perceive a redness like that of a clear sky lit up by the sun's glow. As the inward sign, you experience predominantly bliss in your consciousness and the forty kinds of lustful thought cease. This state is called "increase."

As the red and white elements meet in your heart, your consciousness enters between them. The outward sign is a perception of blackness like that of a clear sky in complete darkness. The inward sign is that your consciousness experiences a state without any thoughts and you faint away into utter darkness. This is called "attainment."

You then emerge for a short while from that swoon into an experience like that of a sky unaffected by any of those three previous conditions. This is the "clear light of the time of the ground"[316] appearing. To recognize it as your own nature and rest in it is what is called "superior transference to the dharmakāya." It is Buddhahood without passing through any intermediate state.

After that point the intermediate state of absolute reality and the intermediate state of becoming progressively unfold, but those stages will not be described here because they are related to the instructions on the main practice.

For those without adequate experience of the path,[317] the best moment to apply the transference is at the beginning of the dissolution process. At that time, completely cut through all attachment to this life and give yourself courage by thinking, "Now that I am dying, I will rely on the instructions of my teacher and fly to the pure lands like an arrow shot by a giant. What a joy this is!"

It will be difficult to remember clearly all the visualizations and other important points of transference, so if you have a companion able to remind you, ask him or her to do so. But in any case, at that moment, drawing on your previous training and applying the instructions of this profound path, the time has come when you really have to put the transference into effect.

Here, then, are the steps of the main practice of transference, which are the same whether you are training yourself in it or using it at the actual moment of death.

3. The steps of the meditation on transference

Sit comfortably on a cushion, with your legs crossed in the vajra-posture, keeping your back completely straight.

3.1 THE PRELIMINARIES

First, go completely through all the preliminaries, clearly and in detail, starting with the *Calling the Teacher from Afar* and continuing up to the moment of dissolution in the Guru Yoga.

3.2 THE MAIN VISUALIZATION

Visualize that your ordinary body,[318] in an instant, becomes that of Vajra Yoginī. She is red, with one face and two arms, standing with her two legs together, her right foot raised in the "walking posture." Her three eyes are looking up toward the sky. For the purposes of these instructions on transference, visualize her with an attractive expression, at once peaceful and slightly wrathful. With her right hand high in the air, she rattles the small skull-drum that awakens beings from the sleep of ignorance and confusion. With her left she holds at her hip the curved knife that severs the three poisons at the root. She is naked except for a garland of flowers and ornaments of bone. Like a tent of red silk, she appears but has no substance or reality. All this is the *outer empty enclosure* of the body.

Running down the centre of your erect body, visualize the central channel, like a pillar in an empty house. It is called the "central" channel because it stands in the very axis of the body, without leaning to the left or the right. It has four characteristics. It is blue like a film of indigo, symbolizing the unchanging dharmakāya. Its fabric is as fine as a lotus petal, symbolizing the tenuousness of the obscuring veils arising from habitual tendencies. It is as bright as the flame of a sesame-oil lamp, symbolizing the dispelling of the darkness of ignorance. And it is as straight as a segment of bamboo, indicating that it never leads to lower or wrong paths. Its upper end opens straight out into the aperture of Brahmā on the top of the head, like an open skylight, to symbolize that it is the pathway to liberation and higher rebirths, while its lower end is closed off four fingers below the navel without any opening, to symbolize that all access to saṁsāra and lower rebirths is sealed. All this is the *inner empty enclosure* of the central channel.

Now visualize a swelling in the central channel at the level of the heart, like a knot in a bamboo stem. Above this knot, visualize the bindu of energy, light green in colour, active and vibrant. Just above it is the essence of your mind-consciousness, the red syllable *hrīḥ*, with the long vowel sign and two dots for the *visarga*,* fluttering and vibrating like a flag in the wind. This represents your mind awareness.[319]

* A Sanskrit sign pronounced as a hard "h." In Tibetan usage it simply lengthens the syllable, and is written as two small circles one above the other, which symbolize wisdom and means.

In the air a cubit above your head visualize a jewelled throne, held up by eight great peacocks. Upon it is a multicoloured lotus and the discs of the sun and moon, one upon the other, making a three-layered cushion. Seated on the cushion is your glorious root teacher, incomparable treasure of compassion, in essence embodying all the Buddhas of the past, present and future, and in form the bhagavān Buddha and Protector, Amitābha. He is red, like a mountain of rubies embraced by a thousand suns. He has one face. His two hands rest in the gesture of meditation, holding a begging bowl filled with wisdom nectar of immortality. Clad in the three monastic robes, the attire of a supreme nirmāṇakāya[320] observing pure conduct, his body bears the thirty-two major and eighty minor marks, such as the *uṣṇīṣa* on the crown of his head and wheels marked on the soles of his feet, and is bathed in a brilliant radiance from which immeasurable rays of light shine forth.

To Amitābha's right is the noble Lord Avalokiteśvara, embodiment of all the Buddhas' compassion, white, with one face and four arms. The hands of his two upper arms are touching together, palm to palm, at his heart. His lower right hand moves the beads of a white crystal rosary and his lower left hand is holding the long stem of a white lotus whose flower, near his ear, has all its petals open.

To Amitābha's left is Vajrapāṇi, Lord of Secrets, embodiment of all the Buddhas' power and strength. He is blue, and in his two hands, crossed over at his heart, he is holding a vajra and bell.

Both of these deities are wearing the thirteen sambhogakāya ornaments.* Amitābha is seated, his legs crossed in the vajra posture. This symbolizes that he dwells in the extremes of neither saṁsāra nor nirvāṇa. The two Bodhisattvas are standing, which symbolizes that they never tire of working for the benefit of beings.

Around these three principal deities all the lineage teachers of the profound path of transference are gathered like a mass of clouds in a clear sky. They turn their faces with love towards you and all other beings. They gaze at you with smiling eyes, thinking of you with joy. Think of them as the great guides who liberate you and all other beings from the sufferings of saṁsāra and the lower realms, leading you to the pure land of great bliss. Visualize according to the text, starting from:

My ordinary body[318] *becomes that of Vajra Yoginī ...*

down to:

* See page 267

... Gazing skyward with her three eyes.

Then from:

In the centre of her body runs the central channel ...

as far as the words:

... Her body perfect with all the major and minor marks.

Then, with total faith and trust, your whole body tingling and tears streaming from your eyes, repeat as many times as possible the prayer:

Bhagavān, Tathāgata, Arhat, utterly perfect Buddha, protector Amitābha, I prostrate before you. I make offerings to you. In you I take my refuge.

Then recite the next prayer three times in full, starting from:

Emaho ! In this place, the spontaneously appearing absolute Akaniṣṭha ...

as far as:

... May I capture the stronghold of the expanse of dharmakāya!

Next, recite three times the last part, starting from:

With devotion in my mind ...

Finally, recite three times the last line alone:

May I capture the stronghold of the expanse of dharmakāya!

While you pray, concentrate solely upon the syllable *hrīh*, the representation of your mind-awareness, with such devotion for your teacher and protector, Amitābha, that your eyes fill with tears.

Now comes the ritual for ejecting consciousness. As you recite "Hrīh, Hrīh," five times from the back of your palate, the red syllable *hrīh*, representing your mind-awareness, is lifted upward by the vibrant light-green bindu of energy,[321] which rises higher and higher, vibrating all the while. As it emerges from the aperture of Brahmā at the top of your head, call out "Hik!" and visualize the bindu shooting up, like an arrow shot by a giant, and dissolving into Buddha Amitābha's heart.

Go through the process seven, twenty-one or more times, visualizing the *hrīh* in your heart and repeating "Hik!" as before. In other traditions one says "Hik!" as the consciousness shoots up and "Ka" as it comes back down, but in this tradition we do not say "Ka" for the descent.

Then go through the ritual as before as many times as suits you, starting with:

Bhagavān ... protector Amitābha ...

reciting the prayers and practising the technique of ejection and the rest. Then once again, recite three or seven times from:

Bhagavān ... protector Amitābha ...

down as far as:

... I make offerings to you. In you I take my refuge.

Follow this with the condensed transference prayer called *Inserting the Grass-stalk*, written by the treasure-discoverer Nyi Da Sangye[322] and transmitted through the lineage of Dzogchen Monastery:

Buddha Amitābha, I prostrate before you;
Padmasambhava of Oḍḍiyāna, I pray to you;
Gracious root teacher, hold me with your compassion!
Root and lineage teachers, guide me on the path.
Bless me that I may master the profound path of transference.
Bless me that this short path of transference may take me to the realm of celestial enjoyment.[323]
Bless me and others that as soon as this life is over,
We may be reborn in the Land of Great Bliss!

Recite this prayer three times, and then repeat the last line three times. Continue practising the technique of ejection for as long as it suits you, as before. Then start again from:

Bhagavān, Tathāgata ...

and recite the transference prayer from the *Sky Doctrines*, transmitted through the lineage of Palyul monastery:[324]

Emaho! Most marvellous protector Amitābha,
Great Compassionate One and powerful Vajrapāṇi,
With one-pointed mind, for myself and others I beseech you:
Bless us that we may master the profound path of transference.
Bless us that, when the time comes for us to die,
Our consciousness may be transferred to the state of great bliss!

Say this prayer three times, repeating the last two lines again three more times. Then practise the technique of ejection as before.

These last two prayers are not part of the texts of instruction on the *Heart-essence of the Vast Expanse* and were not transmitted by Rigdzin Jigme Lingpa, but came down through Dzogchen Rinpoche, via Gochen Monastery, and through other intermediaries. They form part of the transmissions received by Kyabjé Dodrup Chen Rinpoche, who united them into a single stream. He used them himself, as did my own venerable teacher. Dodrup Chen Rinpoche also inherited the Kagyü lineage of instructions on transference going back to Gampopa. In the transference prayer-book he compiled, some prayers by Gampopa are therefore to be found, although those particular prayers are not ones my own teacher was in the habit of reciting. In any case, the visualization process in all these different traditions is exactly the same, so beyond any doubt the streams of instructions were united to become one great river. My venerable teacher received them many times from Kyabjé Dodrup Chen Rinpoche. I feel that all those who received them from him must also have received the Kagyü tradition of transference instructions at the same time, and are therefore authorized to recite the corresponding lineage and other prayers. Whether or not the two condensed prayers given here are identical to those in Dodrup Chen Rinpoche's collection, they differ only very slightly from other versions and I have therefore written them down just as my venerable teacher taught them.

Once, my teacher was giving the transmission of the *Sky Doctrines* transference tradition. While he was performing transference for a large crowd, some people did not catch the phrase he added, "... all of these (*di nam*), when the time comes for them to die;" so now some say "... this life's perceptions (*dir nang*) ...," and others say "... hence (*di ne*) ...," both of which are, in my opinion, slightly incorrect.

When you have gone through the practice many times and the time comes to end your session, seal it in the expanse of the five kāyas by saying "P'et!" five times. Then rest in equanimity in the natural state without contriving anything.

All the lineage teachers above your head dissolve into the three main figures; the two Bodhisattvas dissolve into Amitābha; Amitābha dissolves into light and then into you. Immediately visualize yourself as the Buddha Protector Amitayus, red, with one face, two hands and two legs. He is sitting in the vajra posture. His hands rest in the gesture of meditation, holding a vase of life filled with the wisdom nectar of immortality and topped with a wish-granting tree. He is wearing the thirteen sambhogakāya ornaments.

Recite "Oṁ Amaraṇi Jīvantiye Svāhā" a hundred times, then the dhāraṇi of long life and other mantras. This is to prevent the duration of your life being affected by the practice and—through the truth of interdependence—dispels any obstacles that might threaten it.[325] This part of the practice is not necessary when you perform transference for a dying or already dead person, nor when you do it for real at the moment of your own death.

The signs of success in this practice are described in the root text:

> The head aches; a drop of serum, shining like dew, appears;
> A grass stalk can slowly be pushed in.

Practise assiduously until these signs arise.

To conclude, share the merit and recite the *Prayer for Rebirth in the Pure Land of Bliss* and other prayers.

Unlike the other practices of the generation and perfection phases, these instructions on the profound path of transference do not require a long training period. Signs of success will definitely come after one week. That is why the method is called "the teaching that brings Buddhahood without any meditation," and that is why everyone should take this unsurpassable shortcut as their daily practice.

> *Unable to take care of myself, I mutter incoherently over the dead.*
> *Without practising, I spread the canopy of my interminable teachings.*
> *Bless me and other frauds like me*
> *That we may be able to practise with perseverance.*

Caves near Dzogchen Monastery

In these caves Patrul Rinpoche spent many years in meditation. The lower one is "Yamāntaka's Terrifying Palace" (see page 374) where he was staying when he wrote *The Words of My Perfect Teacher*.

Conclusion

These instructions contain twelve principal points, of which the first six concern the ordinary, outer preliminaries:

1. To use this human life for what is truly important by reflecting on how difficult it is to find the freedoms and advantages.
2. To goad oneself to diligence by reflecting on life's impermanence.
3. To develop the determination to be free and an attitude of compassion by recognizing that the nature of the whole of saṁsāra is suffering.
4. To renounce evil and adopt good in whatever one does through a detailed understanding of the effects of actions.
5. To be more and more eager for the fruit through remembering the benefits of liberation.
6. By following an authentic spiritual friend, to train oneself to emulate his realization and his actions.

The next five concern the extraordinary, inner preliminaries:

1. To lay the foundation for liberation by taking refuge in the Three Jewels.
2. To establish a framework for the innumerable activities of a

Bodhisattva by arousing the sublime bodhicitta.

3. To confess harmful actions and downfalls, the root of all evil, through the four strengths, using the meditation and recitation on Vajrasattva.
4. To accumulate merit and wisdom, the source of all spiritual progress, by offering the pure lands of the three kāyas in the form of a maṇḍala.
5. To arouse within yourself the supreme wisdom of realization by praying to the teacher, the source of every blessing.

Finally, in case death should arrive suddenly before the path has been completed, a link to the pure lands is created through the transference of consciousness, bringing Buddhahood without meditation.

These preliminary practices may also be presented as follows. Through the four reflections that turn the mind from saṁsāra and through an understanding of the benefits of liberation, you awaken a sincere determination to be free, which opens up access to the whole of the path. Through following a spiritual friend, the source of all good qualities, you create the conditions favourable to the path. Through taking refuge as the foundation, arousing bodhicitta and training in the practice of the six transcendent perfections, you are led along the authentic path of the perfect and omniscient Buddhas.

There are other instructions that are known for their explanations of the three kinds of perception,[326] the three levels of beings' ability, the Mahāmudrā according to the tradition of the sūtras[327] and so forth, but all the essential points of the paths found in them are united here in this present work.

However, purification and accumulation using the two supreme methods, namely Vajrasattva practice and the offering of the maṇḍala; Guru Yoga, the secret path of profound blessings; and the instructions on the transference that brings Buddhahood without meditation—all these are peerless teachings particular to this way of explaining the practice.

After these practices, one enters the extraordinary main path of the vajra core-teaching of the *Heart-Essence*, for which there are special preliminary practices leading to the three kāyas, to mind, and to awareness. Then, once one has been introduced to the absolute through the empowerment of the creativity of awareness,[328] there are naked instructions based on the evolution of one's own experience.*

In writing down these instructions I have not been guided primarily by aesthetic or literary considerations. My main aim has simply been to faithfully record the oral instructions of my revered teacher in a way that is easy to understand and useful for the mind. I have done my best not to spoil them by mixing in my own words or ideas.

On separate occasions, my teacher also used to give numerous special instructions for exposing hidden faults, and I have added whatever I have been able to remember of these in the most appropriate places. Do not take them as a window through which to observe others' faults, but rather as a mirror for examining your own. Look carefully within yourself to see whether or not you have those hidden faults. If you do, recognize them and banish them. Correct your mind and set it at ease on the right path. As Atīśa said:

> The best spiritual friend is one who attacks your hidden faults.
> The best instructions are the ones that hit those faults.
> The best friends are mindfulness and vigilance.
> The best incentives are enemies, obstacles and the sufferings of illness.
> The best method is not to fabricate anything.

It is extremely important to bring the instructions to bear on your hidden faults, to use the Dharma to correct your mind, to maintain mindfulness and vigilance all the time, to take upon yourself full responsibility for whatever happens, never to let even a single negative thought run loose, and to use the teachings to tame your mind. If you can do all that, you will be doing yourself a favour. The Dharma will be of benefit to your mind, and following a teacher will begin to have real meaning. Atīśa also says:

> The best way you can help others is to lead them to take up Dharma.
> The best way they can receive that help is to turn their minds to Dharma.

In short, you now have the freedoms and advantages of human existence. You have met an authentic teacher and received the profound instructions. The opportunity to attain Buddhahood by putting the nine vehicles

* This paragraph refers to the practices specific to the Great Perfection.

of the teachings into practice is now yours. It is now that you can establish a strategy for all your future lives—or now that you can abandon yourself to chance. It is now that you can turn your mind to good—or now that you can abandon it to evil. This very moment is the watershed between the right and wrong direction of your entire existence. This opportunity is like finding something to eat when you have only had one meal in a hundred throughout your whole life. So make use of the Dharma to free yourself while you still can, taking death as your spur at all times. Cut short your plans for this life, and diligently try to practise good and give up evil—even at risk of your life. Follow an authentic teacher and accept whatever he tells you without hesitation. Give yourself, in body and mind, to the Three Jewels. When happiness comes, recognize it as their compassion. When suffering comes, recognize it as the result of your own past actions. Apply yourself to the practices of accumulation and purification with the perfectly pure motivation of bodhicitta. Ultimately, through immaculate devotion and samaya, unite your mind indissolubly with that of a sublime teacher in an authentic lineage. Capture the stronghold of the absolute in this very life, courageously taking on the responsibility of freeing all beings, our old mothers, from saṁsāra's dungeon. This includes all the most crucial instructions.

The pith instructions from the threefold lineage in a river of nectar,
The sweet ambrosia from the lips of a teacher of this true tradition,
The essential points of the practice of the nine vehicles,
Are all collected here, without error or adulteration.

These good words are like well-cooked food,
With all the chaff of fancy phrases winnowed away,
Seasoned with savoury crucial points of deepest practice
In the cooking-juice of instructions based on experience.

These good words are like a skilful farmer
Who, through the wasteland of an evil nature, rank with the three poisons,
Drives the adamantine ploughshare of the teachings, unearthing all hidden faults,
And irrigates skilfully with the water of authentic Dharma.

These good words are like an abundant harvest.

In the fertile soil of determination to be free of saṁsāra,
The seed of bodhicitta is carefully sown
And nurtured with merit and purification, to yield the fruit of spiritual attainments.

These good words are like a kindly nanny.
Watching her charges for hidden faults and uprooting them,
She skilfully exhorts them to good a hundred times,
Ever concerned only to help them improve.

They are not just words; they have a meaning that is especially profound;
They are still warm with the breath of my peerless teacher.
Those who take them as the jewel of their heart
Have certainly taken the true, pure path.

These good teachings are the Bodhisattvas' special skill,
A sacred text written without elegance or poetry
But using everyday language to teach the authentic path,
So that the benefits and the practice may be taken to heart.

Extensive explanatory texts full of copious detail
Do not easily fit in the cramped space of limited minds.
High discourses on philosophical views and profound doctrines
Are hard to put into practice for the weak intellects of our decadent age.

This is why this text, condensed and easy to understand,
A golden elixir to soak into minute openings in narrow minds,
A lamp to light up the gloom of those of feeble wits,
Like an imperturbable instructor, imparts the right meaning clearly on its own.

For the savant who loves verbose discourse,
For the great teacher not seeing what is in the the texts and oral tradition as applying to himself,
To have drunk the nectar of these excellent pith-instructions
Will without doubt revitalize the heart of their practice.

For the hermit who meditates without guidance as if throwing stones in the dark,
For the adept who boasts of all the practice he has done,
For the bogus siddha who has never faced up to his own limits,
This path will cure the disease in their hearts.

This text is not some confection of invented phrases,
A cleverly painted rainbow of fanciful words
By some erudite expert superficially versed in complex texts,
Having nothing to do with the words of my kind teacher.

Of this my vajra-brothers can still bear witness,
For not yet in the distant past is that good age,
A blessed time for Tibet and for the world—
The lifetime of that Buddha in reality, my peerless teacher.

It was that noble being's activity that inspired me
To compile a collection of his authentic words.
This imprint of my devotion and good intention
Should merit great rejoicing by my brothers, and even by the gods.

Fortunate beings living in future times, too:
Please feel the same devotion when you read this text
As you would on meeting my enlightened teacher in person,
For I believe it faithfully conveys the essence of his words.

Whatever merit might accrue from this work
I dedicate to all beings, my mothers of the past,
That they may be sustained by a perfect spiritual friend,
Put his perfect words into practice, and see the excellent fruit.

Especially, may all those nourished on this nectar
From the lips of my peerless teacher, that perfect Buddha,
Together attain perfect Buddhahood;
May I see them setting out and guiding beings.

May the supreme regents of my most kind teacher,
Those who have drunk the nectar of his perfect words
And captivate the fortunate with the intoxicating song of his instructions,
*Long keep their lotus feet firmly upon the vajra throne.**

Henceforth, may I in all my future lives
Be a servant to my perfect teacher and all who follow him;
Pleasing them by fulfilling whatever they might ask
May I be guided as his disciple.

* A poetic expression often employed to wish long life and good health to spiritual teachers.

Until saṁsāra ceases, for every single being,
May I pile up my bodies, my belongings and my merit;
May I serve my old mothers steeped in their afflictions,
And then may they too all take up the perfect Buddha's Dharma.

Meanwhile may the blessings of this precious lineage
Dawn within their hearts like the perfect rising sun.
Having devoted their lives to practice in seclusion,
May they be ever in the presence of the peerless teacher.

This general outer and inner guide to *The Heart-essence of the Vast Expanse* is faithful to the words of my peerless teacher. It arose from the persistent requests of Drönma Tsering, a diligent and highly disciplined fellow disciple, who gave into my keeping some notes in which he had written down everything he could remember. He insisted that I write an explanatory text on the basis of those notes, faithfully recording the teachings of our master. Moreover, Kunzang Thekchok Dorje, a precious *tulku* and representative of the precious and noble teacher and holder of the teaching which brings to maturity and liberates, subsequently repeated the same request two or three times—even providing me with sheets of paper.

Later Kushab Rinpoche Shenpen Thaye Özer[329]—Dharma-sovereign of all doctrines, foremost of all the spiritual sons who hold the lineage of my sublime lord teacher's oral tradition—in turn encouraged me by saying that I must definitely write down the words of our revered teacher in the style in which he taught them, for that would help us all to remember him and revitalize our devotion. I was also encouraged and inspired by a number of my loving vajra brothers and sisters, who are as dear to me as my own eyes and who will surely stay as close to me as a flame and its wick, until we all attain the very heart of enlightenment.

These, then, were the origins of this work, which was written by one to whom Rigdzin Changchub Dorje,[330] that crown ornament of hundreds of incomparable siddhas, gave the name Orgyen Jigme Chökyi Wangpo—but who, behind the embellishment of such a name, is really just Ragged Abu,[331] rough-mannered and burning with the fires of the five poisons.

The text was duly completed at the retreat place, even more remote than the remote Rudam Orgyen Samten Chöling* to which it belongs, known as Yamāntaka's Terrifying Palace—a place splendidly adorned with all the qualities of solitude, where trees bathe their foliage in the warm essence of the rays of the sun while their roots imbibe cool drops of nectar; where vines, thickets, undergrowth, branches and leaves, flowers and fruits of every kind spread forth in filigrees and garlands, filtering the ambrosia of the radiant smile of the Daughter of the Azure Heavens** as it flows down to utterly satisfy the heart.

By the merit of the auspicious completion of this work, may all infinite beings follow this supreme path and be totally liberated into the ground expanse of the primordial Buddha!

* Dzogchen Monastery

** The sun. The elaborate style here, borrowed from the Indian poetic tradition, is traditional for a colophon.

The valley looking towards Dzogchen Monastery
Patrul Rinpoche used to sit on a large flat rock near this spot while he was writing *The Words of My Perfect Teacher.*

Postface

by Jamgon Kongtrul Lodrö Thaye

Om Swasti Siddham
This treasure of Samantabhadra's wisdom, with its six ways of liberation,
Has been unfolded by the mudrā of Sky Yoga of the Vast Expanse.*
Renowned as the *Essence of the Vast Expanse*, glorious with the two accomplishments,
Its great blessings have the power to grant all wishes.

Just to hear the teachings on its preliminary practices explained
Has the power to suddenly transform the minds of living beings.
Following the oral transmission of Jigme Gyalwai Nyugu,
Of everything that Orgyen Chokyi Wangpo taught, this is the essence.

To make available this gift of Dharma, free of all concepts of subject, object and action,
Pema Lekdrup, who has both perfect faith and wealth,
Spiritually and temporally noble secretary of Dergé with its four sections and ten virtues,
Has through this work brought down a rain of inexhaustible Dharma.

By these merits, may this summit teaching of adamantine clear light
Spread and extend throughout the three worlds and remain for a long time.
May all beings connected with it swiftly enjoy the great primordial kingdom
And spontaneously accomplish the welfare of themselves and others.

On the completion of the first corrected draft of the text, this postface was written by Lodro Thaye, who has pure perception of all masters without any sectarian bias. May virtue increase!

* *klong chen nam mkha'i rnal 'byor*, i.e. Jigme Lingpa.

Notes

Abbreviations

DKR	Dilgo Khyentse Rinpoche
ZR	Zenkar Rinpoche
PWR	Pema Wangyal Rinpoche
NT	*Notes on Words of My Perfect Teacher* (see bibliography)
HIST	Dudjom Rinpoche's *Nyingma School of Tibetan Buddhism: Fundamentals and History* (see bibliography)
DICT	*The Great Tibetan-Chinese Dictionary* (see bibliography)
AT	Alternative translation
Skt.	Sanskrit
lit.	literally

1 For beginners, this means avoiding a materialistic or ambitious attitude to the practice. In fact only realized practititioners can practise with true freedom from concepts, but as one's practice matures, freedom from grasping comes progressively.

2 The positive energy of the practice can also be channelled away from enlightenment into other things. NT mentions four circumstances which destroy one's sources of merit. *(dge rtsa)*: 1) Not dedicating the action to the attainment of perfect Buddhahood for the sake of others. 2) Anger: one moment of anger is said to be capable of destroying kalpas of positive actions. 3) Regret: regretting the beneficial actions one has done, even partially. 4) Boasting of one's positive actions to others.

3 NT explains that just as when a drop of water becomes part of the ocean it will continue to exist as long as the ocean exists, when the merit of one's actions is completely dedicated to "the fruit, the ocean of Omniscience," it will not be lost until one has attained complete Buddhahood.

4 "The object of the view (*lta yul*) of both the sūtras and the tantras is the same, i.e. absolute space (*chos kyi dbyings*, Skt. *dharmadhātu*). But with regard to the view itself, a distinction may be made, as when one speaks of seeing a form 'clearly' or of seeing it 'indistinctly.' The Vehicle of Characteristics (the sūtras) establishes the support, the essence, the absolute truth, great emptiness beyond the eight conceptual extremes (*spros mtha'*), but it is not able to realize that its nature is the inseparable union of space and primordial wisdom (*dbyings ye zung 'jug*). As for what is supported, the phenomena of relative reality, the Vehicle of Characteristics establishes them as being interdependent and like a magical illusion. But it does not go further than this impure magical display, to establish the kāyas and wisdoms. The Vehicle of the Secret Mantras, on the other hand, establishes the higher great dharmakāya, the array of kāyas and wisdoms which have always been inseparable, the two absolute truths." NT

5 "In the Vehicle of Characteristics it is not taught that one can attain Enlightenment without abandoning the five objects of desire (*'dod pai yon tan lnga*). But here (in the Resultant Vehicle) one deals with the mind quickly and easily, taking it on the paths in which one does not abandon these five objects, and one can attain the level of Union, the level of Vajradhara, in one life and one body."

6 Beings with sharp faculties are those who are "intelligent enough to be able to realize

the profound view of the Adamantine Vehicle of Secret Mantras and who possess sufficient confidence not to be afraid of vast and powerful actions."

7 According to the Secret Mantrayāna one does not create or develop anything by following the path. One is simply making visible something which is already present—one's own Buddha-nature.

8 One should not see them as ordinary (*rags pa*) beings but as subtle (*phra ba*) or extremely subtle (*shin tu phra ba*) beings." DKR "All in the assembly, whether they realize it or not, are pervaded by the Buddha nature just as sesame seeds are pervaded by oil... So all sentient beings are Buddhas, their utterly pure nature is that of Buddhahood, their primordial essence is that of Buddhahood and their spontaneously present qualities are those of Buddhahood... they are truly Buddhas, visualized as ḍākas and ḍākinīs of the appropriate family. If both teacher and retinue are Buddhas, their Buddhafield is also pure and should be visualized as Akaniṣṭha or another pure land." NT

9 *gsal btab pa* means visualize, but also to bring to mind, to have clearly in one's mind, to refresh one's memory. "Visualizing in this way does not mean telling oneself that a donkey is a horse or that a piece of coal is gold; it means having vividly in one's mind what has always been so from the beginning, that appearances and beings spring from the primal ground, which is the state of Buddhahood." NT

10 "In this kalpa a thousand Buddhas are to appear. However, we have not met those Buddhas who have already come—or if we did meet them they did not succeed in bringing us to liberation. As for the Buddhas of the future, it is still too soon for us to meet them. So without our spiritual teachers we would have no one to help us." DKR

11 The first three are explained in Part Two, Chapter One (page 171). A fourth, irreversible faith, is sometimes added to denote the culmination of faith, when it has become an integral part of one's being.

12 NT says "Whether or not we have received the Dharma, if we have no interest in it we will be like a horse who is offered a bone, or a dog presented with grass." *don gnyer*, "interest," also means "effort," that is to say, not only intellectual interest but also active engagement.

13 These examples from stories of the Buddha's previous lives serve to illustrate the degree of his commitment and should not be taken as recommending extreme asceticism.

14 The sixth sense is mind, since the same psychological reactions are produced by objects which simply arise in thought as by objects perceived by the five physical senses.

15 This refers to ordinary Tibetans, who characteristically have faith in the Dharma and recite the well known mantra, *Oṁ maṇi padme hūṁ*, but who may not have any detailed knowledge of the Buddhist teachings. Here Gyalse Rinpoche is using the term in a slightly derogatory way to provoke his listeners.

16 *grims kyis sgrim la lhod kyis glod.* "This means without distraction, but very relaxed at the same time." DKR. Furthermore, at first it is necessary to rein in the wild thoughts to achieve sustained calm (*zhi gnas*), then one has to relax the mind to allow the expansion of profound insight (*lhag mthong*).

17 "That the way the teachings are expressed are just the words and therefore dispensable is what people say who think they are great Nyingmapa meditators. They think that they can grasp the essential naked meaning without bothering about the words. Pointing to their hearts they will say that this explanation is just words which have no substance and that it is only necessary to understand the essence of mind."

18 The real meaning expresses the truth from the point of view of realized beings. The

expedient meaning refers to teachings intended to lead unrealized beings towards that truth, who would not be able to accept or understand it if it was stated directly. The indirect meaning refers to teachings given to beings to introduce them indirectly to a meaning which is not directly stated.

19 "That is misunderstanding the meaning, imagining, for instance, that from the moment when one has received the teaching of the Secret Mantrayāna one can enjoy sex and alcohol, and perform the practices of union and liberation. To avoid this mistake, one's conduct should be appropriate to the moment (i.e. to the level of spiritual evolution that we have actually reached at the present moment)."

20 AT "an inspiration which is good or bad forever." Here we have followed the explanation of DKR.

21 This refers to a purification practice for the dead in which the dead person is represented by a card bearing their name.

22 The expression *thod pa bor chog ma* literally means "getting rid of the skull," that is, of getting rid of one's body, in the sense of freeing oneself from future rebirths. DKR

23 *'du shes med pa.* AT "without perception." We have followed the explanation of DKR: "The gods without perception have created a blankness in their minds and perceive nothing, as in the state of deep sleep without dreams."

24 *klo kha khra* refers to the large area inhabited by tribal peoples lying to the south of central and eastern Tibet. It includes present-day Arunachal Pradesh, Nagaland and parts of Assam in north-eastern India, as well as parts of north-western Burma.

25 Tibetans habitually call Bodh Gaya *rdo rje ldan*, the Vajra Seat, referring to the spot on which the Buddha sat when he attained enlightenment. It is considered to be the centre of the world.

26 See note 295.

27 These temples were constructed at precise points to subdue the negative forces of Tibet. At the heart of the group was the Rasa Trulnang, the original name for the Jokhang. See also page 342 and note 294.

28 According to NT Padmasambhava means that only in these three periods is the Secret Mantra Vajrayāna revealed on a large scale.

29 Lit. "years," but this does not refer to precise units of time but to periods of growth or decline affected by various causes such as the appearance of a holy being or, conversely, the harmful influence of evil beings. DKR

30 During the period immediately following the promulgation of the teachings, those who practise them attain the fruit almost straight away.

31 During the period of accomplishment there are people who practise the Dharma, but less of them, and their results come more slowly.

32 NT explains that these can crop up suddenly, between one session of practice and the next, or during a session, and destroy one or several of the eighteen freedoms and advantages, like a wolf entering a sheep fold and carrying off one or two of the eighteen sheep within.

33 "These separate one's mind from liberation and omniscience. When one of them occurs, it withers the shoot of enlightenment and cuts one off from the family of liberation." NT

34 A ceremonial parasol carried before a high-ranking lama as a symbol of respect.

35 "The ocean symbolizes the depth and vastness of the three lower realms of rebirth and their infinite sufferings. The blind turtle symbolizes the beings of these three worlds

who are without the two eyes of adopting what is beneficial and abandoning what is harmful. The fact that the turtle only rises to the surface once every hundred years symbolizes the difficulty of escaping from those states. The one hole in the yoke symbolizes the rarity of human and celestial existences. The wind which propels it this way and that represents dependence on favourable circumstances."

36 We have chosen 'Surabhībhadra' as one possible Sanskrit reconstruction of the Tibetan *bde spyod bzang po*, the name of the king for whom Nāgārjuna wrote this text. In fact, although most accounts agree that he was a close friend and patron of Nāgārjuna, the king's identity in historical terms remains uncertain. He was probably of the Śātavāhana line of kings in Āndhra, and while some scholars identify him with Gautamīputra Śatakarṇī, who reigned at the beginning of the 2nd century A.D., others have called him Udayana or Udayī, or identified him with the kings Yajñaśrī or Vikramāditya.

37 This refers to a Tibetan beer prepared by pouring hot water over fermented grain. The barrel containing this preparation would thus be entirely full of grains.

38 The "half" refers to the reign of Mune Tsenpo, who died after reigning for only one year and nine months.

39 He could control his mind in the sense of developing concentration but not in the sense of mastering the negative emotions or realising the nature of mind. From the point of view of Dharma, meditation without the proper orientation is useless.

40 *lam du 'khyer ba*: lit. to take on the path. This means using all situations in daily life as part of the practice. If Gelong Thangpa had taken his negative thoughts on the path by using love as the antidote to aggression, for example, or by seeing the empty nature of the thought as soon as it arose, it would not have led to any harm.

41 *rkyen*: circumstances. The auxiliary cause which allows the deep cause (*rgyu*) to produce its effect. If someone dies in an accident, for instance, the accident itself, the circumstances of that death, are the *rkyen*, and the *rgyu*, the deep cause, is a negative action performed in the past, of which death is the karmic result.

42 *gyur dug*: in Tibetan medicine, this expression refers to foods which are healthy in themselves, but which become toxic or indigestible when eaten in combination with certain other foods.

43 *sha sgren* means meat which is excessively old but not necessarily rotten. Food can be stored for long periods of time in Tibet because of the very particular climatic conditions.

44 If in one's sleep one can remain focused on the clear light which is the natural manifestation of primal awareness, all one's mental experiences will mingle with it and will not be perceived in a deluded fashion.

45 Death will not be followed by an ordinary automatic rebirth caused by past actions.

46 These are the three kinds of diligence explained in detail on pages 245-248. PWR adds: When you have armour-like diligence, nothing can prevent you starting. When you have diligence in action, nothing can interrupt what you are doing. When you have diligence that cannot be stopped, nothing can stop you attaining your goal.

47 The Tibetan term is *chos dred*, lit. "Dharma bear." DICT: "someone who has not been tamed by the Dharma. He knows the Dharma but, not having practised it, his mind has become stiff..." If one approaches Dharma with the wrong attitude, one can acquire a false self-confidence which makes one unreceptive to the teacher and the teachings.

48 These celestial bodies are traditionally considered the dwellings of certain celestial beings, invisible to ordinary humans.

49 *dkor za ba* usually means using funds donated by the faithful, with the particular sense

of using them improperly. Sometimes it refers to the abuse of collective possessions, such as the wealth of a nation, by those in a position of power.

50 Here speech (*ngag*) refers to the subtle power of speech. It is the vehicle for the sound of mantras and can have a power to heal, pacify, subjugate etc., when employed by one who has a certain spiritual training or a particular kind of karma.

51 The magicians hurl various symbolic projectiles at them, such as tormas, mustard seeds or powders, which the pretas perceive as weapons destroying their bodies.

52 Nāgas are a category of beings living under the earth and having miraculous powers. Although they are similar to spirits, they are classed with the animals on account of their serpent-like form. See glossary: "garuḍa"

53 The expression *'du byed kyi sdug sngal* which we have translated as "the suffering of everything composite" is explained as follows: *rgyu rkyen 'du byed nas sdug sngal 'byung*, "when cause and circumstances come together suffering arises." It is considered to be the source of the two other basic kinds of suffering and is described as *khyab pa*, omnipresent or all-pervading, in saṁsāra.

54 The other principal types of birth that occur variously in the six realms are birth from an egg, birth from heat and moisture, and miraculous birth.

55 These are approximate translations of the technical terms used in Tibetan medicine for the first five weekly stages of embryonic development.

56 *las kyi rlung*: the force of previous actions which propels the whole process of saṁsāra.

57 A plate pierced with a hole through which metal is drawn to make wire.

58 In Tibet butter is massaged into the crown of the head of the newborn baby to encourage the fontanelle to close. Although this is considered beneficial to its health, the newborn child is so sensitive that the subtle energies of its body are agitated.

59 For Tibetans, as in many oriental cultures, to step over someone's head (and body, too) is extremely insulting and a source of defilement. For the practitioner of tantra it is a lack of respect for the maṇḍala of the body, which is sacred. However, for a yogī who has realized the ultimate purity of all phenomena in the absolute, all categories of experience have the same taste of emptiness.

60 *las kyi sa pa*, a place where the force of karma is more powerful and its effects are felt more strongly and, in certain cases, sooner. Of the four continents in the universe of traditional cosmology, it is especially in Jambudvīpa that actions produce strong effects, and in which individual experiences are more variable. The inhabitants of the other continents experience the results of past actions, for the most part, rather than creating new causes. Their experiences and lifespans are more fixed.

61 If we are not deceived by favourable circumstances, but realize that they only have as much reality as we accord them, those circumstances can become an aid to the progress of our meditation instead of producing attachments which will obstruct us.

62 It is through observing both good and bad teachers that one can appreciate the good ones. Observing good and bad practitioners helps one to learn how to act oneself.

63 In the same way that outer phenomena appear and disappear in space, mental phenomena arise from the nature of mind (*sems nyid*) and dissolve back within it. They have no independent reality.

64 The realm of the gods is characterized in part by the absence of anger and hatred. So here, in order to be able to fight, the gods of the Heaven of the Thirty-three go to a magic forest which makes them aggressive.

65 The worlds of form and formlessness. See glossary: "three worlds."

66 Lit. "five realms:" an alternative classification of the six realms with the gods and asuras grouped as one.

67 *las su 'char ba*. We have received a number of different explanations of this expression. We have translated it according to the interpretation of DKR as being the equivalent of *las su rung ba*, suitable or workable.

68 Just as a watch tower plays a vital role in a war for observing the enemy and obtaining the victory, the samaya (see glossary) is essential in the Secret Mantrayāna for avoiding obstacles and attaining Buddhahood.

69 Following the progression of the vehicles (Skt. *yāna*) means that externally one follows the discipline of the Śrāvakayāna while internally one practises the Mahāyāna, and secretly one practises the Mantrayāna. Here Patrul Rinpoche means that his teacher, although his mind is wholly beyond saṁsāra, is nonetheless a perfect example to his disciples of how to follow the progressive path.

70 The two other acts with immediate retribution are to cause a schism within the Saṅgha and to shed the blood of a Buddha.

71 In most of Tibetan society of the time, eating meat at every meal would have been considered a sign of wealth and therefore of high status. The guest is acting pretentiously in trying to give the impression that she is unaccustomed to eating anything but meat in her own home.

72 Here Patrul Rinpoche distinguishes between psychic phenomena unrelated to wisdom and the real transcendence of space and time of realized beings, who have attained the three highest Bodhisattva levels. The former are described as being *zag bcas*, "tainted" (by concepts), and the latter as *zag med*, "untainted."

73 "The rites of brahmins" refers to rites performed without the motivation of attaining enlightenment for all beings. Although they are religious rituals they are not considered to lead to ultimate liberation.

74 *dkor nag po:* Because of the very sacredness of the Buddha, Dharma and Saṅgha, the misuse of offerings made to them has especially heavy karmic consequences. Here particular reference is made to the offerings of the faithful for rituals performed for the dead, the sick, etc.

75 *thar pa dang grol ba:* We have translated these two terms here as liberation and freedom, nearly synonymous in English. PWR explains the difference in this context: liberation (*thar pa*) is from saṁsāra, especially the lower realms, while freedom (*grol ba*) is from all the obstacles to omniscience, or enlightenment. In other contexts, *thar pa* can cover both of these meanings, as in Chapter Six.

76 This view is considered incorrect not because it denies a creator, but because it denies the process of causality.

77 This does not mean that one should not question or analyse the teachings. Indeed, the Buddha encouraged such questioning. However, allowing one's opinions to close one's mind to the Buddhist teachings, which often challenge everyday concepts, can actually prevent one from adopting the path that leads to freedom.

78 Since spiritual guides appear according to the past actions of beings, the teacher and his disciples are indissolubly linked. Thus, if the disciples behave inappropriately, the effects rebound—in the relative sphere—on the teacher, reducing the period of his incarnation and creating obstacles for his activity for the benefit of others.

79 Wrong views will render one's attitude narrow. Even one's positive actions will be limited in their effects because one does them without the motivation of attaining

complete enlightenment for the sake of all beings. Moreover if one has no faith in those who transmit the Dharma one will not have the *support* for confession described in Part Two, Chapter Three.

80 This refers to the moment when the karmic energy produced by an action produces its maximum effect, which can be hastened or retarded by the effects of other actions.

81 An slightly different version of this quote is given in Zenkar Rinpoche's edition of the Tibetan text: "To see where you were born before, look at what you are now. To see where you are going to be born next, look at what you do now."

82 Impure generosity is giving with a self-centered attitude, in a miserly fashion or halfheartedly, or giving and then regretting it afterwards. The effect of giving in that way is that one will be wealthy but will not benefit from it.

83 The qualities of a Buddha: the thirty-two major and eighty minor marks, the ten powers, etc.

84 *seng ldeng* is a hardwood, the catechu tree *Acacia catechu*, found all over northern India, Nepal and the valleys of Tibet.

85 see note 36.

86 We have not been able to clarify this phrase. *srog* means the life force which supports heat and consciousness, or the breath. It seems that Surabhībhadra (see note 36) was the patron of Nāgārjuna, who provided him with an elixir of life. If that was the case, perhaps the son, to kill his father, decided to kill Nāgārjuna to prevent him from giving him the elixir.

87 According to legend, Nāgārjuna's head and body took the form of two large stones some distance apart (at Nāgārjunakonda in South India) which gradually draw closer over the centuries. When they reunite, Nāgārjuna will come to life again.

88 In addition to actions which are generally negative, there are actions which the Buddha proscribed for those who had taken particular vows. Here the monk is violating a precept forbidding fully ordained monks to cut vegetation.

89 The circular base upon which piles of rice etc. are placed in the offering of the maṇḍala. To make offerings is part of the process of purification. The maṇḍala offering is explained in detail in Part Two, Chapter Four.

90 Using the Dharma language of the highest views to scorn the principle of cause and effect means to use the teaching of absolute truth as a pretext for doing whatever one wishes, saying there is no difference between good and bad, saṁsāra and nirvāṇa, Buddhas and ordinary beings, and so on.

91 This means whoever is connected with one in any way, positive, negative, or purely incidental. Even a minimal connection with a Bodhisattva, through seeing, hearing, touching, and so on, can bring great benefit and lead to liberation.

92 See Introduction for a brief description of the main practice. "Although all the practices of the main part of the path are not formally described in this book, they are there in essence. The book is complete because it contains the entire meaning of the path." DKR

93 In this chapter, Patrul Rinpoche gives a verse summary of each point, without citing any particular source. These verses are to help the reader or listener to remember them. Direct oral transmission has always had an important place in Buddhism, and Tibetans regularly commit whole volumes of the scriptures to memory. This training enables them to remember oral teachings in detail. The systematic structure of this text, for instance, is in part to enable practitioners to have the instructions constantly available

in their minds.

94 They act unconventionally, with disregard for conventional rules of behaviour, as if their actions were based on true non-conceptual wisdom. In fact they are just fooling themselves.

95 NT specifies that to see one's spiritual teacher as a Buddha one needs to feel: 1) that he is the Buddha in person both in the absolute and relative sense, 2) that all his actions, be they spiritual or worldly, are those of a Buddha, 3) that his kindness towards one exceeds that of the Buddhas, 4) that he embodies the greatest of all refuges, and 5) that if, knowing this, one prays to him without relying on any other aid on the path one will develop the wisdom of realization.

96 *srid pa*: its root meaning is "possibility," whatever can transform into anything else. Thus it represents all the concepts which we project onto reality and which become the illusory world that we perceive. So it can be translated as: becoming, existence, saṁsāra, the world.

97 The perfect horse is one of the possessions of the universal monarch. It knows his wishes before he expresses them. Here the ideal disciple is aware of the intentions of his teacher and in consequence acts appropriately.

98 "To learn the thoughts and actions of the teacher means to acquire all the qualities of his body, speech and mind." DKR. "If one does not first acquire the realization of the teacher, to emulate his actions would be hypocrisy." NT

99 *nor rdzas*: literally, "material wealth." We have often translated this term (and *nor* on its own) as "money," although it could also mean anything precious and valuable, not specifically some form of currency.

100 One of the three great monastic universities of Buddhist India, the others being Nālandā and Odantapurī. The post of "paṇḍita-gatekeeper" of the "gates," or departments, at each cardinal point was given to the scholars most able to defend the Buddhist philosophical position against the challenges of non-Buddhist thinkers presenting themselves for debate. Intense and formalized debating between proponents of different schools of thought was characteristic of this period of high civilization in Northern India.

101 *gyang rim gsum*: "three courses of a clay wall," about three metres. In many parts of Tibet, the walls of houses were built of clay (*gyang*), which was compacted while wet between parallel wooden forms laid along the line of the wall, and allowed to dry. The forms would then be moved up to hold the next course (*rim*) of clay. The wooden boards used as forms were generally about a metre in width. The term *gyang* or *gyang rim* was often used as a rough measure of the depth of snow.

102 A possible explanation of these three sentences is as follows: "Its root is the conquest of the beginning," means that the nature of Buddha which is our original nature cannot be affected by any cause or circumstances. "Its summit is the conquest of attainment" means that one can obtain no higher result. "Its fruit is the conquest of yoga" means that no yoga can give a better result.

103 The tradition based on the teachings originally introduced into Tibet from India in the 8th century came to be known as the Ancient, or Nyingma, Tradition. The tradition based on the new wave of teachings introduced from the 11th century onwards was called the New, or Sarma, Tradition. Milarepa's first teacher, Rongtön Lhaga, belonged to the Nyingma, while Marpa was a translator and accomplished practitioner of the New Tradition teachings.

104 Jetsun Mila wanted to offer the pot filled with barley. To offer an empty vessel is

considered to be inauspicious.

105 The trials that Milarepa had to undergo before receiving the teachings from Marpa, as well as being a purification of past karma, an accumulation of merit and a psychological preparation, also had a bearing on the future of his lineage, each detail having a symbolic significance which, by the principle of interdependence (*rten 'bral*) would affect Milarepa's own future and that of his disciples.

106 To "take refuge" or "go for refuge" has long been the standard English translation for *skyabs su 'gro ba*. The root meaning is to seek protection from a danger, in this case the dangers of samsaric existence.

107 "Why all paths? Because taking refuge is a necessary part of every path of the sūtras and tantras." NT

108 Here faith is simply a spontaneous response. "In this case one does not necessarily know the reasons for one's faith." NT

109 "When one has this kind of faith, one knows why. One has faith because one knows that the Three Jewels, and in particular the spiritual teacher, are an infallible refuge." NT

110 The word "door" (*sgo*) here refers implicitly to faith, as what gives access to the blessings of the Buddha, of Padmasambhava, or of one's teacher. PWR

111 This is the refuge at the level of the Great Perfection.

112 *tshogs zhing*: "the field (i.e. object) for accumulating merit through prostrations, offerings and prayers." DICT. Because of the enlightened qualitites of the Buddha, Dharma and Saṅgha, the effect of any positive action directed towards them has enormous power. See also glossary for field of merit.

113 The lotus symbolizes the purity of the enlightened mind. Although it grows in the mud, its blossom is not stained by it.

114 The number of limbs is specified because the visualized forms of teachers and deities may often have more than one head and more than two arms or legs, each detail having a specific symbolic meaning.

115 The main Bodhisattvas in Buddha Śākyamuni's retinue: Mañjuśrī, Avalokiteśvara, Vajrapāṇi, Maitreya, Ākāśagarbha, Kṣitigarbha, Sarvanivāraṇaviṣkambhin, and Samantabhadra.

116 The thirteen ornaments of the sambhogakāya are listed on page 267.

117 A monk's staff, called *'khar gsil*, literally "ringing staff," consists of a shaft of wood and iron surmounted by two stūpas; below the uppermost hang four wheels and twelve metal rings, whose jangling sound signals the monk's presence. The alms-bowl, usually of metal, is called *lhung bzed*, literally "that which holds what falls".

118 The Dharma protectors are sometimes emanations of Buddhas or Bodhisattvas, and sometimes spirits, gods or demons who have been subjugated by a great spiritual master and bound under oath. The protectors in the first category are free from karma and act out of compassion. Those in the second category are protectors because of their karmic links.

119 "At that moment (of attaining enlightenment) one has the ten strengths and is endowed with the ten powers, so one is free from all fears. As one has the capacity to protect others one no longer needs to take refuge." NT

120 "The only ultimate refuge is the ultimate state of Buddhahood. The Dharma and the Saṅgha are temporary refuges. The Dharma of transmission is the meaning that one has to realize. Once one has realized that meaning correctly, one has no further need of it, just as after crossing a river one no longer needs a boat. As for the Dharma of

realization, as one progresses on the path one leaves behind one's previous realizations, which are in other words deceptive and impermanent.

As for the Saṅgha, Śrāvakas and Pratyekabuddhas do not have the qualities of Bodhisattvas who have attained the sublime levels, and sublime Bodhisattvas do not have the qualities of Buddhas; Bodhisattvas who are ordinary beings still fear the lower realms. Such beings are therefore not a source of refuge in the long term." NT

121 Here the refuge is expressed according to the three different phases of the main practice. See Introduction.

122 To practise systematically it is recommended that one allots a regular period of time, during which one concentrates on the practice without interruption. This might be just once a day, or, in an intensive retreat, for instance, as many as four sessions a day: in the early morning, mid-morning, afternoon and evening.

123 The common (*thun mong*) accomplishments, consist of miraculous powers, etc. and are common to Buddhism and other yogic paths. The supreme (*mchog*) accomplishment is total enlightenment beyond saṁsāra.

124 *rus pa can*, literally meaning "bony," referring here to the expression *snying rus*, lit. "a bone in the heart," meaning bold determination and the courage never to give up.

125 The basic requirement before performing ceremonies to help others is that one should have thoroughly practised the main part of the sādhana in question, which consists of the recitation of the mantra many thousands of times, to purify one's own mind.

126 "Maṇḍala" in this context means the circle of deities visualized and invoked for the practice. In the true Buddhist tradition this is considered as a method for arousing one's own wisdom mind. Here it is being misused as a gross magic rite.

127 Although there are wisdom teachings in the Bön tradition that are very close to Buddhism, what is meant here is the primitive Bön of village sorcerers.

128 Real anger (*zhe sdang rang mtshan pa*) is a negative emotion based on the dualistic notion of "I" and "other." It should be distinguished from the expression of anger displayed by beings who are free from such notions and whose every action is based on compassion for all beings. This wrathful display is a powerful method to help those who are not susceptible to a peaceful approach.

129 An allusion to the story of the building of the Great Stūpa, at Bodhnath, near Kathmandu, by a poultrywoman and her sons. Three of the sons were reborn, as a result of the wishes they made at that time, as the master Padmasambhava, the king Trisong Detsen, and the abbot Śāntarakṣita, who together were responsible for firmly establishing the Dharma in Tibet. This magnificent stūpa is a thriving focus for Tibetan devotees, who know it by the name Jarung Khashor. (For the whole story, see *The Legend of the Great Stūpa*, transl. Keith Dowman, Berkeley, Dharma Publishing 1973.

130 According to the predictions of a brahmin astrologer after the birth of the prince Siddhartha, the child would become either a universal monarch or a Buddha.

131 Different tantras include lions or peacocks in the list instead of dogs or cows. All of these are types of meat that were not normally eaten because they were taboo according to brahmanical thought in ancient India, being either too holy or else unclean. They are therefore specified for practices aiming to break concepts.

132 Certain experiences such as visions, dreams etc. may be, but are not necessarily, signs of progress in the practice. Teachers in Patrul Rinpoche's lineage insist that one should not be fascinated by such experiences. One should rather measure progress by the growth of devotion, compassion and freedom from negative emotions in one's mind.

133 The ten levels and five paths of a Bodhisattva. Here the meaning seems to be progress on the path in general.

134 From the earliest times, the tradition was that Buddhist monks offered the first part of what they received on their daily begging round to the Three Jewels, ate the middle part without discrimination, and gave the last part to the needy.

135 "Arousing bodhicitta" is only one possible translation of *sems bskyed*. The word *bskyed* means to give birth to, to produce, but also to make grow, to develop. The word *sems*, which is an abbreviation of *byang chub kyi sems* (Skt. *bodhicitta*), the "mind of enlightenment," has several levels of meaning. For the beginner, it is simply the intention to liberate all beings. However in a deeper sense, bodhicitta is a synonym of Buddha-nature, (Skt. *Tathāgatagarbha*) and of primal awareness (*rig pa*). At this level it is not something to be produced which was not there before, because it is the fundamental nature of our mind, which has always been with us and only has to be discovered and made manifest. We have chosen "arouse" to try to convey something of both aspects.

136 This is defined by NT as "to promise to attain the fruit."

137 NT says: "The bodhicitta of application is the will to practise the six transcendent perfections, which are the cause or the means of attaining the fruit."

138 "Relative bodhicitta is produced with the support of our thoughts." NT

139 "Absolute bodhicitta is wisdom in which the movements of thought have dissolved." NT

140 Here, for the sake of clarity, we have inserted a heading that is not in the original text.

141 The moon's reflection in water appears vividly but has no true, independent existence. The same is true of what we perceive through the senses, since phenomena are empty of any objective essence. However, we are led astray by the belief that those appearances are objectively real. It is this fundamental confusion which is the basis for the negative emotions which make us wander in saṁsāra.

142 The reason why bodhicitta is so fundamental to the path of enlightenment is because at the absolute level it is the Buddha-nature itself, inherent in all beings, which naturally has limitless love and compassion. The process of relative bodhicitta serves to make that nature manifest. NT says of these two aspects: "The first is the deep cause of attaining Buddhahood, and the second is the circumstantial cause."

143 NT explains that one should first try to arouse bodhicitta for the merest instant, then for two, then three and so on.

144 Guidance according to experience, *nyams khrid*, is a method of teaching in which the teacher first gives just a little instruction. The student puts it into practice and then presents his experience of the practice to the teacher, who then advises him or gives further instruction on that basis, and so on in a continuous interaction.

145 A form of the Bodhisattva Avalokiteśvara, crystalline white in colour.

146 Skt. *uṣṇīṣa*: this protuberance on the crown of the head is one of the physical marks of a Buddha. In the case of Jewel Crest, this mark was present even though he was not a fully enlightened Buddha.

147 The first five perfections are related to the accumulation of merit, while nonetheless being infused with wisdom. It is this that makes generosity and so on "transcendent perfections."

148 Bodhisattvas who have attained the sublime levels have realized emptiness and have vast and pure intentions, which is not the case with ordinary beings.

149 *rang don*, one's own benefit (AT goal), implies the total realization of emptiness, the

dharmakāya, from which the sambhogakāya and nirmāṇakāya then manifest out of compassion to accomplish *gzhan don*, the benefit of others.

150 See glossary: warmth.

151 The medicinal tree symbolizes the bodhicitta, which cures oneself and others of all sufferings.

152 The symbolic offering of the body is explained in Part Two, Chapter Five.

153 This is explained in Part One, Chapter 4, section III (pages 124-126).

154 NT explains that what can be destroyed in this way is the result of positive actions which only produce merit (*bsod nams*), that is to say those which are performed without the three supreme methods.

155 "To keep discipline for a day is more valuable than a hundred years of generosity; to cultivate patience for a day is more valuable than a a hundred years of discipline." NT

156 They were presumably students of one of the Śrāvakayāna schools which hold that there is no truly existing personal self (*gang zag gi bdag med*), but do not recognize the total emptiness of true existence of phenomena (*chos kyi bdag med*).

157 It is the unlimited openness of love and compassion for all beings that allows the mind to open fully to the vastness of the Mahāyāna view.

158 See also note 46.

159 "Avoid falling into an extreme which will bring about excessive fatigue, or practising an exaggerated asceticism which will put an end to your life." NT

160 "One becomes more and more attached to meditative experiences. These are the experience of bliss, in which one feels happy for no reason; the experience of clarity, when the mud of thoughts has settled and one feels like a house that is empty, within and without; the experience of non-thought, in which, when one checks whether any thoughts are arising, one has the impression that there are none to arise. One still clings to the reality of an 'I,' (*gang zag gi bdag*) by thinking of 'my experience.' And one also clings to the reality of the object (*chos kyi bdag*) by thinking there are real experiences to be attached to. This conflicts with the realization of the emptiness of true existence which is the source of liberation." NT. At this stage of concentration, one has only achieved sustained calm (*zhi gnas* Skt. *śamatha*) without profound insight (*lhag mthong* Skt. *vipaśyanā*).

161 Seven point posture of Vairocana - *rnam snang chos bdun,* the seven points of the ideal meditation posture: legs crossed in the vajra posture, back straight, hands in the gesture of meditation, eyes gazing in the direction of the tip of the nose, chin slightly tucked in, shoulders well apart "like a vulture's wings," and the tip of the tongue touching the palate.

162 Keeping the back straight allows the subtle energy (*rlung*) to flow freely in the subtle channels (*rtsa*). There is an intimate relationship between this subtle physical system and the movements of the mind. It is said that the mind rides on this energy like a rider on a horse.

163 The transcendent perfections of means (*thabs*), strength (*stobs*), aspiration (*smon lam*) and primal wisdom (*ye shes*) are added to the usual six to make what are called the ten transcendent perfections.

164 This means neither suppressing thoughts nor following them, nor deliberately trying to alter the state of one's mind or achieve a specific state of meditation. All deluded thoughts are in a sense alterations of the natural flow of awareness.

165 That is, having nothing to be ashamed of in front of the Three Jewels.

166 Concentration is the absence of distractions. The source of distraction is taking appearances as real. To meditate on appearances as deities (which means as pure wisdom manifestations with no concrete reality) is to be concentrated.

167 *nges shes*, lit. "certainties," is used here to mean extreme views, such as eternalism and nihilism, which state that phenomena definitively do or do not exist.

168 "Here *srid pa* (samsaric existence) refers to anything that one believes to be real and to which one is attached." DKR

169 Since the view is the realization of emptiness, the realizer, what is realized and the process of realization are recognized as being without any intrinsic reality. They only appear as the illusory magical display of awareness, empty and naturally radiant.

170 The union of appearances and emptiness, awareness and emptiness, bliss and emptiness, and clarity and emptiness.

171 This means acting without conceptualizing, in the realization that the actor, the action and the object acted upon are all without intrinsic reality.

172 Before embarking on this practice one should have received the empowerment of Vajrasattva from a qualified holder of the lineage. In general, the practices which follow in the rest of the text from this point should only be undertaken under the guidance of a qualified teacher.

173 In the practices of the Vajrayāna one considers the visualized deity as one's own root teacher who represents all the Buddhas of past, present and future. Vajrasattva (Tib. *rdo rje sems dpa'*) is the particular Buddha who, as a Bodhisattva, pledged that whoever recited his mantra would be purified of all their negative actions and obscurations. His name refers to the indestructible purity of the nature of mind.

174 Aṅgulimāla, who had been given a false teaching that he would gain liberation by killing one thousand people and collecting a finger from each, had already killed nine hundred and ninety-nine, and was on his way to complete the thousand by killing his mother when he met the Buddha, whom he tried to kill instead. Because of the Buddha's powers, he was unable to attack him. Then the Buddha spoke to him and turned his mind to the Dharma.

175 Nanda is the example of someone with extreme attachment attaining liberation; Aṅgulimāla is the example of someone with extreme ignorance; Darśaka (another name for Ajātaśatru) is the example of extreme aggression; Śaṅkara is the example of someone with both extreme attachment and extreme anger. Nanda and Aṅgulimāla became Arhats, Darśaka became a Bodhisattva, and Śaṅkara was reborn in a god realm and subsequently attained the path of seeing.

176 NT describes this as the external support.

177 NT describes taking refuge, generating bodhicitta, and especially compassion as the *inner* support.

178 NT speaks of six things to be contemplated for the practice of regret: 1) Time: regretting all the negative actions that one has done from time without beginning until now, during this life, in a particular month, or day, or moment, and so on. 2) Motivation: regretting all acts committed under the sway of desire, aversion and confusion. 3) Accumulation: regretting whatever negativity one has accumulated physically, verbally, or mentally. 4) The nature of the action: regretting both acts which are negative in themselves (such as the ten negative actions, the five acts with immediate retribution, etc.) and particular faults, transgressions of one's vows and so on. 5) Object: regretting all wrong actions, whether directed towards saṁsāra or nirvāṇa. 6) Karma:

regretting all harmful acts and downfalls which have earned one a short life, many illnesses, poverty, fear of enemies and endless wandering in the lower realms.

179 The printing and distribution of sacred books is considered a powerful practice for accumulating merit and purifying obscurations, provided that it is done purely as an offering without any profit.

180 *dag pa dran pa*: This Tibetan expression literally means "remembering the purity." It refers to the fact that every element of visualization is not a mere image but has a particular meaning, and it is important to be aware of this significance as one does the practice. The precise way in which the elements of this practice relate to the four powers is explained a few paragraphs later. Although here we are only dealing with the preliminary practice, many points mentioned in this chapter are useful for the main practice of the generation and perfection phases.

181 In the main practice (see Introduction) one often visualizes oneself in the form of a deity. Here we consider we are ordinary and impure at first, and through the practice we become pure. So at the outset we think of our body as being in its usual everyday form.

182 *ston pa*: This common epithet of the Buddha literally means "revealer," and signifies the teacher who taught the Dharma for the first time in our kalpa and world. Vajrasattva is the first teacher of many traditions of the Vajrayāna in the same way as the Buddha Śākyamuni is the originator of the vehicle of characteristics.

183 Here the vajra and bell symbolize skilful means and wisdom.

184 The shorter of these necklaces comes down to the breast, the longer down to the navel.

185 The female figure symbolizes wisdom, and the male figure skilful means; at another level the female symbolizes emptiness and the male appearance, or again they can symbolize absolute space and primal wisdom. Their sexual union symbolizes that in the state of enlightenment all these are experienced as inseparably one.

186 These are not material channels but the subtle pathways in which the subtle energies of the body flow. The significance of these channels becomes clear when one practises the yogic exercises of the perfection phase of the main practice.

187 As the nectar fills each wheel, one receives a corresponding blessing, as mentioned in each of the lists of four in this paragraph.

188 Literally, "the state of union beyond learning," "union" referring to the union of the rūpakāya and dharmakāya. In the five paths of the Bodhisattva, the path beyond learning is the fifth, and denotes the state of total Buddhahood.

189 These five colours represent the five Buddha families, each representing a particular aspect of wisdom.

190 The words *dag* and *ma dag* here could also be interpreted in terms of reciting all the syllables of the mantra correctly or otherwise. But in view of the explanation in the following paragraph they have been translated as "purity" and "impurity".

191 *bskyed rim gsal 'debs*, the description of the images to be visualized and the different processes of the meditation is recited before proceeding to the actual recitation of the mantra. This is the standard structure of the ritual texts used for the *sādhana* (*sgrub thabs*, lit. means of accomplishment) of any deity. Such texts are used not only for ceremonies in a group for particular purposes, but also for personal practice.

192 The use of tobacco products pollutes the system of subtle channels and energies and thus has a harmful effect on the mind at a deep level.

193 The words of the offering section of the sādhana, which are repeated after the recitation of the mantra and before the conclusion.

194 This image indicates that the use of such offerings is karmically very dangerous and can lead to rebirth in the hells.

195 When one has received an empowerment, the power of the practice should be maintained by a daily practice, even if this is brief. Here the lamas are doing such practices during the ceremony rather than in their own time.

196 The three maṇḍalas of the teacher's body, speech and mind.

197 "Drinking your heart blood" means destroying your life force. The Secret Mantrayāna puts us in touch with our true nature and our most fundamental energies. If we keep the samaya commitments it enables us to progress rapidly. But if we do not, we give rise to a powerful self destructive force. This is called the "vajra ogre" and is the opposite of the wisdom deities.

198 To commit a complete root downfall is to break one of the basic vows of the monastic discipline, consciously, in a situation where it is not impossible to do otherwise.

199 i.e. in which a single figure embodies all the deities. This is explained more fully in the chapter on Guru Yoga.

200 The twofold purity is to possess the purity of the Buddha nature in the first place, and then the purity of having actualized it and achieved Buddhahood. "According to the teachings of the Nyingma tradition, the primordially pure nature which is Buddhahood and the qualities of the three kāyas already dwell within us in their entirety, and we do not need to seek them elsewhere. But if we do not use the two accumulations as auxiliary factors, these qualities will not become manifest. It is like the sun: although its rays illuminate the sky by themselves, it is still necessary for the wind to drive away the clouds which hide it." NT

201 *bsags sbyang rang sar dag kyang*, lit. "even when accumulation and purification are pure in their own place."

202 The directions that follow are sometimes quite technical and are intended to complement an oral explanation, normally accompanied by a demonstration.

203 We make offerings in the presence of the accomplishment maṇḍala, which is used rather as one might use a statue of the Buddha. It symbolizes the perfect Buddhafield of the five Buddhas which represent the five wisdoms. As it is these five wisdoms which we wish to accomplish, this maṇḍala is called the accomplishment maṇḍala.

204 The convention in a maṇḍala is that the front is east, the back is west, and so on. Here the maṇḍala is turned to face the practitioner, so the eastern side is nearest.

205 The *Heart-essence of the Vast Expanse* (*klong chen snying thig*) is one of a number of *Heart-essence* teachings. The most important of these are the *Heart-essence of the Ḍākinī* (*mkha' 'gro snying thig*) and the *Heart-essence of Vimalamitra* (*bi ma snying thig*), transmitted through Yeshe Tsogyal and Vimalamitra respectively. Both these teachings have come down through the lineage of Longchenpa.

206 A ready made "iron fence" is a ring, usually of metal which one uses to contain the first level of offerings of the maṇ ḍ ala. It represents the ring of mountains surrounding the world. In such a case a second ring contains the offerings of the eight goddesses and a third the sun, moon, etc. The ornament for the summit mentioned later is simply a jewel-shaped ornament which one puts on top at the end. These accessories are additions to enhance the offering, which is nonetheless perfectly authentic without them.

207 If you arrange the maṇḍala so that the East is towards you, you should turn the completed maṇḍala round to face the maṇḍala of accomplishment at the end, when you recite, "I offer this maṇḍala ..."

208 The basic explanatory text for these preliminary practices is the *Explanation of the Preliminary Practice of the Heart-essence of the Vast Expanse*, written by Jigme Lingpa. Each element of the maṇḍala has several levels of meaning, corresponding to different levels of practice.

209 Though more ordinary than those which follow, this is nonetheless an offering of an ideal universe, as perceived in the pure vision of highly evolved beings rather than the everyday experience of a universe full of suffering perceived by ordinary deluded perception.

210 *mi mjed 'jig rten*. According to the explanation of DKR which implies another possible spelling (*mi 'byed*, undivided) in this universe the emotions are so strong that beings are never separate from them.

211 *bkod pa chen po lnga*, lit. the five great arrangements. These are the Buddhafields of the Buddhas of the five families.

212 Like Milarepa, who lived in remote places in the mountains where there was no-one to bring him food, and subsisted on a diet of nettles.

213 In this simpler maṇḍala offering one uses only seven piles of grain, to represent Mount Meru, the four continents, the sun and the moon.

214 *zhal zas*: an honorific term for food. In this case an offering of food represented by a type of torma which bears this name.

215 Concepts of subject, object and action.

216 Extracting the essences *(bcud len)*, a method which makes it possible to consume only certain substances and elements in minute quantities, without having to use ordinary food. It is the basis for subtle practices to purify the body and refine the mind.

217 Ascending or descending can be applied to the qualities of different kalpas or refer to a smaller timescale: for instance our present times are an era of degeneration compared to the time of Śākyamuni.

218 The term used here for the body is *phung po*, referring also to the "aggregates", i.e. the psychophysical constituents which interdependently make up what one thinks of as oneself.

219 The Mother: the feminine, wisdom or emptiness, which is described as the mother of all the Buddhas because when one realizes emptiness one becomes Buddha.

220 *ma cig khro ma nag mo*, Skt. *Krodhakali.*

221 The syllable *p'et* (generally pronounced "pay" or "pet", although there are many variations) uttered abruptly, is used to cut through the process of conceptualization.

222 *a thung*, used here by Patrul Rinpoche for the more usual *a shad*, meaning "the a-stroke," a simple line, thicker at one end and pointed, (།) which forms part of the Tibetan letter A (ཨ). In this practice it is upside down, giving it the appearance of a flame. In many practices the *hang* (ཧཾ) is upside down also, although that is not mentioned in our text.

223 Nectar: The Skt. *amṛita*, lit. "the immortal," was translated into Tibetan as *bdud rtsi*, the nectar (*rtsi*) which conquers the demon (*bdud*) of death. It is a symbol of wisdom. Immaculate (*zag med*) means "unsullied by negative emotions."

224 *dpal mgon bdun cu rtsa lnga*, some of the most famous Dharma-protectors of Tibet. They are considered to be emanations of Mahākala.

225 In this practice the tongues of the Buddhas and Bodhisattvas have the symbolic form of a half-vajra, which represents the indestructible wisdom body, extending into a tube of light, representing their ability to accept offerings.

226 Lit. "debts for the castle above and the fields below," that is to say, the debts we owed the lord for his protection when we were tenants and the debts we owed to the farmers for their crops when we were lords.
227 These last four refer to spiritual attainments.
228 See page 69.
229 *snyems*, lit. arrogance, used in this chapter with the very particular meaning of believing in "I."
230 "According to the causal vehicle of characteristics, the four demons are: 1) The demon of the aggregates, *phung po'i bdud*, referring to that which dies. (Without the five aggregates, there would be no support, or basis, for the sufferings of saṁsāra.) 2) The demon of negative emotions, *nyon mongs pa'i bdud*, the causer of death. (These emotions, which arise from the belief in a self, give rise to negative actions. Negative actions give rise to karma and it is due to karma that we helplessly are born and die.) 3) The demon of the Lord of Death, *'chi bdag gi bdud*, which is death itself. (This means death as such, which inevitably follows birth. More subtly it is the natural impermanence of each moment, which is by nature painful.) 4) The demon of the sons of the gods, *lha'i bu yi bdud*, that which prevents us from proceeding towards the state of peace beyond death. (In practice it refers to distraction, thoughts of attachment to external objects.)

"According to the Mantrayāna vehicle, the four demons are: 1) The tangible demon: exterior things and beings which harm our body and mind. 2) The intangible demon: attachment, aversion and confusion and the 84,000 types of negative emotions that give rise to all the sufferings of saṁsāra. 3) The demon of exultation: this means the exultation that one feels when one thinks that one's own spiritual teacher, the teachings one has received and the practices one is engaged in are different, and that one's own vajra brothers and sisters are superior to other people's. More particularly, it is the infatuation that one feels when one achieves the slightest 'warmth' or power of the practice. 4) The demon of conceit is the root of the three others: it is the belief in 'I' and 'mine;' this conceit makes us take the five aggregates as 'me' or 'mine:' if one destroys this demon, all external demons are destroyed by themselves, without doing anything to destroy them."
231 "The venerable mother" means Machik Labdrön, who is speaking in this quotation.
232 Usually symbolically with a four-line verse of teaching.
233 We have used the Sanskrit term as being less unwieldy than the Tibetan (*bla ma'i rnal 'byor*) or English. As well as meaning simply "practice based on the teacher," the term means "uniting with the nature of the teacher's mind."
234 In Buddhist philosophy, emptiness is established on the basis of logical reasoning. This is not a purely intellectual pursuit but a spiritual exercise, using concepts to break concepts.
235 *dpe'i ye shes*. In Anuyoga, for instance, through working with the channels and energies, one experiences bliss-emptiness, which provides an indication of the flavour of the true primal wisdom that always dwells within us but which we are unable to recognize. It is rather like a picture of an elephant which would enable us to recognize a real elephant. In the Great Perfection the nature of mind, the true primal wisdom, is introduced directly.
236 "In what way should one consider him as a Buddha? According to the Lesser Vehicle it is not even necessary to consider one's teacher as a special being or a pratyekabuddha.

To consider him as an ordinary being with certain qualities is enough. For the Bodhisattva path it is enough to consider him as a being who has attained one of the supreme levels, as the nirmāṇakāya of a Buddha or a Bodhisattva who is at least on the great path of accumulating (*tshogs lam chen po*). In the tradition of the Great Perfection, it is inappropriate to consider one's teacher as an ordinary learned person, as an Arhat, as a Bodhisattva on one of the sublime levels, as the nirmāṇakāya of a Buddha or even as the sambhogakāya. One must consider him as the dharmakāya. If one is capable of praying to him with a faith that is utterly constant, one can arouse the wisdom of inner realization without recourse to other paths." NT

237 NT explains in detail as follows: "If one has the devotion to see one's teacher as a Buddha, the wisdom of realization will arise even if one does not practise the generation and perfection phases. This opinion is shared by the New Tradition. Nonetheless, in Mahāyoga and Anuyoga, the generation and perfection phases are the main practice. If one has no conflicts with one's teacher and spiritual companions and practises considering the teacher to be the essence of the deities, the accomplishments are near and the blessing will come swiftly."

238 *sgyu ma ngal gso*, the third work in Longchenpa's *Trilogy of Rest, ngal gso skor gsum*. Longchenpa himself explains that the title can be taken not only as "finding rest from illusion," but also as "finding rest *in* illusion,"—illusion in the latter case being understood as referring to the view of everything as being like a magical display without any inherent reality.

239 Complete surrender to the wisdom nature embodied by the teacher permits a direct communication of that wisdom. Without this process of surrender, there can be no letting go of ego-clinging. This principle applies to all stages of the path, but becomes much more intense and explicit in Guru Yoga. The effectiveness of any path depends on the extent to which it is approached in this way.

240 The merging of appearances and mind (*snang sems 'dres pa*) refers to the realization that all appearances are produced by the creativity of mind, and the true nature of mind is emptiness; this leads one to experience everything in a way that is beyond any subject-object duality, and is characterized as unobstructedly 'naked' and 'penetrating' (*zang thal*). PWR

241 This is a form of the phenomenon known as the rainbow body (*'ja' lus*).

242 Visualizing oneself as a deity enables one to go beyond the limitations of everyday conventional ideas not only of the teacher but also of oneself. NT says: "If one visualizes oneself in one's ordinary form, this idea will prevent the blessings from entering." Also, one visualizes oneself in a female form in relation to the male form of Guru Rinpoche, thus combining the aspects of wisdom and means; and, specifically, by thinking one has the nature of Yeshe Tsogyal, Guru Rinpoche's closest disciple, one creates a *rten 'brel* (interdependent link or auspicious connection) with their extraordinary teacher-disciple relationship.

243 *brtul zhugs kyi spyod pa*: the unconventional lifestyle adopted by the most advanced practitioners as a means of perfecting their confidence in the view. "Having transcended ordinary activities, engaging in extraordinary ones." DICT

244 The deer is a symbol of peacefulness. Avalokiteśvara is commonly depicted with the skin of a deer draped over his shoulders. This hat is trimmed around the border with the skin of a fawn.

245 The intense energies of such places provide a challenge which practitioners can use to

confront their own fears.

246 An exclamation of wonder. "What does one find wonderful? The purity and infinitude of phenomena." NT

247 The Prayer in Seven Lines:

Hūṁ! Born in the north west land of Oḍḍiyāna
On the pollen bed of a lotus stem,
Wondrously, you attained supreme accomplishment.
You are renowned as the Lotus Born,
Surrounded by retinues of many ḍākinīs.
Emulating you, I will perfect myself—
Come then, I pray, bestow your blessings.
Guru Padma Siddhi Hūṁ.

This is the most revered prayer to Padmasambhava. It has many levels of meaning, and in itself constitutes a complete path.

248 So that one does not feel that one is just inventing an artificial visualization, one invites the "real" Padmasambhava and his retinue from his Buddhafield, the Copper-coloured Mountain. These *wisdom deities (ye shes sems dpa'*, Skt. jñānasattva) dissolve into and bless the *samaya deities* (*dam tshig sems dpa'*, samayasattva) that we have already visualized. The same goes for the palace and other elements of the Buddhafield (here, both the deities and their environment, the palace, are included in the term *tam tshig pa*). As we have already seen, Padmasambhava's presence is there all the time. These techniques serve to develop confidence in that experience.

249 "Secret" because the vajra master has a hidden ability to increase the merit of actions. For "field of merit" see note 112 and glossary.

250 "There are three kinds of prostration:

The superior kind is 'encountering the view.' To prostrate with the view means to know that there is no subject, object or action to conceptualize.

The middling kind of prostration is called 'training in meditation.' In this we manifest innumerable bodies, each chanting innumerable songs of praise. One might think that this was a practice of the generation phase, but this is not the case because the innumerable bodies generated are impure, ordinary bodies (and not deities).

The ordinary kind of prostration is 'devotional prostration:' prostrating one's body, reciting prayers with one's speech and experiencing devotion with one's mind. Since devotion is the most important point, one should keep the qualities of the infinite objects of refuge in mind as one is prostrating." NT

Ideally, one should try to incorporate the view of the first type of prostration and the visualization of the second as one practises the third.

251 The "five hundred thousand preliminaries" refers, generally speaking, to the custom of reciting the refuge prayer, bodhicitta prayer, hundred syllable mantra, offering of the maṇḍala, and prayer of the Guru Yoga one hundred thousand times each. However, there are other ways of counting the five practices (to include prostrations, for example), and additional recitations are often added to these basic five.

252 In practice it is usual when accumulating prostrations in this way to extend the body full length.

253 The bag used for transporting butter is already impregnated with grease, so once it has become stiff adding more grease will not help. In the same way, this type of practitioner, who takes the teachings intellectually, and has become blasé, feeling that he has heard

all the teachings before, will not be touched by receiving more teaching, but will only become even more proud.

254 Lit. "the golden foundation of the universe," the base of the universe in traditional cosmology. DKR suggests that in terms of modern cosmology this can be thought of as the earth's core.

255 "Offering should serve as an antidote for attachment and avarice." NT

256 One of the eight Close Sons (see glossary), distinct from the primordial Buddha Samantabhadra.

257 "The confession of negative actions is the antidote to aversion." NT

258 "Those which lead to liberation" refers to positive actions which are done while applying the three supreme methods. Other positive actions only lead to better rebirths.

259 Some details given in NT: "All sources of merit arising from absolute truth are untainted by negative emotions (*zag med*); all those arising from relative truth are tainted (*zag bcas*). All those that are accomplished on the paths of accumulating and joining are tainted; all those accomplished on the paths of seeing and meditation are untainted. All accumulation of merit is tainted; all accumulation of wisdom is untainted."

260 "The antidote for confusion." NT

261 NT describes this as the antidote for wrong views, and adds that to pray for the long life of one's teacher and one's vajra brothers and sisters is a very profound practice which clears away obstacles which threaten our own life.

262 "To enter nirvāṇa" in this context refers to Buddhas or Bodhisattvas ending their activities in our world, and we therefore entreat them to stay and continue these activities for the sake of beings, as did the layman Cunda in the case of Buddha Śākyamuni.

263 "The antidote for uncertainty." NT. If one does not dedicate the positive actions one has done, one does not know what effect they will have.

264 If one performs an act of charity, for instance, without channelling one's intention through dedication and aspiration, that action is described as "without direction" (*lung ma bstan*). There is no knowing what benefit will come of it. However if one makes a wish—for instance, never to lack the necessities of life while practising the Dharma—the action acquires a precise direction and will lead towards the desired goal.

265 One can also dedicate the result of a positive action to a particular person. However, for that act to be really effective, one should dedicate it to all beings including that person.

266 The Tibetan *gsol ba 'debs pa* has here, as in most instances in this text, been translated as "prayer" or "praying". However, it should be understood in the deepest and widest sense of the English word, and perhaps with somewhat different connotations. It literally means to 'cast' or 'hit' (*'debs*) a request (*gsol*), but *gsol* also implies having total reliance and trust in something infallible, and *'debs* a forceful, determined undertaking (PWR). It therefore refers more to the state of mind to be felt—one of total confidence, openness and reliance—than to its expression, as can be understood in this section where the meaning encompasses the receiving of the four empowerments.

267 "What has to be accomplished is the level of the four vajras. The purified channels are the vajra body, or nirmāṇakāya; the purified energies are vajra speech or the sambhogakāya; the purified mind is vajra mind or the dharmakāya; the purified nature (of these three) is vajra inseparability or the svabhavikakāya." NT

268 The term *heruka* is often used for wrathful deities, but in fact refers to any form that represents one's ultimate nature. "*He* represents space (i.e. emptiness), *ka* represents Wisdom, and *ru* the union of the two" NT. The meaning of this passage in the text is

that in whatever Vajrayāna practice one might do, the nature of the principal deity is invariably one's own teacher, who thus is always the most important focus of devotion and source of blessings.

269 After the union of the essence of the mother and father at the moment of conception, the wheel of manifestation forms (this wheel, or *cakra*, is located at the navel once the body is formed). From it appear the three principle channels, which subsequently subdivide into thousands of others. See glossary under "channel" and "wheel."

270 *shes bya bum 'jug*, one of the instructions on the yoga of sleep found in the Great Perfection teachings.

271 At this level, taking perceptions as the path means experiencing them without any concept of an intrinsic reality of either perception or perceiver. The six consciousnesses and their objects become ungraspable, like space. They no longer give rise to attachment and thus are no longer a source of suffering.

272 The empowerment brings one to liberation through maturing one's mindstream.

273 "The ground empowerment is as follows. If one realizes the nature of the mind, which is one's Buddha nature, that is the 'empowerment' of nirvāṇa. If one does not, that is the 'empowerment' of saṁsāra. On the path, empowerment consists of three elements: 1) The *ground empowerment*, in which one is introduced to the maṇḍala of a deity by an authentic spiritual teacher. At that moment, at best one realizes the view of the absolute empowerment. In the middling case, one has the experience of bliss, clarity and non-thought. At least one should experience a certainty that one's body, speech and mind are the three vajras, with a mind undistracted by anything else. An empowerment received in this way will be the support for the path of Vajrayāna. However, to request more and more empowerments till one's head is flattened (by all the ritual-objects placed on it), while one's mind makes no progress at all, cannot serve as a true empowerment.
2) The *path empowerment*. Once one has received the ground empowerment, any further empowerments, whether one receives them from someone else or takes them by oneself, are empowerments on the path of the Vajrayāna, whose function is to repair and purify.
3) The *fruit empowerment* is the "great light ray empowerment," which, from the inseparability of the ground and clear light, and by the power of the wisdom of the absolute empowerment, destroys all obscurations of the habitual tendencies, or tendencies of the three perceptions of clarity, increase, and attainment during transference (at the time of death)."

274 They purify us of attachments to the three worlds of desire, form and formlessness, perfect the qualities of the three kāyas in us and mature in us the wisdom of clear light.

275 Another name for the Copper-coloured Mountain.

276 *spangs rtogs*, the qualities of a Buddha—*freedom* from all obscurations and tendencies, and *realization* of the two kinds of knowledge—knowing all that there is to know and knowing the nature of everything.

277 According to the teachings of Vajrayāna, the Buddha was already fully enlightened when he appeared in the world and all his actions were only a display to teach beings.

278 Mount Malaya, or Malayagiri (*ri ma la ya*), is in Śrī Laṅka and is usually equated with the sacred mountain Sumanakūṭa, now known as Adam's Peak, which is also the site of a footprint of the Buddha and was visited by Guru Rinpoche. In some accounts Mount Malaya is described as "blazing with meteorites" (*gnam lcag 'bar ba*).

279 The Five Excellent Ones of Sublime Nobility (*dam pa'i rigs can dra ma lnga*) were a god (*grags ldan mchog skyong*, Skt. Yaśasvī Varapāla), a nāga (*klu rgyal 'jog po*, the nāga king Takṣaka), a yakṣa (*skar mda' gdong*, Ulkāmukha), a rākṣasa (*blo gros thabs ldan*, Matyaupāyika) and a human being (*dri med grags pa*, Vimalakīrti); alternatively, according to some sources, the god Indra (*rig 'dzin lha dbang rgyal sbyin*) is listed in place of Vimalakīrti.

280 *mdo dgongs 'dus*, also known as *'dus pa mdo*. Although it is called a sūtra, this text is in fact one of the four root tantras of Anuyoga. It was written down in molten beryl by the rākṣasa Matyaupāyika.

281 *rgyud gsang ba'i snying po*, Skt. *Guhyagarbha*, called here the Glorious Secret Tantra (*dpal gsang ba'i rgyud*).

282 The story of Garab Dorje follows in the next section. In spite of his Indian origin, we have kept the Tibetan name, since in the Tibetan tradition his Sanskrit name (Pramodavajra or Prahevajra) is rarely used, and his Tibetan name is more likely to be familiar to readers.

283 Vajrasattva, *rdo rje sems dpa'*: *rdo rje sems* means vajra mind, and here Vajrasattva should be understood in the absolute sense of primal awareness (*rig pa*) which is indestructible.

284 *rgyal thabs spyi lugs*: empowerment without any ritual or visible process, simply the complete and instantaneous transfer of enlightened realization from mind to mind. *spyi lugs*, "pouring," refers to this direct transfer, while *rgyal thabs*, the "conquerors' means," can be understood as referring to Buddhahood and also, metaphorically, to the sovereignty conferred, as by a king to his heir.

285 *yang sprul*: the "emanation of an emanation" because Garab Dorje is an emanation of Vajrasattva, who is himself an emanation of Samantabhadra.

286 The text has a variant reading, *ma brtsol* meaning "without effort." However both mean without mental fabrication or manipulation. ZR

287 *byang sems rdo la gser zhun*.

288 Nyatri Tsenpo was enthroned in the Yarlung valley, one of seven small principalities in central Tibet, probably in the second or third century B.C. (HIST gives 247 BC). His lineage came to be known as the Chögyal dynasty, and later gradually gained control over a substantial portion of the country.

289 Lha-Thothori Nyentsen (374-? A.D.) was the 28th king of the Chögyal dynasty, and the event described is said to have occurred in 433 A.D. These dates are given in DICT and by Dudjom Rinpoche in HIST, in which he adds that a variant of the story, according to which the sūtra and other sacred objects described were brought to Tibet by visiting Indian paṇḍitas, could well be true.

290 The name means "wishfulfilling jewel." For more details, see HIST.

291 *mdo sde za ma tog bkod pa* (Skt. *Āryakāraṇḍavyūha sūtra*), a scripture on Avalokiteśvara to be found in the *Maṇi Kahbum* of Songtsen Gampo.

292 *dpang skong phyag brgya pa'i mdo* (Skt. *Saksipūraṇasūdrakanamā sūtra*).

293 The dates of Songtsen Gampo's life are often given as 609-698, but according to Gendun Chöphel they are 617-650 (see *White Annals* p.13). HIST also places his birth in 617, while other authors give 629.

294 The *gtsug lag khang* or central temple of Lhasa, the Rasa Trulnang, nowadays known as the Jokhang, could only be built after the construction of the four Thadul (*mtha' 'dul*) or Border-Taming and four Yangdul (*yang 'dul*) or Outer Border-Taming temples,

and other temples, on geomantically important sites around Tibet and its borders. For details of the story and sites, see HIST, Vol. 1, page 510 and notes.

295 Princess Wen-Ch'eng Kung-chu, Kongjo to the Tibetans, was the daughter of the T'ang emperor T'ai-tsung. The statue she brought was of Śākyamuni Buddha at the age of twelve, and had been presented to the Chinese emperor by a Buddhist king of Bengal; the Ramoche temple was built in 641 to house it but it was later moved to the Rasa Trulnang (Jokhang), where it is now—the famous Jowo Rinpoche. Queen Tritsun was the daughter of the Nepalese king Aṁśuvarman; the statue she brought was of Buddha Śākyamuni at the age of eight is now in the Ramoche Temple.

296 The legend recounts that this statue (which can still be seen in the Potala in Lhasa) was made from the wood of the sandal tree-trunk in which the five images were found.

297 According to DICT, most scholars give Trisong Detsen's dates as 790-844, although according to Butön he was born in 718 and according to the Baikar Yasel in 730. See note 301 for the problems of dates in this period.

298 *sa 'dul*: a ritual to purify a place and subdue the forces of the earth there, before constructing a building.

299 He can deal with all situations through the ultimate view. ZR

300 The stūpa at Bodhnath, Nepal. See page 196 and note 129.

301 According to Khetsun Zangpo Rinpoche, the dates for the construction of Samye are as follows: In 797, Khenpo Śāntarakṣita consecrates the ground. In 798 he lays the foundations. In 802, Guru Rinpoche leaves India, arriving at Samye in 809. In 810 he reconsecrates the ground, and in 811 lays the foundation stone again. In 814, Samye is completed. Similar dates are given in HIST but with the comment that there might also have been one less 60-year cycle than traditionally calculated between 790 and 953; in other words, all these dates should perhaps be adjusted by subtracting 60 years.

302 Three elements of the teaching of the Great Perfection (*shan 'byed, la bzla ba, rang grol*).

303 Tiny scrolls on which symbols are written from which the treasure discoverer can reveal an entire teaching or cycle of teachings. See Tulku Thondup, *The Hidden Teachings of Tibet*.

304 The three lineages of the "long" *bka' ma* transmission are the mind lineage of the Conquerors (*rgyal ba dgongs pa'i brgyud*), the symbol lineage of the Vidyādharas (*rig 'dzin brda'i brgyud*) and the hearing lineage of ordinary beings (*gang zag snyan brgyud*). The six lineages of the "short" *gter ma* or spiritual treasures transmission are the same three together with the lineage empowered by prayers (*smon lam dbang bskur ba'i brgyud*), the lineage of sealing and entrusting to the ḍākinīs (*mka' 'gro gtad rgya'i brgyud*) and the lineage of prophetically authorized succession (*bka' bab lung bstan gyi brgyud*). In this paragraph Patrul Rinpoche briefly describes the sequence of these last three lineages, which are specific to the spiritual treasures. "Sealing and entrusting to the ḍākinīs" corresponds to the actual concealment of the treasure. For further details see HIST Vol I, page 745. The possession of "nine" transmissions refers to lineages including both bka' ma (three) and gter ma (six) transmissions.

305 All these masters lived well before Jigme Lingpa's time. He met them and received detailed teaching from them in visions. He is noted for the extraordinary learning that he acquired in this way although he had hardly studied at all.

306 Vajradhara (*rdo rje 'chang*) means "Holder of the vajra." The teacher holds the key to our indestructible nature. This is often used as a highly respectful way of referring to

a great teacher.

307 The first line of this saying, *mgo ma tshos gong lce snyabs*, can be understood to refer literally to not starting to taste a head that is being cooked until it is ready (the cooking of yaks' or cows' heads being widespread in Tibet, particularly among the nomad pastoralists). However, 'sticking your tongue out' can imply expressing agreement or acquiescence, and 'the head being cooked' is sometimes used as a metaphor for understanding. An alternative—if less colourful—translation would therefore be "agreeing before you've understood."

308 "The superior transference is practised by the sublime Bodhisattvas who contemplate the truth of absolute reality (*chos nyid kyi bden pa*) on the Path of Seeing, and who have, in this very life, given rise to the view of the unchanging nature as it is (*gnas lugs*) and preserved it day and night without interruption. They practise transference either by following the pith instructions of transferring from the body (*grong 'pho*) and transferring into another body (*grong 'jug*) in the practice of trekchö, or by following those of 'entering the inside of clear light' in the practice of thögal.

"Then there are those beings of very pure samaya who have mastered awareness but who only have control of their perceptions in the daytime, and not at night. When they die and the process of dissolution, as well as the phenomena of 'clarity, increase, and attainment,' have taken place, the clear light of the absolute body at the moment of death appears. That is the 'mother' clear light, the moment of the ground. They are led by the 'child' clear light, which is experienced in this life. When the two clear lights meet they are liberated in the primordial purity, the original ground.

"There are those who have begun to experience the 'development of experiences and appearances' in thögal. At the moment of death, when the clear light of the moment of death appears, they do not recognize it, since they do not have the realization to do so, and are unable to be liberated. But when the intermediate state of Absolute Reality (*chos nyid bar do*) arises they recognize it and remain in oneness with it and are thus liberated in the spontaneous manifestation.

"Both the superior liberation in this life and middling liberation in the intermediate state, are considered as superior transference through the seal of the dharmakāya." NT. (See also note 314).

309 "The middling transference is practised by those who have begun to have the wisdom of the perfection phase. Having reached one of the four clear stages of the path of joining, they have given rise to the wisdom of that path and are capable of entering and leaving an illusory body. Alternatively they have been introduced to the pure manifestation (*rtsal snang*), the inseparable union of the generation and perfection aspect of the deities and have accustomed themselves to it. At the moment of death, as in the moment of dissolution in the generation phase, they dissolve the illusory body into clear light. If in this life they have given rise to the illustrative clear light (*dpe'i 'od gsal*), they will recognize the absolute clear light in the intermediate state, and, as a result, they will manifest as the body of the yidam, the great seal of union which is not yet beyond learning (*slob pa'i zung 'jug phyag rgya chenpo*)." NT

zung 'jug ye shes kyi sku (Skt. *Yuganaddha-Jñanakāya*), the "union wisdom kāya," is the union of rūpakāya and dharmakāya, or, in other words, the indivisibility of appearance and emptiness, or of the generation and perfection phases. "Union" (*zung 'jug*) means the realization that these two aspects of the nature of reality are not two separate things, like the two horns of a cow, but are completely inseparable.

310 This transference is practised by beginners on the path of accumulating who have received empowerment, respected the samayas and have a good understanding of the view, and who use the generation phase as the path but have not mastered it. Although they cannot be liberated in the clear light of the moment of death or in the intermediate state of absolute reality, they can close the way to an unfavourable womb, and choose a favourable rebirth. They are either propelled by their compassion and bodhicitta to a pure Buddhafield, or reborn as an incarnation (see glossary) to parents practising the Dharma. They will be liberated in the next life.

311 Ordinary transference is practised by beginners who only have devotion to the Dharma and have had no sign of success on the path to presage their liberation.

312 The moment when the breath has ceased but the heart has not yet stopped beating.

313 This is the case if one does not have the necessary power of wisdom. Another explanation is that this is not the appropriate way to help the dead.

314 *mkha' spyod gnas su khrid par byed.* This should not to be taken too materialistically. "In fact there is nothing and no-one who leads or is led. It is simply the meeting of the 'mother' and 'child' luminosities." DKR. The 'mother' clear light is that which is our basic nature and dwells in all beings, to which the teacher has introduced us. The 'child' clear light is the continuity of recognition of that nature which we have cultivated in our practice. (See also note 308).

315 The constituents of the body can be grouped into four (sometimes five) inner elements (*khams*): 1) flesh, 2) blood, 3) heat, and 4) breath or energy (*rlung*), (and in some medical treatises, though not here, 5. cavities). These correspond to the four (or five) outer elements: 1) earth, 2) water, 3) fire and 4) air or wind (also *rlung*), (and often 5. space). Both inner and outer elements are best understood as properties or states—solidity, fluidity, temperature, movement and capacity—of both the external world and the body's constituents. The experiences described occur as those properties in their specific role as components of the living body are lost, and merge or "dissolve" back into their wider, generalized context.

316 "At the moment of clarity, the consciousnesses of the five doors (of the senses) (*sgo lnga'i shes pa*) dissolve in the mental consciousness (*yid shes*). At the moment of increase, the mental consciousness dissolves in the mind of the emotions (*nyon yid*). At the moment of attainment, the mind of the emotions dissolves into the ground of all (*kun gzhi*). When one recovers consciousness (the moment known as close attainment) the ground of all dissolves into clear light." NT. At this moment there is a direct experience of the ground clear light. For one who has been introduced to the nature of that ground as the dharmakāya and has stabilized that recognition, this moment is an opportunity for immediate enlightenment, the meeting of the mother and child clear lights. For most people it passes unnoticed in a flash.

317 They do not have the unshakeable stability in the practice and unshakeable confidence in the authentic view necessary to practise the types of transfer described above.

318 Here, for "ordinary body", instead of the term *tha mal lus* which is often used in visualization instructions, the text uses the term *gzhi lus*, lit. "basic" or "fundamental" body. In practical terms the meaning is the same—one's ordinary form—but the implication is that our ordinary body is illusory too. It is the *bar do'i sgyu lus*, the "illusory body of the intermediate state," the ground or basis of all the illusions we are experiencing in this present life—which, no less than the intermediate state of becoming (*srid pa'i bar do*), is also an intermediate state (the *skye gnas bar do*). PWR. See glossary

under 'intermediate state.'

319 Here this term can simply be understood as one's consciousness. ZR

320 This expression here means a Buddha.

321 "What does one mean by energy (*rlung* represented by the green bindu) and mind (*sems* represented by the syllable *hrīḥ*)? The movement aspect is the energy and the knowing aspect is the mind, but in essence they are one and the same." NT

322 A fourteenth century discoverer of spiritual treasures.

323 *mkha spyod*: in general, a celestial realm. Here it is a "great" celestial realm (*mkha spyod chen po*) that is referred to, meaning a type of Buddhafield, manifested for the benefit of beings. A "small" celestial realm (*mkha spyod chung ngu*) can refer to any celestial god-realm. (But see also note 314.)

324 *gnam chos*. The *Namchö* or *Sky Doctrines* is a thirteen-volume collection of teachings received in visions by the prolific treasure-discoverer Mingyur Dorje, who was born in 1645 and died in 1668 at the age of only twenty-three. The *Namchö* lineage is one of the principal practice traditions of the Nyingma monasteries of Palyul and Kathok in Eastern Tibet.

325 Such obstacles arise principally through wrong technique when reciting "Hik" during this practice. "The 'Hik' is a sound which shortens life. As one uses it, one should draw up the air below the navel, stretch the air of the upper part of the body and turn one's eyes sharply upward in the air. If obstacles arise, press down the upper air, release the lower air and stretch the air at the navel, do the vajra recitation of the three syllables (*oṁ aḥ hūṁ*, in concert with inhaling, holding and exhaling), focus your mind on the soles of the feet and look downwards. The obstacles will disappear." NT

326 The preliminaries for the "Path and Fruit" (*lam 'bras*) practice of the Sakya tradition are based on the three kinds of perception (*snang ba gsum*): impure perception (*ma dag pa'i snang ba*), mixed perception experienced by yogīs through practice (*rnal 'byor nyams kyi snang ba*), and pure perception (*dag pa'i snang ba*).

327 As in "The Sublime Continuum" (*rgyud bla ma*, Skt. *Uttaratantraśāstra*) and other texts. ZR

328 Tib. *rig pa rtsal gyi dbang bskur*.

329 Kushab Gemang, Gyalse Shenpen Thaye or Gyalse Rigpa'i Dorje (born 1800), one of the principal lineage-holders of the *Heart-essence of the Vast Expanse*.

330 Changchub Dorje (1745-1821), also known as Jigme Trinle Özer, was the first Dodrup Chen Rinpoche, one of Jigme Lingpa's principal disciples, and blessed Patrul Rinpoche as a child.

331 Orgyen Jigme Chökyi Wangpo is Patrul Rinpoche's personal name. The self-deprecation in this paragraph is traditional. However, it has a particular force coming from Patrul Rinpoche, who showed the same modesty in his way of life.

332 Jamgön Kongtrul the Great (see glossary) was a contemporary of Patrul Rinpoche and of Jamyang Khyentse Wangpo; the three of them knew each other well, having studied together in their youth at the monastery of Shechen in Kham. He was a prolific writer, compiler and editor of books, and wrote this postface after making the textual corrections to Patrul Rinpoche's original manuscript, as it was being prepared for xylograph printing at the great press of Derge.

333 The six ways of liberation (*grol ba drug*) are by seeing, hearing, remembering, touching, tasting and wearing.

Glossary

For abbreviations, see page 377

Abbot - *mkhan po,* in general means someone who gives monastic vows. This title is also given to a person who has attained a high degree of knowledge of the **Dharma** and is in charge of teaching it. It can also simply be the title given to the eldest monk during a traditional summer retreat.

Abhidharma - *mngon pa,* one of the three piṭakas. The foundation of Buddhist psychology and logic. It describes the universe, the different kinds of beings, the steps on the path to enlightenment, refutes mistaken beliefs, etc.

Absolute Space - *chos dbyings,* Skt. *dharmadhātu*, AT: the expanse of reality. From the point of view of realization, all phenomena appear as the expanse of emptiness.

Absolute truth - *don dam bden pa*, Skt. *paramārtha satya*, actual truth perceived through wisdom, without mental fabrications. Its characteristic is to be "beyond mind, unthinkable, inexpressible" (Patrul Rinpoche). See also **relative truth.**

Ācārya - *slob dpon*, 1) teacher. 2) equivalent of spiritual master or lama. See **vajra master.**

Ācārya Padma - *slob dpon padma,* the master Padma, see **Padmasambhava.**

Accomplishment - 1) *dngos grub,* Skt. *siddhi.* "The fruit wished for and obtained through the practice of the instructions." DICT. Common accomplishments can be simply supernatural powers, but in this book the term "accomplishment" almost always refers to the supreme accomplishment, which is enlightenment. 2) *sgrub pa.* In the context of the recitation of mantras, see **approach and accomplishment.**

Adamantine - having the qualities of **vajra.**

Adhicitta - *sems lhag can,* the previous incarnation, in the celestial realms, of **Garab Dorje.**

Akaniṣṭha - *'og min,* lit. "nothing above it." The highest paradise or Buddhafield. There are six different places bearing this name, from the eighth paradise of the gods of the Fourth Concentration up to the absolute Akaniṣṭha, a Buddhafield beyond anything conceivable.

Akṣobhya - *mi bskyod pa*, the Buddha of the Vajra Family. See **five families.**

All victorious banner - *phyogs las rnam par rgyal ba'i rgyal mtshan,* one of the **eight auspicious signs.** It corresponds to the *body* of the Buddha and symbolizes the indestructibility of his teaching.

All Victorious Palace - *rnam rgyal pho brang,* the palace of the god **Indra.**

Ambrosia - *bdud rtsi,* Skt. *amṛita,* lit. the immortal. The nectar (*rtsi*) which conquers the demon (*bdud*) of death. It is a symbol of wisdom.

Amitābha - *'od dpag med,* lit. immeasurable light. The Buddha of the Lotus Family. See **five families.**

Amitāyus - *tshe dpag med,* lit. immeasurable life. The Buddha of longevity.

Amoghasiddhi - *don yod grub pa,* lit. he who accomplishes that which is meaningful. The Buddha of the Action Family. See **five families.**

Ānanda - *kun dga' bo,* a cousin of the Buddha who became his attendant. He was instrumental in the preservation of the teachings after the Buddha had left this world, as he was able to remember everything that he had heard the Buddha say.

Ānandagarbha - *bde mchog snying po,* another name of Adhicitta.

Ancient Tradition - *rnying ma pa,* the followers of the first teachings of Secret Mantra propagated in Tibet by the great master **Padmasambhava** in the 8th century. Patrul Rinpoche belonged to this school.

Ancient Translations - *snga 'gyur,* name given to the first teachings translated from Sanskrit and propagated in Tibet, those of the Ancient, or Nyingmapa Tradition, as opposed to the teachings that were translated and propagated from the 10th century onwards and which gave birth to the New Tradition of Tibetan Buddhism.

Aṅgulimāla - *sor mo threng ba,* one of the Buddha's disciples, who despite having killed nine hundred and ninety nine people, was able, by purifying his negative actions, to attain the level of Arhat. His name means "Garland of Fingers."

Anuyoga - second of the three inner yogas and eighth of the nine vehicles, according to the classification of the Nyingmapa school. In this yoga the main stress is put on the **perfection phase,** particularly meditation on the **channels** and **energies.**

Aperture of Brahmā - *tshang pa'i bu ga,* Skt. *brahmarandra,* point on the top of the head where the **central channel** ends.

Appearances - *snang ba,* see **perceptions.**

Approach and accomplishment - *bsnyen sgrub,* two steps in practices involving the recitation of a **mantra.** In the first, practitioners *approach* the deity that they are visualizing by reciting the **deity**'s mantra. In the second they are familiar enough to identify themselves with the deity.

Arhat - *dgra bcom pa.* To become an Arhat is the final goal of the **Śrāvakayāna.** It is a kind of **nirvāṇa,** beyond rebirth, but falls short of Buddhahood. The Tibetan word literally means one who has subdued the enemies, i.e. **negative emotions.**

Arura and kyurura - *Terminalia chebula* and *Emblica officinalis*, chebulic and emblic myrobolan, medicinal plants. Arura is the emblem of the Medicine Buddha.

Āryadeva - *'phags pa lha* (2nd century), the most famous disciple of **Nāgārjuna**, whose teaching he commented upon in several treatises on Mādhyamika philosophy. See **Middle Way**.

Asaṅga - *thogs med* (4th century), one of the **Six Ornaments**, founder of the Yogachara school and author of many important **śāstras**, in particular the five teachings he received from **Maitreya**.

Atīśa - (982-1054), also known as Dīpaṁkara or Jowo Atīśa (*jo bo a ti sha*). This great Indian master and scholar, one of the main teachers at the famous university of **Vikramaśīla**, was a strict follower of the monastic rule. He received the bodhicitta teachings from many important masters, and in particular from the **Lord of Suvarṇadvīpa** (Dharmakīrti), under whom he studied in Indonesia. He spent the last ten years of his life in Tibet, teaching and taking part in the translation of Buddhist texts. His disciples founded the **Kadampa** school.

Atiyoga - the highest of the three inner yogas, the summit of the Nine Vehicles according to the classification of the **Nyingmapa** School. See **Great Perfection.**

Avalokiteśvara - *spyan ras gzigs* (Chenrezi), one of the **Eight Great Close Sons**. Essence of the speech of all the Buddhas, incarnation of their compassion.

Awareness - *rig pa*, Skt. *vidyā*, the original state of the mind, fresh, vast, luminous, and beyond thought.

Becoming - *srid pa*, the process of samsaric existence. The Tibetan word is often used in the sense of "possibility," and represents all the concepts which we project onto reality and which become the illusory world that we perceive. It is often used as synonym for **saṁsāra** as opposed to *zhi ba*, the peace of **nirvāṇa**.

Beginning - We have used this word to translate *ye* in expressions like *ye nas*, "from the very beginning" or *ye dag* "pure from the beginning." However it should be understood that this does not refer to a first moment of origin or creation in the distant past, but rather to the fact that the pure nature has always been intrinsically present.

Bell - *dril bu,* Skt. *ghaṇṭā*. See **vajra**.

Bhagavān - *bcom ldan 'das*, an epithet of the Buddha. He who has vanquished (*bcom*) the **four demons**, possesses (*ldan*) all the qualities of realization, and is beyond (*'das*) **saṁsāra** and **nirvāṇa**.

Bhṛikuṭī - *jo mo khro gnyer can,* one of the forms of **Tārā**, the female Bodhisattva of compassion. The name means literally "She who has a wrathful frown."

Bile - *mkhris pa*, one of the three humours of the body, whose imbalance creates the different kinds of illness. See also **wind, phlegm.**

Bindu - *thig le*, lit. a circle, sphere, point or drop, but also with a range of more abstract meanings. We have used this Sanskrit term in the chapter on the transference of consciousness to underline the fact that the levels of meaning are multiple; in other contexts we have translated the same word as **essence**.

Bliss (experience) - *bde nyams*, one of the three types of experience in meditation. See **experiences**.

Bliss and emptiness - *bde stong*, bliss experienced without attachment, as being empty.

Blissful (pure land) - *bde ba can,* Skt. *Sukhāvatī*, the Buddhafield of the West, that of Buddha **Amitābha**.

Bodhicitta - *byang chub kyi sems*, lit. the mind of enlightenment. On the relative level, it is the wish to attain Buddhahood for the sake of all beings, as well as the practice of the path of love, compassion, the six transcendent perfections, etc., necessary for achieving that goal. On the absolute level, it is the direct insight into the ultimate nature.

Bodhisattva - *byang chub sems dpa'*, 1. a being who has decided to bring all beings to enlightenment and is practising the Bodhisattva path. 2. a *sublime* Bodhisattva who has attained one of the ten **Bodhisattva levels**.

Bodhisattva Abbot - the title by which **Śāntarakṣita** is sometimes known.

Bodhisattva levels - *'phags pa'i sa*, lit. sublime levels, Skt. *bhūmi*. The ten levels of realization reached by Bodhisattvas on the paths of seeing, meditation and beyond learning. In some classifications additional levels are added. "These levels are sublime because they are far beyond ordinary beings." DICT.

Bodhnath (stūpa) - *bya rung kha shor,* pronounced "Jarungkashor", one of the two great stūpas in the Kathmandu valley. The story of its construction is related to the advent of Buddhism in Tibet and described in the *History of the Jarungkhashor Stūpa,* a terma discovered by Sakya Zangpo (translated by Keith Dowman as *The Legend of the Great Stūpa*, Berkeley, Dharma Publishing, 1973).

Body, speech, mind, qualities and activity - *sku, gsung, thugs, yon tan, phrin las,* five aspects of Buddhahood. Sometimes referred to as the **five kāyas.** See also **five families.**

Bönpo - *bon po,* follower of Bön, the religious tradition prevailing in Tibet before the introduction of Buddhism.

Border country - *mtha' 'khob*, a region in which the teachings are unknown.

Brahmā - *tshangs pa.* In Buddhism Brahmā is not considered as an eternal deity but as the ruler of the gods of the World of Form.

Brahmā-world - *tshang pa'i 'jig rten*, Skt. *brahmāloka,* in general, all the form and formless worlds.

Brahmin - *bram ze*, one of the four castes in ancient Indian society, the priestly caste.

Buddha - *sangs rgyas*, "One who has dispelled (*sangs*) the darkness of the two obscurations and developed (*rgyas*) the two kinds of omniscience (knowing the nature of phenomena and knowing the multiplicity of phenomena)." DICT.

Buddha Nature - *de gshegs snying po,* Skt. *tathāgatagarbha*, the potential of Buddhahood present in every being. AT: essence of Buddhahood.

Burnt offering - *gsur*, an offering made by burning food on coals. It is offered to the Buddhas, the protectors, all beings in general and in particular to wandering spirits and those towards whom we have karmic debts. The usual white *gsur* is prepared with the **three white foods** and the **three sweet foods**. The red *gsur* is prepared with meat.

Calling the teacher from afar - *bla ma rgyang 'bod,* a type of prayer of yearning to one's spiritual teacher.

Cāmaradvīpa - *rnga yab gling,* one of the eight sub-continents in ancient Indian cosmology, to the west of **Jambudvīpa**. This is the south-western continent referred to as the Buddhafield of the **Glorious Copper-coloured Mountain**.

Central channel - *rtsa dbu ma,* Skt. *avadhūti*, the central axis of the subtle body. Its exact description varies according to the particular practice. It represents non-dual wisdom.

Chagme Rinpoche - see **Karma Chagme**.

Chakshingwa, (Geshe) - *lcags shing ba,* a Kadampa geshe, disciple of **Langri Thangpa**.

Channel - *rtsa,* Skt. *nāḍi*, subtle vein in which the subtle **energy** (*rlung*, Skt. *prāṇa*) circulates. The left and right principal channels run from the nostrils to just below the navel, where they join the **central channel**.

Channels and energies (exercises of) - *rtsa rlung gi 'phrul 'khor*, exercises combining visualization, concentration and physical movements, in which the flow of subtle energies through the subtle channels is controlled and directed. These practices should only be attempted with the proper transmission and guidance, after completing the **preliminaries** and achieving some stability in the **generation phase**.

Chekawa Yeshe Dorje - *'chad kha ba ye shes rdo rje* (1101-1175), a famous Kadampa geshe. He systematized the teachings of the Mind Training into seven points, and rendered them more accessible. See *The Great Path of Awakening*, Jamgon Kongtrul, Shambhala, 1987, and *Enlightened Courage*, Dilgo Khyentse, Editions Padmakara, 1992 (worldwide except N. America) and Snow Lion, 1993 (North America only).

Chengawa, (Geshe) - *spyan snga ba* (1038-1103), disciple of **Drom Tönpa**, started the transmission lineage of the Kadampa oral instructions.

Chenrezi - *spyan ras gzigs,* the Tibetan name for **Avalokiteśvara.**

Chö - *gcod,* lit. cutting, destroying. Method of meditation in which one offers one's own body to cut the **four demons** within. **Machik Labdrön** received the chö teachings from the Indian teacher **Padampa Sangye** and from Kyotön Sönam Lama, and propagated them in Tibet.

Chögyal Pakpa - *chos rgyal 'phags pa* (1235-1280), one of the five great scholars of the **Sakya** school known as the Sakya Gongma. He became the preceptor of Mongolian emperor Kublai Khan and regent of Tibet.

Circumambulation - *skor ba*, act of veneration consisting in walking clockwise, concentratedly and with awareness, around a sacred object, e.g. a temple, stūpa, holy mountain, or the house, and even the person, of a spiritual master.

Clarity (experience) - *gsal nyams*, one of the three types of experience in meditation. See **experiences.**

Clarity, increase and attainment - *snang mched thob,* three experiences which occur successively at the moment of death.

Clear light - *'od gsal*, Skt. *prabhāsvara*, spontaneous, luminous (or knowing) aspect of the nature of the mind—or **awareness.**

Clear light of the moment of the ground - *gzhi dus kyi 'od gsal*, "nature of the mind of all beings, pure from the beginning and spontaneously luminous; fundamental continuum (of awareness), potential of Buddhahood." DICT. It can be "introduced" by a realized master to a disciple, who then stabilizes and develops that experience through the profound practices of the **Great Perfection.** Ordinary beings perceive it only for a flash at the moment of death.

Clear Light, (gods of) - *'od gsal gyi lha*, Skt. *Ābhāsvara*, the highest level of the gods of the Second Concentration (in the World of Form).

Clinging - *'dzin pa,* lit. holding, also means to have a belief. Thus "ego clinging" can also be interpreted as "believing in an I."

Common accomplishments - *thun mong gi dngos grub,* supernatural powers coming from meditation, not exclusive to Buddhism, but common to other paths as well. See **accomplishment.**

Concentration - *bsam gtan,* Skt. *dhyāna*, meditative absorption, a state of mind without any distraction. Although it is vital for the meditative practices of the Buddhist path at all levels, it is not sufficient on its own, but must be combined with the correct motivation and view. See also **four concentrations**.

Concept or **Conceptual reference** - *dmigs pa,* any notion of a subject, an object and an action.

Conceptual obscurations - *shes bya'i sgrib pa*, Skt. *jñeyāvaraṇa* "These are the concepts of subject, object and action, which prevent one from attaining omniscience." DICT.

Conditioned - *'dus byas*, Skt. *saṁskṛita*, produced (*byas*) by a combination (*'dus*) of causes and conditions. "Conditioned positive actions are all those done without realizing emptiness," DKR.

Conditioning effect - *dbang gi 'bras bu*, the effect of actions on the environment in which one lives in a future life.

Conqueror - *rgyal ba,* Skt. *jina*, a Buddha.

Consort - 1. *yum,* feminine deity represented in union with a male deity (*yab*). She symbolizes *wisdom* inseparable from *skilful means,* symbolized by the male. They also symbolize the space of emptiness inseparable from awareness. 2. *gsang yum*, lit. secret mother. The wife of a great lama.

Cosmos of a billion universes - *stong gsum*, Skt. *trisahasra*, a cosmos composed of one billion (1000^3) universes like ours and corresponding to the area of activity of one Buddha.

Creativity of awareness - *rig pa'i rtsal,* awareness's inherent and spontaneous ability to manifest phenomena.

Crown protuberance - *gtsug tor*, Skt. *uṣṇīṣa*, a prominence on the head of a Buddha, one of the thirty-two **major marks**.

Dagpo Rinpoche - *dwags po rin po che* (1079-1153), also known as Gampopa, the most famous disciple of **Milarepa** and founder of the Kagyupa monastic order.

Ḍāka - *mkha 'gro*, lit. moving through space, or *dpa' bo*, hero. Tantric equivalent of Bodhisattva. Male equivalent of **ḍākinī.**

Ḍākinī - *mkha' 'gro ma,* lit. moving through space. The feminine principle associated with wisdom. This term has several levels of meaning. There are ordinary ḍākinīs who are beings with a certain degree of spiritual power, and wisdom ḍākinīs who are fully realized. See **three roots**.

Damchen - *dam chen (rdo rje legs pa*), a protector of the Dharma, bound under oath by **Padmasambhava.**

Darśaka - *mthong ldan,* another name of Ajātaśatru, the son of King Bimbisara, king of Magadha and the most important patron of **Śākyamuni** Buddha. Although he had killed his father, he later repented and purified his negative actions to such an extent that he attained the level of a

Bodhisattva.

Degenerate age - *snyigs dus*, Skt. *kāliyuga*, a period of the **five degenerations.**

Deity - *lha*, Skt. *deva*, this term designates a Buddha or wisdom deity, or sometimes a wealth deity or **Dharma protector**. See also **gods.**

Demigod - *lha ma yin*, Skt. *asura*. One of the **six classes of beings**, with jealousy as their predominant emotion.

Demon - *bdud*, Skt. *māra*, term used for terrifying or malevolent energies. However, "what is called a demon is not someone with a gaping mouth and staring wide eyes. It is that which produces all the sufferings of saṁsāra and prevents one from reaching liberation beyond suffering. In short it is that which harms body and mind." NT. See also **four demons.**

Destroyer-of-Saṁsāra - *'khor ba 'jig* , the Buddha Krakucchanda, the first of the thousand Buddhas of this **Good Kalpa**.

Determination to be free - *nges 'byung*, Skt. *niḥsaraṇa* defined as "the mind that wishes to achieve liberation from **saṁsāra**." This term is often translated as "renunciation."

Devadatta - *lhas byin*, a cousin of the Buddha, whose jealousy prevented him from deriving any benefit from the teachings.

Dhāraṇi - *gzungs*, mantra blessed by a Buddha or Bodhisattva which has the power to help beings. There are many in the **sūtras**, often quite long.

Dharma - *chos*. This term has a number of different meanings. In its widest sense it means all that can be known. In this text the term Dharma is used exclusively to indicate the teaching of the Buddha. It has two aspects: the Dharma of transmission (*lung gi chos*), namely the teachings which are actually given, and the Dharma of realization (*rtogs pa'i chos*), or the states of wisdom, etc., which are attained through the application of the teachings. It is often referred to as the "Sublime Dharma" because it liberates beings from suffering. *Dharma* or *chos* can also simply mean "phenomena." When it has this meaning it has been translated as such.

Dharma protector - *chos skyong*, Skt. *dharmapāla*. The Dharma protectors protect the teaching from being diluted and its transmission from being disturbed or distorted. Protectors are sometimes emanations of Buddhas or Bodhisattvas, and sometimes spirits, gods or demons who have been subjugated by a great spiritual master and bound under oath.

Dharmakāya - *chos sku*, lit. Dharma Body. The emptiness aspect of Buddhahood. It can be translated as body of truth, absolute dimension.

Dharmatā - *chos nyid*, "the void nature." DICT.

Dharmodgata - *chos 'phags*, "Sublime Dharma," Bodhisattva from whom **Sadāprarudita** received the teachings on transcendent wisdom.

Dīpaṁkara - **Atīśa**'s ordination name.

Directions - see **ten directions.**

Dissolution (process of) - *thim rim,* a succession of phenomena which occur at the moment of death: the dissolution of the elements, and the three experiences called clarity, increase and attainment.

Distinguishing, clear decision and self-liberation - *shan 'byed, la bzla, rang grol,* three essential points in the Trekchö meditation. Usually they are explained only during the transmission of **Great Perfection** teachings by a qualified Lama.

Dohā - a song in which a siddha (for example, **Saraha** or **Virūpa**) expresses his or her realization.

Downfall - *ltung ba,* "a fault due to the transgression of a rule (monastic or other)." DICT.

Drikung Kyobpa - *'bri gung skyob pa* (1143-1217), the founder of Drikung Monastery and of the Drikung Kagyu school.

Drom Tönpa - *'brom ston pa,* also called *'brom ston rgyal ba'i 'byung gnas* (1005-1064), **Atīśa**'s principal Tibetan disciple, one of the first teachers of the **Kadampa** school and founder of Radreng (*rva sgreng*) Monastery (often pronounced "Reting").

Druk Pema Karpo - *'brug padma dkar po* (16th century), the 3rd Drukchen Rinpoche, great master and writer of the Drukpa Kagyu school and founder of Sangak Chöling Monastery.

Dualistic - *gnyis 'dzin,* lit. grasping at or apprehending two. The concept of "I" and "other."

Ecumenical (movement) - *ris med,* lit. without partiality. Spiritual movement made famous by the great lama Jamyang Khyentse Wangpo as well as Jamgön Kontrul Lodrö Thaye, Lama Mipham, Chogyur Lingpa and Patrul Rinpoche. It is characterized by an attitude of respect for all the teachings and schools of Buddhism.

Effects of actions, *las rgyu 'bras,* Skt. *phala.* See **karma.**

Ego-clinging - see **clinging.**

Egolessness - *bdag med,* Skt. *anātman, nairātmya,* absence of independent or intrinsic existence, either of oneself (*gang zag gi bdag med*) or of external phenomena (*chos kyi bdag med*).

Eight auspicious signs - *bkra shis rtags brgyad,* eight symbols (corresponding to the different parts of the Buddha's body): eternal knot, lotus, canopy, conch, wheel, banner, vase, and golden fish.

Eight Great Charnel-grounds - *dur khrod chen po brgyad,* places of frightening aspect where **ḍākas** and **ḍākinīs** meet. Internally they correspond to the eight consciousnesses (*rnam shes brgyad*).

Eight Great Close Sons - *nye ba'i sras chen brgyad,* the main Bodhisattvas in the retinue of Buddha **Śākyamuni**: Mañjuśrī, Avalokiteśvara, Vajrapāṇi, Maitreya, Kṣitigarbha, Sarvanivāraṇaviṣkambhin, and Samantabhadra. Each fulfils a particular role to help beings. Symbolically they represent the pure state of the eight consciousnesses.

Eight offering goddesses – *mchod pa'i lha mo brgyad*: the Lady of Beauty (*sgeg mo ma*, Skt. Lāsyā), the Lady of Garlands (*phreng ba ma*, Mālā), the Lady of Song (*glu ma*, Gītā), the Lady of Dance (*gar ma*, Nṛtyā), the Lady of Flowers (*me tog ma*, Puṣpā), the Lady of Incense (*bdug spos ma*, Dhūpā), The Lady of Lamps (*snang gsal ma*, Ālokā) and the Lady of Perfume (*dri chab ma*, Gandhā). In the maṇḍala of the peaceful sambhogakāya deities, they are also the consorts of the eight Bodhisattvas (see **Eight Great Close Sons**), and symbolize, respectively, the pure state of the four objects of the sense organs (form, smell, sound and taste) and of the four aspects of thoughts (past, present, future and of undetermined time).

Eight ordinary concerns - *'jig rten chos brgyad*, Skt. *aṣṭalokadharmāḥ*, the normal preoccupations of unrealized people without a clear spiritual perspective. They are: gain and loss, pleasure and pain, praise and criticism, fame and infamy.

Eight perverse acts - *log pa rgyad,* i) criticizing good, ii) praising evil, iii) interrupting the accumulation of merit of a virtuous person, iv) disturbing the minds of those who have devotion, v) giving up one's spiritual master, vi) giving up one's deity, vii) giving up one's vajra brothers and sisters, viii) desecrating a maṇḍala.

Eighty Siddhas - 1. eighty (or eighty four) great siddhas of ancient India whose lives have been recounted by Abhayadatta (see *Buddha's Lions*, Emeryville, Dharma Publishing, 1979). 2. the eighty siddhas of Yerpa in Tibet, disciples of **Padmasambhava** who attained the supreme accomplishment.

Emotions - see **negative emotions.**

Empowerment - *dbang bskur*, Skt. *abhiṣeka*, lit. transfer of power. The authorization to hear, study and practise the teachings of the Vajrayāna. This takes place in a ceremony which may be extremely elaborate or utterly simple. See **four empowerments.**

Emptiness - *stong pa nyid,* Skt. *śūnyatā*, the absence of true existence in all phenomena.

Energy - *rlung,* Skt. *prāṇa*, *vāyu*, lit. wind. Its characteristic is to be "light and mobile." The mind is described as riding on the *rlung* like a rider on a horse. Five different types of *rlung* regulate the functions of the body: i) the ascending energy (*gyen rgyu*), ii) the energy of evacuation (*thur sel*), iii) the fiery energy (*me mnyam*), iv) all-pervading energy (*khyab byed*) and v) the life-supporting energy (*srog 'dzin*).

Enjoying the Emanations of Others - *gzhan 'phrul dbang byed*, Skt. *Paranir-*

mitavaśavartin, the sixth and highest level of the gods of the World of Desire, in which the gods enjoy the things miraculously produced by other gods. See **three worlds**.

Enlightenment - *byang chub*, Skt. *bodhi*, purification (*byang*) of all obscurations and realization (*chub*) of all qualilties.

Enlightenment Tree - *byang chub kyi shing*, the tree under which Buddha **Śākyamuni** attained enlightenment.

Equality - *mnyam pa nyid*, Skt. *samatā*. All things equally have the nature of emptiness.

Essence - *thig le*, Skt. *bindu*, lit. drop. "Essence or seed of the great bliss; in the **channels** there are different kinds, pure or degenerate." DICT. The term *thig le* has a number of different meanings according to the context and type of practice.

Essential nature, natural expression and compassion - *ngo bo, rang bzhin, thugs rje*. View of the **Great Perfection**: the essential nature of the mind and all phenomena is emptiness; the expression of that nature is clarity; its compassion is all-pervasive.

Eternalism - *rtag par lta ba*, Skt. *ātmadṛṣṭi*, *satkāyadṛṣṭi*, the belief in an eternally existing entity, a soul for instance. Considered an extreme philosophical tendency. See **nihilism**.

Excellent Words - *gsung rab*, Skt. *pravacana*, the words of the Buddha.

Exhaustion of phenomena in the real nature - *chos nyid zad pa*, one of the **four visions** or experiences on the path of Thögal. "All phenomena being purified in the maṇḍala of the sole great essence, all things invented by the mind are exhausted in the real nature. Not even grasping to the real nature remains." DICT.

Expedient meaning - *drang don*, Skt. *neyārtha*. The expedient meaning refers to teachings intended to lead unrealized beings towards the truth of the **real meaning**.

Experiences (meditative) - *nyams*, experiences of **bliss**, **clarity**, and **non-thought**. One should not be attached to such experiences or confuse them with the final goal.

Extracting the essences - *bcud len*, a method which makes it possible to consume only certain substances and elements in minute quantities, without having to use ordinary food.

Feast offering - *tshogs kyi 'khor lo*, Skt. *gaṇacakra*, a ritual in which one blesses, offers and consumes food and drink as wisdom nectar.

Field of merit - *tshogs zhing*, the focus, or object, of one's offering, devotion, prayer, prostrations, etc., through which one can perform the necessary accumulations of merit and wisdom. The term usually implies a visualized focus of practice such as the refuge deities, the teacher in Guru Yoga, etc. The fact that one's practice and positive actions are directed towards such an embodiment of the Buddha, Dharma and Saṅgha gives them a much greater power.

Five crimes which are almost as grave (as the five crimes with immediate retribution) - *nye ba'i mtshams med lnga*, i) acting impurely with a female **Arhat**; ii) killing a **Bodhisattva**; iii) killing someone training towards the supreme level; iv) stealing the sustenance of the **Saṅgha**; v) destroying a **stūpa**.

Five crimes with immediate retribution - *mtshams med lnga*, Skt. *pañcānantarīya*, i) killing one's father or ii) one's mother or iii) an Arhat; iv) creating a split in the **Saṅgha**; v) malevolently causing a Buddha to bleed. Someone who has committed one of these five actions takes rebirth in the hell of Ultimate Torment immediately after death, without going through the intermediate state.

Five degenerations - *snyigs ma lnga,* they are the degeneration of i) lifespan ii) negative emotions (the five poisons increase) iii) beings (it is difficult to help them) iv) times (wars and famines proliferate) v) views (false beliefs spread).

Five energies - see **energy**.

Five Families - *rigs lnga*, Skt. *pañcakula*, the Buddha, Vajra, Jewel, Lotus and Action families. The five Buddha Families represent the real nature of all things. For example, the Five **Conquerors** are the real nature of the five aggregates, their Five **Consorts** the real nature of the five elements, the five wisdoms the real nature of the **five poisons**, and so on.

Five hundred thousand preliminaries - *'bum lnga*, five traditional preliminary practices: refuge, bodhicitta, vajrasattva, maṇḍala and guru yoga, performed one hundred thousand times each.

Five kāyas - *sku lnga*, Skt. *pañcakāya*, the **three kāyas** to which are added the Unchanging Vajra Kāya (*mi 'gyur rdo rje'i sku*, Skt. *vajrakāya*) and the Kāya of Perfect Enlightenment (*mngon par byang chub pa'i sku*, Skt. *abhisambodhikāya*). The expression can also refer to the five Buddha families: body, speech, mind, qualities and activity.

Five paths - *lam lnga*, Skt. *pañcamārga*, five successive stages in the path to enlightenment: the **paths of accumulating, joining, seeing,** meditation, and the path beyond learning.

Five perfections - *phun sum tshogs pa lnga*, the perfect teacher, teaching, place, disciples and time.

Five poisons - *dug lnga*, the five negative emotions: 1) bewilderment, *gti mug*, Skt. *moha* (AT: ignorance, confusion), 2) attachment, *'dod chags*, *rāga* (AT: desire), 3) aversion, *zhe sdang*, *dveṣa* (including hatred, anger, etc.),

4) jealousy, *phra dog*, *īrsyā*, and v) pride, *nga rgyal*, *māna*.

Five samayas of relishing - *dang du slang ba'i dam tshig lnga*, five secondary **samayas** in the Great Perfection. They are concerned with the enjoyment of the five meats and the five nectars, substances used by tantric practitioners which are ordinarily considered impure or taboo. See page 207 and note 131.

Five sciences - *rig gnas lnga*, Skt. *pañcavidyā*, the five branches of learning that a paṇḍita must master: 1) the making of things (*gzo rig gnas*, *śilpavidyā*), 2) the repairing of things (includes medicine; *gso ba'i rig gnas*, *cikitsāvidyā*), 3) philology (*sgra' rigs gnas*, *Śabdavidyā*), 4) logic (*gtan tshigs kyi rig gnas*, *hetuvidyā*) and 5) philosophy (*nang don rig gnas*, *adhyātmavidyā*).

Five wisdoms - *ye shes lnga*, five aspects of the wisdom of Buddhahood: the wisdom of the absolute space (*chos dbyings kyi ye shes*, Skt. *dharmadhātujñāna*), mirror-like wisdom (*me long gi ye shes, ādarśajñāna*), the wisdom of equality (*mnyam nyid kyi ye shes*, *samatājñāna*), discriminating wisdom (*so sor rtog pa'i ye shes*, *pratyavekṣaṇājñāna*), and all-accomplishing wisdom (*bya ba grub pa'i ye shes*, *kṛityānuṣṭhānajñāna*). See **five families**.

Four activities - *phrin las bzhi*, four types of activity performed by realized beings to help others and eliminate unfavourable circumstances: pacifying (*zhi ba*), increasing (*sgyas pa*), controlling (*dbang*) and fierce subduing (*drag po*).

Four boundless qualities - *tshad med bzhi*, Skt. *caturaprameya*, unlimited love (*byams pa*, Skt. *maitrī*), compassion (*snying rje*, *karuṇā*), joy (*dga' ba*, *muditā*), and equanimity (*btang snyoms*, *upekṣa*).

Four concentrations - *bsam gtan bzhi*, Skt. *caturdhyāna*, four levels of meditative absorption, the fruit of which is to be reborn in four kinds of god realms in the **World of Form**. However they can also be used on the path of enlightenment.

Four demons - *bdud bzhi*, see note 230, page 393. See also **demon**.

Four elements - *'byung ba bzhi*, Skt. *catur / pañca bhūta*, earth, water, fire and wind or air, as principles of solidity, liquidity, heat and movement.

Four empowerments - *dbang bzhi*, the **vase empowerment**, the **secret empowerment**, the **wisdom empowerment** and the **precious word empowerment**.

Four formless states - *gzugs med bzhi*, four concentrations called infinite space (*nam mkha' mtha' yas*, Skt. *ākāśānantya*), infinite consciousness (*nam shes mtha' yas*, *vijñānāśānantya*), nothing at all (*ci yang med pa*, *akiṁcanya*), and neither existing nor non-existing (*'du shes med 'du shes med min*, *naivasaṁjñāsamjñā*); four god realms corresponding to these concentrations.

Four Great Kings - *rgyal chen rigs bzhi*, Skt. *caturmahārājakāyika*, four gods who are traditionally the protectors of the four directions. Their realm is the first of the six god realms in the **World of Desire**. See **three worlds.**

Four great streams of suffering - *sdug sngal gyi chu bo chen po bzhi*, birth, sickness, old age and death.

Four joys - *dga' ba bzhi*, Skt. *caturānanda*, four increasingly subtle experiences of **bliss** beyond ordinary feelings, connected with the practice of the third, or **wisdom, empowerment.**

Four kāyas - the **three kāyas** plus the *svābhāvikakāya*, *ngo bo nyid kyi sku*, the kāya of the nature as it is, representing the inseparability of the first three.

Four metaphors - *'du shes bzhi.* Thinking of oneself as someone who is sick, of the spiritual friend as the doctor, of the Dharma as the remedy, and of practising his instructions as the way to recover.

Four obscurations - *sgrib bzhi*, the obscurations of i) negative emotions, ii) karmic obscurations, iii) conceptual obscurations and iv) obscurations of habitual tendencies. See **obscurations.**

Four or **six tantra sections** - *rgyud sde bzhi* or *drug*, classification of the **tantras** either into four groups: **Kriyā**, Caryā (or Upa), Yoga and Anuttarayoga (this classification is usual in the **New Translations** schools); or into six groups: Kriyā, Upayoga, Yoga, Mahāyoga, **Anuyoga** and **Atiyoga** (usual in the **Ancient Tradition**).

Four Visions - *snang ba bzhi*, four successive stages in the practice of thögal in the **Great Perfection**: i) dharmatā actually appearing (*chos nyid mngon sum*), ii) increase of experiences and appearences (*nyams snang gong 'phel*), iii) the ultimate reach of awareness (*rig pa tshad phebs*), iv) exhaustion of phenomena beyond mind (*chos zad blo 'das*).

Four ways of attracting beings - *bsdu ba'i ngos po bzhi*, Skt. *catuḥsaṁgrahavastu*, the four ways in which a Bodhisattva attracts disciples: 1) being generous (*sbyin pa*, Skt. *dāna*), 2) speaking in a pleasant manner (*snyan par smra ba*, *priyavāditā*), 3) teaching in accordance with individuals' needs (*don mthun pa*, *samānārthatā*), 4) acting in accordance with what he teaches (*don spyod pa*, *arthacaryā*).

Fruit empowerment - *'bras bu'i dbang*, the empowerment that takes place at the moment of attaining full enlightenment.

Full effect - *rnam smin gyi 'bras bu*, Skt. *vipākaphala*, the point at which an action has its maximum effect, for instance a rebirth in hell.

Gampopa - *sgam po pa*, see **Dagpo Rinpoche.**

Gandharva - *dri za*, lit. smell eaters. Spirit feeding on smells. Also used for beings in the **intermediate state.**

Garab Dorje - *dga' rab rdo rje*, better known by his Tibetan name than by his Sanskrit names, Pramudavajra, Prahevajra, Surativajra or Prajñābhava. The first human teacher in the lineage of the **Great Perfection**.

Garuḍa - *khyung*, a mythical bird of very large size which is able to fly as soon as it is hatched, symbolizing **primal wisdom**. The five colours in which it is sometimes represented symbolize the **five wisdoms**. It is the enemy of the **nāgas**, and is depicted with a snake in its beak, symbolising consuming the negative emotions.

Gelugpa - *dge lugs pa*, one of the schools of the **New Tradition**, founded by Je Tsongkhapa (1357-1419) and at first called the Gandenpa after his seat, the monastery of Ganden.

Generation phase - *bskyed rim*, Skt. *utpattikrama*"meditation yoga through which one purifies oneself of one's habitual clingings to the four kinds of birth and in which one meditates on forms, sounds and thoughts as having the nature of deities, mantras and wisdom." DICT.

Generosity - *sbyin pa*, Skt. *dāna*, lit. giving.

Geshe - *dge bshes*, spiritual friend. The usual term for a **Kadampa** teacher. Later it came to be used for a doctor in philosophy in the **Gelugpa** school.

Ghost - *'dre*, spirit of a dead person or, more generally, harmful spirit.

Glorious Copper-coloured Mountain - *zangs mdog dpal ri*, a **Buddhafield** manifested by **Padmasambhava**, to which he departed when he left Tibet and where he is now still said to be.

Gods - *lha*, the beings of one of the **six realms**, dominated by pride. To avoid confusion we have translated *lha* as "deity" when it means a Buddha or **wisdom deity**.

Gods and demons - *lha 'dre*, refers in general to all the different classes of spirits, whether helpful (*lha*) or harmful (*'dre*).

Gods without perception - *'du shes med pa'i lha*, gods in the Formless World.

Good Kalpa - *bskal pa bzang po*, Skt. *bhadrakalpa*, the present kalpa, called good because it is a kalpa in which one thousand Buddhas appear.

Gotsangpa (Gönpo Dorje) - *rgod tshang pa mgon po rdo rje* (1189-1258), **Kagyupa** master, disciple of Tsangpa Gyare, founder of a branch of the Drukpa Kagyu school and of many monasteries.

Great Compassionate One - *thugs rje chen po*, epithet of **Avalokiteśvara**.

Great Exuberant Lakes - *rol pa'i mtsho chen*, "seven lakes encircling Mount Meru, in which the nāga kings live and play." DICT.

Great Omniscient One - *kun mkhyen chen po*, the title by which **Longchenpa** is frequently known.

Great Outer Oceans - *phyi'i rgya mtsho chen po*, the great oceans which surround Mount Meru and the four continents in the ancient Indian cosmology.

Great Perfection - *dzogs pa chen po*, other name of **Atiyoga**, the summit of the nine vehicles. *Perfection* means that the mind, in its nature, naturally contains all the qualities of the three bodies: its nature is emptiness, the dharmakāya; its natural expression is clarity, the samboghakāya, and its compassion is all-encompassing, the nirmāṇakāya. *Great* means that this perfection is the natural condition of all things. AT: great completeness. The teachings of the Great Perfection are classified in three sections: the mind section (*sems sde*), the space section (*klong sde*), and the pith-instruction section (*man ngag gi sde*). See also Introduction.

Great Vehicle - *theg pa chen po*, Skt. *mahāyāna*, vehicle of the **Bodhisattvas**, great because it aims at full Buddhahood for the sake of all beings.

Ground-of-all - *kun gzhi*, Skt. *ālaya*, abridged form of *kun gzhi rnam par shes pa*, the ground consciousness in which the **habitual tendencies** are stored. It is the basis for the other consciousnesses. Occasionally, in certain teachings, *kun gzhi* is used for the original nature, the **primordial purity** (*ka dag*).

Guru Rinpoche - *gu ru rin po che*, the name by which **Padmasambhava** is most commonly known in Tibet.

Guru yoga - *bla ma'i rnal 'byor*, practice of mixing one's mind with the teacher's mind.

Gyalse Rinpoche - *rgyal sras rin po che*, lit. the Precious Son of the Conquerors. A title given to Thogme Zangpo (1295-1369), a great master of the Nyingma and Sakya traditions and author of the *Thirty Seven Elements of a Bodhisattva's Practice* (*rgyal sras lag len*).

Gyelgong - *rgyal 'gong*, a class of malignant spirits.

Habitual tendencies - *bag chags*, Skt. *vāsanā*, habitual patterns of thought, speech or action created by what one has done in past lives. AT: habits, inclinations, impregnations.

Hearing lineage of ordinary beings - *gang zag snyan brgyud*, lineage of transmission in which it is necessary for the teacher to use words and the disciple to hear them, rather than transmitting the teachings mind-to-mind or using symbols.

Hell - *dmyal ba*, Skt. *naraka*, one of the **six realms**, in which one experiences intense suffering. In the hell realm one generally experiences the effects of actions rather than creating new causes.

He Who Proclaims the Dharma with Inexhaustible Melodious Voice - *sgra dbyangs mi zad pa sgrogs pa*, name of a Buddha.

Hundred Families - *rigs brgya*, the forty-two peaceful and fifty-eight wrathful deities.

Hundred Syllables - *yig brgya*, the mantra of Vajrasattva, representing the essence of the **Hundred Families**.

Illustrative wisdom - *dpe'i ye shes*, wisdom attained through spiritual practice which serves as a pointer to introduce true **primal wisdom**.

Impervious practitioner - *chos dred*, lit. Dharma bear. "Someone who has not been tamed by the Dharma, who knows the Dharma but does not practise it, so that his mind has become stiff ..." DICT. Someone who only has an intellectual understanding, without any real experience, but considers that he or she knows all about the Dharma.

Indra - *brgya byin*, king of the god realm of the **Thirty-three**.

Infinite Aspiration - *mos pa mtha yas*, a future Buddha, the last of the thousand Buddhas who will appear in this present **Good Kalpa**.

Innate (wisdom, joy, etc.) - *lhan skyes*, Skt. *sahaja*, lit. born together, meaning that wisdom, joy, and nirvāṇa in general are latently present even as we experience ignorance, suffering and saṁsāra. The two aspects of one and the same nature are "born together", but perceived as opposites by unenlightened minds.

Inseparable Universe - *mi 'byed 'jig rten*, our world, the field of activity of **Śākyamuni**.

Intermediate state - *bar do*, Skt. *antarābhava*, term used for the various stages of experience between death and the next rebirth, with a wider interpretation that includes the various states of consciousness in life. Four intermediate states are distinguished: 1) the natural intermediate state of this life (*rang bzhin skyes gnas bar do*), 2) the intermediate state of the moment of death (*'chi kha'i bar do*), 3) the **intermediate state of absolute reality** (*chos nyid bar do*), and 4) the **intermediate state of becoming** (*srid pa'i bar do*); or, to make six intermediate states, two more particular states, within the first, can be added: 5) the intermediate state of dream (*rmi lam bar do*) and 6) the intermediate state of meditative concentration (*bsam gtan bar do*).

Intermediate state of absolute reality - *chos nyid bar do*, intermediate state during which absolute reality manifests as pure forms of peaceful or wrathful aspect, according to one's own individual tendencies.

Intermediate state of becoming - *srid pa'i bar do*, the intermediate state during which the force of **karma** propels one towards one's next rebirth in saṁsāra. AT: intermediate state of possibilities, intermediate state of existence.

Jambudvīpa - *'dzam bu gling*, the southern continent, one of the four main "continents" in ancient Indian cosmology, the one in which we live. In some contexts this name refers to South Asia, and in others to the world in a general sense.

Jamgön Kongtrul (the Great), Lodro Thaye - *'jam mgon kong sprul blo gros mtha' yas* (1813-1899) was a great teacher of the non-sectarian movement and was responsible, with Jamyang Khyentse Wangpo, for compiling several great collections of teachings and practices from all traditions, including the *Treasury of Rediscovered Teachings* (*rin chen gter mdzod*).

Jetsun Mila - *rje brtsun mi la* (1040-1123), Tibet's great yogī and poet, whose biography and spiritual songs are among the best loved works in Tibetan Buddhism. One of the foremost disciples of **Marpa**, he is among the great masters at the origin of the **Kagyupa** school.

Jigme Lingpa - *'jigs med gling pa* (1729-1798), see the introduction of this book. He is considered to be a combined emanation of **Vimalamitra, King Trisong Detsen** and Gyalse Lharje. Patrul Rinpoche is often considered to be the emanation of Jigme Lingpa's speech.

Jowo - *jo bo*, lit. lord. A title often used by Tibetans for the Indian paṇḍita **Atīśa.**

Jowo and Śākya - *jo shag rnam gnyis*, Jowo Mikyö Dorje and Jowo Śākyamuni, two statues of the Buddha brought to Tibet respectively by the Nepalese and Chinese princesses whom King **Songtsen Gampo** married in the 7th century.

Jowo Rinpoche - *jo wo rin po che*, a statue representing Buddha **Śākyamuni** at the age of 12, in the Jokhang temple in Lhasa.

Joyful Magic - *'phrul dga'*, Skt. *Nirmāṇarata*, a god realm in the World of Desire (on the fifth level of Gods of Desire) in which the gods can magically produce whatever they need. See **three worlds.**

Joyous Realm - *dga' ldan*, see **Tuṣita heaven.**

Jungpo - *'byung po*, a class of malignant spirits.

Kadampa - *bka' gdams pa*, the first of the schools of the **New Tradition,** which followed the teachings of **Atīśa.** It stressed compassion, study and pure discipline. Its teachings were continued by all the other schools, in particular the **Gelugpa,** which is also known as the New Kadampa school.

Kagyupa - *bka' brgyud pa*, one of the schools of the **New Tradition,** which followed the teachings brought to Tibet from India by **Marpa** the Translator in the 11th century and transmitted to **Milarepa.** There are several branches of the Kagyu school.

Kalpa - *bskal pa.* A great kalpa, which corresponds to a cycle of formation and destruction of a universe, is divided into eighty intermediate kalpas. An intermediate kalpa is composed of one small kalpa during which the span of life, etc., increases and one small kalpa during which it decreases.

Kapāla - *ka pa la*, a bowl made with the top of a skull.

Karma - *las.* We have generally preferred to say "the effects of actions,"

"actions and their effects" or the "principle of cause and effect." Karma literally means simply "action," but is often used loosely to mean the result produced by past actions (*las kyi 'bras bu*, Skt. *karmaphala*).

Karma Chagme - *karma chags med* (16th century), famous lama of the **Kagyupa** school who united the teaching of his school and those of the Nyingmapas and was the tutor of the treasure-discoverer **Namchö Mingyur Dorje.**

Karmapa - *kar ma pa*, name of a series of great lamas of the **Kagyupa** school, whose lineage of reincarnations goes back to Dusum Khyenpa (1110-1193). The Karmapas were the first **tulkus** recognised in Tibet.

Karmic energy - *las kyi rlung*, energy determined by one's karma, as opposed to *ye shes kyi rlung*, the energy connected with wisdom.

Karmic obscurations (obscurations of past actions) - *las kyi sgrib pa*, Skt. *karmāvaraṇa*, obscurations created by negative actions. See obscurations.

Kāśyapa - *'od srung*, the third of the thousand Buddhas of this present kalpa, the one before **Śākyamuni.** Kāśyapa is also the name of one of Śākyamuni's Śrāvaka disciples.

Kātyāyana - Indian Arhat who was a disciple of the Buddha and wrote down one section of the **Abhidharma.**

Kāya - *sku*, see **three kāyas, four kāyas, five kāyas.**

Kharak Gomchung, (Geshe) - *kha rag sgom chung*, an 11th century **Kadampa** lama, disciple of Geshe **Potowa.** His name means "Little Meditator of Kharak," and he was famous for his perseverance and strict application of the teachings. It is said that he received the teachings of the Great Perfection and achieved the rainbow body.

Khampa Lungpa - *khams pa lung pa (sgang sha'kya yon tan)* (1025-1115), a **Kadampa** lama, one of **Drom Tönpa**'s principal disciples.

Khaṭvāṅga - a trident with many symbolic ornaments. See page 316.

Khu, Ngok and Drom - the three main disciples of **Atiśa.** Their full names are Khutön Tsöndru Yungdrung, Ngok Lekpai Sherab, and Drom Gyalwai Jungne (**Drom Tönpa**).

Kīla - *phur ba*, wrathful deity, the activity aspect of all the Buddhas, a manifestation of **Vajrasattva.** Practice related to this deity is based on the four aspects of Kīla, those of the ritual object, compassion, Bodhicitta and awareness-wisdom.

King, Subject and Friend - *rje 'bangs grogs gsum*, King **Trisong Detsen**, the great translator **Vairotsana** and the ḍākinī **Yeshe Tsogyal.**

Kṛiṣṇācārya - *nag po spyod pa*, one of the eighty-four **Mahāsiddhas** of India.

Kriyā (yoga) - *bya ba*, the first of the three outer **tantras**, the fourth of the nine vehicles. In this type of practice the stress is mainly put on correct external behaviour and cleanliness.

Kṣatriya - *rgyal rigs*, one of the four classes of the ancient Indian social system, the class of kings and warriors.

Kuśa - *ku sha*, a kind of grass considered auspicious, because the Buddha sat on a cushion of it when he attained enlightenment.

Lakhe - *gla khe*, kind of tree with a sweet bark.

Lama - *bla ma*, Skt. *guru*, 1. spiritual teacher, explained as the contraction of *bla na med pa*, "nothing superior." 2. often used loosely for Buddhist monks or yogīs in general.

Langri Thangpa, (Geshe) - *glang ri thang pa* (1054-1123), **Kadampa** geshe, disciple of Geshe **Potowa**, author of the *Mind Training in Eight Verses* and founder of the Langthang Monastery.

Lay disciple - *dge bsnyen*, Skt. *upāsaka*, someone who has taken the refuge vows and five other vows (or only some of them): not killing, not lying, not stealing, not indulging in improper sexual conduct, and not taking intoxicants. It is one of the eight categories vows of the **Prātimokṣa**.

Level of union - *zung 'jug gi go 'phang*, the level of **Vajradhara**. The union is that of **dharmakāya** and **rūpakāya**.

Levels - see **Bodhisattva levels**.

Liberation - *thar pa*, Skt. *mokṣa*, 1. freedom from saṁsāra, either as an **Arhat** or as a Buddha. 2. occasionally, *bsgral las byed pa*, performing the action of liberation, a practice to liberate the consciousness of a malignant being into a Buddhafield. See also note 75.

Lingje Repa - *gling rje ras pa* (1128-1188), founder of the Drukpa Kagyu school.

Longchenpa - *klong chen rab 'byams pa* (1308-1363), also called the Omniscient Sovereign or King of Dharma, one of the most extraordinary spiritual masters and scholars of the **Nyingmapa** school. He wrote more than 250 treatises covering almost all of Buddhist theory and practice up to the **Great Perfection**, of which he was among the greatest exponents. Among those that have survived are the famous *Seven Treasures* (*mdzod bdun*), the *Nyingtik Yabzhi* (*snying tig ya bzhi*), the *Trilogy of Rest* (*ngal gso skor gsum*), the *Trilogy of Natural Freedom* (*rang grol skor gsum*), the *Trilogy of Dispelling Darkness* (*mun sel skor gsum*) and the *Miscellaneous Writings* (*gsung thor bu*).

Lord of Death - *'chi bdag*, Yama.

Lord of Secrets - *gsang ba'i bdag po*, an epithet of **Vajrapāṇi**.

Lotus Born - *padma 'byung nas*, see **Padmasambhava**.

Lover of the Stars - *skar ma la dga' ba*, name of a Bodhisattva. He is an example of someone whose selfless aspiration enabled him to accumulate merit in spite of his committing what would normally be considered a negative act.

Lower realms - *ngan song*, the **hells**, the realms of **pretas** and of animals.

Machik Labdrön - *ma cig lab sgron* (1031-1129), a disciple of **Padampa Sangye**, she became the holder of his instructions on the Chö practice.

Mādhyamika - *dbu ma'i lam*, see **Middle Way**.

Mahāyāna - *theg pa chen po*, see **Great Vehicle**.

Mahā (yoga) - the first of the three higher yogas according to the classification of the Dharma into nine vehicles. In this yoga, the main stress is put on the **generation phase** (*bskyed rim*).

Mahākāśyapa - *'od srung chen po*, one of the foremost **śrāvaka** disciples of Buddha **Śākyamuni**, and chief among the first compilers of the **Abhidharma**. After the Buddha had left this world, he became the first patriarch of the Dharma, entrusted with the responsibility for maintaining the teachings and the Saṅgha.

Mahāmudrā - *phyag rgya chen po*, lit. Great Seal. The Great Seal means that the seal of the absolute nature is on everything, that all phenomena belong to the wisdom maṇḍala. This term can be used to denote the teaching, meditation practice or supreme accomplishment.

Mahāsiddha - *grub chen*, a yogī who has reached the supreme accomplishment.

Maitreya - *byams pa*, the Buddha to come, the fifth in this present kalpa. He is also one of the **Eight Great Close Sons**.

Maitrīyogī - *byams pa'i rnal 'byor pa*, one of **Atīśa**'s three principal teachers.

Major and minor marks - *mtshan dang dpe byad*, thirty-two major marks (*mtshan bzang*, Skt. *mahāpuruṣa lakṣaṇa*) and eighty minor ones (*dpe byad*, *ānuvyañjana*) characteristic of a Buddha.

Mamo - *ma mo*, Skt. *mātṛikā*, a kind of dākinī.

Maṇḍala - *dkyil 'khor*, lit. centre and circumference. 1. The universe with the palace of the deity at the centre, as visualized in the practice of the **generation phase**. 2. The visualized ideal universe as an offering.

Mandāravā - a ḍākinī, daughter of the King of Zahor, in India. One of the five principal disciples and **consorts** of **Padmasambhava** and one of the main holders of his teaching.

Māndhātṛi - *nga las nu*, a previous incarnation of the Buddha who became extremely powerful through the power of his past merit, but lost his power due to some evil thoughts.

Mani - the mantra of **Avalokiteśvara** (Chenrezi), *oṁ maṇi padme hūṁ*.

Manifest Joy - *mngon par dga' ba*, Skt. *Abhirati*, name of a kalpa and of the

Buddhafield of Buddha **Akṣobhya**.

Mantra - *sngags*, manifestation of supreme enlightenment in the form of sounds. Syllables which, in the **sādhanas** of the **Secret Mantrayāna,** protect the mind of the practitioner from ordinary perceptions and invoke the wisdom deities.

Mañjuśrī - *'jam dpal dbyangs*, a tenth level **Bodhisattva.** He embodies the knowledge and wisdom of all the Buddhas.

Mañjuśrīmitra - *'jam dpal bshes gnyen*, second human master in the lineage of the **Great Perfection**, a great paṇḍita of **Nālandā** and disciple of **Garab Dorje.**

Māra - *bdud*, demon, see note 230; the tempter in general, that which makes obstacles to spiritual practice and enlightenment.

Marpa - *lho brag mar pa* (1012-1097), great Tibetan master and translator, disciple of Drogmi, **Nāropa**, Maitrīpa and other great siddhas. He brought many **tantras** from India to Tibet and translated them. These teachings were passed down through **Milarepa** and his other disciples, and are the basis of the teachings of the **Kagyu** lineage.

Maudgalyāyana - *mo'u 'gal gyi bu*, one of the two foremost **śrāvaka** disciples of **Śākyamuni** Buddha. He was said to be the one who had the greatest miraculous powers.

Means - *thabs*, see **skilful means.**

Meditate, meditation - *sgom pa*, to let the mind rest on an object of contemplation or reflection, or to maintain the flow of the authentic view.

Melong Dorje - *me long rdo rje* (1243-1303), Tibetan **mahāsiddha,** the teacher of Kumaradza, **Longchenpa**'s teacher.

Merit - *bsod nams*, Skt. *puṇya*, good **karma**, the energy generated by positive actions of body, speech and mind.

Meru, Mount - *ri rgyal po ri rab*, immense mountain, wider at the top than at the bottom, around which the four continents of the world are disposed, according to ancient Indian cosmology.

Middle Way - *dbu ma'i lam*, Skt. *mādhyamika*, teaching on emptiness first expounded by **Nāgārjuna** and considered to be the basis of the **Secret Mantrayāna.** "Middle" means that it is beyond the extreme points of view of nihilism and eternalism.

Milarepa - see **Jetsun Mila.**

Mind lineage of the Conquerors - *rgyal ba dgongs brgyud*, lineage of transmission of the teachings from mind to mind.

Muni - *thub pa*, lit. the Mighty One. An epithet for a Buddha.

Nāda - defined as *chos nyid kyi rang sgra*, the spontaneous sound of dharmatā.

In the syllable *hūṁ* it is represented by a little flame above the circle on top, symbolizing the state of enlightenment, the sole essence, awakened awareness.

Nāga - *klu*, a kind of snakelike being living in the depths of water or under the ground. Although they have miraculous powers they are classified as belonging to the animal realm. See **three worlds**.

Nāgārjuna - *klu sgrub* (1st-2nd century), Indian master, one of the **Six Ornaments**. He expounded the teachings of the **Middle Way** and composed numerous philosophical and medical treatises.

Nālandā - the birthplace near Rājagṛiha of the Buddha's disciple Śāriputra, which much later, starting in the time of the Gupta kings (5th century), became one of the great centres of learning in Buddhist India. It was destroyed around 1200 A.D.

Namchö Mingyur Dorje - *gnam chos mi 'gyur rdo rje*, a famous **treasure discoverer** of the 16th century.

Nanda - *dga' bo*, a cousin of the Buddha who became one of his foremost disciples.

Nāropa - *na ro pa* (1016-1100), Indian paṇḍita and siddha, the disciple of **Tilopa** and teacher of **Marpa** the Translator.

Natural state - *gnas lugs*, Skt. *prakṛiti*, lit. way of abiding. "The nature or condition of everything." DICT.

Nectar - see **ambrosia**.

Negative action - *sdig pa* or *mi dge ba*, Skt. *aśubha*. "That which produces suffering" (Dudjom Rinpoche). AT: harmful action, unwholesome act, evil.

Negative emotions - *nyon mongs pa*, Skt. *kleśa*, "mental phenomena which assail body and mind and lead to harmful actions, creating a state of mental torment." DICT. AT: afflictive emotions, passions, afflictions. Synonym of poison (dug). See **five poisons**.

New Tradition - *gsar ma pa*, the followers of the **tantras** that were translated and propagated from the time of the translator **Rinchen Zangpo** (958-1055) onwards. It designates all the schools of Tibetan Buddhism except for the Nyingmapa, or **Ancient Tradition**.

New Translations - see **New Tradition**.

Nihilism - *chad par lta ba*, Skt. *vibhava dṛṣṭi*, materialism, the view which denies the existence of past and future lives, the principle of cause and effect, and so on.

Nine Expanses - *klong dgu*, nine subdivisions of the Expanse Section (*klong sde*) in the teachings of the **Great Perfection**.

Nirmāṇakāya - *sprul sku*, body of manifestation, the aspect of Buddhahood which manifests out of compassion to help ordinary beings.

Nirvāṇa - *mya ngan las 'das pa*, the state beyond suffering. The conception of nirvāṇa differs in the **Śrāvakayāna**, **Mahāyāna** and **Vajrayāna**.

Non-action - acting without conceptualizing, from the state of realization that the actor, the action and the object acted upon are all without intrinsic reality.

Non-dwelling nirvāṇa - *mi gnas pa'i myang 'das*, total enlightenment, beyond both saṁsāra and nirvāṇa, not "dwelling" in either of them.

Non-thought (experience) - *mi rtog pa'i nyams*, Skt. *avikalpa*, *nirvikalpa*, one of the three types of experience in meditation. A calm state in which there are no thoughts. See **experiences**.

Novice - *dge tshul*, Skt. *śrāmaṇera*. A novice monk holding fewer vows than a fully ordained monk (*dge slong*, Skt. *bhikṣu*).

Nyingmapa - see **Ancient Tradition.**

Obscurations - *sgrib pa*, Skt. āvaraṇa, factors which veil one's Buddha-nature. See also: **two obscurations, four obscurations.**

Obscurations of habitual tendencies - *bag chags kyi sgrib pa*, Skt. *vāsanāvaraṇa*, the habitual tendencies imprinted on the ground-of-all. See **obscurations.**

Obscurations of negative emotions - *nyon mongs kyi sgrib pa*, Skt. *kleśāvaraṇa*, "thoughts (of hatred, attachment etc); they prevent one from attaining liberation." DICT. See obscurations.

Omniscient Dharma-King - epithet of **Longchenpa.**

Once-Come-King - *sngon byung gi rgyal po*, a Buddha in the first **kalpa.**

Orgyenpa (Rinchen Pal) - *o rgyan pa rin chen dpal* (1230-1309), a great siddha of the Drukpa Kagyu tradition, disciple of **Gotsangpa.** He travelled widely, visiting **Oḍḍiyana,** Bodhgaya and China. Among his disciples were Karmapa Rangjung Dorje, Kharchupa and Dawa Senge.

Owner of the ground - *sa bdag*, Skt. *bhūmipati*, a spirit occupying a place.

Padampa Sangye - *pha dam pa sangs rgyas* (11th-12th century), Indian siddha who established the teachings of the Shijepa (*zhi byed pa*) school. Teacher of **Machik Labdrön,** to whom he transmitted the **Chö** teachings. He travelled to Tibet several times.

Padma - the name by which **Padmasambhava** refers to himself. The name means "lotus."

Padma Thötreng - *padma thod phreng rtsal*, lit. Padma garlanded with skulls. One of the names of **Padmasambhava.**

Padmasambhava of Oḍḍiyāna - *o rgyan padma 'byung gnas*, the Lotus-born Teacher from Oḍḍiyāna, often known as **Guru Rinpoche.** During the reign of King **Trisong Detsen**, the great master subjugated the evil forces hostile to the propagation of Buddhism in Tibet, spread the Buddhist teaching of **Vajrayāna** in that country and hid innumerable **spiritual treasures** for the sake of future generations. He is venerated as the Second Buddha whose coming was predicted by the first one, Buddha **Śākyamuni**, to give the special teachings of Vajrayāna.

Palace of Lotus Light - *padma 'od kyi pho brang*, the palace of **Padmasambhava** in the Buddhafield of the **Glorious Copper-coloured Mountain**.

Palmo (nun) - *dge slong ma dpal mo*, famous Indian nun who propagated the practice of Nyung-ne (one-day fast and vow of silence) and attained the supreme accomplishment through the practice of **Avalokiteśvara**.

Palyul (monastery) - *dpal yul*, one of the six great monasteries of the Nyingmapa school.

Paṇḍita - a scholar, someone learned in the five traditional sciences (see: **five sciences**). Particularly used to refer to Indian scholars.

Path of accumulating - *tshogs lam*, Skt. *sambhāramārga*, the first of the five paths towards total enlightenment, according to the Bodhisattva vehicle. On this path one accumulates the causes which will make it possible to proceed towards enlightenment.

Path of joining- *sbyor lam*, Skt. *prayogamārga*, the second of the five paths. On this path one connects oneself to or prepares oneself for seeing the two kinds of absence of self.

Path of seeing - *mthong lam*, Skt. *darśanamārga*, the third of the five paths, according to the Bodhisattva vehicle. It is called this because on it one really sees the two kinds of absence of 'self' (i.e. of true, independent existence), that of the individual and that of phenomena.

Perceptions - *snang ba*, that which appears in the eyes of each individual according to his or her tendencies or spiritual development. NT, quoting Patrul Rinpoche, speaks of three types of perception: 1) deluded perceptions, which arise in the consciouness of the beings of the six realms due to misunderstanding; they are called the impure deluded perceptions of the universe and beings. 2) the perceptions of interdependence (*rten 'brel*), magical illusions (*sgyu ma*), corresponding to the eight similes of illusion which one does not apprehend as real (see page 252); these are the perceptions of the bodhisattvas of the ten levels in their post-meditation state (*rjes thob*). 3) the authentic, perfect, perceptions of wisdom; when one has realized the natural state of everything, the beings and the universe appear as the display of the **kāyas** and wisdoms.

Perfection phase - *rdzogs rim*, Skt. *sampannakrama*. 1. "with characteristics" (*mtshan bcas*), it is the meditation on the **channels** and **energies** of the body visualized as a vajra body. 2. "without characteristics" (*mtshan med*), it is the meditation phase during which the forms visualized in the generation phase are dissolved and one remains in the experience of emptiness.

Phlegm - *bad kan*, one of the three humours according to Tibetan medicine. See also **wind, bile.**

Piṭaka - see **Tripiṭaka.**

Piṭaka, (fourth) - *sde snod bzhi pa*, the piṭaka of the **Secret Mantrayāna.**

Pith-instructions - *man ngag*, Skt. *upadeśa*, instructions explaining the most profound points of the teachings in a condensed and direct way for the purposes of practice.

Positive action - *dge ba*, Skt. *kuśala*. "That which produces happiness" (Dudjom Rinpoche). AT: beneficial act, virtue.

Potowa, (Geshe) - *po to ba* (1031-1105), one of the **Three Brothers,** the three foremost disciples of **Drom Tönpa** (the founder of the **Kadampa** school).

Prātimokṣa - *so sor thar pa*, lit. individual liberation. The vows of individual liberation are the eight categories of vows taught in the **Vinaya,** from the simple one day vow up to the complete vows of fully ordained monks. See **three vows.**

Pratyekabuddha - *rang sangs rgyas*, "someone reaching the end of saṁsāra without the help of a spiritual master. By studying the nature of interdependent origination, he realizes the absence of true existence of the self and half-realizes the absence of true existence of phenomena." DICT.

Precious canopy - *rin po che'i gdugs*, one of the **eight auspicious signs,** it corresponds to the Buddha's head and symbolizes protection from negative actions.

Precious Master of Oḍḍiyāna - *o rgyan rin po che*, one of the names of **Padmasambhava.**

Precious word empowerment - *tshig dbang rin po che*, the fourth **empowerment** "which eliminates the defilements of body, speech, mind and habitual tendencies, enables one to meditate on the natural Great Perfection and sows the seed for obtaining vajra wisdom and the svabhavikakāya." DICT.

Preliminaries - *sngon 'gro*. See **five hundred thousand preliminaries.**

Preparation, main part and conclusion - *sbyor dngos rjes gsum*, the three supreme methods for any practice: 1) beginning by checking that one has the compassionate motivation, 2) practising without materialistic concepts, and 3) ending by dedicating the merit to the enlightenment of all beings.

Preta - *yi dvags*, AT: hungry spirit, spirit, hungry ghost.

Primal wisdom - *ye shes*, Skt. *jñāna*, "the knowing (*shes pa*) that has always been present since the beginning (*ye nas*), awareness, clarity-emptiness, naturally dwelling in the mindstream of all beings." DICT.

Primordial purity - *ka dag*, the nature of Buddhahood, present in all beings, the purity of which can never be spoiled.

Principle of cause and effect - *las rgyu 'bras*, lit. action, cause and fruit. Process by which every action produces a corresponding effect. See **karma**.

Profound insight - *lhag mthong*, Skt. *vipaśyanā*, "to see with the eye of wisdom the particular nature of things." DICT.

Prostration - *phyag 'tshal ba*, gesture of reverence, in which the forehead, the two hands and the two knees touch the ground.

Protectors - see **Dharma protectors**.

Protectors of the Three Families - *rigs gsum mgon po*, the Bodhisattvas **Mañjuśrī, Avalokiteśvara** and **Vajrapāṇi**. The three families are respectively those of the body, speech and mind of the Buddha.

Puchungwa, (Geshe) - *phu chung ba*, one of the **Three Brothers**.

Pūrṇakāśyapa - *'od srung rdzogs byed*, a leading **tīrthika** master at the time of the Buddha.

Pure land - *dag pa'i zhing*, a place or world manifested by a Buddha or great Bodhisattva through the spontaneous qualities of his realization. There, beings can progress towards enlightenment without falling back into the lower realms of saṁsāra. Also, any place whatsoever, when it is perceived as a pure manifestation of spontaneous wisdom.

Pure Land of Bliss - *bde ba can*, Skt. *Sukhāvatī*, the **Buddhafield** of **Amitābha**.

Pure levels (three) - *dag pa sa gsum*, the eighth, ninth and tenth **Bodhisattva levels**, thus called because Bodhisattvas on these levels are totally free from the **obscuration of negative emotions** (*nyon sgrib*).

Pure perception - *dag snang*, "the perception of all the world and its contents as a pure Buddhafield, as the display of kāyas and wisdoms." DICT.

Rākṣasa - *srin po*, a kind of malignant spirit that eats human flesh.

Ratnasambhava - *rin chen 'byung gnas*, the Buddha of the Jewel Family. See **five families**.

Real meaning - *nges don*, Skt. *nītārtha*, direct expression of truth from the point of view of realized beings. See also **expedient meaning**.

Realm - see **six realms**.

Refuge - 1) *skyabs yul*, the object in which one takes refuge. 2) *skyabs 'gro*, the practice of taking refuge.

Relative truth - *kun rdzob bden pa*, Skt. *saṁvṛiti satya*, the apparent truth perceived and taken as real by the deluded mind.

Repa Shiwa Ö - *ras pa zhi ba 'od*, one of the main disciples of **Milarepa**.

Rinchen Zangpo - *rin chen bzang po* (958-1055), the most famous translator of the second propagation of Buddhism in Tibet, when the **New Tradition** began.

Ṛiṣi - *drang srong*, 1) sage, hermit, saint, particularly the famous sages of Indian myth, who had enormous longevity and magical powers. 2) name of a constellation.

Root teacher - *rtsa ba'i bla ma*, 1) the principal, or first, spiritual teacher from whom one has received empowerments, commentaries and pith instructions. 2) the teacher who has introduced one to the nature of the mind.

Royal posture - *rgyal po'i rol stabs*, sitting posture with the right leg half stretched and the left drawn in.

Rūpakāya - *gzugs sku*, Body of Form, which includes the **sambhogakāya** and **nirmāṇakāya** together.

Sadāprarudita - *rtag tu ngu*, a Bodhisattva whose name means "Ever Weeping", on account of the numerous tears he shed in his quest to receive the teachings on transcendent wisdom.

Śākyamuni - *sha kya thub pa*, the Buddha of our time, who lived around the 5th century B.C.

Sakyapa - *sa skya pa*, one of the schools of the **New Tradition**, founded by Khön Könchok Gyalpo (1034-1102).

Samantabhadra - *kun tu bzang po*, 1) the original Buddha (Adibuddha), he who has never fallen into delusion, the Dharmakāya Buddha represented as a naked figure, deep blue like the sky, in union with Samantabhadrī, as a symbol of awareness-emptiness, the pure, absolute nature ever present and unobstructed. The source of the lineage of the tantra transmissions of the Nyingma school. 2) Bodhisattva Samantabhadra, one of the **Eight Great Close Sons**, renowned for the way in which, through the power of his concentration, he miraculously multiplied the offerings he made.

Samaya - *dam tshig*, lit. promise. Sacred links between teacher and disciple, and also between disciples, in the **Vajrayāna**. The Sanskrit word samaya can mean: agreement, engagement, convention, precept, boundary, etc. Although there are many detailed obligations, the most essential samaya is to consider the teacher's body, speech and mind as pure.

Samaya object or substance - *dam tshig gi rdzas*, object or ingredient which is necessary for or enhances the practices of the Vajrayāna.

Sambhogakāya - *longs spyod rdzogs pa'i sku*, Body of Perfect Enjoyment, the spontaneously luminous aspect of Buddhahood, only perceptible to highly realized beings.

Saṁsāra - *'khor ba*, the cycle of existence in which one is endlessly propelled by negative emotions and the karmic force of one's actions from one state of rebirth to another.

Saṁvarasara - *bde mchog snying po*, one of **Mañjuśrī**'s names.

Samye - *bsam yas*, the first monastery in Tibet, in the Tsangpo valley south-east of Lhasa, built during the time of King **Trisong Detsen**. The name means "inconceivable."

Samye Chimpu - *bsam yas mchims phu*, name of a group of hermitages situated on the mountainside above **Samye** Monastery, where many great Buddhist masters have attained accomplishment.

Saṅgha - *dge 'dun*. In its broad meaning it refers to all the practitioners of the Buddha's teaching. It can have a more restricted meaning according to the context, referring to ordained monks, Arhats, Bodhisattvas, etc.

Śaṅkara - *bde byed*, example of a man whose strong desire and hatred led him to kill his mother. He repented and, having purified his negative actions, was reborn in a god realm.

Śāntarakṣita - *zhi ba mtsho*, also called the Bodhisattva Abbot. This great Indian **paṇḍita** of the **Mahāyāna** school was abbot of the Buddhist university of **Nālandā** and author of a number of philosophical commentaries, such as the *Ornament of the Middle Way* (*dbu ma rgyan*, Skt. *Madhyamakālṁkāra-kārikā*). He was invited to Tibet by King **Trisong Detsen** to consecrate the site of the first Tibetan monastery at **Samye** and ordained the first Tibetan monks.

Śāntideva - *zhi ba lha* (7th century), the great Indian poet and **mahāsiddha**, who astounded the monks of his monastery of **Nālandā** with his famous poem on the practice of bodhicitta, the Bodhicaryāvatāra (*spyod 'jug*), or *The Way of the Bodhisattva*.

Saraha - *sa ra ha*, Indian **mahāsiddha**, author of three cycles of **dohās**.

Śāriputra - *sha ri'i bu*, one of the two foremost **Śrāvaka** disciples of Buddha **Śākyamuni**.

Sarvanivāraṇaviṣkambhin - *sgrib pa rnam sel*, one of the **Eight Great Close Sons** of Buddha **Śākyamuni**.

Śāstra - *bstan bcos*, a commentary on the Buddha's teachings.

Sattvavajra - *sems dpa' rdo rje*, a name given to **Vajrapāṇi**.

Śāvaripa - *sha ba ri pa* or *ri khrod dbang phyug*, one of the eighty-four **mahāsiddhas** of India. He was a hunter from a hill tribe in Bengal, and along with his two wives became a disciple of **Nāgārjuna**.

Second Buddha - *sangs rgyas gnyis pa*, an epithet of **Padmasambhava**.

Secret empowerment - *gsang dbang*. The second **empowerment**, "which purifies the defilements of speech, enables one to meditate on the channels and energies and to recite mantras, and sows the seed for obtaining vajra speech and the sambhogakāya." DICT.

Secret Mantrayāna - *gsang ngags kyi theg pa*, a branch of the **Great Vehicle**

which uses the special techniques of the **tantras** to pursue the path of enlightenment for all beings more rapidly. Synonym of **Vajrayāna.**

Seven attributes of royalty - *rgyal srid sna bdun*, Skt. *saptaratna*,seven possessions of a **universal monarch**, each of which has a symbolic significance. They are the precious golden wheel, precious wishfulfilling jewel, precious queen, precious minister, precious elephant, precious horse and precious general.

Seven branches - *yan lag bdun*, Skt. *saptāṅga*, a form of prayer which comprises seven parts: prostration, offering, confession, rejoicing, requesting the teachers to turn the wheel of Dharma, requesting them not to pass into nirvāṇa, and dedication of merit.

Seven noble riches - *'phags pa'i nor bdun*, Skt. *saptadhanam*, faith, discipline, generosity, learning, conscientiousness, modesty and wisdom.

Seven point maṇḍala - *mandal so bdun ma*, maṇḍala comprising Mount Meru, the four continents, the sun and the moon.

Seven point posture of Vairocana - *rnam snang chos bdun*, Skt. *saptadharma-vairocana*, the seven points of the ideal meditation posture: legs crossed in the vajra posture, back straight, hands in the gesture of meditation, eyes gazing along the nose, chin slightly tucked in, shoulders well apart "like a vulture's wings", and the tip of the tongue touching the palate.

Shang Rinpoche - *bla ma zhang rin po che (brtson 'grus grags pa)* (1121-1193), a great **Kagyupa** lama, founder of the Tsalpa Kagyu branch.

Shapkyu - *zhabs kyu*, lit. foot hook. A sign in the shape of a hook which is put under consonants to represent the *u* sound.

Sharawa - *sha ra ba (yon tan grags)* (1070-1141), name of a **Kadampa** geshe, disciple of Geshe **Potowa**.

Shübu Palgyi Senge - *shud bu dpal gyi seng ge*, one of the **twenty five disciples** of **Padmasambhava.**

Siddha - *grub thob*, lit. one who has attained the accomplishments. Someone who has attained the fruit of the practice of the **Secret Mantrayāna.**

Siddhi - *dngos grub*, see **accomplishment.**

Six classes of beings - *'gro drug*, see **six realms of existence.**

Six consciousnesses - *rnam shes tshogs drug*, Skt. *ṣaḍvijñānakāya*, lit. six gatherings of consciousness, meaning the gathering of a sense object, of a sense organ and of a consciousness. They are the vision, hearing, smell, taste, touch and mental consciousnesses.

Six Ornaments - *rgyan drug*, the six great commentators of the Buddha's teachings: **Nāgārjuna**, **Āryadeva**, **Asaṅga**, Vasubandhu, Dignāga and Dharmakīrti.

Six realms of existence - *'gro drug*, Skt. *ṣaḍgati*, six modes of existence caused and dominated by a particular mental poison: the realms of **hells** (anger), of **pretas** (miserliness), of animals (bewilderment or ignorance), of humans (desire), of **demigods** or asuras (jealousy), and of **gods** (pride). They correspond to deluded perceptions produced by beings' **karma** and apprehended as real. One also speaks of five realms (*'gro lnga*, Skt. *pañcagati*), counting gods and demigods together as one realm.

Six transcendent perfections - *pha rol tu phyin pa drug*, Skt. *ṣaḍ pāramitā*: transcendent generosity (*sbyin pa'i pha rol tu phyin pa*, Skt. *dāna-pāramitā*), transcendent discipline (*tshul khrims gyi pha rol tu phyin pa*, *Śīla-pāramitā*), transcendent patience (*bzod pa'i pha rol tu phyin pa*, *kṣānti-pāramitā*), transcendent diligence (*brtson 'grus kyi pha rol tu phyin pa*, *vīrya-pāramitā*), transcendent concentration (*bsam gtan gyi pha rol tu phyin pa*, *dhyāna-pāramitā*) and transcendent wisdom (*shes rab kyi pha rol tu phyin pa*, *prajñā-pāramitā*). See also **transcendent perfection.**

Skilful Means - *thabs*, Skt. *upāya*, spontaneous, altruistic activity born from wisdom.

Skull cup - *thod phor*, Skt. *kapāla*. The top of a skull is used in certain rituals and by some yogīs as a bowl. It symbolizes egolessness.

Small skull drum - *thod pa'i ḍa ma ru*, small doublesided drum made of two skull-tops.

Smṛtijñāna - (10th-11th century), famous Indian master and **paṇḍita** who contributed to the translation into Tibetan and correction of certain tantras and commentaries. His death, in Tibet, marks the end of the period of the **Old Translations.**

So, Zur and Nub - *so zur gnubs*, the family names of three great masters who were the early holders of the lineage of the Nyingma Kahma (long transmission from master to disciple of the Nyingma teachings, as opposed to the Terma, or **spiritual treasures** hidden, then revealed, sometimes a very long time later). Their full names were So Yeshe Wangchuk, Zur Shakya Jungne and Nub Chen Sangye Yeshe.

Songtsen Gampo - *srong btsan sgam po* (617-698), 33rd king of Tibet and one of the three great religious kings. It was during his time that the first Buddhist temples were built.

Source of good - *dge ba'i rtsa ba*, Skt. *kuśalamūla*, positive actions which are like the roots (*rtsa ba*) of merit or good (*dge ba*).

Spiritual companions - *chos grogs*, students of the same teacher, or with whom one has received teaching. It is considered vital to have harmonious relations with such people, particularly in the **Vajrayāna.**

Spiritual friend - *dge ba'i gshes gnyen*, Skt. *kalyāṇamitra*, a synonym for spiritual teacher.

Spiritual treasure - *gter ma*, teachings, with statues and other objects, that were hidden by **Padmasambhava, Yeshe Tsogyal** and others in earth, rocks, lakes and trees, or even in more subtle locations such as space or mind for the sake of future generations, and then rediscovered in miraculous ways by incarnations of Padmasambhava's disciples, the treasure discoverers.

Śrāvaka - *nyan thos*, a follower of the root vehicle of Buddhism whose goal is to attain liberation from the sufferings of saṁsāra as an **Arhat**. Unlike the followers of the **Great Vehicle**, the Śrāvakas do not aspire to full enlightenment for the sake of all beings.

Śrāvakayāna - *nyan thos kyi theg pa*, the vehicle of the **Śrāvakas**.

Śrī Siṁha - *dpal gyi seng ge* (4th century), the third human teacher in the lineage of transmission of the **Great Perfection** teachings, disciple of **Mañjuśrīmitra**.

Śroṇa (Śroṇajāt) - *gro byin skyes*, a **vīṇā** player who became a disciple of the Buddha and gained the ability to visit other realms, notably those of the **pretas**.

Study - *thos pa*, lit. listening. Traditionally, listening to the teachings was the main way of learning in Tibet. Before studying from a text, it is important to receive the aural transmission by actually hearing the teacher's words. The term "study" should therefore be understood as rather more than simply reading a text.

Stūpa - *mchod rten*, lit. support of offering, symbolic representation of the Buddha's mind. The most typical Buddhist monument, which often has a wide square base, a rounded mid-section, and a tall conical upper section topped by a sun and moon. Stūpas frequently contain the relics of enlightened beings. They vary in size from tiny clay models to the vast stūpas at Borobodur in Indonesia and Bodha in Nepal.

Sublime being - *skyes bu dam pa*, "realized being who has the capacity to act for the benefit of others on a vast scale." DICT.

Sublime Compassionate One - *'phags pa thugs rje chen po*, one of the names given to **Avalokiteśvara** (Chenrezi), the Bodhisattva of compassion.

Sublime levels - see **Bodhisattva levels**.

Sugata - *bde bar gshegs pa*, lit. gone to happiness: a Buddha. "Someone who, using the happy path of the Bodhisattva vehicle, reaches the happy fruit: perfect Buddhahood." DICT.

Sunakṣatra - *legs pa'i skar ma*, the Buddha's cousin, who, despite spending twenty-five years as the Buddha's attendant and knowing all his teachings by heart, was still unable to see any good qualities in him. He died shortly after leaving the Buddha and was reborn as a preta.

Supreme accomplishment - *mchog gi dngos grub*, see **accomplishment**.

Sustained calm - *zhi gnas*, Skt. *śamatha*, the basis of all concentrations. "The distraction of the mind by other objects having been calmed (*zhi*), the mind stays (*gnas*) without wavering in concentration." DICT.

Sūtra - *mdo*, a concise text spoken by the Buddha; one of the Three Piṭakas. See **Tripiṭaka**.

Suvarṇadvīpa (Lord of) - *gser gling pa*, a Buddhist master, Dharmakīrti, who lived in Sumatra in the 10th century. **Atīśa** considered him as the most important of the teachers from whom he received the teachings on **bodhicitta**.

Svābhāvikakāya - *ngo bo nyid kyi sku*, the Body of the Essential Nature; the fourth kāya, the aspect of inseparability of the first three, **Dharmakāya**, **Sambhogakāya** and **Nirmāṇakāya**.

Symbol lineage of the Vidyādharas - *rig 'dzin brda yi brgyud*, lineage of transmission of the teachings by means of gestures or symbols.

Tainted (action) - *zag bcas*, Skt. *sāsrava*, done with the **three concepts** of subject, object and action.

Tangka - *thang ka*, a Tibetan scroll painting.

Tangtong Gyalpo - *thang stong rgyal po* (1385-1509), famous Tibetan siddha who travelled extensively in China, Tibet and other eastern countries, built numerous temples and metal bridges and founded monasteries at Derge and elsewhere.

Tantra - *rgyud*, text based on the original purity of the nature of mind, whose fruit is the realization of that nature. The root texts of the **Vajrayāna** teachings.

Tantric - related to the **tantras**, to the **Vajrayāna**.

Tārā - *sgrol ma*, female **Bodhisattva** born from a tear of **Avalokiteśvara**; female manifestation of great compassion.

Tathāgata - *bde bzhin gshegs pa*, one who has reached the real nature, a Buddha.

Ten directions - *phyogs bcu*, the four cardinal points, the four intermediate ones, the zenith and the nadir.

Tendencies - see **habitual tendencies**.

Tenma - *rten ma bcu gnyis*, twelve female local deities who took the vow, in the presence of Padmasambhava, to protect the Dharma.

Theurang - *the'u rang*, a kind of spirit appearing like a small dwarf with only one leg.

Thirty-five Buddhas - *sangs rgyas so lnga* or *bde gshegs so lnga*, the Thirty-five Buddhas of Confession, representing the omnipresence of the Buddhas, ready to purify beings from their faults in all thirty-five directions of space (the four main directions, the four intermediate directions, then the eight and sixteen subdirections, the centre, the nadir and the zenith).

Thirty-three - *gsum cu rtsa gsum*, Skt. *Trāyastriṁśa*, a god realm in the World of Desire, the abode of **Indra** and his thirty-two ministers. See **three worlds**.

Thought - *rnam rtog*, Skt. *vikalpanā*, in general, whatever arises in the mind in a **dualistic** mode.

Threatening mudrā - *sdigs mdzubs*, Skt. *tarjanī mudrā*, threatening gesture, pointing with the forefinger and little finger.

Three Brothers - *sku mched gsum*, the three principal disciples of **Drom Tönpa**: **Potowa, Chengawa** and **Puchungwa**.

Three concepts - *'khor gsum*, subject, object and action, perceived as having a real and independent existence.

Three Jewels - *dkon mchog gsum*, Skt. *triratna*, the **Buddha**, the **Dharma** and the **Saṅgha**.

Three kāyas - *sku gsum*, Skt. *trikāya*, lit. the Three Bodies: the three aspects of Buddhahood: **dharmakāya, sambhogakāya** and **nirmāṇakāya.**

Three maṇḍalas - *dkyil 'khor gsum*, the maṇḍalas of body, speech and mind as manifestations of the primordial nature: forms as deity, sounds as **mantra** and thoughts as wisdom.

Three poisons - *dug gsum*, the three **negative emotions** of bewilderment, attachment and aversion. See **five poisons**.

Three Roots - *rtsa gsum*, the **lama**, root or source of blessings; the **yidam**, source of accomplishments; and the **ḍākinī** (or **protectors**), source of activities.

Three supreme methods - *dam pa gsum*. See **preparation, main part and conclusion**.

Three sweet foods - *mngar gsum*, sugar, molasses and honey.

Three times - *dus gsum*, Skt. *trikāla*, past, present and future.

Three vows - *sdom pa gsum*, Skt. *trisaṁvara*, the vows of **Prātimokṣa**, the precepts of the **Bodhisattvas** and the **samayas** of the **Secret Mantrayāna**.

Three white foods - *dkar gsum*, milk, butter and curd, which are traditionally considered as very pure foods.

Three worlds - 1) *khams gsum*, the world of desire, the world of form and the world of formlessness. The first contains the beings of the **hell, preta**, animal, human and **demigod** realms, and some of the god realms. The second two are god realms with a rarified experience which is the result of certain types of intense concentration (see **worldly concentrations**). 2) Occasionally used to translate *sa gsum*, Skt. *tribhvana*, lit. the three levels, i) above the earth (*sa bla*), ii) on the earth (*sa steng*) and iii) below the earth (*sa 'og*); they are called respectively the realms of gods, of humans and of **nāgas**.

Threefold training - *bslab pa gsum*, Skt. *triśikṣā*, discipline (*tshul khrims*, *śīla*), concentration (*ting nges 'dzin*, *citta*) and wisdom (*shes rab*, *prajñā*).

Thusness - *de bzhin nyid*, Skt. *tathatā*, "the nature of things, emptiness." DKR.

Tilopa - *ti lo pa*, one of the eighty four **mahāsiddhas** of India. Teacher of **Nāropa**.

Tingdzin Zangpo (Nyang) - *myang ting 'dzin bzang po* (9th century), Tibetan **mahāsiddha**, disciple of **Vimalamitra** (from whom he received the entire teachings of the *Heart-essence*) and of **Padmasambhava**. He is said to have been the first Tibetan to attain the rainbow body of the great transference (*'ja' lus 'pho ba chen po*), the greatest accomplishment of the **Great Perfection**.

Tīrthika - *mu stegs pa*, a proponent of extreme philosophical views such as **nihilism** and **eternalism**. Often used for the schools of philosophical and religious thought in India that were opposed to Buddhism.

Tönpa (Geshe) (1005-1064), another name of **Drom Tönpa**.

Torma - *gtor ma*, a ritual object, often modelled from flour and butter, which can be the symbol of a deity, a maṇḍala, an offering, or occasionally a weapon to fight negative forces.

Total enlightenment - *rdzogs pa'i byang chub*, Skt. *sambodhi*, complete Buddhahood.

Trakpa Gyaltsen - *grags pa rgyal mtshan* (1147-1216), one of the five great scholars of the **Sakya** school, who are known as the Sakya Gongma.

Transcendent perfection - *pha rol tu phyin pa*, Skt. *pāramitā*. The six methods of training in the bodhicitta of application. They are transcendent because they are accompanied by the wisdom of emptiness. See also **six transcendent perfections**.

Transference - *'pho ba*, 1) passing from one place to another, transmigrating (after death). 2) practice for directing the transference of consciousness at the time of death.

Treasure - see **spiritual treasure**.

Treasure discoverer - *gter ston*, see **spiritual treasure**.

Tripiṭaka - *sde snod gsum*, The three collections of the Buddha's teachings, **Vinaya, Sūtra** and **Abhidharma.** The **Vajrayāna** teachings are sometimes considered as a fourth piṭaka. Tripiṭaka means "the three baskets," so called because the palm-leaf folios on which the scriptures were originally written were collected and stored in baskets.

Trisong Detsen - *khri srong sde'u btsan* (790-844), 38th king of Tibet, second of the three great religious kings. It was due to his efforts that the great masters came from India and established Buddhism firmly in Tibet.

Tsampa - *tsam pa*, flour made from roasted barley or other grains. A staple food in Tibet.

Tsa-tsa - *tsa tsa*, a small clay **stūpa**, Buddha, or other figure, made with a mould.

Tulku - *sprul sku*, the Tibetan translation of the Skt. **nirmāṇakāya**, also used as an honorific title and general term for recognized incarnations of lamas, who are found, usually in childhood, and brought up to inherit the lineage and often the monastic foundations of their predecessors.

Tuṣita heaven - *dga' ldan*, (fourth level) realm of the gods of the World of Desire, in which Buddha **Śākyamuni** took a final rebirth before appearing in this world. At present **Maitreya**, the future Buddha, is in the Tuṣita heaven teaching the Mahāyāna. See **three worlds**.

Twelve categories of teaching in the piṭakas - *sde snod bcu gnyis*, lit. twelve piṭakas, also called the Twelve Branches of Excellent Speech (*gsung rab yan lag bcu gnyis*). The twelve types of teaching given by the Buddha correspond to twelve types of text: condensed (*mdo sde*, Skt. *sūtra*), melodious (*dbyangs bsnyan*, *geya*), prophetic (*lung bstan*, *vyākaraṇa*), verse (*tshigs bcad*, *gāthā*), spoken with a purpose (*ched brjod*, *udāna*), conversatory (*gleng gzhi*, *nidāna* - questions, talks, etc.), concerning his past lives (*skyes rab*, *jātaka*), marvellous (*rmad byung*, *adbhutadharma*), establishing a truth (*gtan babs*, *upadeśa*), biographical or "expressing realization" (*rtogs brjod*, *avadāna*), historical (*de ltar byung*, *itivṛittaka*), and very detailed (*shin tu rgyas pa*, *vaipulya*).

Twelve qualities of full training - *sbyangs pa'i yon tan bcu gnyis*, Skt. *dvādaśadhūtaguṇa*, twelve ascetic practices of **śrāvakas** and **pratyekabuddhas**, such as eating only once a day, living in solitude, possessing only the three monastic garments, etc.

Twelve Vajra Laughs - *rdo rje gad mo bcu gnyis*, a teaching of the **Great Perfection**.

Twenty One Genyen - *dge bsnyen nyer gcig*, a group of spirits who were subdued by **Padmasambhava** and became protectors of the Dharma.

Twenty-five disciples - *rje 'bang nyer lnga*, the greatest Tibetan disciples of **Padmasambhava**. All of them attained the supreme accomplishment. The most famous were King **Trisong Detsen**, **Yeshe Tsogyal**, and **Vairotsana**. Many of the great masters of Tibetan Buddhism are emanations of the twenty-five disciples.

Two accumulations - *tshogs gnyis*, Skt. *sambhāradvaya*, the accumulation of merit (*bsod nams*, Skt. *puṇya*) and that of wisdom (*ye shes*, *jñāna*).

Two obscurations - *sgrib gnyis*, the **obscurations of negative emotions** and **conceptual obscurations.** See also **obscurations** and **four obscurations.**

Two Supreme Ones - *mchog gnyis*, Guṇaprabha (*yon tan 'od*) and Śākyaprabha (*sha kya 'od*).

Two truths - *bden pa gnyis*, the **absolute** and **relative truths.**

Twofold goal - *don gnyis*, one's own goal, benefit or welfare (*rang don*) and that of others (*gzhan don*). Often understood in the ultimate sense of the goal for oneself being achieved by the realization of emptiness, the **dharmakāya**, and the goal for others by compassion manifesting as the **rūpakāya.**

Twofold purity - *dag pa gnyis*, original purity (*rang bzhin ye dag*), which is the Buddha nature in all beings, and purity from all adventitious stains (*blo bur phral dag*). Only a Buddha has this second purity as well.

Oḍḍiyāna - *o rgyan*, a ḍākinī land which is the birthplace of **Padmasambhava.** According to some it is located between present-day Afghanistan and Kashmir. It is also the birthplace of **Garab Dorje.** The use of "Oḍḍiyāna" coupled with titles such as "Great One," "Second Buddha," "Great Master," and so on invariably refers to **Padmasambhava.**

Unaltered - *ma bcos pa*, Skt. *naisargika*, left in its original state, without manipulations or fabrications.

Unexcelled, the - *'og min*, Skt. *Akaniṣṭha*, see **Akaniṣṭha.**

Universal monarch - *'khor lo sgyur ba'i rgyal po*, Skt. *cakravartin*, 1) a king ruling over a world system. 2) an emperor.

Untainted (action) - *zag med*, Skt. *anāsrava*, done without concepts of subject, object and action.

Vairocana - *rnam par snang mdzad*, the Buddha of the Buddha family. See **five families.**

Vairotsana - *bai ro tsa na*, Tibet's greatest translator and one of the first seven monks to be ordained in Tibet. He was one of the principal disciples of **Padmasambhava** and of **Śrī Siṁha.**

Vaiśākha - *sa ga zla ba*, the fourth month of the Tibetan lunar calendar. It is on the fifteenth of that month that the Buddha was born, attained enlightenment and passed into nirvāṇa.

Vaiśravaṇa - *rnam thos sras*, one of the **Four Great Kings** (whose god realm is the first in the World of Desire), guardian of the North and god of wealth.

Vajra - *rdo rje*, AT: diamond, adamantine thunderbolt. Symbol of unchanging and indestructible wisdom capable of penetrating through everything. Ritual instrument symbolizing compassion, skilful means, awareness. Always associated with the bell, *dril bu*, Skt. *ghaṇṭā*, the symbol of wisdom, emptiness. For the vajra's form see illustration of Vajrasattva who holds the vajra in his right hand and the bell in his left.

Vajra brothers and sisters - *rdo rje spun*, students of the same teacher, or with whom one has received **Vajrayāna** teachings. See **spiritual companions.**

Vajra master - *rdo rje slob spon*, Skt. *vajrācārya*, "the spiritual master who introduces one to a maṇḍala of the Secret Mantrayāna and gives the liberating instructions." DICT.

Vajra of Joy - *dgyes pa rdo rje*, a name of **Garab Dorje.**

Vajra of Laughter - *bzhad pa rdo rje*, another name of **Garab Dorje.**

Vajra posture - *rdo rje dkyil krung*, Skt. *vajrāsana*, meditation posture with the legs crossed and the feet resting on the thighs.

Vajra recitation - *rdo rje bzlas pa*, recitation of mantras in concert with inhalation, holding and exhalation.

Vajra Seat - *rdo rje gdan*, Skt. *Vajrāsana*, the place in India (the present name is Bodh Gaya) where all the Buddhas of this kalpa are to attain enlightenment.

Vajra song - *rdo rje mgur*, song (*mgur*) expressing the inner experiences of a yogī, his realization of the ultimate indestructible (vajra) nature.

Vajra Yoginī - *rdo rje rnal 'byor ma*, a female sambhogakāya form of Buddha.

Vajradhara - *rdo rje 'chang*, lit. vajra holder. In the **New Tradition,** he is the primordial Buddha, source of all the tantras. In the **Ancient Tradition,** Vajradhara represents the principle of the Teacher as enlightened holder of the Vajrayāna teachings.

Vajradhātvīśvarī - *rdo rje dbyings 'phugs ma*, one of the **consorts** of the Buddhas of the **Five Families.**

Vajrapāṇi - *phyag na rdo rje*, one of the **Eight Great Close Sons.**

Vajrasattva - *rdo rje sems dpa'*, the Buddha who embodies the **Hundred Families.** The practice of Vajrasattva and recitation of his mantra are particularly effective for purifying negative actions. In the lineage of the **Great Perfection** he is the **sambhogakāya** Buddha.

Vajrayāna - *rdo rje theg pa*, see **Secret Mantrayāna.**

Vase empowerment - *bum dbang*, the first **empowerment** "that purifies the defilements of the body, enables one to meditate on the generation phase and sows the seed for obtaining the vajra body and the nirmāṇakāya." DICT.

Vase of great treasure - *gter chen po'i bum pa*, one of the **eight auspicious signs.** It corresponds to the throat of the Buddha and symbolizes the teachings that fulfil all desires.

Vehicle - *theg pa*, Skt. *yāna*, the means for travelling the path to enlightenment.

Vidyādhara - *rig 'dzin*, knowledge holder. "One who through profound means holds the deities, mantras, and the wisdom of great bliss." DICT. In the **Nyingmapa** Tradition there are four levels of vidyādhara: (i) totally matured (*rnam smin*), (ii) mastering the duration of his life (*tshe dbang*), (iii) mahāmudrā (*phyag chen*), and (iv) spontaneously accomplished (*lhun grub*).

View - *lta ba*, Skt. *dṛṣṭi*, 1) point of view, belief. 2) the authentic point of view, the real knowledge of the natural state of all phenomena.

Vikramaśīla - one of the most famous Buddhist universities of India, destroyed in the 12th century.

Vimalamitra - *dri med bshes bnyen*, one of the most learned Indian Buddhist masters. He went to Tibet in the 9th century, where he taught extensively, and composed and translated numerous Sanskrit texts. The quintessence of his teaching is known as the *Vima Nyingtig*, one of the *Heart-essence* teachings of the **Great Perfection**.

Vīṇā - an Indian musical instrument, with strings that are plucked.

Vinaya - *'dul ba*, one of the Three **Piṭakas**, containing teachings about monastic dicipline and ethics in general.

Vipaśyin - *rnam par gzigs*, the first of the six Buddhas who preceded Buddha **Śākyamuni**.

Virūpa - one of the eighty-four **mahāsiddhas** of India. An important source of the teachings of the **Sakyapa** tradition.

Walking posture - *mnyam pa'i 'dor stabs*, standing posture with the two legs together but the right foot slightly forward (symbolizing eagerness to help other beings).

Warmth (sign of) - *drod rtags*, a sign that the practice is beginning to work. (When a fire produces heat, it means that it has started properly.) This expression does not particularly refer to an experience of physical heat.

Water torma - *chu gtor*, an offering made with water, milk and grains.

Wealth deity - *nor lha*, a deity that one propitiates to increase wealth.

Wheel - *'khor lo*, Skt. *cakra*, one of the centres of energy at different points on the **central channel**, from which radiate the small subtle channels going to all parts of the body. Generally there are considered to be four or five of these wheels.

Wheel of Dharma - *chos kyi 'khor lo*, Skt. *dharmacakra*, the symbol of the Buddha's teaching. To turn the wheel of the Dharma means to teach the Dharma. During his lifetime, the Buddha gave three major series of teachings, which are referred to as the first, second and third turnings.

Wind - 1. see **energy**. 2. one of the three humours according to Tibetan medicine. See also **bile, phlegm**.

Wisdom - *shes rab*, Skt. *prajña*, the ability to understand correctly, usually with the particular sense of understanding emptiness. AT: discerning wisdom. See also **primal wisdom**.

Wisdom empowerment - *shes rab kyi dbang*, the third empowerment "that purifies the defilements of the mind, enables one to meditate on the perfection phase and sows the seed for obtaining the vajra mind and the dharmakāya." DICT.

Wish-fulfilling jewel - *yid bzhin nor bu*, Skt. *cintāmaṇi*, a fabulous jewel found in realms of the gods or nāgas which fulfills all one's wishes.

Wish-fulfilling tree - *dpag bsam gyi shing*, magical tree which has its root in the **demigod** realm but bears its fruit in the realm of the gods of the **Thirty-three**.

Without Fighting - *'thab bral*, Skt. *Yāma*, name of a god realm of the World of Desire, so called because it is high enough for the gods there not to have to fight with the demigods. See **three worlds**.

Worldly concentrations - concentrations leading not to enlightenment but only to rebirth in god realms. See **four concentrations**.

Wrathful Black True Mother - *ma cig khros ma nag mo*, Skt. *Krodhakālī*, lit. the one mother wrathful and black. A manifestation of Samantabhadrī in wrathful sambhogakāya form, an aspect of Vajravarāhī (rdo rje phag mo).

Wrong view - *log lta*, Skt. *mithyādṛiṣṭi*, AT: false belief, particularly a view that will lead one to courses of action that bring more suffering.

Yakṣa - *gnod sbyin*, a class of spirits.

Yama - *gshin rje*, the Lord of Death.

Yamāntaka - *gshin rje bshed*, wrathful form of **Mañjuśrī**.

Yellow scroll - *shog ser*, piece of paper (not necessarily yellow) on which the texts of **spiritual treasures** are written.

Yeshe Tsogyal - *ye shes mtsho rgyal*, **Padmasambhava**'s mystic **consort** and greatest disciple. She served him perfectly, and helped him to propagate his teachings, in particular concealing **spiritual treasures** to be rediscovered later for the sake of future disciples.

Yidam - *yi dam*, Skt. *devatā*, *iṣṭadevatā*, a deity representing enlightenment, in a male or female, peaceful or wrathful form corresponding to one's individual nature. The yidam is the source of accomplishments. See **three roots**.

Yoga - *rnal 'byor*, practice, lit. a method for uniting (*'byor*) with the natural state (*rnal ma*).

Yogī or **yoginī** *rnal 'byor pa* or *rnal 'byor ma*, someone who practises **yoga**, a spiritual practitioner.

Bibliography

1. Texts cited by Patrul Rinpoche

Advice to King Surabhībhadra – rgyal po bde spyod la gdams pa, an alternative name for Nāgārjuna's *Suhṛllekha* or *Letter to a Friend* (*bshes sbring*). (See note 36).

Array of Ati - a ti bkod pa, a tantra.

Cloud of Jewels - Ratnamegha-sūtra, mdo sde dkon mchog sprin, a sūtra thought to be the first one translated into Tibetan (by Tönmi Sambhota).

Collection of Deliberate Sayings - Udānavarga, ched du brjod pa'i tshoms. This is the Mahāyāna equivalent of the Pali Dhammapada, and contains teachings which were given spontaneously by the Buddha in the interests of maintaining the doctrine, rather than in answer to the questions of specific individuals.

Condensed Transcendent Wisdom - Prajñāpāramitā-saṁcayagāthā, phar phyin bsdus pa, name of a śāstra by Āryaśūra.

Confession of Downfalls - ltung gshags, another name for the *Sūtra in Three Parts.*

Detailed Commentary on the Condensed Meaning - dgongs 'dus rnam bshad, commentary written by Jigme Lingpa on the cycle of practices called *bla ma dgongs 'dus* by Sangye Lingpa.

Dharma Practice that Spontaneously Liberates Habitual Clingings - chos spyod bag chags rang grol, a section of the *zhi khro* by Karma Lingpa.

Diamond Cutter Sūtra - Vajracchedikā-sūtra, rdo rje gcod pa.

Dohās (of Saraha) - Dohākośa, do ha mdzod.

Dohās (of Virūpa) - Dohākośa, do ha mdzod.

Eight Great Marvellous Verses - ngo tshar ba'i tshig chen brgyad, eight exclamations through which the Great Perfection tantras express the ultimate nature of the great omnipresent perfection.

Eight Verses of Langri Thangpa - glang thang pa'i tshig brgyad ma, eight stanzas on the bodhicitta practice of mind training.

Essential Ornament - snying po'i rgyan, a tantra.

Finding Rest from Illusion - sgyu ma ngal gso, a treatise by Longchenpa showing how all phenomena correspond to the eight similes of illusion. Th third book in his *Trilogy of Rest, ngal gso skor gsum.*

Finding Rest in the Nature of Mind - sems nyid ngal gso, a work by Longchenpa. The first book in his *Trilogy of Rest, ngal gso skor gsum.*

Five Teachings of Maitreya - *byams chos sde lnga*, five texts taught by the Buddha Maitreya to Asaṅga in the Tuṣita heaven: *Abhisamaya-alaṁkāra (mngon rtogs rgyan)*, *Mahāyāna-sūtra-alaṁkāra* (*mdo sde rgyan*), *Madhyānta-vibhaṅga* (*dbus mtha' rnam 'byed*), *Dharma-dharmatā-vibhaṅga* (*chos dang chos nyid rnam 'byed*) and *Uttara-tantra-śāstra* (*rgyud bla ma*).

Five Treatises on the Middle Way - *dbu ma rig pa'i tshogs*, five treatises on Mādhyamika philosophy by Nāgārjuna: *Prajñā-mūla-madhyamaka-kārikā* (*dbus ma rtsa ba shes rab*), *Yukti-ṣaṣṭikā-kārikā* (*rigs pa drug cu pa*), *Vaidalya-sūtra* (*zhib mo rnam 'thag*), *śūnyatā-saptati-kārikā* (*stong nyid bdun cu pa*), *Vigraha-vyāvartanī-kārikā* (*rtsod pa bzlog pa*).

Heart-essence - *snying thig*, quintessence of the teachings of the pith instruction section (*man ngag sde*) in the Great Perfection. Its two main transmission lineages are those of Vimalamitra and Padmasambhava. The most well-known heart essences are *bi ma snying thig*, *mkha' 'gro snying thig* and *klong chen snying thig*.

Heart-Essence of the Vast Expanse - *klong chen snying gi thig le*, a treasure rediscovered by Jigme Lingpa, one of the most famous heart essence teachings. Published by Lama Ngödrup for H.H. Dilgo Khyentse Rinpoche, Paro, Bhutan, 1972, 4 volumes.

Hevajra tantra - *Hevajra-tantra-rāja*, *rgyud brtags gnyis*.

Immaculate Sūtra - *dri ma med pa'i mdo*.

Inserting the Grass-stalk - *'pho ba 'jag 'dzugs ma*, a prayer by Nyi Da Sangye, recited in the practice of transference.

Instructions on Bodhicitta Written on Stone in Gold - *byang sems rdo la gser zhun*, probably the text called *rdo la gser zhun* belonging to the Mind Section (*sems sde*) of the Great Perfection, in the Collection of Nyingma Tantras (*rnying ma rgyud 'bum*).

Jātakas - *skyes rabs*, a section of the Buddha's teachings in which he told the stories of his previous lives.

Jewel Garland - *Ratnāvalī*, *rin chen phreng ba*, name of a śāstra written by Nāgārjuna.

Letter of Consolation - *Śokavinodana*, *mya ngan bsal ba'i springs yig*, a śāstra by Aśvaghoṣa.

Moon Lamp Sūtra - *Candrapradīpa-sūtra*, *zla ba sgron me'i mdo*, another name for the *Sūtra of the King of Concentration*, *Samādhirāja-sūtra*, *ting 'dzin rgyal po*.

Nirvāṇa Sūtra - *Mahāparinirvāṇa-sūtra*, *mya ngan las 'das pa'i mdo*.

Powerful Secret - *gnyan po gsang ba*, the first name given to the sūtra that King Lha-Thothori Nyentsen is said to have discovered on the roof of his palace (in 433 A.D.). It was later called the ***Sūtra of a Hundred Invoca-***

tions and Prostrations. It also generally refers to the apparition of different objects, among which was this sūtra, announcing the beginning of Buddhism in Tibet.

Prayer in Seven Lines - *tshig bdun gsol 'debs*, the most famous prayer invoking Padmasambhava and sung for the first time by ḍākinīs at the moment of the Master's birth. It had several levels of meanings and contains the essence of all the teachings. See note 247.

Prayer of Good Actions - *Bhadracaryāpraṇidhāna*, *bzang spyod smon lam*, a prayer spoken by the Buddha in the *Avataṁsaka-Sūtra*, *phal po che* and almost always recited at the end of rituals.

Prayer of Sukhāvatī - *bde ba can gyi smon lam*, a prayer to take rebirth in the pure land of Buddha Amitābha. The most famous is one written by Karma Chakme.

Prayer of the Copper-coloured Mountain - *zangs bdog dpal ri'i smon lam,* a prayer to be reborn in the Buddhafield of Padmasambhava.

Precious Supreme Path - *lam mchog rin po che*, a text by Gampopa.

Seven Treasures - *mdzod bdun*, a set of works by Longchenpa: 1) *The Precious Treasure of Absolute Space*, *chos dbyings rin po che'i mdzod*; 2) *The Precious Wish-Fulfilling Treasure: a Commentary on the Pith Instructions of the Great Vehicle*, *theg pa chen po'i man ngag gi bstan bcos yid bzhin rin po che'i mdzod*; 3) *The Precious Treasure of the Supreme Vehicle*, *theg pa'i mchog rin po che'i mdzod*; 4) *The Precious Treasure of Pith Instructions*, *man ngag rin po che'i mdzod*; 5) *The Precious Treasure of Words and Meaning that Illuminate the Three Abodes of the Secret Unsurpassable Luminous Adamantine Essence*, *gsang ba bla na med pa 'od gsal rdo rje snying po'i gnas gsum gsal bar byed pa'i tshig don rin po che'i mdzod*; 6) *The Precious Treasure of Philosophical Doctrines thet Illuminate the Meaning of All Vehicles*, *theg pa mtha' dag gi don gsal bar byed pa grub pa'i mtha' rin po che'i mdzod*; and 7) *The Precious Treasure of the Natural State*, *gnas lugs rin po che'i mdzod.*

Seventy Stanzas on Refuge - *skyabs 'gro bdun bcu pa.*

Sūtra Arranged like a Tree - *Gaṇḍhavyūha-sūtra*, *sdong po bkod pa*, section of the *Avataṁsaka Sūtra*, *phal po che.*

Sūtra Designed like a Jewel Chest - *Ārya-ratna-kāraṇḍavyūha-sūtra, mdo sde za ma tog bkod pa*, in the *Maṇi Kahbum* of Songtsen Gampo.

Sūtra in Three Parts - *Triskandha-sūtra*, *phung po gsum.*

Sūtra of a Hundred Actions - *Karmaśataka-sūtra*, *mdo sde las brgya pa.*

Sūtra of a Hundred Invocations and Prostrations - *Saksi-pūraṇa-sūdraka-namā-sūtra*, *dpang skong phyag brgya pa,* name of a sūtra in the Kangyur that seems to be the first Buddhist book that appeared in Tibet (on the roof of the palace of king Lhathothori Nyentsen, in the middle of the 5th century). It was translated into Tibetan by Thönmi Sambhota.

Sūtra of Great Liberation - *thar pa chen po'i mdo.*

Sūtra of Instructions to the King - *Rājāvavādaka-sūtra, rgyal po la gdams pa.*

Sūtra of Sublime Dharma of Clear Recollection - *Saddharmanu-smṛityu-pasthāna-sūtra, dam pa'i chos dran pa nye bar bzhag pa'i mdo.*

Sūtra of the Condensed Meaning - *mdo dgongs pa 'dus pa*, one of the four root tantras of Anuyoga.

Sūtra of the Heart of the Sun - *nyi ma'i snying po'i mdo.*

Sūtra of the Wise and the Foolish - *Damomūrkha-sūtra, mdzangs blun gyi mdo.*

Sūtra Requested by Sāgaramati - *Sāgaramati-paripṛicchā-sūtra, blo gros rgya mtshos zhus pa'i mdo.*

Sūtra that Perfectly Encapsulates the Dharma - *Dharmasaṅgīti-sūtra, chos yang dag par sdud pa'i mdo.*

Tantra of the Array of Samayas - *Samaya-vyūha, dam tshig bkod pa'i rgyud*, a tantra common to both Mahāyoga and Anuyoga.

Tantra of Immaculate Confession - *dri med gshags pa'i rgyud.*

Tantra of the Secret Essence - *Guhyagarbha-tantra, rgyud gsang ba'i snying po*, also called *dpal gsang ba'i rgyud*, the root tantra of Mahāyoga.

Tantra of the Union of Sun and Moon - *nyi zla kha sbyor.*

Tantra of Thorough Comprehension of the Instructions on all Dharma Practices - *chos spyod thams cad kyi man ngag mngon par rtogs pa'i rgyud.*

Torch of the Three Methods - *Nayatraya-pradīpa, tshul gsum sgron me*, name of a śāstra composed by Tripiṭakamāla.

Transcendent Wisdom in Eight Thousand Verses - *Aṣṭasāhasrikā-prajñāpāramitā, shes rab kyi pha rol tu phyin pa brgyad stong pa* (abbreviated as *brgyad stong pa*).

Treasury of Precious Qualities - *yon tan rin po che'i mdzod*, the famous treatise by Jigme Lingpa, in which he expounds the entire Buddhist path, from the Śrāvakayāna teachings up to the Great Perfection.

Vows of the Five Families - *rigs lnga'i sdom pa*, name of a tantra.

Way of the Bodhisattva - *Bodhicaryāvatāra, byang chub sems dpa'i spyod pa la 'jug pa*, famous treatise by Śāntideva describing the Bodhisattva path.

Well Explained Reasoning - *Vyākhyā-yukti, rnam bshad rig pa*, name of a śāstra by Vasubandhu.

Wish-granting Treasure - *yid bzhin mdzod*, abbreviated name of 2) of the *Seven Treasures* (*mdzod bdun*) by Longchenpa (see above).

2. Reference Work for the Notes and Glossary

rdzogs pa chen po klong chen snying thig gi sgnon 'gro'i khrid yig kun bzang bla ma'i shal lung gi zin bris (*Notes on* The Words of my Perfect Teacher), Ngawang Pelzang (*ngag dbang dpal zang*), alias Khenpo Ngakchung, who was the close disciple of Nyoshul Lungtok Tenpai Nyima, himself the close disciple of Patrul Rinpoche. Tibetan text republished by Thubten Nyima, Zenkar Rinpoche, Minorities Publishing House, Chengdu, China. This collection of explanatory notes, which expands in detail selected points from the present text, is being translated into English under the direction of Alla Zenkar Rinpoche (and with the participation of members of the Padmakara Translation Group) and is due to be published during 1988 by Dipamkara, 367A Holloway Road, London N7 0RN, U.K.

3. Works of Patrul Rinpoche

Collected Works of dPal sprul O rgyan 'Jigs med Chos kyi dBang po, (Tibetan text), reproduced from H.H. Dudjom Rinpoche's xylographic collection by Sonam Kazi, 6 Volumes, Gangtok, 1971. *kun bzang bla ma'i shal lung* is in Volume 5 of this collection. *thog mtha' bar gsum dge ba'i gtam lta sgom spyod gsum mnyams len dam pa'i snying nor* (*The Heart-Treasure of the Enlightened Ones, a Discourse Virtuous in the Beginning, Middle and End*) is in vol. 6, pp. 195-209.

Collected Works of dPal sprul O rgyan 'Jigs med Chos kyi dBang po, (Tibetan text), reproduced from a newly calligraphed set of manuscripts, edited by Thubten Nyima, Zenkar Rinpoche, and published by the Office for the Kangyur and Tangyur, Chengdu, China, 1988.

rdzogs pa chen po klong chen snying thig gi sgnon 'gro'i khrid yig kun bzang bla ma'i shal lung, (Tibetan text in bound paperback format). Edited by Thubten Nyima, Zenkar Rinpoche, si khron mi rigs dpe skrun khang (Ethnic Minorities Publishing House), Chengdu, China, 1988.

Le Chemin de la Grande Perfection, French translation of *kun bzang bla ma'i shal lung*, Padmakara Translation Group, Peyzac-le-Moustier, Editions Padmakara, 1987, 2nd edition 1997.

Kün-Zang La-May Zhal Lung, Patrul Rinpoche (translated Kazi Sonam Topgay), Upper Montclair (New Jersey), Diamond Lotus Publishing, 1989-1993. 3 volumes.

Tantric Practice in Nying-ma, Khetsun Sangpo Rinbochay (translated Jeffrey Hopkins), Ithaca, Gabriel/Snow Lion, 1982. (Prepared from oral teachings based on Patrul Rinpoche's *Kunzang Lamai Shelung*).

Propitious Speech from the Beginning, Middle and End (*thog mtha' bar gsum dge ba'i gtam lta sgom spyod gsum mnyams len dam pa'i snying nor*) Patrul Rinpoche, (translated Thinley Norbu), Jewel Publishing House, 1984.

Heart Treasure of the Enlightened Ones (*thog mtha' bar gsum dge ba'i gtam lta sgom spyod gsum mnyams len dam pa'i snying nor*), Patrul Rinpoche, commented by Dilgo Khyentse, (translated by the Padmakara Translation Group), Boston, Shambhala, 1992. Includes a brief biography of Patrul Rinpoche.

4. Biographies of Patrul Rinpoche

Praise to Patrul Rinpoche, (*rgyal-ba'i myu-gu chos-kyi dbang-po rjes-su dran-pa'i ngag-gi 'phreng-ba bkra-shis bil-ba'i ljong bzang kun tu dga'-ba'i tshal*), Jamyang Khyentse Wangpo ('jams-dbyangs mkhyen-brtse'i dbang-po.) Appended to vol. 6 of *Collected Works* pp. 245-250.

The Dew-Drop of Amṛita (*mtshungs bral rgyal-ba'i myu-gu o-rgyan jigs-med chos-kyi dbang-po'i rtogs-brjod tsam gleng-ba bdud rtsi'i zil thig*), The Third Dodrup Chen, Tenpai Nyima (mdo-grub bstan-pa'i nyi-ma), vol. 4 of *Collected Writings*, pp. 101-136, published by Dodrup Sangye, Gangtok, Sikkim, 1972.

The Elixir of Faith (*o-rgyan 'jigs-med chos kyi dbang-po'i rnam-thar dad-pa'i gsos sman bdud rtsi'i bum bcud*), Khenpo Kunpel (*mkhan-chen kun-bzang dpal-ldan*), vol. 2 of *Collected Writings* (*gsung-'bum*) of mKhan-chen Kun-bzang dPal-ldan, pp. 353-484. Published by H.H. Dilgo Khyentse Rinpoche, Bhutan, 1986. Forthcoming in English and French translations by the Padmakara Translation Group under the title *The Life and Teachings of Patrul Rinpoche*.

5. Secondary sources

This list consists of works cited in the notes and glossary only, and is not intended to be an exhaustive bibliography of relevant works.

Dzogchen Innermost Essence Preliminary Practice, Jigme Lingpa (translated Tulku Thondup), Dharamsala, Library of Tibetan Works and Archives, 1982.

Enlightened Courage, Dilgo Khyentse, Peyzac-le-Moustier (France), Editions Padmakara, 1992.

Great Path of Awakening, Jamgon Kongtrul (translated K. McLeod), Boston, Shambhala, 1987.

Hidden Teachings of Tibet, an explanation of the terma tradition of the Nyingma school of Buddhism, Tulku Thondup Rinpoche, London, Wisdom 1986.

Legend of the Great Stūpa, translated Keith Dowman, Berkeley, Dharma Publishing, 1973.

Nyingma School of Tibetan Buddhism: its Fundamentals and History, Dudjom Rinpoche (translated Dorje and Kapstein), Boston, Wisdom, 1991.

Tantric Tradition of the Nyingmapa, Tulku Thondup, Marion, Buddhayana, 1984.

Index

The Padmakara Translation Group

The Padmakara Translation Group is devoted to the accurate and literate translation of texts and spoken material into Western languages by trained Western translators, under the guidance of authoritative Tibetan scholars, principally Taklung Tsetrul Pema Wangyal Rinpoche and Jigme Khyentse Rinpoche, in a context of sustained study and discussion.

Translations into English

The Excellent Path of Enlightenment, Dilgo Khyentse, Editions Padmakara, 1987

The Wish-Fulfilling Jewel, Dilgo Khyentse, Shambhala, 1988

Dilgo Khyentse Rinpoche, Editions Padmakara, 1990

Enlightened Courage, Dilgo Khyentse, Ed. Padmakara, 1992 (North American edition: Snow Lion Publications, 1994)

The Heart Treasure of the Enlightened Ones, Dilgo Khyentse and Patrul Rinpoche, Shambhala, 1992

A Flash of Lightning in the Dark of Night, the Dalai Lama, Shambhala, 1993

Wisdom: Two Buddhist Commentaries, Khenchen Kunzang Palden and Minyak Kunzang Sönam, Editions Padmakara, 1993.

The Words of My Perfect Teacher, Patrul Rinpoche, International Sacred Literature Trust - HarperCollins, 1994, 2nd edition Sage Altamira, 1998

The Life of Shabkar: Autobiography of a Tibetan Yogi, SUNY Press, 1994

Journey to Enlightenment, Matthieu Ricard, Aperture, 1996

The Way of the Bodhisattva (Bodhicaryāvatāra), Śāntideva, Shambhala, 1997

The Lady of the Lotus-Born, Gyalwa Changchup and Namkhai Nyingpo, Shambhala, 1998

Translations into French

Le Chemin de la Grande Perfection, Patrul Rinpotché, Editions Padmakara, 1987, 2nd edition 1997

Dilgo Khyentsé Rinpotché, Editions Padmakara, 1990

Au Seuil de l'Eveil, Dilgo Khyentsé, Editions Padmakara, 1991

La Marche vers l'Eveil (*Bodhicaryāvatāra*), Śāntidéva, Editions Padmakara, 1992

Comme un éclair déchire la nuit, Dalaï Lama, Ed. Albin Michel, 1992

Audace et compassion, Dilgo Khyentsé, Editions Padmakara, 1993

Comprendre la vacuité, Khentchen Kunzang Palden and Minyak Kunzang Seunam, Editions Padmakara, 1993.

La Vie de Yéshé Tsogyal, souveraine du Tibet, Gyalwa Tchangtchoub et Namkhai Nyingpo, Editions Padmakara, 1995

Le Goût unique du bonheur et de la souffrance, Djigmé Tenpai Nyima, Editions Padmakara, 1995

La Fontaine de grâce, Dilgo Khyentsé, Editions Padmakara, 1995

Le Trésor du coeur des êtres éveillés, Dilgo Khyentsé, Seuil, 1995

Diamants de sagesse, Péma Wangyal, Editions Padmakara, 1996

L'Esprit du Tibet, Matthieu Ricard, Seuil, 1996

Translations into German

Der Friede beginnt in dir, Dalai Lama, O.W.Barth Verlag, 1994

Das Herzjuwel der Erleuchteten, Dilgo Khyentse, Theseus Verlag, 1994

Die geheimen Dakini-Lehren, Padmasambhava, O.W.Barth Verlag, 1995

Die sieben tibetischen Geistesübungen, Dilgo Khentse, O.W.Barth Verlag, 1996

Translations into Spanish

Compasión Intrépida, Dilgo Khyentse, Ediciones Dharma, 1994

Note (end 1997): a translation of *The Words of My Perfect Teacher* into Spanish is nearing completion; a translation into German has started; and a translation into Italian is planned for the near future.

If you are interested in our activities, please contact us at:

Padmakara Translation Group
24290 Saint-Léon-sur-Vézère
France

Gönpo Lekden

Gönpo Maning Nagpo

Ekajaṭī

Khyabjuk Rāhula

Damchen Dorje Lekpa

Tseringma

It is traditional in Tibetan books to have pictures of the Dharma Protectors at the end.